ASCII	PRINTS	HEX
64	@	40
65	A	41
66	B	42
67	C	43
68	D	44
69	E	45
70	F	46
71	G	47
72	H	48
73	I	49
74	J	4A
75	K	4B
76	L	4C
77	M	4D
78	N	4E
79	O	4F
80	P	50
81	Q	51
82	R	52
83	S	53
84	T	54
85	U	55
86	V	56
87	W	57
88	X	58
89	Y	59
90	Z	5A
91	[	5B
92	\	5C
93	]	5D
94	^	5E
95	_	5F

ASCII	PRINTS	HEX
96	`	60
97	a	61
98	b	62
99	c	63
100	d	64
101	e	65
102	f	66
103	g	67
104	h	68
105	i	69
106	j	6A
107	k	6B
108	l	6C
109	m	6D
110	n	6E
111	o	6F
112	p	70
113	q	71
114	r	72
115	s	73
116	t	74
117	u	75
118	v	76
119	w	77
120	x	78
121	y	79
122	z	7A
123	{	7B
124	:	7C
125	}	7D
126	~	7E
127	△	7F

MS-DOS Power User's Guide
Volume II

MS-DOS® Power User's Guide

Volume II

Martin Waterhouse
Jonathan Kamin

SAN FRANCISCO • PARIS • DÜSSELDORF • LONDON

Cover art by Thomas Ingalls + Associates
Series design by Jeffrey James Giese
Chapter art and layout by Suzanne Albertson

To Fiona and Nancy,
for putting up with us

You do not have to eat lunch.
—James L. Flood

ACKNOWLEDGMENTS

A work of this nature is never the exclusive product of those whose names appear on the cover. This volume would not even exist without the persistent efforts of Dr. R. S. Langer and Dianne King of SYBEX, who coerced it into being out of nothingness. It was given shape and coherence through the editorial efforts of Fran Grimble, Valerie Robbins, and Barbara Gordon; and technical accuracy by Dan Tauber and Dennis Bourque.

Many individuals gave generously of their time to help us understand and find our way through the complexities in which we found ourselves embroiled. Among those deserving special mention are Dan Sweeney of Quarterdeck Office Systems, Coleen Haworth of Digital Research, Bernard Penney of Seaware, Kevin Kearney of Mansfield Software Group, Wendy Shulman and Mark Skiba of Inset Systems, David Matthews of Datastorm Technologies, John Butler of Microsoft, Enrique LaRoche, Alex Soya, and Morgan Witthoft. In addition, we owe thanks to many CompuServe subscribers for their hints and tips in response to our queries.

The high-resolution screens in this book were captured and edited with Hijaak and InSet, generously donated by Inset Systems. Most of the diagrams originated in GEM Draw Plus, for which we owe thanks to Gale Steiner of Digital Research. Therese Myers, President of Quarter-deck Office Systems, contributed a copy of DESQview, which not only was a subject of discussion but an active contributor to the creation of this work. Shelley Sofer, President of All Computers, loaned us an All ChargeCard to work with. Paul Chase valiantly attempted to install it. Debra Globe of Compaq ensured that we had the latest release of DOS to use. We have undoubtedly forgotten others, and hope they consider themselves thanked.

In addition, we owe a debt to many on the staff at SYBEX for turning the stuff of ideas into a set of pages with a cover: Jocelyn Reynolds word processed the manuscript, Kristen Iverson proofread it, Jeff Giese designed the book and completed the diagrams, Suzanne Albertson put it together, Olivia Shinomoto typeset it, Sonja Schenk created the screen reproductions, and Anne Leach compiled the index.

CONTENTS AT A GLANCE

TABLE OF CONTENTS

10: MULTITASKING OPERATING SYSTEMS

INTRODUCTION

MS-DOS is the most popular operating system for computers using the 8088, 8086, 80286, and 80386 microprocessors—in other words, the IBM PC and its various clones, compatibles, and extensions. This set of programs tells the microprocessor how to communicate with the computer's peripheral devices and how to run programs. (From the point of view of the microprocessor, disk drives, serial and parallel ports, and memory are peripheral devices.) Without an operating system, the computer can do almost nothing. Replace one operating system with another, and you give your computer a different set of preconceptions.

DOS includes much more than the simple commands everyone needs to know to copy files and disks, and perform basic file-management chores. Indeed, it includes most of the facilities needed to enable programmers to write the most sophisticated application programs.

The MS-DOS Power User's Guide, Volume II follows a previous volume that introduced all the facilities of MS-DOS and PC-DOS that you, as a user, can employ to control your computer. The current volume delves deeper into the mysteries of the operating system from the user's point of view. We have attempted to go beyond the limitations of DOS, to show you what you can add to your system to make DOS work better and faster, to run multiple processes at once, and to link your computer with others.

The current volume is valid for all releases of MS-DOS and PC-DOS from 2.0 through 3.3. However, we focus primarily on the facilities available in releases 3.2 and 3.3.

The book is in three parts. After a review of where DOS has come from and where it is going in Chapter 1, Part I shows you the ways you can enhance and extend DOS, Part II shows you how to run multiple processes, and Part III takes you into the world of connectivity.

Chapter 2, *Enhancing Your Batch Programs*, introduces two extensions to the native DOS batch language presented in Volume I: Personal REXX and Extended Batch Language. These languages give you all the facilities of a true programming language, yet interact effectively with DOS. We also review the latest additions to the native batch language.

Chapter 3, *Controlling the Video Display*, takes you into the labyrinthine world of video adapters, display memory, and video modes and standards. We give you an overview of the development of these modes and standards, suggest ways to avoid problems, and present some utilities that can help you gain full control over what appears on your screen.

Printers have come a long way since the first 12cps daisywheel models. In Chapter 4, *Extending Your Printer's Capabilities*, we discuss the variety of types of printers now available, and present some software with which you can control and program them.

In Chapter 5, *Turbocharging DOS*, we explore the ways you can increase the speed of your system through enhancing the keyboard, the screen, and the disk I/O.

Chapter 6, *Controlling the Structure of Your Disks*, reviews some of the material from Chapter 2 of Volume I in order to take you where no sensible person should go: right into the boot record and file allocation table. We show you how to address these areas of the disk so that you can control the size of your hard disk's root directory and data clusters. Through a few simple changes, you can drastically increase the amount of data a hard disk can hold. We also discuss ways of optimizing the speed of your hard disk for your system.

Security of your data is the focus of Chapter 7, *Protecting Your Data*. We discuss methods of hiding directories, encrypting files, limiting access to your computer, and defending yourself against destructive programs.

Part II begins with Chapter 8 in which we introduce the main features of several windowed operating environments. These programs let you switch freely between programs in memory, share data among programs, and otherwise make it easier to use what you already have. Chapter 9 explores the capabilities of these environments in greater depth.

Chapter 10 introduces *Multitasking Operating Systems*—systems that let you run more than one program at a time. We explain two methods by which multitasking is achieved, and present three alternatives to DOS as ways of achieving it. We also note how these systems interact with DOS, and how you can use the environments introduced in Chapter 8 to run multiple programs.

In Part III we show you myriad ways to link your computer to others. Chapter 11, *Ways of Connecting Computers*, gives an overview of the field, with special emphasis on local-area networks. Chapter 12 is an *Introduction to Serial Communications*, which is the basis for all telecommunications. We present the many factors involved in telecommunicating to help you avoid its numerous pitfalls. In Chapter 13, *Using Telecommunications*, we take you step by step through a series of telecommunications tasks: sending files to another computer by direct link, sending files over the phone lines and communicating directly with other PCs, using E-Mail, and getting the most out of electronic bulletin boards and online services.

Chapter 14, *Installing and Using Networks*, explores local-area networks in greater depth. Since every networking situation is different, we cannot present you with a complete guide. However, to give you some of the feel of what's involved, we take you though installing two different types of networks. We also give you a sample of how to use an IBM token-ring network, so you get a sense of what it's like to be connected. In addition, we present some general guidelines for managing a shared environment and provide two examples of situations in which a network can boost productivity.

Chapter 15, *Accessing Mainframes and Minicomputers*, explores the methods, benefits, and dangers of linking your PC to mainframes and minicomputers. We discuss the advantages and disadvantages of working on a large network and look ahead to the connectivity of the future.

Finally, the appendices present reference material. Appendix A lists the source code for the assembly-language programs in the book.

Appendix B does the same for the Turbo Pascal programs. Appendix C lists sources of software mentioned in the book. Appendix D presents reference tables of ANSI escape sequences. Appendix E is a series of ASCII tables, including all displayable characters in the standard character set; control characters; extended ASCII codes for key combinations and special keys; and box and border characters.

ABOUT THE PROGRAM LISTINGS

There are four types of program listings provided in this book:

- ▲ Batch programs
- ▲ DEBUG script files
- ▲ Turbo Pascal programs
- ▲ Assembly-language programs

We'll present the requirements for entering the various listings, then explain the typographics, syntax, and naming conventions used in the book.

Batch Programs

Many of the programs in this book are batch files, which are programs that automate the execution of DOS commands. The text in batch files *must* consist of the standard ASCII characters (the standard alphanumeric characters, and the symbols that you can type from the keyboard), or DOS will not be able to execute them. For a complete table of ASCII characters, including the extended ASCII character set (ASCII codes 128 through 255), see Table E.1 in Appendix E. Several of the batch programs display menus.

Script Files

To aid those of you who do not program in assembly language or Turbo Pascal, we have presented *script file* versions of all the programs. To create a script file, you must enter the text as a standard ASCII text file, just as you do with a batch file. You do not have to know anything about programming to use these script files, but you do have to type accurately.

The script files are used as input for DEBUG. To create the working programs represented by the script files, make sure that both DEBUG and the script file are in your current directory or on your search path, and enter a command of the form

DEBUG<*FILENAME.EXT*

where *FILENAME.EXT* is the name of the script file. The script file tells DEBUG to assemble the program from the code and write the result to a .COM file. If you have created the script file correctly, DEBUG should do all the work for you. If you haven't, your computer may well lock up.

Be very sure to end every line with a carriage return, including the blank line near the end and the last line. Otherwise, your computer *will* lock up.

If the program doesn't behave as it should, you can debug it by *unassembling* it. Invoke DEBUG and then enter the command

U100

The screen should display the same code as appears in the book, with two extra columns of figures. If the entire program does not appear, press U again. If the screen doesn't match the program in the book, you have made an error in the script file. See Volume I Chapter 3 for a full introduction to DEBUG.

Assembly-Language and Turbo Pascal Programs

To create the assembly-language programs in Appendix A, you need the IBM or Microsoft Macro Assembler. To create the Turbo Pascal programs in Appendix B, you need the Turbo Pascal compiler. These programs will not run unless they are turned into executable code by the appropriate software tool, and then linked with a linker. Unlike the script files, however, they are fully commented. Thus, if you are just learning to program, you can enter the programs as script files, and then study their logic by examining the source code.

How the Programs Are Listed

The programs all appear in separate, boxed listings. In the listings of batch files, each line is preceded by a number, which is followed by a colon and a space. *Do not type in these line numbers and colons!* They are merely for reference, so that specific lines can be referred to in text, and so that you can keep your place when entering the programs. The other types of programs do not have numbered lines.

HOW TO ENTER THE PROGRAMS

All the programs, regardless of their type, must be entered as ASCII text files. This means that they cannot contain any of the control codes that a word processing program normally inserts in the text.

The simpler files can be entered using the COPY CON command. However, once your files extend beyond two or three lines, or you want to edit them, this command becomes inadequate. Moreover, you will need to be able to insert Escape characters into some of these files, and it is extremely difficult, if not impossible, to do so using COPY CON.

Most word processors or text editors can be made to create ASCII text files of the type required. DOS's resident line editor, EDLIN, although clumsy, is adequate for all the programs in the book. With it, you can enter the Escape character, and any control characters that are needed.

Control Characters

When control characters are discussed in text, they are referred to by name; e.g., Ctrl-S, Ctrl-C, and Ctrl-[. When they appear in program listings, however, they appear as the character preceded by a caret mark:

```
^S ^C ^[
```

How you enter them depends on the program you use to create the listing. Some word processors cannot accept any such codes, because they use these characters as commands. Some of them will accept only a few of the control characters, while still others will accept all of them.

Escape Characters

The Escape character (ASCII 27) is a special control character, equivalent to Ctrl-[. When the Escape character is required in a program listing, it appears either as ^[or as a ← (its graphic representation in Table E.1). It precedes most codes sent to the printer as well as codes known as ANSI escape sequences, which are explained fully in Volume I, Chapter 9 and reviewed in Chapter 3. (A complete reference appears in Appendix D.)

Again, how you enter this character depends on the software you use. Generally, if you can insert a control character into a file by preceding it with a command key (such as Ctrl-P in WordStar), you can insert an Escape character either by following the command key with a [character, or by pressing the Escape key.

If You Don't Want to Type in the Listings

If you'd rather not type in the listings, all the programs that appear in this book, along with most of the public-domain utility programs we discuss, are available on disk. To obtain a copy of the disk, see the back of the book.

CONVENTIONS USED IN THIS BOOK

All file names, path names, and DOS commands appear entirely in uppercase characters. However, you can enter them in uppercase, lowercase, or a combination of both.

The file name *FILENAME.EXT* is a generic name, representing any file. If several file names are used as part of a command, the form

    FILE1.EXT FILE2.EXT. . .FILEN.EXT

is used.

When sample syntax is given for a command, anything in square brackets is optional, and anything in italics is generic. Thus, for example, when you see the command

    CHKDSK [*drive*]

you must type

    CHKDSK

and you may optionally follow it by a drive specifier, such as A: or C:. Do not type the word *drive* or the brackets. You must always press Return after entering a command.

Throughout the book, marginal symbols will help you to find important information. The symbol

denotes information pertaining to a specific release of DOS, or to a particular hardware configuration. It always appears with a notation as to the relevant version. The symbol

indicates a hint that will smooth out a process, or make some technique easier to use. The symbol

denotes a warning regarding something to avoid: an undesirable consequence of a technique or command, or a mistake that can be easily made.

THE SYSTEM ASSUMED BY THIS BOOK

In order to make full use of this book, your computer system should have the following components:

- DOS 2.0 or later (DOS 3.1 or later preferred)
- 640K of system memory
- Two or more disk drives, including either two diskette drives (of any type), or one diskette drive and a hard disk
- A printer
- A monitor with an appropriate adapter
- A serial port or a modem
- Expansion memory beyond 640K

If you have an EGA adapter and monitor, you will find many hints on ways to use them. We also address the issues of extended and expanded memory at some length, although you can do many of the things we describe without it.

WHERE IS
DOS TODAY?

1

TRYING TO KEEP UP TO DATE with DOS can be almost a full-time career. Microsoft presents a new release of MS-DOS approximately every six to nine months. In the six-year lifetime of MS-DOS we have seen versions 1.0, 1.05, 1.1, 2.0, 2.1, 2.11, 3.0, 3.1, 3.2, 3.3, 3.31, and even 4.0 (in Europe). In addition, many computer manufacturers have released their own versions of DOS. Some of these releases are stripped-down versions of a standard release, with only the bare minimum of commands needed to run the computer. Other manufacturers have included extra commands and facilities. Still others have made some minor changes. For example, Epson and ITT have different FORMAT commands for hard disks and diskettes. Sperry and Compaq include commands that allow you to use all of a hard disk that is larger than 32MB for DOS. Some manufacturers' versions of MS-DOS include many more menus and messages than others.

This book will focus primarily on DOS 3.X. Since there are significant additions to each iteration of DOS 3.X, they bear reviewing here.

DOS 3.0

Release 3.0 of MS-DOS had numerous additions and enhancements. Most importantly, the third generation of MS-DOS is designed to work with the faster processor chip and high-density drives of the AT series of computers. In addition, facilities were added to allow the user to configure the keyboard and the style of date and time display for different languages. A GRAFTABL program, which permits the display of graphics characters on graphics screens, makes possible the display of those foreign-language characters with ASCII codes higher than 127.

A third new feature involves file sharing and block locking, so that files can be shared by several users at the same time without the risk of "deadly embrace." Finally, software was included to create a RAM disk in a portion of memory. (The assembly-language code to create this program has been present in several generations of the DOS manual, but only with release 3.0 was it actually made available on disk.)

DOS 3.1

Two significant additions were made to DOS with release 3.1. First, enhancements were added to many commands to make them compatible with local-area networks. Second, two new commands were added, JOIN and SUBST, to allow the user to reassign drives to directories, and to combine drives. These features made it easier to use software that was not designed with tree-structured directories in mind.

DOS 3.2

As with all previous revisions of DOS, DOS 3.2 was created to deal with a hardware change. In this instance, there were two: double-sided 3½-inch microfloppy diskettes, such as are used on some laptop computers; and external hard-disk drives. Most obviously, DISKCOMP, DISKCOPY, and FORMAT were made to operate effectively on microfloppies. These disks hold 720K.

In addition, several other commands were enhanced. To reduce the chance of formatting the default drive by accident, the FORMAT command no longer functions without parameters. The ATTRIB command, which in earlier releases of DOS 3.X set or cleared the read-only bit of the attribute byte, is now able to set or clear the archive bit. The SELECT command (present only in some manufacturers' versions of 3.2) formats a diskette, copies the DOS files onto it, and establishes default nationality formats and keyboards.

DOS 3.2 also includes two new external file-management commands: XCOPY and REPLACE. These commands allow fast and selective copying of files. They provide many options not available with the COPY command.

To supplement the local-area network support added in release 3.1, DOS 3.2 also supports token-ring networks.

In addition, MS-DOS 3.2, but not PC-DOS 3.2, includes the APPEND external command. (IBM included the APPEND command with its network software, but not with DOS.) This command creates a search path for data files as well as program files. There were also minor enhancements to other commands.

DOS 3.3

DOS 3.3 was released for IBM's PS/2 series of computers. This release includes many new commands for dealing with the new hardware. Most obviously (as usual), the FORMAT, DISKCOMP, and DISKCOPY commands can now address another storage medium—1.44MB microfloppy diskettes. There are special files for addressing new types of screens. In addition, a complex system has been introduced for selecting foreign-language character sets and keyboards. The MODE command has been enhanced to handle serial communications at 19,200 bps and address up to four serial ports. Previous versions of DOS could go only as high as 9600 baud and could address only two serial ports. In addition, DOS 3.3 is better able to address new display types, such as the VGA (video graphics array) on the PS/2 computers and the LCD display used on many laptops. Finally, the APPEND command is now available in PC-DOS as well as MS-DOS.

DOS 3.31

As of this writing, only Compaq has a release 3.31 of DOS. This DOS differs from earlier releases primarily in the features of the FDISK command. In this release, FDISK can format a hard disk that is larger than 32MB as a single volume. However, the documentation warns you that your software may not be able to deal with this larger volume size. (For a discussion of why hard-disk volumes have been limited to 32MB, see Chapter 5.)

As a result of each hardware manufacturer tailoring DOS to the requirements of its computers, there are literally dozens of versions of each release of MS-DOS. For example, we have used no less than 11 versions of MS-DOS 3.1: IBM, Epson, Zenith, Toshiba, Panasonic, Computerland, Compaq, GriD, ITT, Sperry, and Businessland/Wyse.

COMPATIBILITY AMONG VERSIONS

Generally, programs written to run in conjunction with earlier versions of DOS will run just as well with later versions. The converse, however, may not be true. If you have a program that says it requires DOS 2.0 or later, don't expect it to run with DOS 1.1.

What is considerably more problematic is compatibility between versions of the programs that make up DOS itself, and between different manufacturers' versions of DOS and different computers. Running the external programs from, say, DOS 2.1 while your computer is operating under the control of DOS 3.1 will probably result in the error message

Incorrect DOS version

You'll get the same message if you try to run external programs from DOS 3.1 while your computer is under the control of DOS 2.1. The external programs in the various DOS releases are tailored to match the characteristics of the system files and COMMAND.COM, which have changed significantly from one release to the next. Therefore, you should not try to mix different versions of DOS.

As a rule, programs written to run with earlier versions of DOS will run with later versions. However, they will not take advantage of all the options included in later versions. On the other hand, there is no guarantee that programs written to run under later versions of DOS will run with earlier versions. Indeed, few programs today will still run with DOS 1.X, although most will run with DOS 2.0 or later.

In the years between 1981 and 1987, the architecture of the IBM PC/XT and PC/AT became stable enough that differences between these versions were barely perceptible. We have had no noticeable problems running Compaq DOS on a Computerland AT nor running Epson DOS or PC-DOS on a nameless Taiwanese clone.

If your computer is 100 percent IBM-compatible, you can probably use any release of PC-DOS that you like, as well as the version of MS-DOS supplied by your computer's manufacturer. If compatibility is any less than 100 percent, you can expect occasional trouble and unpredictable results.

In this book, the term *MS-DOS* will refer to a master version of MS-DOS, which is the basis for all versions with a given release number. This version is released to computer manufacturers, but is theoretically unobtainable by ordinary users except from computer manufacturers. (In actual fact, we bought a copy of MS-DOS 3.2, in Microsoft's typical blue box, off the shelf at a neighborhood computer store, and we've seen MS-DOS 3.3 in the same format.) The term DOS refers collectively to all versions—or all versions with a given release number—including PC-DOS. When a different name, such as PC-DOS, is used, it refers to a specific computer manufacturer's released version.

At the lowest level, all computers that use MS-DOS or PC-DOS can use the same data files. Of course, it may be difficult to exchange them because of differences in the media. With 5¼ and 3½ inch disks in 360K, 720K, 800K, 1.2MB, and 1.44MB formats, you may not be able to move files from one computer to another very easily, even if they use the same operating system. (See Chapter 13 for ways to deal with this problem.)

WHAT VERSION OF DOS DO I NEED?

If you want to use the examples in this book, you should be using DOS 2.0 or later. We will point out any examples that require DOS 3.X.

There is no reason why you should not use one of the 3.X versions on an 8088-based computer. Many significant features of the newer releases are of use to 8088, 8086, and 80286 users. The newer DOS releases do take quite a bit more memory, so applications that need over 600K to run may be unable to fit in the space left after DOS loads itself.

To further illustrate this point, Table 1.1 shows the relative size of DOS from release 2.0 through 3.3. The figures suggest that if DOS were to continue on its present course, you would eventually use an entire 640K to simply load the operating system.

		IBMBIO.COM	IBMDOS.COM	COMMAND.COM	TOTAL K
	2.X	4	18	18	40
	3.0	9	19	22	50
DOS RELEASE	3.1	10	28	24	62
	3.2	16	28	24	68
	3.3	22	30	25	77

Table 1.1 ▲ *Memory Use of DOS Releases (K).*

WHERE WILL DOS GO FROM HERE?

The next operating system for the PC family of computers, OS/2, has already been released by IBM and Microsoft. OS/2 will allow true multitasking and address significantly larger amounts of memory. Notice that the *D* has been dropped, suggesting that the new system is not precisely a *disk* operating system. This is only part of the story.

OS/2 represents an alternative concept in microcomputer operating systems. It will include functions currently available in large-scale environments such as UNIX. In addition to multitasking and large-scale memory addressing, OS/2 will use a special graphics-based user interface called a *presentation manager*. The result is a far cry from the old

    A>

prompt. Microsoft will use a version of Windows as the presentation manager, and IBM is expected to use something that will look like Windows. (For a discussion of Windows, see Chapter 8. For more on OS/2, see Chapter 9.)

Microsoft has committed itself to continued development of MS-DOS for computers using the 8086 and 8088 processors, and it will be sufficient for many 80286-based systems as well. OS/2 will be predominantly for fast 80286- and 80386-based machines.

One of the major differences between MS-DOS and OS/2 is the way the two operating systems communicate with your hardware. DOS communicates with your hardware through a series of *services* that make up the *BIOS,* or Basic Input/Output System. The BIOS comprises a program in special ROM chips on your motherboard. However, these services tend to be inefficient for some applications and don't work for some purposes. Therefore, many "poorly behaved" programs avoid using BIOS services and write directly to the hardware. As a result, they may not work properly on some computers, whose BIOS does not match that of IBM. Both application programs and device drivers can behave poorly. DOS cannot protect memory from poorly behaved programs. OS/2, on the other hand, uses the features of the 80286 processor to protect one program's memory from another.

OS/2 requires customized device drivers to address your hardware. These drivers are provided by the hardware manufacturer. They ensure that OS/2 will be compatible with your system. The only way OS/2 can address the hardware is via a device driver. If an appliction attempts to access hardware directly, OS/2 will abort the application.

Figure 1.1 shows how OS/2 and DOS interface with the hardware.

No doubt many major computer manufacturers will charter Microsoft to produce OS/2 drivers for their 80286- and 80386-based computers. Smaller manufacturers of clones may have to use the most generic components in order to use a common set of OS/2 drivers. The PS/2 computers

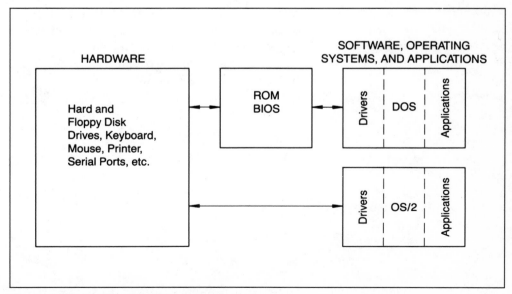

Figure 1.1 ▲ *OS/2 and DOS Hardware Interfaces.*

using 80206 and 80306 chips incorporate a great deal of customized circuitry. This makes it increasingly difficult for smaller manufacturers to rely on IBM's version of the operating system and its device drivers.

Does the emergence of OS/2 mean the end of DOS? This seems unlikely. One reason is that there are still millions of fully functional PCs using the 8088, 8086, and NEC V-20 microprocessors, which will be unable to run OS/2. Another fact that bodes well for DOS is that the IBM Extended Edition of OS/2 is estimated to cost six times as much as DOS. Applications that run under OS/2 will no doubt be priced similarly.

OS/2 was designed primarily to break the 640K barrier and to allow multitasking and virtual memory addressing. However, taking advantage of these features brings some major problems. To use OS/2 on most existing 80286 and 80386 computers you will need at least 1.5MB of RAM. A pointing device such as a mouse will be helpful as well. A high-resolution graphics adapter (EGA or VGA) and monitor are highly recommended. You will also need a large, fast hard disk. The operating system itself requires over a megabyte of hard-disk storage and will not run from a diskette. OS/2 seems to be intended for the corporate market.

We believe DOS is a low-cost alternative that will continue to be the only operating system used by the majority of PC owners. Perhaps if OS/2—and, more importantly, OS/2 applications—drop significantly in price, DOS may be supplanted on newer computers. However, DOS will still serve the needs of most of us for the immediate future and will be in use for many years to come. It is a powerful operating system, and we believe DOS will be continually enhanced to use the features of new hardware.

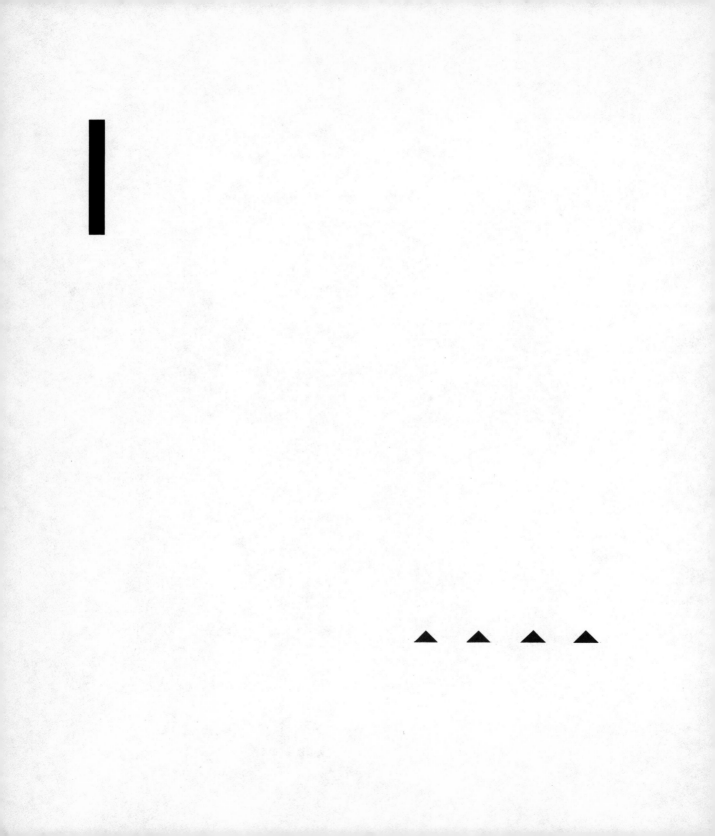

PART I

EXTENDING DOS

Enhancing Your Batch Programs

VOLUME I OF THIS WORK presented a complete overview of the DOS batch programming language. Included were many advanced features that you could use to make your computer perform exactly as you wanted. Many other works also discuss the batch language, and we recommend that you become very familiar with the batch language before considering the extensions and alternatives discussed in this chapter. For those of you who find the batch language has too many limitations for your needs, this chapter explores some solutions.

Having used the batch language for many years, we have seen it develop into a useful way of grouping commands and still allowing some flexibility. However, batch files, even in the latest version of DOS, are little more than a simple substitute for typing commands directly into the machine for immediate action.

It would be nice if we could have an operating-system language that works closely with DOS commands and programs, yet has extremely powerful variable handling, looping , and program control. For example, setting up a simple loop containing a number of commands that iterates N times—where N is a parameter passed to the batch file—is extremely difficult. Another limitation of batch files is that they can't manipulate lines of text, break up long words, or group words together. They also can't do simple arithmetic. These tasks are quite easy with an extended batch language.

EXTENDED BATCH LANGUAGES

There are several extensions to the batch language on the market. We'll look at two of them here: EBL, which stands for Extended Batch Language, and Personal REXX, which stands for REstructured eXtended eXecutive, an executive PC language based on an IBM mainframe product that is used under the VM/CMS operating system. These two extended batch languages give you the same facilities in all versions of DOS from 2.1 through 3.3.

Because EBL is a shareware product, it is an excellent introduction to powerful batch procedures. You can try it and see if you like it before you pay any fees. If EBL proves to be what you are looking for, then for a relatively low cost you can purchase complete documentation and additional functions. If EBL is not powerful enough for your requirements, then you may prefer Personal REXX. REXX is an extremely powerful extension and alternative to the DOS batch language. If you want to learn how to program on the PC you may even find REXX useful as an interim language.

EBL

Extended Batch Language (EBL), from Seaware, is an executive or command programming language for DOS. It is rather like having a high-level language available from the DOS prompt. The minimum requirements are the same as for this book—an IBM PC or compatible, and DOS 2.0 or later. EBL gives you greater control over the processing of DOS commands than does the standard DOS batch language. EBL includes these features:

- ▲ Loop and control structures
- ▲ String functions, including analysis of string length, parsing, and using parts of strings
- ▲ Many types of variables in addition to the DOS replaceable parameters
- ▲ Error traps
- ▲ The ability to accept single-keystroke input in response to a prompt

▲ Control of screen color without using ANSI.SYS

▲ True conditional branching

▲ A trace facility you can use not only to debug, but to learn

▲ Extensive string-handling operations (parsing, substring, length, etc.)

▲ Mathematical functions

▲ Special features for handling return codes, which DOS uses the ERRORLEVEL command to process

▲ The ability to use both DOS and EBL commands in the same program

In many ways EBL is as powerful as BASIC or Pascal, but it is easier to learn. In contrast, although the DOS batch language has improved with each release of DOS, its ability to use variables and to direct program control has remained primitive. With the facilities of EBL, it is extremely easy to construct working menus—much easier than with ANSI.SYS, for example.

There are many benefits to using a language like EBL. For example, suppose you need to execute a communications program to log on to a bulletin board to get some financial data, download the data, import it to a Lotus 1-2-3 spreadsheet, and execute a 1-2-3 macro to print a graph. Unfortunately, as often happens, the bulletin board's phone could be busy for many hours. It would be nice to crank up the process and leave it to execute. One way to achieve this is by using EBL.

If you are a system programmer who needs to perform many sequences of tasks between the linker, compilers, debuggers, and editors, you could use EBL to create an automated procedure to provide these functions. For example, you may want to try several different library combinations to see which one works. EBL could read the return code for each link. If it is not zero, EBL could instruct the computer to try a different combination of libraries. You could also program EBL to perform other functions depending on messages received from any program.

As another example, suppose that you need to switch frequently among word processing, spreadsheet, and accounting programs. You could use EBL to do this automatically. In addition, you could create a menu system and help files to assist users in a variety of ways.

In a networking environment, EBL can simulate users at many terminals performing real tasks. By executing EBL procedures on each workstation, you can simulate users logging on, using shared databases,
transferring large files, printing documents, and sending messages. This
makes it easy to test the load on the system.

EBL has many other impressive features. One is that you can modify
EBL itself. When you become a registered user, you receive the Turbo
Pascal source code to EBL, which you can modify to your specific needs.
EBL is also compatible with many other operating environments: PC
Network, TopView, Windows, and DESQview can all run in conjunc-
tion with EBL.

To use EBL, you must have a program called BAT.COM in your current directory or on your search path. To have a batch program use EBL,
make the command

> BAT /P

its first line. Thereafter you can use any batch or EBL commands in your
batch files.

There are two ways to distinguish between EBL commands and their
DOS equivalents. The /P switch tells EBL to process any commands
shared by both DOS and EBL as EBL commands. Alternatively, you can
preface any command specific to EBL with

> BAT

For example, to use EBL's TYPE command to display text on the screen
you could enter a command such as

> BAT TYPE Display this text on the screen

If you also include DOS external commands in your file, you should
use the /S switch. This switch tells EBL to use the DOS command shell
when it encounters commands that it doesn't recognize. Batch programs that start with BAT /P instead of BAT /P/S, and also contain
DOS external commands, will generate a mess of syntax errors.

The BAT command places the file BAT.COM in memory, and it stays
there once it is loaded. It is not reloaded with every invocation. If you
find that EBL is not processing your DOS commands properly,
you should use the BAT preface for your EBL commands, and enter the
DOS commands in the normal manner.

Listing 2.1 is one of Seaware's EBL batch file samples, called EDIT-SET.BAT. This program allows you to search for and modify DOS environment strings. The first line gives away the fact that this is no ordinary batch file because it is a

BAT /P

command. As explained above, this command invokes EBL's processor.

```
 1: bat /p * Edit DOS Environment settings...
 2:
 3: *      (c) Copyright 1986 by Seaware Corp.
 4: *
 5:      if %1/ = / goto -tell
 6:      /U %1 = %1 |/U-
 7:      trace.off
 8:      shell set >editset$.dat
 9:      <editset$.dat
10:
11: -read.line
12:      read.parsed %0
13:      if %0 ? %1= = 1 then goto -found.var.match
14:      if %0 <> ^Z then goto -read.line
15:      <
16:      type Environment variable ''' %1 ''' was not found!
17:      type Current settings are: |type
18:      shell type editset$.dat
19:      shell del  editset$.dat
20:      exit
21: -found.var.match
22:      <
23:      stack Set %0;
24:      shell del  editset$.dat
25:      exit
26:
27: -tell      begtype
```

Listing 2.1 ▲ *EDITSET.BAT.*

To invoke this program, enter

EDITSET *variable*

where *variable* is an environment variable. This batch file will let you edit or change any DOS environment variables. The environment always contains the variables PATH, PROMPT, and COMSPEC, although you can add others with the SET command. (See the section on environment variables later in this chapter.)

EDITSET.BAT will put the current setting on the DOS command line. You can then use the built-in editor for the DOS command line, or another DOS-prompt editor such as DOSEDIT to rewrite the command, changing the value of the variable. It's much easier to use this program with a DOS command-line editor such as DOSEDIT.

Personal REXX

As mentioned earlier, REXX is derived from the IBM mainframe VM/CMS environment. It was the third generation of a batch language for that environment. Sadly, there was no PC equivalent until Mansfield Software produced a version of REXX for the PC in 1984. At first glance, REXX looks like any other programming language. However, its programs work with DOS as though they were batch files.

The biggest advantage of Personal REXX is its concision. DOS batch files that might take a hundred lines or more can be written with a handful of REXX commands. In addition to all the features of EBL, Personal REXX includes many functions that can tell you a great deal about your hardware. You can even address memory locations and ports directly.

You can use REXX either as a memory-resident program or a transient program. In either case, you begin by loading a program called RXINTMGR.COM. This is the REXX Interrupt Manager. Once the manager is loaded, you invoke it by entering a command of the form

REXX *PROGRAM*

where *PROGRAM* is the name of the file to execute. REXX programs normally have the extension .REX. However, you can specify the extension on the command line if you use a different one.

To make it resident, you simply enter the command

REXX /R

You must then invoke your programs with a command of the form

RX *PROGRAM*

The programs will load much more quickly with REXX in resident mode. However, as with all resident programs you must give up some of your RAM—in this case, about 115K. You can remove REXX from memory with the command

RX /U

REXX does not automatically pass over DOS commands, as EBL does. Rather, to execute a DOS command in a REXX program, you must enclose it in quotes.

If you have expanded memory, REXX takes advantage of it. After REXX executes a program or procedure, the program stays in memory in case it is needed again. However, if expanded memory is available, REXX will store the code there, rather than in base memory, leaving the latter free for other procedures. This is useful if you have a routine that is called repeatedly. It also speeds up execution of long programs.

Listing 2.2 illustrates a simple REXX procedure to tell you what equipment is installed in your computer. This example shows how REXX's special functions use low-level DOS routines normally accessible only via a high-level language or assembly-language routines.

```
 1: /* SYSTEM Status indicator an example of some REXX functions */
 2: 'cls'                                   /* Use a DOS clear
screen command*/
 3: call scrwrite  1, 5, 'REXX sample system status'
 4: call scrwrite  4,5,'Total number of drives    -'
 5: call scrwrite  4,40,pcdisk(N)           /* Get all drives*/
 6:
 7: call scrwrite  6,5,'Number of Floppy Drives  -'
 8: call scrwrite  6,40,pcfloppy()          /* How many floppies?*/
 9:
10: call scrwrite  8,5,'Number of Game ports      -'
11: call scrwrite  8,40,pcgame()            /* Game port?*/
12:
13: call scrwrite  10,5,'Number of Parallel ports-'
14: call scrwrite  10,40,pcparallel()       /* Number of printer ports*/
15:
16: call scrwrite  12,5,'Number of Serial ports  -'
17: call scrwrite  12,40,pcserial()         /* Number of comm ports*/
18:
19: call scrwrite  14,5,'Amount of memory in K    -'
20: call scrwrite  14,40,pcram()            /* RAM in 1024 blocks*/
21:
22: call scrwrite  16,5,'Date of system ROM       -'
23: call scrwrite  16,40,pcromdate()        /* Get ROM date.*/
24:
25: call scrwrite  18,5,'System type           -'
26: pct = pctype()
27:   select
28:       when pct = -1 then call scrwrite  18,40,'Unknown PC type'
29:       when pct =  0 then call scrwrite  18,40,'IBM PC'
30:       when pct =  1 then call scrwrite  18,40,'IBM PC/XT or Portable'
31:       when pct =  2 then call scrwrite  18,40,'IBM PCjr'
32:       when pct =  3 then call scrwrite  18,40,'IBM PC/AT'
33:       when pct =  4 then call scrwrite  18,40,'IBM XT/286'
34:       when pct =  5 then call scrwrite  18,40,'IBM PC Convertible'
35:       when pct = 30 then call scrwrite  18,40,'IBM PS/2 Model 30'
36:       when pct = 50 then call scrwrite  18,40,'IBM PS/2 Model 50'
37:       when pct = 60 then call scrwrite  18,40,'IBM PS/2 Model 60'
38:       when pct = 80 then call scrwrite  18,40,'IBM PS/2 Model 80'
39:       otherwise call scrwrite   18,40,'PC compatible'
40:   end
41: call cursor 24, 1 /* Place cursor at bottom of screen*/
42: exit
```

Listing 2.2 ▲ *EQUIP.REX.*

Here is a line-by-line explanation of how this program works.

1:      The program title is included as a comment. Comments in REXX are set off by the characters /* at the beginning and */ at the end.

2: Executes the DOS CLS function.

3: Displays a simple message using the SCRWRITE function, which places the cursor at a particular point on the screen before displaying a message. This command line places the cursor at row 1, column 5.

4: Displays a message at row 4, column 5.

5: This line performs two functions. It executes the REXX function PCDISK, which returns the number of logical drives available. However, it first uses the SCRWRITE function to place the cursor at row 4, column 40. Thus, the message displayed is the *result* of the function, rather than the function itself.

7–23: These lines have the same effect as lines 4 and 5, but display different messages and execute different functions. Each function reveals something different about the installed hardware.

25: This line displays the number associated with the particular type of computer, which the PCTYPE function returns. This is often called a *signature*. This example tests only for various types of IBM computers. However, other manufacturers such as Compaq also have their unique signatures. (Some compatibles use the same number as their IBM equivalent, so the signature returned by this part of the program may not accurately reflect the type of computer on which it is executed.)

26–40: This section of the program represents what is called a *select/case structure* in many programming languages. This is a control structure that allows your program to choose among a number of alternative actions, based on the value held by the controlling variable or expression. In this instance, the controlling variable is PCT, which receives the value of the PCTYPE function. Each WHEN command tests the value of PCT. If the returned value matches the one expressed in the WHEN statement, the command following THEN is executed. If no match is found, then whatever follows the command OTHERWISE in line 39 is executed.

41: To keep the DOS command line from appearing in the middle of the display, the CURSOR function places the last line at the bottom of the screen.

42: Returns control to DOS.

REXX, EBL, and DOS Compared

As DOS becomes more complex, you have to spend more and more time delving in DOS manuals and books like this to use even the most basic DOS commands. As Volume 1 showed, you can simplify matters by creating separate batch files to execute different versions of a command. Another way of handling the problem is to create menus. We'll construct a menu for the DOS FORMAT command. Since there are now so many disk media available, and since each works with different versions of DOS, it would be useful if you could choose the type of format you want from a menu instead of looking up a mess of switches.

Listing 2.3 shows such a menu constructed in REXX and named FMT.REX. This program displays a menu from which you can choose among the more popular formatting options for DOS 3.3. It works on PS/2, AT, and standard PC computers, and it will format 1.44MB and 720K 3½-inch disks as well as 1.2MB and 360K 5¼-inch disks.

The entire program is a loop. It gives you a choice of format commands. The menu reappears after each command is executed. To end the program, enter a lowercase x and the menu disappears.

Here are the procedures used in this program:

2: The start of a loop. This command waits for a lowercase x to be pressed.

3: Instead of using a DOS CLS command, as we did in EQUIP.REX, the SCRWRITE function clears the screen by filling all 2000 character cells with a blue background color.

4: Displays a message in magenta on a white background.

5: Places the cursor out of the way in the lower-left corner of the screen.

6–15: These lines display the menu. The series of commas after the text hold places for parameters that affect the way the

```
    1: /* MS-DOS Format Command Menu.*/
    2: do until key = 'x'
    3: call scrwrite 1,1,,2000,,30
    4: call scrwrite 23,9,' Select a formatting option (lowerc
ase "x" to return to DOS) ',,,117
    5: call cursor 25,1
    6: call scrwrite 2,10,'F1  - Default format drive A, boota
ble',,,30
    7: call scrwrite 4,10,'F2  - Default format drive B, boota
ble',,,30
    8: call scrwrite 6,10,'F3  - Default format drive A, non-b
ootable',,,30
    9: call scrwrite 8,10,'F4  - Default format drive B, non-b
ootable',,,30
   10: call scrwrite 10,10,'F5  - Double density 2.44 MB drive
A, non-bootable',,,30
   11: call scrwrite 12,10,'F6  - Double density 2.44 MB drive
A, bootable',,,30
   12: call scrwrite 14,10,'F7  - 360K format in 2.2MB A, non-
bootable--RISKY!',,,30
   13: call scrwrite 16,10,'F8  - Largest single-sided format,
drive A',,,30
   14: call scrwrite 18,10,'F9  - Largest single-sided format,
drive B',,,30
   15: call scrwrite 20,9,'F10 - 8-sector format for any vers
ion of DOS, drive A',,,30
   16: key = inkey()
   17:    if length(key) = 2 then do
   18:       fk = c2d(substr(key,2,1))-58
   19:       call scrwrite 1,1,,2000,,0
   20:       select
   21:          when fk = 1  then 'format a:/s/v'
   22:          when fk = 2  then 'format b:/s/v'
   23:          when fk = 3  then 'format a:/v':
   24:          when fk = 4  then 'format b:/v'
   25:          when fk = 5  then 'format a:/v/n:9/t:80'
   26:          when fk = 6  then 'format a:/s/v/n:9/t:80'
   27:          when fk = 7  then 'format a:/v/4'
   28:          when fk = 8  then 'format a:/v/1'
   29:          when fk = 9  then 'format b:/v/1'
   30:          when fk = 10 then 'format a:/b'
   31:       end
   32:    end
   33: end
   34: exit
```

Listing 2.3 ▲ *FMT.REX.*

line looks. The final parameter is a number that translates into a combination of foreground and background colors. This code produces bright yellow on blue.

16:   The INKEY function is used to capture any keys pressed.

17:   Rejects any key that is not a function key.

18, 19: The character-to-decimal function (c2d) subtracts 58 from the key value. This allows us to use the values 1 through 10 instead of 59 through 68 in the select/case structure that follows.

20–31: A select/case structure that executes the appropriate version of the FORMAT command for each menu option.

The menu produced by this program appears in Figure 2.1.

For comparison, programs roughly equivalent to the FMT.REX program in the EBL and native DOS batch languages follow. FMTEBL.BAT, shown in Listing 2.4, is the EBL version of the same program.

```
    F1  - Default format drive A, bootable

    F2  - Default format drive B, bootable

    F3  - Default format drive A, non-bootable

    F4  - Default format drive B, non-bootable

    F5  - Double density 1.44 MB drive A, non-bootable

    F6  - Double density 1.44 MB drive A, bootable

    F7  - 360K format in 1.2MB A, non-bootable--RISKY!

    F8  - Largest single-sided format, drive A

    F9  - Largest single-sided format, drive B

    F10 - 8-sector format for any version of DOS, drive A


    Select a formatting option (lowercase "x" to return to DOS)
```

Figure 2.1 ▲ *Menu Displayed by FMT.REX.*

You can position the cursor in EBL using the LOCATE command, just as you can with the SCRWRITE command in REXX. In this example, we have used the commands BEGTYPE and END to display a block of text, instead of displaying the text line by line. (We could have done the same in REXX with the SAY command.) EBL has an INKEY function similar to REXX's, but for variety we have used the READ function. Therefore, this version of the program uses the number keys rather than the function keys.

When EBL clears the screen, it clears to the default colors, even if you give it colors to use with the COLOR command. Therefore, we have constructed a loop to clear the screen to blue. This loop writes a string of 80 space characters (i.e., one line) to the screen 25 times.

```
 1: bat /p /s
 2: * The next line is a string of 80 space characters
 3: %a = "                                                                               "

 4: color 1E
 5: -entry
 6: %b = 1
 7: locate 1 1
 8: -clear
 9: type %a
10: %b = %b + 1
11: if %b >25 then goto -endclear
12: goto -clear
13: -endclear
14: color 75
15: locate 10 23
16: type  Select a formatting option ("X" to return to DOS)
17: color 1E
18: locate 1 1
19: begtype
20:
21:
22:          1 - Default format drive A, bootable
23:
24:          2 - Default format drive B, bootable
25:
26:          3 - Default format drive A, non-bootable
27:
28:          4 - Default format drive B, non-bootable
29:
30:          5 - Double density 2.44 MB drive A, non-bootable
31:
32:          6 - Double density 2.44 MB drive A, bootable
33:
34:          7 - 360K format in 2.2MB drive A, non-bootable--RISKY!
35:
36:          8 - Largest single-sided format, drive A
37:
38:          9 - Largest single-sided format, drive A
39:
40:          0 - 8-sector format for any version of DOS, drive A
41:
42: end
43: locate 1 24
44: read %1
45:          if %1 = 1 format a:/s/v
46:          if %1 = 2 format b:/s/v
47:          if %1 = 3 format a:/v
48:          if %1 = 4 format b:/v
49:          if %1 = 5 format a:/s/v:9/t:80
50:          if %1 = 6 format a:/s/v/n:9/t:80
51:          if %1 = 7 format a:/v/4
52:          if %1 = 8 format a:/v/1
53:          if %1 = 9 format b:/v/1
54:          if %1 = 10 format a:/b
55:          if %1 = x exit
56:          if %1 = X exit
57: goto -entry
```

Listing 2.4 ▲ *FMTEBL.BAT.*

To run this program, you must have BAT.COM in the current directory or on the search path. Here is how this program operates:

1:     Invokes the EBL processor, and tells it to let DOS process any external DOS commands.

2:     A comment, indicated by the leading asterisk.

3:      Creates a string of 80 space characters and assigns it to the variable %a.

4:      Sets the screen colors to bright yellow on blue by assigning a value to the COLOR command.

5:      -entry is a *label,* indicating the beginning of a loop within the batch file.

6–13:   This is the routine that clears the screen to blue. First a counter variable (%b) is established, and set to 1. Then the cursor is moved to the home position with the LOCATE command. The label -clear marks the beginning of a loop. Within this loop, the space string is written to the screen and the counter is incremented until the 25th line is reached. When the counter reaches 25, the loop is exited.

14–16:   These lines display the prompt message near the bottom of the screen, in magenta on a white background. Notice that the row and column parameters of the LOCATE command are in the opposite order from those of the SCRNWRITE command in REXX. The COLOR parameters in EBL are actually easier to decipher (if you can read hex) than those in REXX. The first hex digit represents the standard color codes for background (0–7) and the second the standard codes for foreground (0– 15, or 0–F hex). In REXX, the color codes are the decimal equivalent of the hexadecimal number represented by the combination of these digits, which doesn't make a whole lot of sense.

17–18:   Restores the default colors of yellow on blue, and repositions the cursor at home.

19–42:   These lines, set off by the BEGTYPE and END commands, create the menu display.

43:      Repositions the cursor.

44:      The read %1 is an input command; it assigns whatever you type to the variable %1.

45–54: EBL does not have a select/case structure. Therefore, a series of IF statements tests %1 for each of the acceptable values. When a match is found, EBL executes the appropriate DOS command by loading a secondary command processor.

55–57: If an uppercase or lowercase X is entered, the program ends. If anything else is entered, the program returns to the -entry label and starts over.

The display produced by this program appears in Figure 2.2. Notice that you can't put extra spaces around the prompt message, as we did in the REXX version.

```
1  - Default format drive A, bootable

2  - Default format drive B, bootable

3  - Default format drive A, non-bootable

4  - Default format drive B, non-bootable

5  - Double density 1.44 MB drive A, non-bootable

6  - Double density 1.44 MB drive A, bootable

7  - 360K format in 1.2MB drive A, non-bootable--RISKY!

8  - Largest single-sided format, drive A

9  - Largest single-sided format, drive A

0  - 8-sector format for any version of DOS, drive A

Select a formatting option ("X" to return to DOS)
```

Figure 2.2 ▲ *Menu Displayed by FMTEBL.BAT.*

The DOS batch file version of the same menu uses ANSI escape sequences to assign the various format commands to the function keys. It also uses ANSI escape sequences to control color, and to position text on the screen. The DOS version actually uses fewer lines of code (only 28). However, it requires four files, and it is much harder to understand than the other versions. Moreover, the facilities provided by

ANSI.SYS for controlling the screen and accepting input are considerably weaker than those of EBL and REXX.

We begin with a short batch file, FMT.BAT, shown in Listing 2.5. This file does nothing more than use the TYPE command to execute ANSI escape sequences in two files, and change the prompt. The FKEYS.FMT file, which appears in Listing 2.6, contains the sequences to program the function keys. FMT.MNU, shown in Listing 2.7, contains the sequences that create the menu screen.

The first line of FMT.MNU contains escape sequences that color and clear the screen, and position the cursor. Each line of text is preceded by an escape sequence to position it on the screen. The last line, line 12,

```
1: ECHO OFF
2: TYPE FKEYS.FMT
3: TYPE FMT.MNU
4: PROMPT Your Choice MM^P
```

Listing 2.5 ▲ *FMT.BAT.*

```
1: ^[[0;104;"TYPE FMT.MNU";13p
2: ^[[0;113;"CLRKEYS";13p
3: ^[[0;59;"FORMAT A:/S/V";13p ^[[0;60;"FORMAT B:/S/V";13p
4: ^[[0;61;"FORMAT A:/V";13p ^[[0;62;"FORMAT B:/V";13p
5: ^[[0;63;"FORMAT A:/V/N:9/T:80";13p ^[[0;64;"FORMAT A:/S/V/N:9/T:80";13
6: ^[[0;65;"FORMAT A:/V/4";13p ^[[0;66;"FORMAT A:/V/1";13p
7: ^[[0;67;"FORMAT B:/V/1";13p ^[[0;68;"FORMAT A:/B";13p
```

Listing 2.6 ▲ *FKEYS.FMT.*

```
 1: ^[[3h^[[1;33;44m^[[2J
 2: ^[[2;10HF1 - Default format drive A, bootable
 3: ^[[4;10HF2 - Default format drive B, bootable
 4: ^[[6;10HF3 - Default format drive A, non-bootable
 5: ^[[8;10HF4 - Default format drive B, non-bootable
 6: ^[[10;10HF5 - Double density disk in 2.44 MB drive A,
non-bootable
 7: ^[[12;10HF6 - Double density disk in 2.44 MB drive A,
bootable
 8: ^[[14;10HF7 - 360K format in 2.2MB drive A, non-bootab
le--RISKY!
 9: ^[[16;10HF8 - Largest single-sided format, drive A
10: ^[[18;10HF9 - Largest single-sided format, drive B
11: ^[[20;9HF10 - 8-sector format for any version of DOS, d
rive A
12: ^[0;35;47m^[[22;9H Press Alt-F1 to redisplay menu, Alt-
F10 to quit. ^[1;33;44m
```

Listing 2.7 ▲ *FMT.MNU.*

begins with a sequence to display the prompt message in magenta on white, and ends with one to restore the original colors of yellow on blue.

Although the menu itself is as attractive as those produced by the other languages (see Figure 2.3), it is not so easy to use. This is partly because the batch program does not retain control once it is executed— it merely reprograms the keys. Therefore, your input has to be entered at a DOS prompt, rather than within a program.

```
    F1 - Default format drive A, bootable

    F2  - Default format drive B, bootable

    F3  - Default format drive A, non-bootable

    F4  - Default format drive B, non-bootable

    F5  - Double density disk in 1.44 MB drive A, non-bootable

    F6  - Double density disk in 1.44 MB drive A, bootable

    F7  - 360K format in 1.2MB drive A, non-bootable--RISKY!

    F8  - Largest single-sided format, drive A

    F9  - Largest single-sided format, drive B

    F10 - 8 sector format for any version of DOS, drive A
    ╞══════════════════════════════════════════════════════╡
    │ Press Alt-F1 to redisplay menu, Alt-F10 to quit. │
Your Choice ⟹ _
```

Figure 2.3 ▲ *Menu Displayed by FMT.MNU.*

We had to use two files (FMT.MNU and FKEYS.FMT) because each time the FORMAT command is executed, the screen scrolls. We had to have a way to bring back the menu. To do this, we assigned the command to display the menu file, FMT.MNU, to function key Alt-F1 in line 1 of FKEYS.FMT. Line 2 of FKEYS.FMT programs the Alt-F10 key to call the fourth file, CLRKEYS.BAT, which appears in Listing 2.8. This file clears all the function-key assignments and restores the normal prompt.

```
1: ECHO OFF
2: ECHO ^[[0;59;0;59p^[[0;60;0;60p^[[0;61;0;61p^[[0;62;0;62p^[[0;63;0;63p
3: ECHO ^[[0;64;0;64p^[[0;65;0;65p^[[0;66;0;66p^[[0;67;0;67p^[[0;68;0;68p
4: ECHO ^[[0;104;0;104p^[[0;113;0;113p^[[2J
5: PROMPT $p$g
```

Listing 2.8 ▲ *CLRKEYS.BAT.*

(Of course, the screen scrolls in the other two versions of the program as well. However, the looping structures provided by these languages allow us to redisplay the menu as part of the program.)

 Warning: ANSI escape sequences can be unpredictable. In an earlier version of this set of programs, we had the sequences that program the Alt-F1 and Alt-F10 keys at the end of FKEYS.FMT, on a single line. On one of the computers where we tested the program, the Alt-F1 sequence appeared not to have been recognized, and the result of pressing the Alt-F10 key combination was not the correct string. There is no explanation for this. None at all. None. We have experienced similar bizarre effects with ANSI sequences on some computers that worked perfectly well on others.

REPLACING COMMAND.COM

If an extended batch language doesn't do the trick for you then it may pay you to replace COMMAND.COM entirely. If you decide to do this, remember that you will need to maintain compatibility with DOS. If you upgrade to a later release of DOS, you will undoubtedly also have to replace your replacement of COMMAND.COM.

Command Plus

Command Plus is a relatively inexpensive DOS command processor published by ESP Software Systems. It replaces DOS's COMMAND-.COM directly, but is fully compatible with it and offers a wealth of extended features. Everything that runs on DOS versions 2.0 through 3.3 works under Command Plus. Command Plus offers significantly enhanced COPY, DEL, and DIR commands and adds a sophisticated BROWSE command. Among other features, it lets you give commands alternative names, and you can enter several commands on a single command line. It also includes a shell programming language and a command stack that lets you recall any of the last 48 commands entered. You can scroll these commands using the cursor keys and re-execute any of the them.

BROWSE, an excellent alternative to the TYPE command, lets you scroll backwards and forwards through text files and search for strings.

With Command Plus's logging facility, you can keep track of all use of the computer. This is most useful for protecting yourself from the IRS, but it has other purposes as well. Command Plus lets you use wild-card patterns to include or exclude file names in a command. For example, the command

    DIR *.[ch]

displays all files with a C or H extension.

DIR itself is also an improvement over COMMAND.COM's DIR. You can display multiple file specifications and hidden files. For example, the command

    DIR *.EXE *.COM *.BAT

will display only EXE, COM, and batch files.

SCRIPT is an interpretive command file processor that has many features similar to EBL. However, because Command Plus is resident, SCRIPT can be used without loading the interpreter first.

Command Plus is not for the casual user, but its flexibility and extent will be sure to attract a large following. It is almost as if someone has looked at where DOS has come over the past four or five versions and projected it ahead to a far off future version.

SOME BATCH PROGRAMMING TIPS AND UTILITIES

Calling One File from Another

DOS 3.3
One of the nicest new batch features of DOS 3.3 is the CALL command. This command allows you to call one batch file from within

another and return safely to the original. In earlier versions of DOS, you could do this with the COMMAND /C command. This worked adequately. However, if your second batch file made any modifications to the environment, those modifications would be lost before you could use them, because the environment created by the COMMAND /C command would disappear when you returned to the original batch file. With the CALL command, this is no longer true.

Batch files can even call themselves, but you must be careful to ensure that the procedure terminates at some point, or you'll have an endless loop that repeats until all your memory is used up or you hit Ctrl-Break, whichever comes first. (Of course, you can always call a batch file from within itself with the %0 parameter in any version of DOS.) Listing 2.9 shows a way to use the CALL command.

```
 1: ECHO OFF
 2: MYPROG1
 3: IF ERRORLEVEL 0 IF NOT ERRORLEVEL 1 ECHO Program successful!
 4: IF ERRORLEVEL 0 IF NOT ERRORLEVEL 1 GOTO endit
 5: IF ERRORLEVEL 1 IF NOT ERRORLEVEL 2 CALL RET1
 6: IF ERRORLEVEL 2 IF NOT ERRORLEVEL 3 CALL RET2
 7: IF ERRORLEVEL 3 CALL RET3
 8: GOTO abnex
 9: :abnex
10: ECHO MYPROG1 ended abnormally--error routine completed.
11: :endit
```

Listing 2.9 ▲ *ERTEST.BAT.*

This program assumes that MYPROG2.COM generates an exit code that can be tested with the ERRORLEVEL command. This command, you may remember, works on a "greater-than-or-equal-to" basis. Therefore, you must be sure not to test for higher error codes when you have already responded to lower ones. Hence, the nested IF statements in lines 3 through 6. Line 4, in particular, is necessary because if the program generated the exit code 0, when everything behaved as it should, you would want to skip all the error routines. Since 1, 2, and 3 are all higher than 0, they would all be executed if the program didn't skip these lines. The programs RET1.BAT, RET2.BAT, and RET3.BAT would all contain separate routines for different error conditions.

Taking Advantage of Environment Variables

A very useful feature of the batch language since DOS 2.0 is its ability to look at and modify environment variables. Finally, in the DOS 3.3

manual, this feature had been documented as being "officially" available. Using this facility, you can see what PATH, COMSPEC, or anything assigned using the SET command has been set to.

An environment variable is set using the SET command with syntax of the form

SET *variable = value*

You can then examine the *value* assigned to *variable* in a batch file by referring to the variable name surrounded by percent signs or to the value preceded by a percent sign. For example, if you included

%COMSPEC%

in a batch file, the batch file would refer to the name of the current command processor.

You can also use this facility to change the path on the fly, and save the old path. Have you ever been greeted with the message

Bad command or filename

Who hasn't? In many cases this could mean that your path is set to

C:\;C:\DOS;C:\BATCH;C:\UTIL

but the file you want is neither on that path nor in the current directory. To fix the problem, you would normally type PATH, see what it's set to, and retype the entire path adding the needed directory to the end of it. Instead, you could use the program NEWPATH.BAT, shown in Listing 2.10, to save your current path and create a new temporary one. When you're done with the program in the missing directory, use OLD-PATH.BAT, shown in Listing 2.11, to restore the original path. (Alternatively, you could use EXTPATH.BAT from Volume 1, Chapter 14. You could then use SYSRESET.BAT from Chapter 9 of that volume to restore the original path.)

To use NEWPATH.BAT, type

NEWPATH [*drive*]\ *path*

where \ *path* is the name of the directory you want to put on the search path. You can optionally include the drive specifier. In this program, the variable %PATH% is used to read the current path. The list of directories on the path is then reassigned to a new variable, OLDPATH, which is also kept in the environment. When you want to change back, you execute OLDPATH.BAT, which reverses the procedure, assigning

```
1: SET OLDPATH=%PATH%
2: PATH %1
```

Listing 2.10 ▲ *NEWPATH.BAT.*

```
1: SET PATH=%OLDPATH%
2: SET OLDPATH=
```

Listing 2.11 ▲ *OLDPATH.BAT.*

the value of %OLDPATH%, i.e., the original path, to the PATH variable, and clearing the OLDPATH variable.

Of course, if you stuff your environment with such long strings, you may soon see the message

Out of environment space

and none of this will work.

To cure this problem, you can enlarge the environment using either the SHELL command with the /E: switch in your CONFIG.SYS file, or the COMMAND command with the /E: switch. Follow the /E: switch with a number equaling the intended size of the environment in DOS 3.3, or a number that will equal the intended size of the environment when multiplied by 16 in DOS 3.2. For further details, see Volume I, Chapter 8.

Suppressing Messages

DOS 3.3
Another useful addition to the batch language in DOS 3.3 is that you can now suppress the display of any line in a batch file by placing the @ character at its beginning. Even if you use ECHO OFF as the first line

ECHO OFF

is still displayed. If you use

@ECHO OFF

instead, then nothing is displayed. The @ character will also suppress REM lines.

 Warning: This new feature may cause you problems if you have files with names such as @XXX.COM or @YYY.EXE. Don't be surprised if you see a

File not found

message, because the @ characters will be stripped off by the batch interpreter.

Delaying Program Execution

How often have you needed to start a process on your PC sometime in the late evening long after everyone has left the office? For example, you might need to shut down a network, send a file over a telephone line when it's least expensive, or perform a tape backup. The program STARTAT.COM is a simple program that you can create using an assembler or DEBUG. You can use it in a batch file to pause execution until a specified time. The program STRTTIME.BAT, which appears in Listing 2.12, shows how to use STARTAT.COM. STRTTIME.BAT will wait until the system clock reads 23:20:00 to execute the rest of your batch file.

```
1: ECHO OFF
2: STARTAT 23:20:00
3: ECHO Begin Process....
```

Listing 2.12 ▲ *STRTTIME.BAT.*

Listing 2.13 is the script file STARTAT.DEB. You can use it to create the utility by typing it in nondocument mode, and then, being sure that DEBUG is on the search path, entering

DEBUG < STARTAT.DEB

If you program in assembly language, you will find the source code and documentation in Appendix A.

```
N STARTAT.COM
F 102 L 85 0
A 100
JMP     0187
OR      AL,[BX+SI]

A 187
MOV     SI,0080
MOV     DI,0104
MOV     CX,0080
CLD
REPZ
MOVSB
CMP     BYTE PTR [0104],09
JNZ     01F6
MOV     AL,[0106]
CMP     AL,30
JL      1F6
CMP     AL,32
JG      1F6
SUB     AL,30
MUL     BYTE PTR [0103]
MOV     [0184],AL
MOV     AL,[0107]
CMP     AL,30
JL      1F6
CMP     AL,39
JG      1F6
SUB     AL,30
ADD     [0184],AL
MOV     AL,[0184]
CMP     AL,17
JG      1F6
MOV     AL,[0108]
CMP     AL,3A
JNZ     01F6
MOV     AL,[0109]
CMP     AL,30
JL      1F6
CMP     AL,35
JG      1F6
SUB     AL,30
MUL     BYTE PTR [0103]
ADD     [0185],AL
MOV     AL,[010A]
CMP     AL,30
JL      1F6
CMP     AL,39
JG      1F6
SUB     AL,30
ADD     [0185],AL
JMP     0200
NOP
MOV     DX,0255
MOV     AH,09
INT     21
JMP     024F
NOP
MOV     AL,[010B]
CMP     AL,3A
JNZ     01F6
MOV     AL,[010C]
CMP     AL,30
JL      1F6
CMP     AL,35
```

```
JG      1F6
SUB     AL,30
MUL     BYTE PTR [0103]
ADD     [0186],AL
MOV     AL,[010D]
CMP     AL,30
JL      1F6
CMP     AL,39
JG      1F6
SUB     AL,30
ADD     [0186],AL
MOV     DX,0274
MOV     AH,09
INT     21
SUB     AX,AX
MOV     AH,2C
INT     21
MOV     AL,[0184]
CMP     AL,CH
JNZ     0234
MOV     AL,[0185]
CMP     AL,CL
JNZ     0234
MOV     AL,[0186]
CMP     AL,DH
JNZ     0234
XOR     AL,AL
MOV     AH,4C
INT     21
INC     SI
DB      6F
JB      02C6
DB      61
JZ      027C
DB      69
JNB     027F
CMP     AH,[BX+SI]
PUSH    BX
PUSH    SP
INC     CX
PUSH    DX
PUSH    SP
INC     CX
PUSH    SP
AND     [BX+SI+48],CL
CMP     CL,[DI+4D]
CMP     DL,[BP+DI+53]
OR      CL,[DI]
AND     AL,57
DB      61
DB      69
JZ      02E2
DB      6E
DB      67
CS:
CS:
CS:
OR      CL,[DI]
AND     AL,32

RCX
181
W
Q
```

Listing 2.13 ▲ *STARTAT.DEB.*

The assembler STARTAT program is very small (about 400 bytes). In Appendix A you will find the assembler source code, and in Appendix B, a Turbo Pascal version with some extra features. The code for the Turbo

Pascal version is considerably shorter, but the compiled program is significantly bigger than the assembler version (it's about 11K). The screen is cleared and both the start time and current time are displayed.

CONTROLLING THE VIDEO DISPLAY

THERE ARE SO MANY video standards today that conforming your software to your graphics card and monitor is a major portion of the installation procedure for most popular software packages. The fact that you can choose among dozens of video adapter boards is something of a mixed blessing. On the one hand, you can draw incredibly detailed designs with a CAD (computer-aided design) program. On the other hand, your CAD program may be designed for one specific graphics card, and you may need a different board for other day-to-day functions.

In this chapter, we'll look at the variety of video display adapters available, consider some of the advantages and disadvantages of each, and advise you on how to minimize conflicts. We'll examine the various types of adapters in some detail, paying attention to the types of display available on each.

In addition, you'll learn some techniques for resolving conflicts between various display types, and between your hardware and your software. Finally, we'll examine screen-driver software, which can give you a great deal of additional control over the behavior of your screen. But first, a brief history of the display standards that have been available for MS-DOS computers.

A BRIEF HISTORY OF VIDEO GRAPHICS

In November 1981, IBM introduced the IBM PC. At the same time, they introduced two graphics standards: *monochrome*—a high-resolution, text-only display—and *color graphics*. Text generated by the monochrome display adapter (MDA) was clear enough to stare at for hours. The color graphics adapter (CGA) was originally intended as a supplement to the monochrome standard for displaying primitive graphics in color. However, it also produced text on a 25-row-×-80-column screen, as did the MDA. Although it could display text in 16 colors, it could also produce eyestrain.

In the beginning, monochrome was much more popular than color. However, the absence of a way to display graphics on the monochrome screen was a drawback. In 1983, Hercules introduced its mono-graphics card, which offered mixed high-resolution (720 × 348) text and graphics at a reasonable cost. Needless to say, it became quite popular.

Although several color graphics alternatives reached the market, none was accepted as a standard until IBM introduced the enhanced graphics adapter (EGA) in September 1984. This display adapter presented several significant improvements over the CGA: higher resolution, more colors, legible color text, and monochrome graphics—all with a single adapter. In addition, it could produce a reasonable facsimile of the CGA display. Shortly thereafter, many firms began producing EGA-compatible cards.

IBM introduced another display adapter, the professional graphics adapter (PGA) at the same time as the EGA. It had still higher resolution and still more colors than the EGA. However, it wasn't compatible with existing standards, and it required a very high-resolution monitor. It never caught on, and has since been discontinued.

More recent EGA-compatible boards included features not part of the original EGA standard—specifically, greater compatibility with the CGA standard and higher screen resolution. These boards are sometimes called extended EGA (EEGA) boards. The latest enhancements include automatic synchronization with whatever monitor is attached to the board. Even with all of these enhanced features, the price has continued to fall. As a result EEGA boards have been widely accepted. These cards will all work perfectly well with a standard EGA monitor. To make full use of the additional modes provided in the EEGA boards, you must have a *multisync* or *multiscan* monitor. These monitors can adapt their displays to a variety of resolutions, depending on the signal they receive.

In April 1987, IBM announced the Personal System/2 series of computers (PS/2), which included a new video standard. This new standard, the video graphics array (VGA), was built into the motherboard of their new computers. At the same time, IBM introduced a VGA card that could be used in older PCs.

The VGA represents a radical departure from earlier video standards. Until the VGA, the signal produced by all the adapter boards was a *digital* signal; that is, colors were treated discretely, because they were represented by different digital codes. There was no way to create a true blend of colors. The VGA, in contrast, has an *analog* signal, which treats color as a smoothly varying quantity. This makes it possible, in theory, to display any shade of any color. Although the VGA's resolution, at 640 × 480, seems only a fractional improvement over the EGA, the palette now gives you access to 256,000 colors. Moreover, the VGA can mimic the MGA, CGA, EGA, and MCGA adapters quite successfully.

Board manufacturers are trying to make new boards that will produce true VGA signals. However, because of the VGA's analog signal, matching the number of screen lines and number of available colors is not sufficient. Moreover, older enhanced color monitors—the kind designed to use EGA adapters—will not work with it. The multisync or multiscan monitors generally accept some form of analog signal. Thus, most of them will probably work with the VGA if you can get a cable to connect the monitor to the VGA's nonstandard socket.

CHARACTERISTICS OF DIFFERENT VIDEO ADAPTERS

At present there are five principal types of video adapter boards, or integrated subsystems:

- ▲ The monochrome display adapter (MDA)
- ▲ The color graphics adapter (CGA)
- ▲ The Hercules graphics adapter—also known as the monochrome graphics display adapter (MGDA)
- ▲ The enhanced graphics adapter (EGA)
- ▲ The video graphics array (VGA), both on the IBM PS/2 and in a more limited version on the PC*jr*

All of these boards, except the MDA, can display both graphics and text in one form or another. We'll now cover in detail what these adapters can and cannot do.

Graphics adapters do part of their work by storing information regarding what appears on the screen in a portion of RAM. Some of your computer's built-in RAM is reserved for this purpose, and the display adapters have additional built-in memory to supplement it. One of the principal differences among the various adapters is the amount of memory they include.

The Monochrome Display Adapter

The monochrome display adapter (MDA) was originally intended for business applications, while color was for the hobbyist. You could get good text quality at a relatively low cost with a monochrome display. Even today, many PCs have only an MDA and a compatible monitor.

The MDA cannot produce graphics because it has only 4K of memory on the board. This is just enough memory to store information about the 4000 character spaces on the screen. Thus, there is no place to store information about individual screen pixels, and the only kind of graphics you can display is character-based bar charts. The only DOS graphics mode you can use is 80-column text. This is what is produced by the DOS command

MODE MONO

The Color Graphics Adapter

The color graphics adapter (CGA) offers rudimentary color graphics. The board includes 16K of memory, enough to store information on 640 × 200 pixels in two colors. Because 640 × 200 is relatively low resolution, graphics images appear somewhat grainy. The CGA has seven display modes:

- ▲ 40-column black and white text
- ▲ 80-column black and white text
- ▲ 40-column color text

▲ 80-column color text

▲ 320 × 200 pixel color graphics

▲ 320 × 200 pixel black and white graphics

▲ 640 × 200 two-color graphics

You can choose any of the text modes with the commands

```
MODE BW40
MODE BW80
MODE CO40
MODE CO80
```

respectively. You cannot establish the graphics modes directly from DOS, but you can often reference them from your programs. Normally, you will not have any problems selecting a CGA mode.

The Monochrome Graphics Adapter

Before the Hercules adapter was introduced, the only way to display both text and graphics adequately was to use two separate adapters, one MDA and one CGA, with an appropriate monitor attached to each. (Some people compromised on a single CGA monitor.) This was a serious problem for business users who wanted to display Lotus 1-2-3 graphs. The Hercules card not only offered the same sharp text on the monochrome screen, but also a gray-scale shaded graphics display. Because this product is not produced by IBM or Microsoft, nor by the computer manufacturers, none of the parameters of the DOS MODE command address it directly. Instead, you control it with a separate program supplied with the card.

The Enhanced Graphics Adapter

The enhanced graphics adapter (EGA) was an incremental step toward better resolution and a greater range of color. It required much more video memory to achieve this result. IBM offered several options ranging from 64K to 256K, allowing a maximum resolution of 640 × 360. The new video modes, and the emulation of older modes, are produced by the *video BIOS*. This is code placed in ROM chips on the board.

When IBM introduced the board, it was expensive, did not allow composite graphics, and was not fully downwardly compatible with the CGA standard. More disturbingly, the capabilities of the board were not understood by the majority of software developers. However, many manufacturers quickly made improvements.

The EGA is supposed to incorporate all earlier display standards, including monochrome. It can even display graphics on monochrome screens, in rather the same way that the Hercules card does. Unfortunately, software written to use the Hercules card had to be rewritten to use an EGA card with a monochrome monitor, although it would work if you had a multisync or multiscan monitor.

The EGA produces the same seven modes as the CGA, the monochrome mode, and four additional graphics modes. One major enhancement of the EGA is that you can customize the display character set. On the CGA and MDA, characters are produced by a hardware-based character generator. On the EGA, the character set is mapped into a memory area that can be programmed. (For a program that you can use for this purpose, see the discussion of Display Master at the end of this chapter.)

Unless your manufacturer's version of DOS includes additional modes, DOS's MODE command can address only the five modes CO80, CO40, BW40, BW80, and MONO. Some manufacturers of EGA cards include software with their cards that allows you to address additional modes, and switch among them. The software may be either a program to be executed at the DOS prompt, or a device driver to place in your CONFIG.SYS file. If your application programs are designed to use these additional modes, they may be able to use them automatically when you have set the graphics card to them. If not, the application programs may include device drivers that you can install to make the programs use the additional modes.

The Multicolor Graphics Array

With the introduction of the PS/2 computers, IBM released a multicolor graphics array with the Model 30. Unfortunately, the initials MCGA are used for this type of adapter as well as the Hercules type. The IBM MCGA's maximum resolution of 640 × 480 is in two colors or 320 × 200 with 256 colors. It can also display monochrome text.

The MCGA is largely compatible with the CGA, except that it cannot generate a border color. The MCGA cannot emulate any of the EGA graphics modes; however, you can customize its character fonts.

The Video Graphics Array

The VGA is built into the PS/2 Models 50, 60, and 80 and is available as an option board for PC/AT models. The VGA specification is quickly gaining acceptance as the graphics display system of choice by virtue of the many vendors offering compatible boards and monitors. The VGA consists of 256K of video memory and a video digital-to-analog converter, also called a DAC.

The VGA produces all the EGA and PS/2 MCGA video modes. The only mode unique to the VGA is a 640-×-480, 16-color graphics mode. The VGA represents only an incremental improvement in resolution over the EGA, especially since many boards now available can produce resolutions of 1000 × 1000 or greater. The significant improvement is in the analog signal and the number of colors. In addition, the VGA will switch automatically to the mode being used by a program. Thus, you should never need the DOS MODE command to control the display when a VGA is installed.

THE VIDEO MODES

Most software will set your hardware to the video mode it needs in order to run properly. However, you can set the video mode yourself with the MODE command. The five video parameters available with the MODE command have already been discussed. If you use the ANSI.SYS device driver (see later in this chapter for a summary, and Chapter 9 of Volume I for a detailed discussion), you can set these modes by placing the appropriate ANSI escape sequences in an ECHO or PROMPT statement in a batch file.

Table 3.1 gives a summary of the video modes currently in use, and Table 3.2 shows which modes are available with which types of adapters. Note that the column labeled "Text Resolution" in Table 3.1 represents the dimensions of a single character cell in pixels.

VIDEO MODE DECIMAL	HEX	TYPE	COLORS	RESOLUTION GRAPHICS	TEXT	DOS MODE
0	0	Text	16[a]	360 × 400	9 × 16	BW40
1	1	Text	16[a]	360 × 400	9 × 16	CO40
2	2	Text	16	720 × 400	9 × 16	BW80
3	3	Text	16	720 × 400	9 × 16	CO80
4	4	Graphics	4	320 × 200	8 × 8	
5	5	Graphics	4[b]	320 × 200	8 × 8	
6	6	Graphics	2	640 × 200	8 × 8	
7	7	Text	Mono	720 × 400	9 × 16	MONO
8	8	Graphics	4			
9	9	Graphics	4[b]			
10	A	Graphics	2			
11[d]	B					
12[d]	C					
13	D	Graphics	16	320 × 200	8 × 8	
14	E	Graphics	16	640 × 200	8 × 8	
15	F	Graphics	Mono	640 × 350	8 × 16	
16	10	Graphics	16	640 × 350	8 × 16	
17	11	Graphics	2	640 × 480	8 × 16	
18	12	Graphics	16	640 × 480	8 × 16	
19	13	Graphics	256[c]	320 × 200	8 × 8	

[a] From a palette of 64 colors.

[b] Gray shades.

[c] From a palette of 256,000 colors.

[d] Reserved for font loading.

Table 3.1 ▲ *Video Modes.*

ADAPTER		VIDEO MODE																			
		0	1	2	3	4	5	6	7	8	9	10	11	12	13	14	15	16	17	18	19
MDA									x												
CGA		x	x	x	x	x	x	x													
EGA		x	x	x	x	x	x	x							x	x	x	x			
EEGA		x	x	x	x	x	x	x							x	x	x	x	x	x	
VGA		x	x	x	x	x	x	x							x	x	x	x	x	x	x
PCjr								x	x	x											

Table 3.2 ▲ *Modes Available on Video Adapters.*

RESOLVING CONFLICTS BETWEEN VIDEO HARDWARE AND SOFTWARE

The ease with which you can shift from one software package to another depends in part on your having installed your video adapters properly, and in part on having installed your software properly for your hardware.

If your adapter is not one of the types listed in Table 3.2, you may well have problems running many of the programs on the market today. One very common problem is that you can display text, but are unable to display graphics. Other problems are more subtle, and can take many forms.

One major cause for incompatibilities between video hardware and software involves the memory areas addressed by the card. Figure 3.1 illustrates the memory locations used by several types of video adapters relative to the system RAM, which begins at 640K (hex address A000).

This is most likely to cause problems if you have more than one graphics card installed in your system and both use a given memory area. To avoid this problem you may have to set a jumper on one of the cards to disable the BIOS. The software supplied with some EGA cards can handle this problem for you automatically.

If you haven't installed your software properly, or if it is poorly designed, you can run into serious problems. One of the most frustrating situations that you can encounter is discovering that a program you

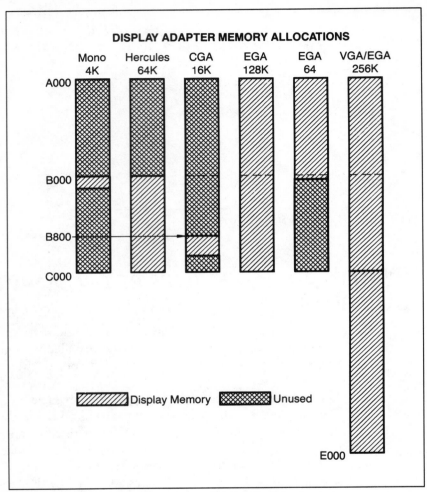

Figure 3.1 ▲ *Memory Locations Used by Different Video Adapters.*

want to use appears to be incompatible with your video card. This can stem from a number of circumstances:

▲ You may not have installed the software drivers for your video card when you installed your software.

▲ Your video card may not have enough memory on it to run your application.

▲ Your video card may not be set to the correct mode.

▲ Your video card may have a BIOS that is incompatible with IBM's. (The original EGA BIOS had some bugs, which some manufacturers of clones dutifully copied. Others attempted to correct the bugs, with results other than those intended.)

▲ Your video card may conflict with another card in your system.

The first problem is most likely to arise when you are in such a hurry to get your new software up and running that you don't bother to read the manual. These situations may also follow a trip to the discount PC store, where the salesman shows you the latest whizzbang software but doesn't bother to tell you that you need some obscure video card or nightmarishly complex setup procedures to use it.

The problem of not enough memory is likely to occur only with the original IBM EGA adapter. This card had only 64K of onboard memory. Virtually all other EGA cards have 256K. If you have one of the original EGA cards, and are not sure how much memory is installed on it, you can find out with the program EGASIZE.COM, which you can create with the script file EGASIZE.DEB shown in Listing 3.1. Fully annotated assembler code appears in Appendix A.

This program returns an exit code of 0 if you have 64K. For each additional 64K, the exit code increments by 1. To use this program, run the program EGAMEM.BAT, shown in Listing 3.2.

```
N EGASIZE.COM
A 0100
JMP     0103
NOP
MOV     AH,12
MOV     AL,00
MOV     BL,10
MOV     BH,00
MOV     CX,0000
INT     10
MOV     AH,00
MOV     AL,BL
MOV     AH,4C
INT     21
RETF

RCX
19
W
Q
```

Listing 3.1 ▲ *EGASIZE.DEB.*

```
 1: ECHO OFF
 2: EGASIZE
 3: IF ERRORLEVEL 3 ECHO You have 256K of memory on your EGA.
 4: IF ERRORLEVEL 3 GOTO end
 5: IF ERRORLEVEL 2 GOTO 192k
 6: IF NOT ERRORLEVEL 1 GOTO 64k
 7: ECHO You have 128K of memory on your EGA.
 8: ECHO EGA daughterboard installed with 1 bank of memory.
 9: GOTO end
10: :192k
11: ECHO You have 192K of memory on your EGA.
12: ECHO EGA daughterboard installed with 2 banks of memory.
13: GOTO end
14: :64k
15: ECHO You have 64K of memory on your EGA.
16: ECHO You will be unable to run MS Windows in High Resolution.
17: :end
```

Listing 3.2 ▲ *EGAMEM.BAT.*

This batch file is a fairly straightforward exit-code test. In line 6, instead of directing execution to a module if the exit code is 1, we have saved a few lines of code by making that the default. If the exit code is not 1, i.e., if it is 0, the messages for 64K of EGA memory are displayed. If it is 1, the messages immediately following the exit-code tests are displayed.

The incorrect mode problem may stem from one of two sources. Usually, your software will set your adapter to the correct mode. However, some poorly designed programs assume you will have done so yourself before loading the program. The second possibility is that you have not installed your board correctly. There may be jumpers or switches to set to tell the board what kind of computer it's running in, or what kind of monitor is attached to it. Check the manual that came with the board if all else fails. In other cases, the problem may be that you simply don't have enough memory on your card. There may even be conflicts with other boards in the machine.

If you have an incompatible BIOS, you will probably encounter problems such as the cursor disappearing in CGA mode, or you may find some of your colors—that are supposed to be different—are indistinguishable.

Determining the Current Video Adapter

When installing software on a machine, frequently the first thing you are asked is what type of display adapter you have. In the case of the EGA and similar cards, it is also important to know how much memory is installed. It may also be important to know to what mode the previous program set the adapter, because not all programs reset the video adapter automatically.

The script file VMODE.DEB, shown in Listing 3.3, will create a program to help you find out the type of display adapter you have installed and the mode it is set to. To create VMODE.COM, type in VMODE-.DEB exactly as it appears. Be sure to enter a carriage return after each line, including the blank one, and at the end of the file. After making sure that DEBUG is on your search path or in the current directory, enter the command

DEBUG<VMODE.DEB

You can examine the complete assembler source code in Appendix A if you are interested.

```
N VMODE.COM
A 0100
JMP     0103
NOP
MOV     AH,0F
MOV     AL,00
MOV     CX,0000
INT     10
MOV     AH,4C
INT     21
RETF

RCX
11
W
Q
```

Listing 3.3 ▲ *VMODE.DEB.*

VMODE.COM generates an exit code equivalent to the video mode as shown in Table 3.1. To use it, run VIDMODE.BAT, which appears in Listing 3.4. This program displays a message telling you the video mode to which your adapter is set.

If you are a programmer, you may prefer to use the Turbo Pascal program, WHATVID.PAS. Its source code appears in Appendix B. This program does not require a batch file. Instead, it generates a three-line message telling you the type of monitor you are using, the current video mode, and the type of adapter to which your monitor is attached. For example, the program might display the following message:

Monitor type: Color
80 column color text.
EGA with 256K installed

```
 1: ECHO OFF
 2: VMODE
 3: IF ERRORLEVEL 0 IF NOT ERRORLEVEL 1 ECHO 40 x 25 text black & white CGA
 4: IF ERRORLEVEL 1 IF NOT ERRORLEVEL 2 ECHO 40 x 25 text 16-color CGA
 5: IF ERRORLEVEL 2 IF NOT ERRORLEVEL 3 ECHO 80 x 25 text black & white CGA
 6: IF ERRORLEVEL 3 IF NOT ERRORLEVEL 4 ECHO 80-column color text
 7: IF ERRORLEVEL 4 IF NOT ERRORLEVEL 5 ECHO 320 x 200 4-color CGA
 8: IF ERRORLEVEL 5 IF NOT ERRORLEVEL 6 ECHO 320 x 200 4-shade Gray-scale
CGA
 9: IF ERRORLEVEL 6 IF NOT ERRORLEVEL 7 ECHO 640 x 200 2-color CGA
10: IF ERRORLEVEL 7 IF NOT ERRORLEVEL 8 ECHO Monochrome
11: IF ERRORLEVEL 8 IF NOT ERRORLEVEL 9 ECHO 160 x 200 16-color PCjr
12: IF ERRORLEVEL 9 IF NOT ERRORLEVEL 10 ECHO 320 x 200 16-color PCjr
13: IF ERRORLEVEL 10 IF NOT ERRORLEVEL 11 ECHO 640 x 200 4-color PCjr
14: IF ERRORLEVEL 11 IF NOT ERRORLEVEL 12 ECHO ** EGA Internal use
15: IF ERRORLEVEL 12 IF NOT ERRORLEVEL 13 ECHO ** EGA Internal use
16: IF ERRORLEVEL 13 IF NOT ERRORLEVEL 14 ECHO 320 x 200 16-color EGA
17: IF ERRORLEVEL 14 IF NOT ERRORLEVEL 15 ECHO 640 x 200 16-color EGA
18: IF ERRORLEVEL 15 IF NOT ERRORLEVEL 16 ECHO 640 x 350 Monographics EGA
19: IF ERRORLEVEL 16 IF NOT ERRORLEVEL 17 ECHO 640 x 350 64-color EGA
20: IF ERRORLEVEL 17 IF NOT ERRORLEVEL 18 ECHO 640 x 480 2-color VGA
21: IF ERRORLEVEL 18 IF NOT ERRORLEVEL 19 ECHO 640 x 480 16-color VGA
22: IF ERRORLEVEL 19 ECHO 640 x 480 256-color VGA
```

Listing 3.4 ▲ *VIDMODE.BAT.*

The code looks at the video setup in stages, first seeing if it is set to color or monochrome. This first step will work for almost all video cards on the market today. The second step looks to see if the system is a PS/2 or has a VGA adapter. The third step tests to see if the adapter is an MDA, CGA, PC*jr*, or EGA display adapter. Finally, the program tests whether the computer is a 3270-type PC or PC/AT and tests for the existence of graphics capability. This part is optional, because most 3270 PCs are found in large corporations.

Setting Your Adapter Mode

Having discovered what video setting is currently active, you can initialize the video adapter to a limited number of settings using either the DOS MODE command, or special control strings within ANSI.SYS. To give you access to a wider range of modes, you can use SETVID-.COM, which you can create from the script file SETVID.DEB, shown in Listing 3.5.

Using this program may require some care. For example, attempting to set a standard PC color graphics card to a PC*jr* mode may cause the computer to lock up. To use this program, enter the command

SETVID *N*

```
N SETVID.COM
F 0105 0184 0
A 0100
JMP       0185

A 185
MOV       SI,0080
MOV       DI,0104
MOV       CX,0080
CLD
REPZ
MOVSB
MOV       BL,[0106]
CMP       BL,30
JL        01CA
CMP       BL,39
JG        01CA
SUB       BL,30
MOV       AL,[0107]
CMP       AL,30
JL        01B9
MOV       [0184],AL
MOV       AL,BL
MUL       BYTE PTR [0103]
ADD       [0184],AL
JMP       01BD
NOP
MOV       [0184],BL
MOV       AH,00
MOV       AL,[0184]
MOV       CX,0000
INT       10
JMP       01CC
NOP
MOV       AL,01
MOV       AH,4C
MOV       AL,00
INT       21
RETF

RCX
D3
W
Q
```

Listing 3.5 ▲ *SETVID.DEB.*

where N is the decimal number of any of the video modes from 0 through 19. The command may or may not have the desired effect, depending on whether the hardware you have installed can display it, whether your manufacturer's version of DOS supports it, and whether you have installed the proper device drivers. (Some modes, such as 132-column text, cannot be displayed without a special device driver installed in your CONFIG.SYS file.)

If the mode you select blows up your screen, you can probably get back to something normal by executing the program again with a parameter that you know is acceptable. You may have to type the command blind, but it should work.

Changing the Size and Shape of Your Cursor

You may often find that your cursor disappears, perhaps because either a program removed it or the background is too bright. You can bring it back by changing the size and height of the cursor. Many people have asked Martin for ways to change the shape of the cursor and to control its blinking. This is one of those "good news and bad news" situations. Unfortunately, the blink is built into the hardware, so you can't turn it off. However, the good news is that it you can change the cursor size and starting height with a simple program. You can create CURSOR.COM by using the DEBUG script file shown in Listing 3.6 and following the directions for the other script files in this chapter. (Assembler source code appears in Appendix A.)

To execute this program, enter a command of the form

CURSOR *SSEE*

where *SS* is a two-digit decimal number representing the starting line of the cursor (usually between 01 and 10), and *EE* is a two-digit decimal number representing the ending line (usually between 01 and 11). Note that some adapters permit fewer lines. The CGA, for example, can have only up to seven lines. The program is not foolproof. It checks only to see that the top line is above the bottom line. For example, to set the standard cursor on a CGA, you would enter

CURSOR 0607

A Turbo Pascal version of the program, SETCURSR.PAS, appears in Appendix B. This version takes two parameters, one at the starting line and a second at the ending line. You can execute SETCURSR.COM either from a DOS prompt or from within a batch file. To execute it from within a batch file, use a command of the form

SETCURSR *start end*

where *start* is the top line of the cursor and *end* is the bottom line.

To run the program from a DOS prompt, enter the command

SETCURSR

You will then be prompted for a starting and ending line.

```
N CURSOR.COM
F 0105 0184 0
A 0100
JMP     0186

A 0185
ADD     [BP+0080],BH
MOV     DI,0104
MOV     CX,0080
CLD
REPZ
MOVSB
MOV     AL,[0106]
CMP     AL,30
JL      01EB
CMP     AL,39
JG      01EB
SUB     AL,30
MUL     BYTE PTR [0103]
MOV     [0184],AL
MOV     AL,[0107]
CMP     AL,30
JL      01EB
CMP     AL,39
JG      01EB
SUB     AL,30
ADD     [0184],AL
MOV     AL,[0108]
CMP     AL,30
JL      01EB
CMP     AL,39
JG      01EB
SUB     AL,30
MUL     BYTE PTR [0103]
MOV     [0185],AL
MOV     AL,[0109]
CMP     AL,30
JL      01EB
CMP     AL,39
JG      01EB
SUB     AL,30
ADD     [0185],AL
MOV     AH,01
MOV     CH,[0184]
MOV     CL,[0185]
INT     10
JMP     01ED
NOP
MOV     AL,01
MOV     AH,4C
MOV     AL,00
INT     21
RETF

RCX
F4
W
Q
```

Listing 3.6 ▲ *CURSOR.DEB.*

SCREEN DRIVERS

To give you greater control of your screen, no matter what kind of video adapter you have, you can use *screen driver* software. These programs allow you to address your screen directly in one way or another.

ANSI.SYS

DOS includes a screen driver of its own—ANSI.SYS. To use it you must load it into memory by adding the command

DEVICE = ANSI.SYS

to your CONFIG.SYS file. If the ANSI.SYS file is not in the boot directory, precede it with the name of the drive and/or directory in which it is located, for example:

DEVICE = C:\DOS\ANSI.SYS

Many application programs must have ANSI.SYS loaded to address the screen and keyboard properly. ANSI.SYS is designed to allow the PC to be used as a remote terminal. Many communications programs require ANSI.SYS.

In many ways, ANSI.SYS is essential on computers that use MS-DOS but are not IBM-compatible. It enables these computers to use a common set of screen-control characters. In addition, the ANSI.SYS driver monitors the keyboard to be sure that it conforms to DOS's requirements. Data from programs that read input from the keyboard or write to the screen directly, bypass the ANSI driver.

Essentially, ANSI.SYS has three functions:

▲ Positioning the cursor on the screen.

▲ Controlling colors and other aspects of the graphics display on your screen.

▲ Allowing you to assign special meanings to the keys on the keyboard, including both swapping key positions and assigning string values to the keys.

It performs these functions through special character codes called *escape sequences.*

What Is an Escape Sequence? An escape sequence recognized by ANSI.SYS usually has the following four elements:

▲ The Escape character

▲ A left bracket

▲ A numeric parameter

▲ A terminating code explaining the function of the sequence

For example, a sequence to set the cursor at the upper-left corner of the screen takes the form

^ [[1,1f

where 1,1 is the horizontal and vertical position of the cursor, and f is the code telling ANSI.SYS that this is the horizontal-and-vertical position sequence. For a full discussion of the ANSI.SYS driver, see Volume I, Chapter 9. For complete tables of ANSI escape sequences, see Appendix D.

Warning: If your editor or word processor displays the escape character as ^ [, it's easy to miss the second left bracket. If you do, the sequence won't work properly. It's also important to use the correct case of the terminating code. ANSI.SYS is quite particular about the case of its codes, and if you enter a code that should be uppercase in lowercase, or vice versa, the actual character you entered will be displayed on the screen, and the sequence will not work.

Figure 3.2 illustrates some typical device drivers. In particular, two drivers supplied with DOS— ANSI.SYS and VDISK.SYS. In effect, when these device drivers are loaded they become a part of DOS. They inform DOS about the kinds of events they process, and DOS then directs events of those types to the device drivers for processing. For example, ANSI.SYS intercepts data going to the screen; if it recognizes any character sequences, it translates them into screen color, cursor position, and so forth. VDISK.SYS intercepts calls for disk processing and routes them to the VDISK driver. If the call requests it, VDISK will write to the RAM disk it has created rather than to a physical disk.

You can send ANSI escape sequences by executing a program that uses standard DOS output services to display data, by embedding them in PROMPT or ECHO statements, or simply by using the TYPE command to display a file containing them.

There are several drawbacks to relying on ANSI.SYS. Most importantly, it processes escape sequences extremely slowly. What ANSI.SYS offers is sometimes much less than what you need. Also, when you use

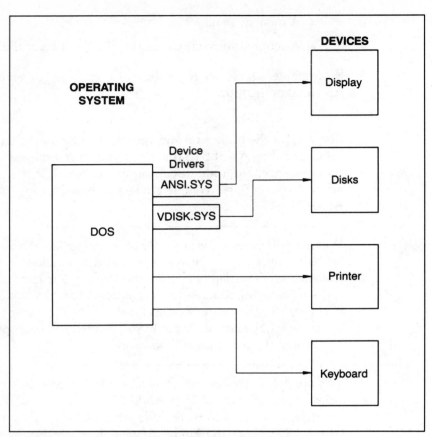

Figure 3.2 ▲ *How a Console Driver Works.*

programs that bypass DOS services, you can't be sure that conflicts or loss of data will not occur.

However, the ANSI driver employs a good concept. Fortunately, there are some alternative drivers available that offer significant advantages over ANSI.SYS while maintaining compatibility. One particularly useful alternative is a public-domain driver called NANSI.SYS. Another is a complete EGA-control package called Display Master, which includes a console driver specifically for the EGA.

NANSI.SYS

NANSI.SYS, placed into the public domain by Daniel Kegel, is a good alternative to ANSI.SYS. It accepts the same escape sequences, but it operates much faster. NANSI.SYS has some additional commands that greatly extend your control of the console. Its operation is identical otherwise except that you load it with the command

DEVICE = NANSI.SYS

in your CONFIG.SYS file.

These are the principal additional features of NANSI.SYS:

- ▲ Significantly faster operation than ANSI.SYS
- ▲ Simpler key reassignment
- ▲ Special support for EGAs
- ▲ A character filter
- ▲ It changes the beep produced by Ctrl-G to a less irritating sound

Both ANSI.SYS and NANSI.SYS use IBM video BIOS to control the screen. However, NANSI.SYS bypasses the BIOS if the screen is in a text mode. This allows it to react much more quickly in some circumstances. Table 3.3 provides a list of the escape sequences in NANSI-.SYS that are not available in ANSI.SYS.

SEQUENCE	EFFECT
^ [[NL	Inserts N blank lines at the cursor line
^ [[NM	Deletes N lines including the cursor line
^ [[N@	Inserts N space characters at the cursor
^ [[NP	Deletes N characters, including the character under the cursor
^ [[C;Dy	Replaces all instances of character C with character D in output

Table 3.3 ▲ *NANSI.SYS Escape Sequences.*

The difference in NANSI's handling of key reassignment is in the way it clears reassignments. To reset keys that you have reassigned, enter the original code for the key with no parameter, and it will be restored to its default meaning.

The character filter replaces all instances of a given character with a different character in output, as Table 3.3 shows. It does not rewrite the file on disk. You might use it to print a character that appears on a daisy-wheel printer but doesn't have an ASCII code. To cancel the effect of a filter sequence, enter the sequence

^ [[y

If you have an enhanced graphics adapter installed, you can address three additional video modes using a video mode sequence. You use this same sequence to make an EGA display 43 rows of text. To enter 43-line mode, you first choose your text mode and then use the parameter **43** for a second video mode sequence. For example, to display 43 rows of 80-column color text, issue the sequence

^ [[= 3h ^ [[= 43h

To return to a 25-row screen, issue one of the standard text mode sequences without following it with the 43-row sequence. Thus, to return to 25-row color text, just issue the sequence

^ [[= 3h

NANSI.SYS ignores mode 43 unless there is an EGA in your computer. (In bit-mapped modes, the cursor is simulated with a small blob—the Ctrl-V graphics character.) Table 3.4 lists the parameters available for the video-mode escape sequence.

NANSI.SYS conforms completely to ANSI standard X3.64. Thus, you can use ANSI X3.64 control sequences to make the IBM-PC console look like a DEC VT-100 to any application program. This is useful with some telecommunications programs and terminal-emulation programs. Many such programs emulate the DEC VT-100 terminal, and they will handle your screen and keyboard more efficiently if they think they are running on a VT-100. It will also let you extend a dumb terminal emulator to include support for the VT-100 standard.

Display Master

Display Master from Intersecting Concepts is a somewhat different kettle of fish. It includes both a device driver and a control program, and it allows you very precise control of an EGA with an appropriate monitor.

PARAMETER	EFFECT
0	40 × 25 black & white text
1	40 × 25 color text
2	80 × 25 black & white text
3	80 × 25 color text
4	320 × 200 graphics (4 bits/pixel)
5	320 × 200 graphics (1 bit/pixel)
6	640 × 200 graphics (1 bit/pixel)
7	Toggles word wrap
13	320 × 200 graphics (4 bits/pixel—EGA only)
14	640 × 200 graphics (4 bits/pixel—EGA only)
16	640 × 350 graphics (4 bits/pixel—EGA only)

Table 3.4 ▲ *NANSI.SYS Video Mode Parameters.*

The control program lets you:

▲ Choose the number of rows and columns of text for your monitor to display

▲ Change the DOS default colors at will

▲ Map any of the 64 EGA colors, or any of the 256,000 VGA colors, to the 16 palette colors that can be used in text mode

▲ Produce underlined characters on screen in the color of your choice

▲ Edit the actual character fonts used on your screen

▲ Choose the shape of your cursor

You can make any of these changes (except editing the character fonts) either by entering commands on the command line or by invoking the control program and selecting from menus. Figure 3.3 shows Display Master's main menu, which is also its help screen.

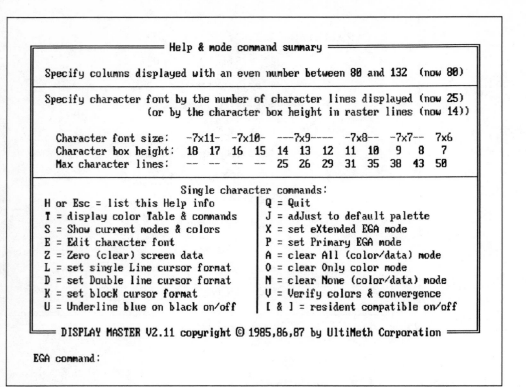

```
═══════════ Help & mode command summary ═══════════

Specify columns displayed with an even number between 80 and 132   (now 80)

Specify character font by the number of character lines displayed (now 25)
           (or by the character box height in raster lines (now 14))

 Character font size:   -7x11-  -7x10-  ---7x9-----  -7x8--  -7x7--  7x6
 Character box height:  18  17  16  15  14  13  12  11  10   9   8   7
 Max character lines:   --  --  --  --  25  26  29  31  35  38  43  50

                    Single character commands:
H or Esc = list this Help info      │ Q = Quit
T = display color Table & commands  │ J = adJust to default palette
S = Show current modes & colors     │ X = set eXtended EGA mode
E = Edit character font             │ P = set Primary EGA mode
Z = Zero (clear) screen data        │ A = clear All (color/data) mode
L = set single Line cursor format   │ O = clear Only color mode
D = set Double line cursor format   │ N = clear None (color/data) mode
K = set blocK cursor format         │ V = Verify colors & convergence
U = Underline blue on black on/off  │ [ & ] = resident compatible on/off

═══ DISPLAY MASTER V2.11 copyright © 1985,86,87 by UltiMeth Corporation ═══

EGA command:
```

Figure 3.3 ▲ *Display Master's Main Menu.*

To use Display Master, you install the device driver, DM.SYS, in your CONFIG.SYS file. If you wish, you can install a default screen size and foreground and background colors at the same time. If you have already installed another console driver, you should remove it. If you have expanded memory, you can configure the device driver to store character fonts there, so you use up less conventional memory. The program DM.COM is the control program, which you execute at a DOS prompt.

The package includes special screen drivers for Framework and for Lotus programs, a patch to make dBASE III PLUS work in whatever number of rows you choose, programs to load and save screen fonts, and a program to set up various applications to work with Display Master. You invoke the latter in a batch file that loads the application. It will not work if you have changed the name of the executable file, however.

Display Master gives you somewhat more flexibility than most of the alternatives. Normally, EGA cards give you a choice of 25 or 43 rows of text. With Display Master and a standard EGA and monitor, you can display text in any number of rows from 25 to 43. If you have an enhanced EGA and multiscan monitor, you can display as many as 70 rows of text with 80 columns, or 50 rows of text up to 132 characters long, in two-character increments.

Of course, when you get characters this small, they become very hard to read. It's useful to be able to switch into, say, a 70-×-132-character screen to get a broad view of a spreadsheet, but you wouldn't want to spend much time working with it. On the other hand, the 35-line mode produces an extremely readable display, and you can see a full page of double-spaced text at a time. Legibility is even greater if you edit the character set to produce a sans-serif font with the Font Editor, shown in Figure 3.4. This is part of the main control program—the only part that you must use the menu to access. Figure 3.5 shows this font used in WordStar 4.0 on a 35-line screen. As you can see, it's quite easy to read.

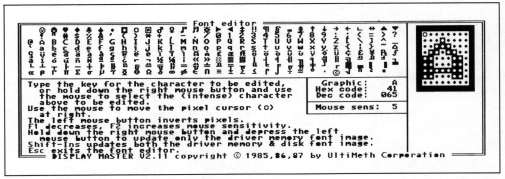

Figure 3.4 ▲ *The Display Master Font Editor.*

The size of the character cells is such that it's most efficient to choose 25, 35, 43, 50, or 70 rows of text. If you choose, say, 31 lines, the text will be the same size as for 35 lines, but the bottom four lines will be blank.

You select your palette by assigning color combinations to the sixteen default colors. Every color except black is represented by its first letter. Black is represented by a period. The high-intensity colors use the same codes, but are prefaced with an I.

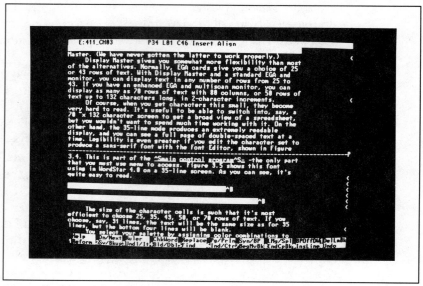

Figure 3.5 ▲ *A 35-Line Screen with a Sans-Serif Font.*

You set your colors on Display Master's Palette screen. With an EGA, you adjust the intensity of red, blue, and green for each color by selecting a value from 0 to 3. With a VGA, the settings range from 0 to 63 for each hue. Once you have a palette that you like, you can save it to a file with a single command. Indeed, the easiest way to establish Display Master settings for any given program is to invoke DM.COM, adjust *all* the settings to be suitable to the application, and then save the results to a file. You can establish a default number of lines and columns, cursor size, screen-clearing mode (needed for some programs that use nonstandard ways of getting characters on the screen) and color palette, and whether to use underlining, for any program. For example, a batch file that invoked Lotus 1-2-3 might include the following commands:

```
DM L123.DM
CD\LOTUS
123
DM LDEFAULT.DM
```

For this to work, the directory that holds the Display Master files must be appended, or else the files must be in the current directory.

If you want complete—and easy—control of your EGA or VGA, you will find it in Display Master. You may quickly come to wonder how you ever did without it. And with a minimum of effort, you will learn a great deal about how the EGA works.

EXTENDING YOUR PRINTER'S CAPABILITIES

B EFORE 1984, the only print quality that could be considered letter quality came from daisywheel printers. Unfortunately, daisywheel printers are noisy and slow, require attention, and cannot print graphics.

There is very little you can do to control the output you get from a daisywheel printer. Most of them let you print text with underlining, boldfacing or doublestriking as well as unemphasized. You can control horizontal and vertical spacing to a degree. However, to go beyond that, all you can do is embed control codes in word-processed text that make the printer stop so that you can switch to a different wheel. This way you can at least place italic and regular text in the same document.

The dot-matrix printer has for some time been the most common type of printer used with personal computers. It has always had the advantages of being fast and relatively flexible. In addition, most dot-matrix printers can print graphics images. However, before 1984, no dot-matrix printers produced print that you could study without getting eyestrain.

Despite the absence of letter-quality print, the popularity of the dot-matrix printer stemmed from its flexibility. Most dot-matrix printers give you a choice of at least two fonts and several type sizes, besides the standard lines-per-inch and characters-per-inch controls. In addition, by using escape sequences, you can program most of them to change type styles. Many of the more recent models (especially those with a 24-pin print head) can also produce print that rivals the output of a daisywheel printer.

Laser printer technology for PCs is a form of cross-breeding between the expensive mainframe laser printers, such as the Xerox 9700, and photocopier technology. Canon was the first to introduce a low-cost laser printer engine with its LBP-CX, in 1983. Hewlett-Packard became one of the first American companies to market a laser printer when it placed the Canon engine in its HP LaserJet, in 1984.

Laser printers allow you a great deal more control over the appearance of the printed page than do other types of printers. You might even think of them as specialized desktop computers with a high-quality output device attached. Indeed, the HP LaserJet is controlled by a Motorola 68000 chip, the same chip that powers Apple's Macintosh.

Two other types of printers are also available: inkjet printers and thermal transfer printers. Inkjet printers are quiet and have fewer moving parts than daisywheel or dot-matrix printers. Unfortunately, if you don't use special paper, the output is smudgy. Thermal transfer printers have only one advantage—superb color. However, they are extremely slow, and the materials they use are expensive. Generally, these two types of printers are controlled via escape sequences.

WAYS OF CONTROLLING PRINTERS

There are two types of control strings that most printers understand. Among the ASCII characters are several control characters that have specific meaning for almost all printers. Table 4.1 shows these ASCII characters, which work with everything from daisywheels to laser printers.

In addition Ctrl-K is VT or Vertical Tab, Ctrl-N is SI or Shift-In, and Ctrl-O is SO, or Shift-Out. However, not all printers recognize these codes. Epson printers use Ctrl-N to turn on enlarged print and Ctrl-O to turn on condensed print, but other manufacturers use different codes.

To control other aspects of print appearance, most printers use *escape sequences*. These are series of characters preceded by an Escape character. You may think of Escape as a key on your keyboard, and in fact it is. However, as you can see from Table 4.1, it is also an ASCII character (ASCII 27). Escape sequences begin with an Escape character and are followed by one or more text or control characters.

We have already discussed escape sequences in connection with ANSI.SYS and NANSI.SYS in Chapter 2. Printers use escape

CONTROL CHARACTER	ASCII NAME	CODE DECIMAL	HEX	EFFECT
^ H	BS	9	09	Backspace
^ I	HT	8	08	Horizontal tab
^ J	LF	10	0A	Line feed
^ L	FF	12	0C	Form feed
^ M	CR	13	0D	Carriage return
^ [	ESC	27	1B	Escape

Table 4.1 ▲ *ASCII Printer Control Codes.*

sequences in the same way. When a printer receives an Escape character, it treats the characters immediately following the Escape character as commands, rather than as text. All characters following the Escape character are processed as commands until one appears that the printer does not recognize. It then prints this character, and all subsequent characters, until another Escape character is encountered.

Because laser printers can do so much more than dot-matrix or daisywheel printers, making effective use of them requires a great deal more in the way of commands. Where you could embed a few simple escape sequences in your text to control daisywheel or dot-matrix printers, you need to use a *printer definition language* to make full use of a laser printer.

In this chapter, we'll introduce you to two types of utilities: print-enhancement software, which enlarges the range of print styles available from a dot-matrix printer; and printer-control software, which increases your control over the flow of data to your printer. In addition, we'll give you an overview of the two principal printer definition languages used for controlling laser printers.

PRINT-ENHANCEMENT SOFTWARE

Print enhancement software comes in many guises. It may enhance the appearance of the print, or make it easier to use a printer's native escape sequences. It may be transient or RAM-resident, and it may offer you a menu or insist on command-line switches.

Unfortunately, because each printer manufacturer uses different escape sequences for the same purposes, most print-enhancement software is specific to a single type of printer. Since Epson was for many years the leading manufacturer of printers, and because IBM's printers were slightly modified Epsons, some manufacturers chose to make their printers "Epson-compatible" to one degree or another. As a result of Epson's predominance, most print-enhancement software is specific to Epson printers and those that use the same escape sequences.

Fontasy

Fontasy, published by Prosoft, lets you embellish text with attractive fonts and icons. In its current release, 2.0, Fontasy includes 28 fonts, and 275 more are available separately. In addition, many more are in the public domain, as are many items of compatible clip art. Fontasy's fonts can include symbols, icons, or complex graphics, as well as text characters.

Fontasy is a WYSIWYG (what you see is what you get) application that uses sophisticated but easy-to-use tools and a built-in editor to let you manipulate combined text and graphics. Fontasy has excellent menus, on-line help, and multiple view screens for your work.

Because you see what will be printed on the screen before you print it, you may be able to get your printed output right on the first try. You can begin with any ASCII file and then modify the text or embellish the output with some really dramatic effects, as Figure 4.1 illustrates.

Fontasy works with all the following types of printers:

- ▲ C.Itoh 1550, 1570, and 8510
- ▲ Radio Shack DMP400/500, DMP105/200, and DMP2100/2100P
- ▲ Epson FX, JX, LX, and MX series
- ▲ Epson LQ1500
- ▲ Gemini 10X, 15X, and most Star printers
- ▲ HP ThinkJet
- ▲ HP LaserJet, LaserJet Plus, and LaserJet II

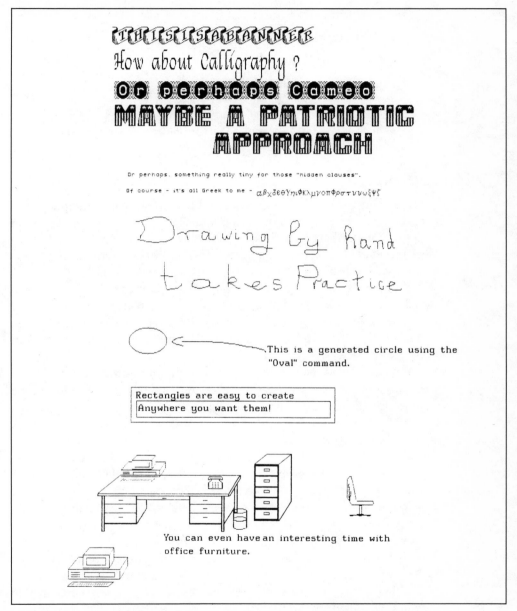

Figure 4.1 ▲ *A Sample Fontasy Printout.*

▲ IBM Graphics Printer

▲ IBM Proprinter

▲ IBM Color Printer

▲ Okidata Microline 92, 93, and 84-II

▲ Ricoh Laser series

▲ Toshiba 351, 1340, and 1351 (in IBM graphics mode)

Imageprint

Imageprint is a shareware program published by Image Computer Systems. It allows you to produce high-quality characters on any Epson or Epson-compatible dot-matrix printer. You can use it with any ASCII file with remarkable results. You invoke Imageprint at a DOS prompt. You can use it to print files or what you enter at the keyboard.

To make use of your printer's options, you embed control codes preceded by a backslash. For example, \W will switch your printer to doublewide mode, and \U will turn on unidirectional printing. As you can see, the commands are considerably more mnemonic than standard escape sequences.

You can control page format with dot commands that select left and right margins, right-justification, even and odd page gutters, automatic centering, headers, footers, six or eight lines per inch, and line spacing. (If you use WordStar, some of the dot commands will be quite familiar.)

With Imageprint, you can use a primitive line editor such as EDLIN and still create an attractively formatted document. Imageprint works with all Epson printers (except the LQ series), the IBM Graphics printer and Proprinter, and printers that are compatible with any of these.

To see how Imageprint works, take a look at Figures 4.2 and 4.3. Figure 4.2 shows a sample piece of text with Imageprint's commands included. Figure 4.3 shows the resulting printout.

To determine whether your printer is compatible, see if the codes ^[Z*NN* and ^[Y*NN* produce quad-density graphics and high-speed, double-density graphics, respectively, and if ^[3*N* sets vertical line spacing in 216ths of an inch.

```
.en
Let's demonstrate some of the backslash commands:
.lf
\wThe\w \bquick\b \w\hbrown\w\h \ifox\i jumped  \^over\n  \b\ithe\b\i
\wlazy\w \ucow\u. \i\uThe\i\u  \uquick\u  \bbrown\b  \h\ifox\h\i
\i\bjumped\i\b \h\^over\h\n \i\b\wthe\i\b\w \vlazy\n \i\u\w\bcow\i\u\w\b.
Notice that the space the backslash commands take up in the file is
accounted for when left and right justifying text. The extra width
generated by the double width command is also accounted for.
```

Figure 4.2 ▲ *Text with Imageprint Commands.*

```
Let's demonstrate some of the backslash commands:

The  quick  brown  fox jumped over the lazy cow. The quick brown fox
jumped over the lazy cow. Notice that the  space  the  backslash  commands
take  up  in  the file is accounted for when left and right justifying text. The
extra width generated by the double width command is also accounted for.
```

Figure 4.3 ▲ *Printout of Formatted Text Using Imageprint.*

Imageprint allows you to print any characters in the MS-DOS extended character set in letter quality.

One of the major drawbacks to Imageprint is that the program uses several passes of the print head and also slows down the print head to ensure accuracy. However, it will probably still be faster than a daisy-wheel printer.

Imageprint provides three levels of printer quality:

▲ *Medium-quality three-pass print.* This produces low-resolution print at the printer's standard speed. It is useful for memos and reports that don't need high-quality print.

▲ *High-quality three-pass print.* This produces near-letter-quality print at half the printer's standard speed.

▲ *High-quality six-pass print.* This produces true letter-quality print at half the printer's standard speed.

Imageprint lets you use several different fonts, just like the more expensive dot-matrix and laser printers. The available fonts are illustrated in Figure 4.4.

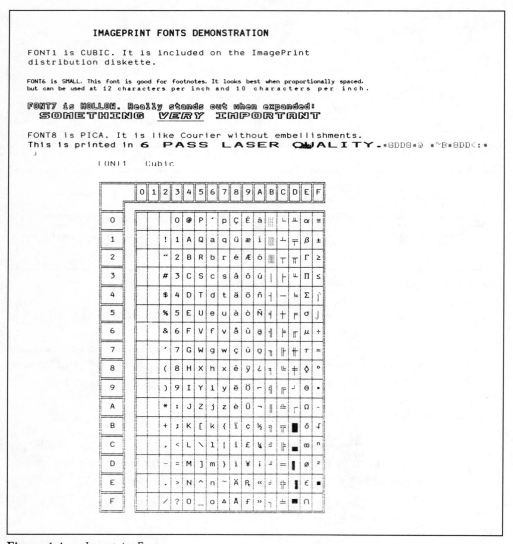

Figure 4.4 ▲ *Imageprint Fonts.*

PRINTER CONTROL SOFTWARE

The DOS PRINT command is a form of printer control software. It lets you print a group of files from disk while you are performing other tasks. But that is essentially all that the DOS PRINT command does. If you want your output to be formatted, you must include all the formatting information in your file. Printer control software generally gives you a great deal more flexibility than the PRINT command. Most especially, it lets you format the output to the page as it is printed.

TDPRT

TDPRT (Tools-Disk-Printer) is a generalized printer utility that performs functions similar to those of the PRINT command, but it is far more powerful and easier to use. It is a shareware product from Saxman Software.

TDPRT enables you to print text files with excellent control over page format and printer features. If you use an Epson FX or NEC P3 printer you need not even set up the program, because it recognizes their escape sequences. If you have another type of printer, a CONFIGURE option lets you enter the correct escape sequences for your printer and add three additional ones of your choice. You enter the escape sequences and control codes via a special configuration menu. Each code is entered as a slash, followed by the decimal ASCII code of the Escape or control character, followed by any other necessary characters. For example, italic print is activated on an Epson printer by the sequence ^ [4. You would enter this sequence as

/0274

To invoke TDPRT, you enter a command of the form

TDPRT *FILE1.EXT FILE2.EXT. . .FILEN.EXT.* **[/***option***]**

and the program will search all directories on the path for the files. The file names may include full path specifications and wild-card characters. Up to ten file names may be entered. The options are entered as one- or two-letter codes. For example, to print a document called TEXTFILE.ASC, starting on page 3 and ending on page 7, in emphasized elite print, you would enter

TDPRT TEXTFILE.ASC /FROMP3 /TOP7 /EM /E

The following list should be sufficient to give you an idea of what you can do with TDPRT.

   ▲ You can print your text with a default heading (the file name and page number), your own heading, or no heading.

▲ You can place a ruler line on each page.

▲ You can have the print head skip over the perforations on continuous-feed paper.

▲ You can select six or eight lines per inch.

▲ You can print your text with line numbers.

▲ You can print your text with page numbers.

▲ You can print a specified range of lines or pages.

▲ You can choose whether lines too long for the page will wrap to the next line or be truncated.

▲ You can set the form length (in inches).

▲ You can set the page width (in characters).

▲ You can set the left margin (in characters).

▲ You can change the width of tabs from the default of 8.

▲ You can print the formatted output to disk.

▲ If you use PRINT, you can place the file to be printed in the print queue.

TDPRT offers a vast number of options for both the NEC P3 and FX series of printers. With a little help from your printer's documentation, you can set up TDPRT for almost any printer.

Pro-Set

Pro-Set is a utility program to send control codes and escape sequences to an IBM Proprinter. You can run it either as a transient or a RAM-resident program. Pro-Set was written by Fred Willshaw and is in the public domain.

You use Pro-Set by issuing a command of the following form at a DOS prompt:

PRO-SET [R = C C = C V = C K = NN S = N]

Table 4.2 shows the values for Pro-Set's switches, and their effects.

SWITCH	VALUE	EFFECT
R	R	Run as resident utility
	B	Run in Batch (transient) mode
C	C	Color
	N	No color
V	Y	Beep on display of menu
	N	No beep on display of menu

Table 4.2 ▲ *Pro-Set Switch Values.*

K=*NN* and S=*N* are used to select the hot-key combination used to invoke the program. *NN* and *N* are the keyboard scan codes for the two keys that make up the combination. It is fortunate that the documentation includes a table of scan codes, because they are hard to find elsewhere. Figure 4.5 shows Pro-Set's main menu. As you can see, you invoke the control sequences from this menu.

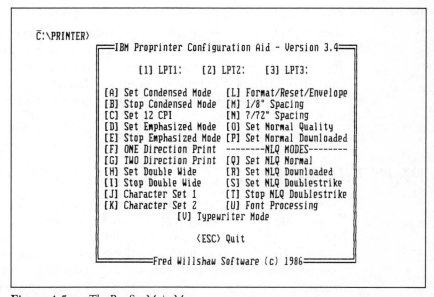

```
C:\PRINTER>
                 ═══IBM Proprinter Configuration Aid - Version 3.4═══

                    [1] LPT1:    [2] LPT2:    [3] LPT3:

                 [A] Set Condensed Mode    [L] Format/Reset/Envelope
                 [B] Stop Condensed Mode   [M] 1/8" Spacing
                 [C] Set 12 CPI            [N] 7/72" Spacing
                 [D] Set Emphasized Mode   [O] Set Normal Quality
                 [E] Stop Emphasized Mode  [P] Set Normal Downloaded
                 [F] ONE Direction Print   --------NLQ MODES--------
                 [G] TWO Direction Print   [Q] Set NLQ Normal
                 [H] Set Double Wide       [R] Set NLQ Downloaded
                 [I] Stop Double Wide      [S] Set NLQ Doublestrike
                 [J] Character Set 1       [T] Stop NLQ Doublestrike
                 [X] Character Set 2       [U] Font Processing
                          [V] Typewriter Mode

                           <ESC> Quit

                 ═══════Fred Willshaw Software (c) 1986═══════
```

Figure 4.5 ▲ *The Pro-Set Main Menu.*

Norton LP

If you use The Norton Utilities, you already have a printer control program: LP, or Line Print. Like the other programs discussed, LP can format your pages, add headers, print a specified number of lines or pages, and send escape and control codes to the printer. In Volume I, we looked at a short program to print the documentation that comes in READ.ME files on disk in a format that would fit in the standard $5^1/2$-×-$8^1/2$-inch binder. A variation of this file might contain the single line

LP %1 /T3/B15/HEADER2/L3/132

This command sets the top margin to 3 and the bottom margin to 15; selects header style 2 (the current time and date, the file name, and the time and date of the file in the directory); sets the left margin to three columns; and sets print at 132 characters per line (i.e., condensed mode). Of course, inevitably, some of these switches work only with Epson-compatible printers. However, you can replace the /132 switch with the additional code

/SET:\PRINTER\CONDENSD

This tells LP to look in a file called CONDENSD on the \PRINTER directory for the escape sequence to put the printer in condensed mode.

In addition to its other capabilities, LP can redirect output to any device or to a file, can print multiple files if you use a wild-card pattern, and can print all of your printer's extended characters. However, if they don't match the MS-DOS character set, you may be a bit surprised by the results.

PRINTER DEFINITION LANGUAGES

Controlling laser printers requires extensive and complex instructions. While a dot-matrix printer's type is limited in size by the size of the print head, a laser printer can create almost infinite variations in the printed output. Therefore, you need something more complex than escape sequences to gain full control of these complex devices. The two principal languages for controlling laser printers are Printer Command Language

(PCL), developed by Hewlett-Packard for its LaserJet printers, and Post-Script, developed by Adobe Systems for other systems and used extensively on the Apple LaserWriters.

Printer Command Language (PCL)

Hewlett-Packard developed PCL to present a consistent control structure for all HP printers. It was also adopted by other printer manufacturers who wanted their printers to be compatible with Hewlett-Packard's.

The term "language" is not particularly accurate, because PCL is made up of what at first appears to be extended Epson control codes. Unfortunately, however, PCL and Epson sequences are not interchangeable. (For a printer definition language that is more like a language, you will need to look at PostScript.)

PCL was intended to address a broad range of printers. Therefore, its features are divided into four levels, each of which includes the simpler levels:

▲ *Level I, Print and Space* is designed for simple printers. It does little more than send the ASCII control codes.

▲ *Level II* provides the minimum level of support for HP printers. It adds such basic formatting commands as boldface and underlining.

▲ *Level III* produces letter-quality print. It is designed for office and word processing use. It allows you to select among fonts and type styles.

▲ *Level IV* is designed for desktop publishing and includes complete page-formatting features.

The PCL codes resemble escape sequences. However, the escape sequences for laser printers tend to be quite long. Unlike dot-matrix printer escape sequences, PCL sequences tend to be grouped into long packets. An Escape character turns them on and another special character terminates the control string.

Table 4.3 shows part of the HP LaserJet escape sequences as implemented under PCL.

CONTROL CODE OR ESCAPE SEQUENCE	DEFINITION
^N	Selects primary font
^O	Selects secondary font
^[&FNS	Stores or recalls cursor position
^[=	Sends a half line feed
^[&10O	Portrait orientation
^[(0U	Selects ASCII symbols (other codes are available)
^[(s0P	Selects fixed, not proportional spacing
^[(sNNH	NN characters per inch
^[(sNNV	NN point size
^[(s0S	Upright characters
^[(s3T	Courier type face

Table 4.3 ▲ *Sample PCL Escape Sequences.*

You can switch among fonts dynamically within a document. For example, suppose we wanted to switch to a font that is portrait, ASCII, 10 cpi, and 12 point fixed, using upright bold Courier characters. We could enter the string

   ^[&10O ^[(0U ^[(s0p10h12V0S3B3T

in our document. In this string, the following codes are activated:

   ^[&10O   Use portrait orientation

   ^[(0U   Use the characters represented by the ASCII code

   ^[s0P   Spacing is fixed rather than proportional

   ^[s10H   10 characters per inch

   ^[s12V   12 point height

   ^[s0S   Characters are upright rather than sideways relative to the orientation of the page

    ^ [(s3B   Print in boldface

    ^ [(s3T   Use the Courier font

The sequence is actually a compressed form of the string. It combines sequences that contain the same two characters following the Escape character—in this case (s. As you can see from the above example, PCL is not easy to use, but it does give you a great deal of control over the HP LaserJet printers.

Luckily, many of today's word processors will embed these control strings into your documents for you, if they have a printer driver for the LaserJet. Alternatively, several utility packages can simplify PCL for you. We will discuss two of them here.

LaserJet Setup Utility   The LaserJet Setup Utility is a shareware product by Guy Gallo. It lets you select fonts, pitch, cartridge types, and other aspects of your LaserJet from a menu. You can run it either as a transient program or as a 79K RAM-resident program.

The LaserJet Setup Utility uses a pull-down menu with submenus, as Figure 4.6 shows. Menu items can be selected by moving the cursor to them or by entering the character that is capitalized in the command.

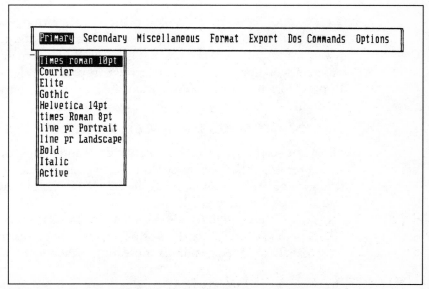

Figure 4.6 ▲ *LaserJet Setup Utility Main Menu.*

You cannot select every possible option. Only the more popular options from each cartridge are available. Table 4.4 shows which options can be selected for the most popular cartridges.

Other commands are selected from a series of submenus including printer reset, page eject, feed options, line wrapping, multiple copies, page length, font testing, and custom printer code inclusion. Formatting options can be selected to control left and right margins, print pitch, lines per inch or page, and orientation.

One submenu lets you enter DOS commands to change directories; change the current drive; copy, rename, and erase files; print files; and see how much disk space is available. An additional submenu selects and sets up text for printing as address labels, or directly on envelopes. Also included is a notepad, which can be useful for taking notes about what options you selected for printing a given file. Of course, this utility also accepts all of PCL's special printer commands.

The RAM-resident version can be unloaded and you can select the hot key to invoke it. LaserJet Setup Utility does not require any special installation and it configures itself to your screen. However, you may have problems reading some text on monochrome graphics monitors. Therefore, the program includes an option for making a monochrome screen the default.

LJ2UP   LJ2UP version 2.0 is a printer utility that will print the equivalent of two pages of ASCII text side by side on one piece of paper. It was written by Joe Barnhard and is in the public domain. To use this program, you must have a font cartridge in your LaserJet with a "Line Printer" font in landscape form. Many font cartridges contain this font.

You invoke LJ2UP with a command of the form

   LJ2UP [-DT*NPVSONAME*I] *FILE1.EXT FILE2.EXT. . .FILE*N*.EXT*

File names can contain wild-card characters and path specifications. If you enter any other character after the hyphen character, LJ2UP will display a command summary. Table 4.5 shows the optional switches, and their effects and default values.

LJ2UP is very helpful for some common tasks that are difficult to complete on a LaserJet, such as printing out program listings, printing long text files for proofreading, or creating database reports.

CARTRIDGE NUMBER	OPTIONS
92286A	Courier 10 point, 12 pitch - Roman-8
	a. Bold and italic for Courier 10
	b. Line Printer (16.66 cpi) landscape
92286L	Courier 10 point, 12 pitch
	a. Bold and italic for Courier 10
	b. Line Printer (16.66 cpi) in both landscape and portrait
92286B	Times Roman 10 point, proportional - USACII
	a. Times Roman 10 point regular, bold, italic
	b. Times Roman 8 point (no bold or italic)
	c. Helvetica 14.4 point (bold only);
	d. Line Printer (landscape) 16.6 cpi
92286F	Times Roman 10 point TMS proportional
	a. Same as 92286B except the Line Printer font is portrait instead of landscape.
92286D	Prestige Elite - 10 point, 12 pitch
	a. **Note:** This cartridge overrides Courier 10 as the default for the LaserJet. Resetting the printer invokes Prestige Elite 10 point, 12 cpi with the Roman-8 character set.
	b. USACII is available from the Font menu.
	c. Bold and italic.
92286E	Letter Gothic 12 point, 12 pitch
	a. Bold and italic
	b. Like Prestige Elite, this font overrides the Courier 10 default.

Table 4.4 ▲ *Fonts Supported by LaserJet Setup Utility.*

SWITCH	DEFAULT	EFFECT
d	ON	Suppresses date/time stamp on page bottom
tN	8	Sets tab stops every N columns
pN	56	Sets print length to N lines (adds two lines for date stamp)
v	ON	Turns OFF the vertical line that separates pages
s	OFF	Enables PC/Forth "screenfile" mode
oNAME	PRN	Redirects the output to a device or file
i		"IBM" file mode: 66 lines/page, no form-feeds

Table 4.5 ▲ *LJ2UP Option Switches.*

PostScript

PostScript, by Adobe Systems, is called a *page description language*, because it treats an entire page as a printable object, whether it contains text, graphics, or both. PostScript printer drivers are increasingly being included with popular software packages such as Aldus' Page-Maker and WordPerfect. At the other end, you have to have a Post-Script processor built into your printer. All Apple LaserWriters include a PostScript engine, and you can get one in special versions of other high-quality laser printers, and even in typesetting machines.

PostScript functions as an interpreter, similar to BASIC. In BASIC, you type in a series of instructions, BASIC interprets their meaning and converts them to instructions that the computer can deal with. With PostScript, your instructions are embedded in your document. When you send your document to a PostScript device, the device can interpret and create a graphics representation of each entire page.

Unlike all other printer definition languages that use special code sequences, PostScript uses commands that look like English to control the output. PostScript treats characters, symbols, and images the same—as graphics objects to be painted on a page. Thus, graphics operations such as stretching, bending, and resizing can be performed on every object, the same way, with the same effect.

With the spread of Microsoft Windows, Digital Research's GEM, and OS/2—all graphics interfaces—the ability to print graphics has become critical. A graphics-based user environment has been in use for some years with Apple's Macintosh, which in some respects has matured nicely, although until recently the Macintosh worked strictly in monochrome, and today's environments demand color. Luckily, PostScript can easily address color printers.

In its simplest form, PostScript has an interactive mode in which you enter commands directly. Alternatively, you can send the printer a file consisting of a series of PostScript commands, rather like a program. When in interactive mode, PostScript simply displays the prompt

PS>

If you don't enjoy programming, you won't like using PostScript in its interactive mode. If you do enjoy programming, PostScript has many features of a true programming language: variables, mathematical operators, line drawing operators, stacks, arrays, strings, logical relationships, string functions, and much more.

Just to give you the feel of a bit of PostScript, Listing 4.1 tells the PostScript engine to draw a line.

```
1: %Sample line draw
2: /inch
3:   def
4:     {        72 mul      }
5: 2 inch 5 inch moveto
6: 3 inch 3 inch lineto
7: stroke
8: showpage
9: %End of sample
```

Listing 4.1 ▲ *Drawing a Line in PostScript.*

Here is a brief description of how this code works:

1: A comment, indicated by the % character.

2: Tells PostScript to use inches as its unit of measurement.

3–4: Tells PostScript to define an inch as a multiple of 72 columns.

5: Moves a position pointer to a point two inches from the left edge of the page and five inches from the bottom.

6:   Sets up a line from the current pointer position to a point three inches from the left and three inches from the bottom.

7:   Draws the specified line.

8:   Ejects the printed page from the printer.

9:   Another comment.

Notice that the commands use a form of *reverse Polish notation;* you give the values first, then say what you want done with them. Thus, the command 2 inch 5 inch moveto first establishes the coordinates relative to the lower-left corner of the page, and then tells the pointer to move to that location.

While this is an actual example, it only gives you an idea of what a tiny piece of PostScript looks like. For a complete introduction, see the excellent *Understanding PostScript Programming,* by David A. Holzgang (SYBEX, 1987).

TURBOCHARGING
DOS

CHAPTER

5

BECAUSE OF THE NATURE of computer hardware, not everything in a computer operates at the same speed. In this chapter, we'll review some of the reasons why your computer may not be working as fast as you think it is, and we'll take a look at some inexpensive utilities that can help you optimize your computer's performance.

BARRIERS TO PEAK PERFORMANCE

You may feel that running ATs and 386 PCs at 12, 16, or even 20 MHz will greatly improve your productivity. However, there are factors that keep the improvement from being as great as you might think it is. While your computer's microprocessor may be blazingly fast, the overall speed of your system is affected by all the devices involved: the disks, the screen, the keyboard, and the serial and parallel ports. The interaction between the processor and these other devices involves input and output, or I/O. Whenever data has to move between the processor and one of these other devices, the speed at which I/O takes place ultimately determines the speed at which data is processed.

Let's look at the factors involved in speed in a little more detail. If your processor runs at 10MHz, this means that the CPU completes an operating cycle ten million times per second. Since a single instruction on the 80286 family of chips takes anywhere from two to over twenty cycles, a CPU in an AT-class MS-DOS computer can run at around

1 MIPS (millions of instructions per second). Computers with an 80386 processor typically operate at 2 MIPS or higher.

The speed at which memory operates is also a factor. Many different types of RAM chips are available today: dynamic, static, and static column are perhaps the most common. The addressing speed of dynamic memory ranges from 120 to 250 nanoseconds. Static and static-column memory can be addressed at from 60 to 150 nanoseconds. To get some perspective, a nanosecond is a billionth of a second. Therefore, such chips can keep up with CPU speeds.

In fact, the most popular forms of low-cost memory run a little slower than the CPU itself. You may become aware of this when you find a reference to *wait states* in your computer's documentation. Wait states slow the CPU down enough to synchronize with the rate at which memory can be accessed. Zero-wait-state computers have either a slow CPU or expensive, high-performance memory. ROM memory and memory used in video cards are extremely slow. When the CPU accesses these types of memory, it usually needs from three to thirty wait states.

Disk I/O speeds are several orders of magnitude lower. Even an extremely fast hard disk (one rated at 20 milliseconds) is about 100,000 times slower than inexpensive RAM chips. Luckily, the hard disk does not use the same access procedures as RAM. As a rule, large blocks of data are read from the hard disk at one time; once the heads are positioned at the start of a block, they can read it quickly. Diskette drives are considerably slower than hard disks.

To summarize, DOS accesses even the slowest memory much more quickly than it does the fastest hard disk. I/O to the serial or parallel port is significantly slower than disk I/O. However, it's still faster than the rate at which you can type. Therefore, you are the slowest component in the chain.

There's not much we can do about your typing speed. But we'll look now at some utilities that can improve the performance of your keyboard, your screen, and your disk drivers.

KEYBOARD PERFORMANCE

You may wonder what can be improved in the area of keyboard performance. The keyboard can already accept characters faster than most of us can type, so why bother? Because we can type sequences of commands a lot faster than DOS can carry them out.

Consider a fairly typical computer session in which you copy and delete files; format a diskette; and use a spreadsheet, a word processor, and a communications program. The only way you can normally get DOS to do any of these jobs is via the keyboard; in this respect, the keyboard is the most important device on your PC.

DOS includes two features that speed up the keyboard: the type-ahead buffer and the auto-repeat function. The type-ahead buffer temporarily holds up to 15 keystrokes until the computer can process them. For example, you could enter the command

COPY *.* A:

and DOS would begin copying all files from your current drive to drive A. Using the type-ahead buffer, you could immediately enter another command such as

ERASE *.BAT

If you do, what you type does not appear on the screen immediately. This is because DOS is still processing the COPY command you previously gave it. However, as soon as DOS has finished copying the files,

ERASE *.BAT

will appear on the screen, and DOS will execute that command. You could continue to enter text until you heard a beep to tell you the buffer was full.

The auto-repeat function comes into play when you hold down a key for longer than half a second. The character is entered continuously until you release the key. For example, if you are using a word processor and want to enter a line of asterisks, you would simply hold down the asterisk key. The way you can hold down a cursor-movement key to keep the cursor moving also illustrates the auto-repeat function. Unfortunately, auto-repeat and keyboard buffering can often confuse you.

Suppose, for example, that you want to move six cells to the right in a spreadsheet, but you have just changed a formula and the spreadsheet is recalculating. The recalculation begins when you leave the cell. When the spreadsheet is small, you will not notice a problem. With a larger spreadsheet, recalculation takes longer. You hold down the cursor-right key expecting to move six cells to the right and nothing happens. You continue to hold down the key. When you release it, your cell pointer is suddenly way off to the right in deep space. The keyboard buffer has probably stored 15 cursor-rights, of which you only wanted six. That's why there are utilities available that can make the auto-repeat and keyboard-buffering functions work for you instead of against you.

Cruise Control

One useful and inexpensive utility that we have used to overcome these difficulties is Cruise Control from Revolution Software. Cruise Control's main features are Anti-Skid Braking and Screen Runner. Anti-Skid Braking checks your application to see how fast it processes keystrokes, then it lowers the autorepeat rate to match, so that the cursor doesn't overrun its destination. Screen Runner, on the other hand, increases cursor movement to the highest speed that your application can tolerate. In most cases this speeds up auto-repeat dramatically, which is particularly valuable when navigating a large spreadsheet or a long document in a word processor.

Cruise Control is RAM-resident; it takes only 4400 bytes and is compatible with most of the popular applications. To provide further compatibility, Cruise Control uses what Revolution Software calls a "Control Strategy." You have a choice of three strategies, one for Microsoft Access, a second for WordStar 3.31, and a third for most other applications.

Like most RAM-resident programs, Cruise Control has a *hot key*—the 5 key on the numeric keypad. In addition, you can change it.

You can increase or decrease the speed to which Cruise Control sets the auto-repeat function by pressing the hot key and plus (to speed up) or minus (to slow down) the function. Cruise Control also allows you to repeat keys using a form of hands-free operation. First you press and release the hot key, then you press and release the key (or Alt-key combination) you want to repeat. Press any key and the hands-free repetition will cease. All other operations use a combination of the hot key and another key. To change the rate at which characters repeat in the hands-free mode, press the gray plus or minus key while Cruise Control is operating.

Cruise Control includes two other facilities. You can use a hot-key combination to insert a date or time in your choice of formats. You can also activate a screen-blanking utility at will with a hot-key combination. Many programs will turn off your screen after a specified period during which no keystrokes have been entered. This is the only one we know of that lets you blank the screen at will.

Cruise Control uses no pop-up menus or windows because it doesn't need them. The only feedback it gives you is a clicking sound when you successfully change the auto-repeat rate.

KEYBOOST

KEYBOOST is part of a set of utilities called PolyBoost, published by Polytron. KEYBOOST gives you the same kinds of improvements in performance as you get with Cruise Control, but it doesn't let you change speeds on the fly and it doesn't prevent the cursor from overrunning its intended position.

Instead of using a hot key, you specify KEYBOOST's parameters on the command line when you load it. You can set auto-repeat only to slow, medium, or fast. (DOS's normal rate is slow.) You can also set the delay period before a key starts repeating to either slow, medium, or fast. (The DOS default is equivalent to medium.)

You can add key clicks at your choice of seven volume levels. The volume of the click is based on processor speed, so that level 3 would be loud on a PC, average on an AT, and quiet on a 386 PC.

KEYBOOST can also modify the duration of sounds and beeps produced by your software. It does this by clipping the sounds to one tenth of a second.

You can configure KEYBOOST to increase the size of the type-ahead buffer. When enabled, the buffer will be increased to 128 bytes from the default DOS size of 15 bytes. If you do increase the type-ahead buffer, you can get lost while paging through a spreadsheet. To prevent this, you can optionally install a buffer flush key combination.

KEYBOOST also includes a command-line editor that goes significantly beyond the DOS editing keys. When it's installed, you can recall and edit up to the last 15 commands (however, the DOS F3 key is disabled). KEYBOOST uses the up-arrow key to step back through earlier commands, and the down-arrow key to step forward. You can edit the command line with the left-arrow, right-arrow, Ins, Del, and Backspace keys.

VKeyrate

VKeyrate is yet another keyboard accelerator. It is included in the Mace Utilities package, which was discussed extensively in Volume I. VKeyrate speeds up the auto-repeat rate, as do the other utilities discussed here. However, it gives you much more precise control, with 31 possible speed settings. You can also modify the delay time before a key starts repeating. The times are measured in milliseconds. The delay can vary from 250 (¼ second) to 500 (½ second). Surprisingly, changes as low as 50 milliseconds are quite noticeable.

Warning: There are some programs that are incompatible with any change in keyboard handling. If you increase the keyboard buffer and try to use SuperKey, for example, every character you type will appear on the screen twice, or even three times. Not only is the result very hard to read, but you run into an awful lot of

Bad command or file name

messages.

SCREEN PERFORMANCE

The way DOS and your computer's BIOS handle getting characters onto the screen is not especially efficient. This is one reason that so many popular programs bypass the BIOS screen routines and write directly to the screen instead. The speed at which the screen is updated is even slower if ANSI.SYS is installed, because it takes some additional time to process each escape sequence. NANSI.SYS, described in Chapter 3, is one alternative that writes to the screen somewhat faster than ANSI.SYS. However, there is a great deal more you can do to improve screen performance, even in circumstances that do not involve a console driver. Described below are two utilities that improve screen performance.

SCREEN BOOST

SCREEN BOOST is another item in the PolyBoost collection of utilities. The package includes two versions of this utility. You use the one appropriate to your display adapter. CGABOOST is for use on the original CGA adapter and CGA compatibles. CRTBOOST is for EGA, MDA, and Hercules boards. CGABOOST includes special routines for eliminating the screen flicker that is fairly common on CGA screens. Because the other adapters do not flicker, CRTBOOST does not include the routines to address the problem, thereby reducing the amount of memory it needs.

You can control the degree to which either program speeds up the rate at which the screen is refreshed. There are six levels. Level 1 is primarily for programs that employ slow screen device drivers such as ANSI.SYS. If this is not your problem, select the speed that is most comfortable for you. We have found that a boost rate of 4 or more causes monochrome monitors and LCD panels to become blurred when scrolling. If you use boost level 6, Ctrl-Break, Ctrl-C (for stop), and Ctrl-Num Lock (pause) are disabled. At level 5 or 6, CGABOOST will begin to exhibit a slight degree of screen flicker. Graphics modes (see Chapter 3) and software that writes directly to the screen do not benefit from boosting.

VScreen

VScreen is part of the Mace Utilities package. It actually overrides the regular PC BIOS video routines, increasing the speed of screen handling by a factor of 2 or 3. VScreen does not work with graphics or programs that write directly to the screen. It is effective on EGA, CGA, and MDA systems; however, VGA performance is not improved.

SPEEDING UP DISK I/O

Many software products speed up disk I/O using a method called *disk caching*. In this section, we'll look at several caching programs, and we'll consider the advantages and disadvantages of caching.

Disk caching is based on the premise that you are likely to want to access a file that you accessed recently. This is true not only for data files such as databases, which you might search several times in a row, but also for program overlays and for the files that DOS uses to locate other files: the FAT, the subdirectories, and especially the root directory. A disk cache is a portion of memory that stores the most recently accessed data. When you begin an operation that requires reading something from disk, the cache program will look in its memory buffer to see if the data you need is there before accessing the disk. Since memory is so much faster than disks, any data that can be retrieved from the cache will be available to you much more quickly than data that must be read from the disk.

DOS itself includes a rudimentary form of disk caching. To use it, you install a BUFFERS command in CONFIG.SYS (see Volume I, Chapter 8 for details). The BUFFERS command sets aside an area in memory to hold data read from disk. When a BUFFERS command is installed, a program accesses the memory buffers before going to disk when it needs to read some data. If the data is not in the buffer, DOS finds the file and fills up the buffer, to capacity if necessary, and then waits until the program has read all the data. This process continues until all the data requests from the program have been satisfied. When the buffer is full, the first data read in will be replaced with new data. Most commercial disk-caching software also uses this first-in first-out method of deciding what to discard when more cache memory is needed.

The degree to which caching will improve performance depends on the way you work. For example, if you typically process large files in different subdirectories only once each, caching won't do much for you. If you use many files in a small number of subdirectories, or the same few files over and over, you will see a great enhancement in speed with caching installed.

The benefits of caching are twofold. In addition to speeding up file access, caching also reduces wear and tear on your hard disk. The same is true for caching a diskette drive. A cache can actually reduce the number of times a disk is accessed by $1/3$ to $2/3$.

Many caches not only read the desired cluster for the requested file but, while the head is positioned over a particular track, read the entire track. Some commercial cache programs also cache disk writes. This is not what it appears to be. When a program writes to disk, the data actually does get transferred to the disk. However, if the caching program caches writes, the data is stored in the cache, and then the cache is written to disk.

Where Does the Cache Go?

As you probably know, you can have two different types of RAM on a standard PC, and up to three types on an AT or 386 PC. Standard memory, also called *conventional* or *base* memory, is the up-to-640K in which you run your programs. If you have a memory card with an expanded memory driver (either the Lotus-Intel-Microsoft EMS standard or the AST-Quadram-Ashton-Tate EEMS standard), you have a second type of memory—*expanded* memory. This memory is used by some programs that create large data files, such as Lotus 1-2-3 and Framework II, for storing data. (The EEMS memory can be used for other things as well, as you'll see in Chapter 8.) The third type of memory, available with the 80286 and 80386 processors, is *extended* memory.

DOS doesn't know about user memory above 640K, and the 8088 processor found on standard PCs can't address it. The expanded memory driver is designed to make extra memory available to software in spite of DOS. Extended memory is addressable by the 80286 and 80386 chips, but DOS still doesn't know what to do with it: in fact, DOS doesn't even know it's there.

If you have either of the latter types of memory, you can ask your caching program to place the cache buffer in that memory. This leaves a lot more room for running your programs than would be available with a cache buffer in standard memory. However, the caching program itself will always occupy some conventional memory.

One consideration in choosing a cache program, therefore, is whether it can be removed from memory. Some caches are loaded as device drivers. This type can only be unloaded by removing the command that loads it from the CONFIG.SYS file and rebooting. Other cache programs are loaded from a DOS prompt, and remain resident. Still others include a command that allows you to remove them. If you sometimes run programs that require all available memory, or if you have programs that are incompatible with caches, be sure that you select a caching program that can be unloaded.

Caches versus RAM Disks

You can also cut down on access to a physical disk by using a RAM disk. As you know, DOS treats RAM disks just as if they were physical disks. They are quite useful if you know ahead of time what files you want to access quickly. They are especially useful for overlay files and for batch files, as you saw in Volume I.

Unfortunately, RAM disks, being nothing more than a specially configured portion of memory, will disappear if the power goes off even for a moment. (There are exceptions, however. See Volume I, Chapter 13 for a full discussion.) Moreover, because DOS treats RAM disks just like any other disks, you can accidentally erase files or trash their FATs. This makes it essential that you frequently back up any data files from a RAM disk to a more substantial medium. See Volume I, Chapter 13 for a presentation of ways to simplify this process. Caches don't suffer from these particular maladies.

How Big a Cache?

The ideal size for a cache depends on how you work and what equipment you have. If you have only conventional memory, you must be sure that you have enough memory to run your software after you have loaded your device drivers, RAM-resident programs, and cache.

If you have extended memory, you can use it all for a cache, unless you also want to use a RAM disk in that memory. If you have expanded memory, you may also have print spoolers and RAM disks using some of that memory. You should be sure that you have enough expanded memory left for the programs that use it after you create the cache. If you cannot allocate at least 40K to a cache, you might as well use the buffers created by the BUFFERS command.

Let's look now at some of the commercially available caching programs.

VCache

VCache comes as three separate programs among the Mace Utilities. CACHE places the cache buffer in conventional memory, CACHE-AT places it in extended memory, and CACHE-EM uses expanded memory. You can specify the disks to be cached and include as many hard disks as are in your computer. You should also specify the size of the cache. If you use VCache regularly, you may find it especially convenient to place the parameters in a batch file, so you don't have to keep looking them up. The program CACHE.BAT, shown in Listing 5.1, is an example of such a batch file. It is designed to place a cache in expanded memory for two hard drives, but to allow you to set the size of the cache when you load it.

```
1: ECHO OFF
2: IF %1@==@ ECHO ^G You must specify the size of the cache in KBytes!
3: IF NOT %1@==@ \MACE\CACHE-EM %1 /C /D
```

Listing 5.1 ▲ *CACHE.BAT, Version 1.*

You invoke CACHE.BAT with a command such as

CACHE 640

If you do not specify a parameter, the program will remind you to do so.

VCache can be used with removable hard-disk systems—Bernoulli and Syquest systems—if you use the /R (removable) switch when invoking the program. This parameter tells VCache to flush out all of a removable cartridge's cached data before it can be removed. You can expect disk performance to improve by 300 percent. Benchmarks have shown that VCache is between three and six times faster than VDISK. VCache works adequately with DOS BUFFERS so there should be no need to change these in your CONFIG.SYS file.

VCache has the additional advantage that you can remove it from memory by invoking it again with the /Q (quit) switch. If you have loaded other RAM-resident programs after it, VCache is well enough behaved to simply stop caching, rather than unloading itself and leaving a gap in memory.

Warning: Generally speaking, the bigger the cache you can have the better. However, you sometimes have to pay a price. If you use VCache to create a cache buffer in extended or expanded memory, the size of the controlling program in conventional memory increases with the size of the cache. For example, a 512K cache in expanded memory is controlled by only 15K in conventional memory, but a 3MB cache requires 51K to control it.

In addition to the hard-disk-caching utilities, Mace includes a floppy-disk cache program called VKette. This is a much simpler program to use. It allocates 26K of base memory to its cache. It will cache all your diskette drives, and it can speed up file copying by a factor of 8. This utility is particularly useful with the DOS BACKUP command.

Warning: VKette is terminally incompatible with some disk controller cards and some clone BIOS routines. Once you access a diskette, VKette always keeps a copy of its root directory and FAT in memory. In some hardware environments, it won't let go of that copy under any circumstances. This is particularly infuriating, not to mention outrageous, when you change disks. There is no way to read or write to the new disk, because VKette convinces DOS that the disk hasn't been changed. If you encounter this problem, just don't use VKette.

The buffer size limits for each version of VCache are summarized in Table 5.1.

PROGRAM	MEMORY TYPE	MINIMUM BUFFER SIZE	MAXIMUM BUFFER SIZE	DEFAULT BUFFER SIZE
CACHE	Conventional	64K	512K	Conventional memory less 128K
CACHE-AT	Extended	64K	8MB	All available
CACHE-EM	Expanded	64K	8MB	All available
VKette	Conventional	26K	26K	26K

Table 5.1 ▲ *VCache Options.*

PolyBoost

The PolyBoost utility package includes separate caching programs for hard disks and floppy disks, and for various types of memory. DSKBOOST is for hard disks and FPYBOOST for floppy disks using conventional memory. To place the caches in expanded memory, use EMMBOOST and FPMBOOST. To use extended memory, load EXT-BOOST and FPXBOOST. PolyBoost's hard-disk caches can support up to a 33MB disk.

With these caching programs, you must reduce the number of buffers created by the BUFFERS command in your CONFIG.SYS file to 2. With PolyBoost, each disk to be cached must have its own cache buffer and control program. For example, you could allocate a 64K cache to hard disk C and a 128K cache to hard disk D. (You cannot cache more than two hard disks.) You must also have separate caches for each diskette drive you want to cache.

The version of CACHE.BAT shown in Listing 5.2 will install a buffer for diskette drive A in conventional memory, one for hard disk C in expanded memory, and a third for hard disk D in extended memory. The number parameter represents the size of the buffer in kilobytes.

```
1:  ECHO OFF
2:  FPYBOOST A: 32
3:  EMMBOOST H1 384
4:  EXTBOOST H2 640
```

Listing 5.2 ▲ *CACHE.BAT, Version 2.*

This design has two unfortunate consequences: If you cache more than one disk, the caching program takes up considerably more of your conventional memory, no matter where the cache buffers are located; and it's not congenial to a style of working in which you switch frequently between two hard disks. On the other hand, if you dedicate a set amount of memory to individual disks, the program doesn't need the overhead required to apportion pieces of cache space to each hard disk. Another advantage of this design is that you can use different types of memory for different caches. The operating limits for each version of PolyBoost's disk caches are outlined in Table 5.2.

PROGRAM	MEMORY TYPE	MINIMUM BUFFER SIZE	MAXIMUM BUFFER SIZE
DSKBOOST	Conventional	5K	500K
FPYBOOST	Conventional	5K	500K
EMMBOOST	Expanded	16K	2MB
FPMBOOST	Expanded	16K	2MB
EXTBOOST	Extended	16K	2MB
FPXBOOST	Extended	16K	2MB

Table 5.2 ▲ *PolyBoost Memory Options.*

PC-Cache

If you use the PC Tools utility package you can use PC-Cache, a caching program included in the package. Unlike the other programs discussed, PC-Cache will cache all the floppy- and hard-disk drives in your system, unless you use the /I switch to tell it to ignore a specific drive. You can specify the size and location of the cache using other parameters. To place the buffer in conventional memory, use the parameter /SIZE*NNN*K, where *NNN* is the size of the cache buffer in kilobytes. In conventional memory, the default is 64K and the maximum is 512K. To place the buffer in expanded memory, use the /SIZEXP*NNN*K parameter. To place it in extended memory, use the /SIZEXT*NNN*K parameter. If the buffer is not in conventional memory, you can use as much extended or expanded memory as you have, if you wish.

In addition, you can specify the address at which the cache buffer should start in extended memory, which may avoid conflicts with some programs that use extended memory. You can also set a maximum number of sectors to be read into the cache at one time. This can be helpful for some applications. When a large program is loaded, it may use all of the cache, thus slowing down operations when you load the program's data files. PC-Cache cannot be unloaded from memory.

IBMCACHE

IBMCACHE is available only to users of IBM's PS/2 model 50, 60, and 80 machines, as it is included on these computers' setup disks. If you have one of these computers, you may as well use the cache program that you received free of charge.

IBMCACHE is designed to improve upon the performance of the traditional BUFFERS command in CONFIG.SYS. It performs sector caching in the same way as VCache, PolyBoost, and PC-Cache, but it does not provide write caching. The program is supplied in two parts: IBMCACHE.SYS, a hidden file on the PS/2's reference diskette; and IBMCACHE.COM, used to copy the driver to your hard disk and modify CONFIG.SYS to suit your requirements. For reasons we have yet to discover, IBM really doesn't want you to install this program on your own. However, we once copied the installed file to an AT, where it functioned perfectly well.

IBMCACHE can use either extended or expanded memory and can be configured in size from 16K to 512K in conventional memory or 16K to 15MB in extended memory. You can also set the number of disk sectors read at one time to two, four, or eight. Because IBMCACHE doesn't cache writes, if you modify a file you will have to access it from disk again if you want to read it.

Some Words of Warning

Obviously, there are caveats associated with a cached environment. The greatest potential danger is that you might be returned to a ready state while the disk is still being written to. This could be disastrous if the cache was updating either the FAT or directory file!

As we explained earlier, the files most likely to be cached are directories and the FAT. If something goes wrong while a file is being written, or if your software interferes with the internal operation of the cache, you can be in serious trouble. The Mace Utilities, which includes VCache and VKette; and PC Tools, which includes PC-Cache, have "safety nets" for just this sort of situation. One part of these packages is a program that stows a spare copy of the FAT and the root directory in a location from which they can be retrieved later. Of course, nothing is foolproof, so the only safe way to use caches is to back up your disks first.

Due to the inherent dangers in caching, and because caching involves modifications of the disk BIOS, you should be extremely careful if your disk setup is nonstandard. For example, disks that have nonstandard FATs or use nonDOS partitions greater than 32MB may encounter some problems. The best rule-of-thumb is to first back up your hard disk, then install the cache and try it with all the software you use regularly, but with expendable data files. Continue to back up the disk as often as possible, but keep the backup that you made before installing the cache. You can never be certain that there will not be a latent incompatibility between your backup software and the cache.

Indeed, there are several operations you should never perform with a cache active, unless you know in advance that the cache will work with the program you are using. In particular, you should not back up or optimize your hard disk while a cache is active. The one exception we know about is PC-Cache which is fully compatible with both the disk-optimizing and backup utilities included in PC Tools.

Unfortunately, you cannot cache a network virtual disk because DOS doesn't treat it the same way as a regular disk. However, you could try to cache the files on the server machine. Many networks have built-in tuning algorithms, which perform some of the same functions that a disk cache does, so you may experience conflicts. As always, back up your server and try it but be thorough and check with the vendor or manufacturer about any known conflicts.

An additional problem can come up if you place the buffer in AT extended memory, as you can with VCache, PolyBoost, and PC-Cache. Unfortunately, DOS includes no standards or memory-management protocol for extended memory. Thus, it is always possible that another program using extended memory may overwrite your cache area. (This is why PC-Cache lets you specify the starting address of the buffer.) AutoCAD, for example, is known to write indiscriminately to extended memory. The only program that can safely share extended memory with AutoCAD is IBM's VDISK, because the source code is freely available and most software developers are able to avoid conflicts with it.

You can also run into conflicts with programs that use expanded memory if the cache buffer is in expanded memory. Some programs make calls to the expanded memory manager when they start up to find out how much expanded memory is installed. They will assume that any such memory not allocated to RAM disks is available. For example, if you open a file in ThinkTank while there is a cache buffer in expanded memory, the file is virtually guaranteed both to blow up and to use up all of your available disk space.

Another potential problem looming on the horizon is that access to extended memory is through the BIOS and, unless compatible AT manufacturers have implemented the extended memory services accurately, conflicts could arise. BIOS compatibility in the extended memory area has not been fully tested, because it isn't supported by DOS and few programs make use of it.

Despite the dangers, caching is still worthwhile. By eliminating from 20 to 60 percent of your disk accesses you will dramatically improve performance. In fact, if you use the BUFFERS command in your CONFIG.SYS file, you are already using rudimentary disk caching. Problems with disk caching usually only trap the unwary. We hope that by letting you know of the potential hazards we have helped you steer clear of them.

CONTROLLING THE STRUCTURE OF YOUR DISKS

WHENEVER YOU RUN OUT of hard disk space, it's always at the worst possible time. This chapter presents some techniques for using the storage space on your disks more efficiently. But first we present some information on the parts of a disk and the system areas, some of which was also discussed in Volume I of this series. If you are familiar with the material in Volume I, you will find the coverage here more extensive and will be able to move on quickly to the practical task of restructuring your hard disks.

THE PARTS OF A DISK

All disks—hard or floppy—have certain parts. Every disk is laid out in *sectors*, which are grouped into *clusters* and arranged in concentric rings called *tracks*. The rings at a given distance from the edge on all sides of a disk are collectively referred to as a *cylinder*. Beyond this point, the terminology for hard disks and floppy disks diverges, because they are structured differently. A floppy disk can have only one or two usable *sides*. A hard disk, however, may consist of several *platters*, each of which has two sides. Every side of every platter of a hard disk has its own read/write head. Diskette drives—at least since the earliest PCs—have two read/write heads, one for each side.

In addition to these parts, hard disks are divided into *partitions*, the largest unit addressable by DOS. We'll go into these terms in some detail here.

Sides and Platters

Sides and platters are the only units of a disk that are physically observable. All the others are simply magnetic patterns. The term *sides* is used to refer to diskettes, which have two of them, numbered 0 and 1. You can format side 0 only or both sides 0 and 1.

Hard disks generally have several platters, each of which has two sides. On hard disks, the sides of the platters are referred to as *heads*. This is something of a misnomer. The head is actually the piece of hardware that reads data from the disk and writes data to it. However, since there is one head for each side of each platter, it is a convenient terminology.

Tracks and Cylinders

Tracks are imaginary concentric rings on disk surfaces. They exist as a pattern in the magnetic storage medium; you can't actually see them. Tracks are created by the FORMAT command, which organizes the storage medium so that it can retain data in a form that DOS understands.

The number of tracks on a disk depends on the number of sides on the disk, the magnetic density of the medium, and the width of the read/write head. Standard 5¼-inch floppy disks have 40 tracks per side. High-density diskettes have 80 tracks per side. The tracks are separated from each other by a gap in which no data is stored. DOS numbers the first track on *each* side or platter of a disk as track 0. A track is referred to by both its side or head and its track number. Thus, when the FORMAT command in DOS 3.X formats a disk, it displays a message of the form

```
Formatting. . .
Head: N Cylinder: NN
```

You'll notice that the head number cycles through every available head (two for a diskette, usually more for a hard disk) before the cylinder number changes. The actual size of a cylinder depends on the density of the storage medium and the number of heads. Figure 6.1 illustrates the relationship of the tracks to the read/write head.

Sectors

Each track on a disk is divided into sectors. A disk sector is the smallest amount of disk storage space that DOS can read or write at one time. Every

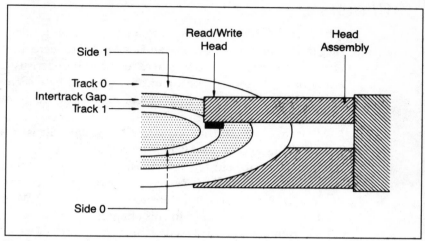

Figure 6.1 ▲ *Disk Tracks.*

type of disk formatted by DOS uses a sector size of 512 bytes. If you use RAM disks, however, you can give them smaller or larger sector sizes.

Each track is divided into the same number of sectors. On 5¼-inch double-density diskettes, you may have eight or nine sectors per track. (You can choose the number of sectors via switches to the FORMAT command.) High-density diskettes have 15. Hard disks typically have 17, although this number may vary from one manufacturer to another.

The sectors are numbered following different schemes, depending on the purpose. The ROM BIOS numbers the sectors on each track beginning with 1. However, for most purposes—including DOS's—the sectors are numbered using a different scheme. These *logical,* or *relative* sectors are numbered consecutively across the entire disk, beginning with 0. These numbers start on side (or head) 0, track 0, and continue on side (or head) 1, track 0. When numbers have been assigned to all the sectors in the first cylinder (the first track on all heads), the next number is given to the first sector on head 0, track 1.

As you will see later, this is not strictly true for hard disks, although it is true for diskettes. Hard disks use an interleave factor—to be explained shortly—which results in the consecutively numbered sectors not appearing next to one another physically.

Clusters

Although DOS can read or write a single sector, it allocates space for files in clusters. A cluster contains one or more sectors. Standard diskettes have clusters of two 512-byte sectors. High-density diskettes generally have clusters consisting of only one 512-byte sector. Hard disks generally have clusters of four or eight sectors, although you can change this, as you'll see later.

What this means is that no matter how small a file is, it will occupy at least one cluster on a disk. If a file is one byte larger than a single cluster, it will take up two clusters. Obviously, then, the efficiency of your disk storage depends to a large degree on the relationship between the typical length of your files and the size of your clusters. We'll explore this relationship in depth later in this chapter.

DOS numbers the clusters on a disk consecutively, beginning with 2. There are no clusters numbered 1 or 0. The first sector to be included in a numbered cluster appears *after* the DOS reserved area, which includes the partition table on a hard disk, the boot record, two copies of the file allocation table, and the root directory. (These terms are all discussed later in this chapter.)

One way to find out the size of a hard disk's clusters is to take these steps:

1. Enter a DIR command.

2. Write down the number of "bytes free" as indicated in the last line of the directory display.

3. Write a small file—one byte is sufficient. In any case, it should not be over 512 bytes.

4. Enter the DIR command again.

5. Note the number of bytes free again.

6. Subtract the second number from the first. This will give you the number of bytes in a cluster.

7. Divide the result by 512 to determine the number of sectors per cluster.

Alternatively, the program CLUSTERS.COM will tell you the size of your clusters directly. To create it, use the script file CLUSTERS.DEB, shown in Listing 6.1. If you prefer, you can use the Turbo Pascal program CLUSTERS.PAS, which appears in Appendix B.

```
A 100
JMP    010B
NOP
ADD    [BX+SI],AL
ADD    [BX+SI],AL
ADD    [BX+SI],AL
ADD    [BX+SI],AL
MOV    AH,36
MOV    DL,00
INT    21
MOV    [0103],AX
MOV    [0105],BX
MOV    [0107],CX
MOV    [0109],DX
MOV    CL,04
SHR    AX,CL
CALL   01E9
MOV    AX,[0103]
AND    AH,0F
CALL   01E9
MOV    AX,[0103]
MOV    AH,AL
MOV    CL,04
SHR    AX,CL
CALL   01E9
MOV    AX,[0103]
MOV    AH,AL
AND    AH,0F
CALL   01E9
MOV    DX,01FB
CALL   01E4
MOV    AX,[0105]
MOV    CL,04
SHR    AX,CL
CALL   01E9
MOV    AX,[0105]
AND    AH,0F
CALL   01E9
MOV    AX,[0105]
MOV    AH,AL
MOV    CL,04
SHR    AX,CL
CALL   01E9
MOV    AX,[0105]
MOV    AH,AL
AND    AH,0F
CALL   01E9
MOV    DX,0218
CALL   01E4
MOV    AX,[0107]
MOV    CL,04
SHR    AX,CL
CALL   01E9
MOV    AX,[0107]
AND    AH,0F
CALL   01E9
MOV    AX,[0107]
AND    AX,00F0
MOV    CL,04
SHL    AX,CL
CALL   01E9
MOV    AX,[0107]
MOV    AH,AL
AND    AH,0F
CALL   01E9
MOV    DX,0234
CALL   01E4
MOV    AX,[0109]
MOV    CL,04
SHR    AX,CL
CALL   01E9
MOV    AX,[0109]
AND    AH,0F
CALL   01E9

MOV    AX,[0109]
AND    AX,00F0
MOV    CL,04
SHL    AX,CL
CALL   01E9
MOV    AX,[0109]
MOV    AH,AL
AND    AH,0F
CALL   01E9
MOV    DX,024F
CALL   01E4
MOV    AH,00
INT    21
RETF
MOV    AH,09
INT    21
RET
CMP    AH,09
JBE    01F1
ADD    AH,07
ADD    AH,30
MOV    DL,AH
MOV    AH,02
INT    21
RET
AND    [BX+SI],CH
DEC    AX
INC    BP
POP    AX
SUB    [BX+SI],SP
PUSH   BX
DB     65
DB     63
JZ     0276
JB     027C
AND    [BX+SI+65],DH
JB     022E
DB     63
DB     6C
JNZ    0285
JZ     0279
JB     0220
OR     AX,2024
SUB    [BX+SI+45],CL
POP    AX
SUB    [BX+SI],SP
INC    CX
JBE    0283
DB     69
DB     6C
DB     61
DB     62
DB     6C
DB     65
AND    [BP+DI+6C],AH
JNZ    02A0
JZ     0294
JB     02A4
OR     CL,[DI]
AND    AL,20
SUB    [BX+SI+45],CL
POP    AX
SUB    [BX+SI],SP
INC    DX
JNS    02B2
DB     65
JNB    0261
JO     02A8
JB     0265
DB     63
DB     6C
JNZ    02BC
JZ     02B0
JB     0257
```

Listing 6.1 ▲ *CLUSTERS.DEB.*

```
OR    AX,2024
SUB   [BX+SI+45],CL
POP   AX
SUB   [BX+SI],SP
INC   BX
DB    6C
JNZ   02CD
JZ    02C1
JB    02D1
AND   [BX+SI+65],DH
JB    0283
```

```
DB    64
JB    02CF
JBE   02CD
OR    CL,[DI]
AND   AL,00

N CLUSTERS.COM
RCX
16B
W
Q
```

Listing 6.1 ▲ *CLUSTERS.DEB (continued).*

Both versions of CLUSTERS will give you statistics on the *current drive only*. To get a report on some other drive, you must first log onto that drive, and then invoke the program. The version of CLUSTERS.COM created by this script file will produce a report similar to the following:

```
0008   (HEX)  Sectors per cluster
0B0C   (HEX)  Available clusters
0200   (HEX)  Bytes per cluster
0FE9   (HEX)  Clusters per drive
```

The Turbo Pascal version in Appendix B converts the results to decimal. Thus, its report for the same disk looks like this:

```
Bytes per sector    : 512
Clusters per drive  : 4073
Available clusters  : 2828
Bytes per cluster   : 4096
```

Partitions

Partitions are the largest unit of storage space that DOS releases through 3.3 can address. The maximum size of a partition is 32MB, which is also the maximum length of a file. This limit is based on the structure of the file allocation table, as we'll explain shortly. The file allocation table holds the address of every cluster on a disk. It is normally set up so that it can hold no more than 16,000 addresses, which is the number of 2K clusters in 32MB.

In DOS releases through 3.2 you can have only one DOS partition on a hard disk, although you can assign partitions to other operating systems. For example, a 70MB hard disk could be divided up into one 32MB DOS partition, one 32MB UNIX partition, and one 6MB XENIX partition.

DOS 3.3 for the first time allowed the creation of several DOS partitions without using third-party software. DOS 3.31 also allows the creation of larger partitions. It does so by creating larger sectors and clusters. However, many software packages cannot deal with larger sectors, and will therefore be unable to write to disks that have larger partitions. Figure 6.2 shows a hard disk partitioned into three logical DOS drives using DOS 3.3.

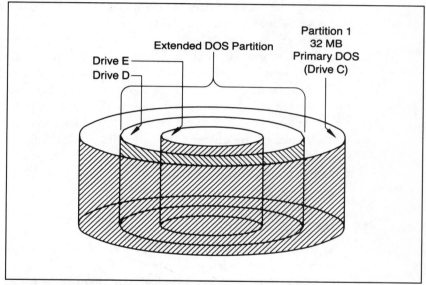

Figure 6.2 ▲ *Sample Partitioning of a 70MB Hard Disk.*

One partition is always the *active* partition. This is the partition containing the operating system that boots the computer. You create the partitions and select the active partition with the FDISK external program. You can create up to four partitions on a hard disk. Each will be treated by DOS as a separate logical drive and will have its own drive specifier.

FDISK records the size of the partitions, the operating system assigned to each, and the active partition in a *partition table* on track 0 of side 0 of head 0. Nothing else appears on that track. The logical structure of the disk begins on track 0 of head 1.

With the advent of larger storage units, various software publishers released programs that could patch DOS to allow for larger partitions, or allow you to create additional partitions for DOS. Some computer manufacturers included such programs in their versions of DOS as well.

Two of these programs, SpeedStor from Storage Dimensions, and Disk Manager from Ontrack, are often packaged with large hard disks. They allow you to create up to four partitions that DOS can read, or to create partitions larger than 32MB. However, FDISK will not recognize these partitions as DOS partitions. Neither will one of these programs recognize the other's partitions, although they can delete them. Moreover, you won't be able to access the partitions without a special device driver in your CONFIG.SYS file, and we had some serious problems with the device drivers. However, if your DOS does not permit this kind of partitioning, these programs will overcome the 32MB limit for you.

If you do not use DOS 3.3, and you want to assign to DOS all of a hard disk that is larger than 32MB, you will have to use a utility program such as SpeedStor. If you don't actually need a disk larger than 32MB for a single file, you are better off with several logical drives of 32MB or less. There are two reasons. First, the less you alter the operating system (which is in effect what the device driver does) the better. The results of the changes are unpredictable and may be unpleasant. Second, even though you may have forced DOS to address a larger disk, some of your software probably can't deal with the larger sectors.

The Interleave Factor

As already noted, on a hard disk, consecutively numbered sectors may not be physically next to one another. There is a good reason for this. A hard disk spins very fast. A typical hard-disk platter rotates at 3600 revolutions per minute. However, as you already know, DOS reads or writes one sector at a time. By the time the read/write head has read or written a complete sector and transferred the data to its destination, several sectors may have passed under the head. Therefore, the next sector cannot be read (or written) until the disk completes a revolution.

To compensate for this time delay, an *interleave factor* is introduced. When the disk is physically, or low-level, formatted, the BIOS assigns sector numbers to the disk. You can arrange to have the numbers assigned so that consecutive logical sector numbers are, say, three sectors apart physically. The disk would then have an interleave factor of 3. If the correct interleave factor is established, the head is ready to read the next logical sector as soon as the sector appears under the head. Figure 6.3 illustrates schematically the relationship of logical and physical sectors with different interleave factors.

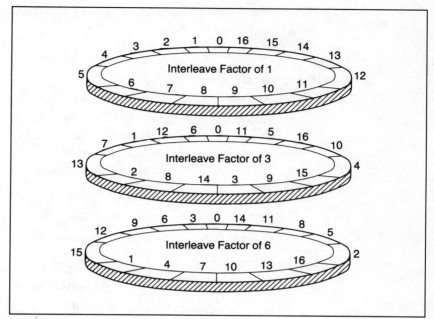

Figure 6.3 ▲ *Interleave Factors of 1, 3, and 6.*

The interleave factor established at the factory may not actually be the best for your system. Typically, a factor of 6 is used for drives to be placed in an XT or clone, and 3 is used for drives to be placed in an AT or clone. PS/2's use 1, i.e., none. With dual or triple speed processors, however, and with some types of drive controllers, this interleave factor may be much too low. An interleave of 3 may be fine on a 6MHz AT; but if your computer switches among speeds of, say, 8, 10, and 13MHz, your interleave factor may be slowing down your work instead of speeding it up.

Obviously, matching the interleave factor to the speed of your disk drive controller and your processor will do a great deal to keep your system efficient. However, it is not easy to change the interleave factor. Later in the chapter, we'll present ways of doing so, and a few caveats.

THE SYSTEM AREAS

In addition to the partition table on hard disks, DOS reserves a portion of the beginning of every disk for its own purposes. This area is divided into three parts: the boot record, two copies of the file allocation table, and the root directory.

The Boot Record

DOS sector 0 (BIOS side 0, track 0, sector 1) is called the *boot record*. The main function of the boot record is to start your computer. It contains the names of the hidden system files, some basic disk error messages, and a short program to load the system files into memory.

The boot record also contains a great deal of information about the disk, including:

▲ The version of DOS used to format the disk

▲ The number of bytes per sector

▲ The number of sectors per cluster, per track, and per disk

▲ The number of sectors taken by the system areas

▲ The number of copies of the FAT (normally 2), and its size in sectors

▲ The maximum number of entries the root directory can hold

▲ The total number of sectors on the disk

▲ The number of sides on the disk

One very important part of the boot record is the *BIOS parameter block*, or BPB. This data area is used mostly by device drivers that need to know the physical disk characteristics. This allows a device driver to calculate a physical disk address from a logical sector number. We will show you how to make use of this area shortly.

The File Allocation Table

After the boot record are two copies of the *file allocation table*, or FAT. This is a map of the disk, keyed to the file names in the directory. It includes information concerning which sectors are unusable, which ones are in use, and which ones are available. It consists of a series of disk sector addresses. If a sector is part of a file, the sector's address in the FAT shows either the location of the next sector in the file, or an indication that it is the last sector in the file. The addresses are stored as 12-bit binary numbers in DOS 2.X, and as 16-bit binary numbers in DOS 3.X. The FAT is proportional to the size of the disk, because it must be able to reference every cluster on the disk.

Directories

Immediately following the FATs is the *root directory*. Its length is proportional to the size of the disk. A double-sided, double-density 5¼-inch diskette's root directory can hold 112 entries. On most hard disks, the root directory can hold 512 entries. Each directory sector has room for 16 entries. If your disk has a volume name, it takes up one entry in the directory. So does each hidden file on your disk, and the name of each subdirectory.

Subdirectories can appear anywhere on the disk, and they can be of any length. All directories contain the following items of information about each file:

- ▲ The file name
- ▲ The file name extension
- ▲ The file's length in bytes
- ▲ The address of the first cluster of the file
- ▲ The date the file was created or last updated
- ▲ The time the file was created or last updated

The Relationship between the FAT and the Directories

DOS uses both a directory entry and addresses in the FAT to read from or write to a file. When DOS reads a file, it first gets the starting cluster number from the directory entry. Then it looks at the address of that cluster in the file allocation table to find the address of the next cluster in the file, and so on, until it finds an end-of-file indicator instead of an address.

When DOS writes a file, it first looks at the directory to see if a file by that name already exists. If so, it deallocates the file's clusters in the file allocation table. Then it looks at the file allocation table to find the first empty cluster. It writes to that cluster, and then checks the file allocation table to find the next empty cluster. It then writes the address of the second cluster in the address of the first cluster. It repeats this procedure for each successive cluster, until the entire file has been written. It then writes the end-of-file indicator in the address of the last cluster.

 Warning: This means that if you are writing a file for which there is not enough room, you not only won't be able to write the file, but you will lose your previous copy on the target disk.

When DOS deletes a file, it does not do anything to the data clusters where the data is written. It merely deallocates the file's clusters in the file allocation table. This is what makes it possible to undelete files, provided you have the proper utility software on hand.

CHANGING A HARD DISK'S CHARACTERISTICS

With the information you now have, and with DEBUG or a byte editor, you should be able to alter the length of the root directory, the cluster size, and the interleave factor of a hard disk. The following sections will show you how to perform each of these operations.

These steps may seem like too much effort just to save some space. However, if you have short files and your hard disk is almost full, you can reclaim as much as a megabyte or two using these techniques.

 Warning: These techniques are not for the faint of heart and should be undertaken only with fear and loathing aforethought. With one minor exception, all of these procedures involve formatting the hard disk, or at least one volume of it. And because of the nature of the changes you will make, it is probable that a format-recovery program won't work. Moreover, you should be prepared to spend lots of time experimenting. And under no circumstances should you attempt these operations unless you have made a fresh backup of your *complete* hard disk. If the disk has multiple volumes, back them all up.

This last point is more important than it seems. It is possible to trash your disk so badly that the only way to recover is to use FDISK to delete the partition, and then create a new one. If you have created multiple DOS volumes using DOS 3.3 or 3.31, and you make a mistake in your primary DOS partition, you will not be able to delete it unless you first delete all the volumes.

Changing the Cluster Size

DOS establishes the size of a disk's clusters when it formats the disk. On a diskette, this depends on the size of the diskette. On a hard disk, it depends on the size of the partition. If the disk was formatted using DOS 3.X, a partition of less then 20MB will have 4K clusters. This means that even the smallest file uses 4096 bytes of storage space. Partitions larger than 20MB have 2K clusters. However, what DOS thinks is the ideal cluster size for a disk may not be the best cluster size for you.

Figure 6.4 shows what can happen if the relationship between the typical length of your files and the size of your clusters is not what it should be. As you can see, with a cluster size of 4096 bytes (eight sectors), a 133-byte file and a 4095-byte file would each take a single cluster. The shorter file is given a great deal of storage space that it doesn't need. On the other hand, a 4097-byte file will take two full clusters, wasting even more storage space.

If your files tend to be large, say 100K or so, the odd few kilobytes of wasted space won't make much difference. Moreover, if your files are usually very large, it is faster to read them from disk 8K at a time than 4K or 2K at a time. However, if your files tend to be in the 256-byte range, 100K of files will use 400K of disk space. This means an average of 3840 bytes of wasted space per file.

Now we'll tell you what you can do about this situation. If you change the cluster size, you necessarily change the number of clusters available on the disk. In order to address all of the clusters, you must change the size of the FAT so that it holds the appropriate number of addresses. You make these changes by altering the boot record. This is the step that can make the disk unusable if you flub it, so be careful. We'll begin by seeing what a boot record looks like. Figure 6.5 shows the boot record of an 8MB partition formatted with Compaq DOS 3.31 displayed in DEBUG.

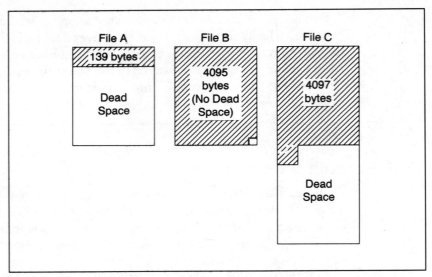

Figure 6.4 ▲ *The Relationship between File Size and Cluster Size.*

```
C:\>DEBUG
-L0 2 0 1
-D0
5F3E:0000  EB 28 90 49 42 4D 20 20-33 2E 33 00 02 08 01 00   .(.IBM  3.3.....
5F3E:0010  02 00 02 AF 3F F8 06 00-11 00 08 00 11 00 00 00   ....?..........
5F3E:0020  00 00 00 00 00 00 00 00-00 00 FA 33 ED B8 C0 07   ...........3....
5F3E:0030  8E D8 C4 1E 1C 00 88 16-FD 01 0A D2 79 08 89 1E   ............y...
5F3E:0040  24 00 8C 06 26 00 8E C5-8E D5 BC 00 7C FC 1E 36   $...&.......|..6
5F3E:0050  C5 36 78 00 BF 2A 7C B9-0B 00 F3 A4 1F C6 06 2E   .6x..*|........
5F3E:0060  00 0F BF 78 00 B8 2A 7C-AB 91 AB FB 8A 16 FD 01   ...x..*|........
5F3E:0070  CD 13 A0 10 00 98 F7 26-16 00 03 06 0E 00 E8 73   .......&.......s
-D
5F3E:0080  00 E8 79 00 BB 00 05 53-E8 A0 00 5F BE 71 01 B9   ..y....S..._.q..
5F3E:0090  0B 00 90 F3 A6 75 57 83-C7 15 B1 0B 90 90 F3 A6   .....uW.........
5F3E:00A0  75 4C 26 8B 47 1C 99 8B-0E 0B 00 03 C1 48 F7 F1   uL&.G........H..
5F3E:00B0  3D 14 00 7F 02 B0 14 96-A1 11 00 B1 04 D3 E8 E8   =...............
5F3E:00C0  32 00 FF 36 24 00 C4 1E-6D 01 E8 30 00 E8 5B 00   2..6$...m..0..[.
5F3E:00D0  2B F0 76 0D E8 1D 00 52-F7 26 0B 00 03 D8 5A EB   +.v....R.&....Z.
5F3E:00E0  E9 5B 8A 2E 15 00 8A 16-FD 01 FF 2E 6D 01 BE 8B   .[..........m...
5F3E:00F0  01 EB 54 90 01 06 24 00-11 2E 26 00 C3 A1 18 00   ..T..$...&.....
-D
5F3E:0100  F6 26 1A 00 91 A1 24 00-8B 16 26 00 F7 F1 92 8B   .&....$...&.....
5F3E:0110  0E 18 00 F6 F1 2A CC 91-FE C5 86 E9 D0 CE D0 CE   .....*..........
5F3E:0120  0A F1 86 F2 87 CA 8A 16-FD 01 C3 BF 05 00 B8 01   ................
5F3E:0130  02 CD 13 72 03 B0 01 C3-80 FC 11 74 F8 33 C0 CD   ...r.......t.3..
5F3E:0140  13 4F 75 EA BE D5 01 E8-1D 00 BE AB 01 E8 17 00   .Ou.............
5F3E:0150  33 C0 CD 16 36 C7 06 72-04 34 12 EA 00 00 FF FF   3...6..r.4......
5F3E:0160  B4 0E BB 07 00 CD 10 AC-3C 24 75 F4 C3 00 00 70   ........<$u....p
5F3E:0170  00 49 42 4D 42 49 4F 20-43 4F 4D 49 42 4D 44      .IBMBIO  COMIBMD
-D
5F3E:0180  4F 53 20 20 43 4F 4D 00-00 00 00 0A 0D 4E 6F 6E   OS  COM......Non
5F3E:0190  2D 53 79 73 74 65 6D 20-64 69 73 6B 20 6F 72 20   -System disk or
5F3E:01A0  64 69 73 6B 20 65 72 72-6F 72 24 00 0D 52 65 70   disk error$..Rep
5F3E:01B0  6C 61 63 65 20 61 6E 64-20 73 74 72 69 6B 65 20   lace and strike
5F3E:01C0  61 6E 79 20 6B 65 79 20-77 68 65 6E 20 72 65 61   any key when rea
5F3E:01D0  64 79 0A 0D 24 00 0D 44-44 69 73 6B 20 62 6F 6F 74   dy..$..Disk boot
5F3E:01E0  20 66 61 69 6C 75 72 65-24 43 6F 70 72 2E 20 43    failure$Copr. C
5F3E:01F0  4F 4D 50 41 51 20 31 39-38 33 2D 38 37 80 55 AA   OMPAQ 1983-87.U.
```

Figure 6.5 ▲ *A DOS 3.31 Boot Record.*

What we're going to do is to *back up the hard disk*, format it, alter the boot record and possibly the file allocation table, and then format the disk again. The extra formats are essential for letting DOS know about the changes you have made. Let's go over this step by step. We'll tell you how to do it using DEBUG, and then we'll give you an overview of how to do it with a byte editor, which is actually much easier.

First back up your hard disk, using whatever backup procedure you prefer. The next step will erase all the data.

Next, turn off the computer. Boot it from a DOS diskette that includes FORMAT.COM. Enter the FORMAT command with *no switches*, specifying the hard drive you want to format.

When the format is complete, invoke DEBUG. If you're lucky, it will be on the same diskette. We'll now edit the boot record.

To begin, use the Load command

L 0 *N* 0 1

where *N* is the logical number of the drive. (As far as DEBUG is concerned, drives are numbered beginning with 0. Thus, drive C is 2, drive D is 3, etc.) If you want to look at the entire boot record, enter the Dump command and the starting address:

D 0

Then enter the Dump command three more times. This will produce a display similar to Figure 6.5.

We will be using only the part of the boot record called the BIOS parameter block, which follows the identification of the DOS release at the beginning of the sector. This block occupies bytes 0B through 17 hex. Table 6.1 shows how the data is stored in this block.

Once you have loaded the boot record in DEBUG, you can display the BPB by entering the command

D B 17

If the disk were the one from which Figure 6.5 was drawn, you would see what appears in Figure 6.6. These few bytes contain all the information you need.

Entering the New Cluster Size   The bytes with which you will actually work are bytes 0D, 16, and 17. Notice that, as expected, the current value in byte 0D is 08, meaning eight sectors (of 512 bytes) per

DATA	LOCATION (HEX)
Bytes per sector	0B, 0C
Sectors per cluster	0D
Number of reserved sectors	0E, 0F
Number of FAT copies	10
Number of root entries in directory	11, 12
Total sectors in logical volume	13, 14
Media descriptor byte	15
Number of sectors per FAT	16, 17

Table 6.1 ▲ *Structure of the BIOS Parameter Block.*

```
-D0B 17
5F3E:0000                                    00 02 08 01 00      .....
5F3E:0010   02 00 02 AF 3F F8 06 00               ....?. .
-
```

Figure 6.6 ▲ *The BPB of the Same Disk.*

cluster. Table 6.2 shows the values to enter in byte 0D to create other usable cluster sizes.

To enter the value, type

    ED

You will see a display of the current value, followed by a period, which is DEBUG's prompt to enter a new value. On this disk, you would see

    -ED
    5F3E:000D 08._

This is simply the address of the byte in memory, and the value it now holds. You then enter the new value, and press Return.

Changing the Size of the FAT   Now comes the hard part. DOS creates a FAT large enough to hold an address for every cluster on the disk. If you have reduced the size of a cluster, you have increased their number. You must therefore increase the size of the FAT to hold an appropriate number

BPB VALUE	BYTES PER CLUSTER
1	512
2	1024
4	2048
8	4096
10	8192

Table 6.2 ▲ *BPB Values for Different Cluster Sizes.*

of entries. In DOS 2.X, and on diskettes, FAT entries are 12 bits long. On hard disks in DOS 3.X they are typically 16 bits long. However, on a volume of 10MB or less, they may be 12 bits under DOS 3.X as well. You must enter a new value to change the size of the FAT. This means you have to calculate the size that the FAT should be.

You will want 16-bit FAT entries, so the fat must be large enough to hold two bytes for each sector. Each FAT sector can hold 256 such entries. So first, you have to figure out how many clusters will be on the disk after you change the cluster size. One megabyte is 1,024,000 bytes. Multiply this number by the number of megabytes in the volume. For example:

$$8 \times 1,024,000 = 8,192,000$$

Now divide this number by the number of bytes that will be in a cluster. If you're aiming for 2K clusters, the equation might be

$$8,192,000 / 2048 = 4000$$

If you want 1K clusters, it's

$$8,192,000 / 1024 = 8000$$

To find out how many sectors should be in each FAT, divide the result by 256. For 2K clusters, it's

$$4000 / 256 = 15.625$$

Round the result *up* to the nearest whole number. In this case, it would be 16. Next, convert the result to hex. This example is easy, because decimal 16 is hex 10. If you have a converting calculator, such as the one in SideKick, it can save you an awful lot of trouble at this point. If the result is less than 256 decimal (100 hex), enter it in byte 16, and press the space bar. If your screen shows something like this

```
-E16
5F3E:0016 06.10
00._
```

then press Return. If some number other than 00 appears, enter a 0 and press Return.

If the number is larger than 256, you must enter it using the notorious Intel low-byte high-byte format. In this format, the two bytes representing the number take the form

byte1 + (byte2 × 100H)

Bytes 1 and 2 of this value are bytes 16 and 17 of the boot record. To enter the value, take these steps:

1. Divide the number to be entered by 256.

2. Convert the result to hex.

3. Enter the result in byte 17.

4. Convert the remainder to hex.

5. Enter the result in byte 16.

Once you have calculated the correct hex values, you can enter the two values by entering the command

```
E16
```

If you then enter the remainder in byte 16 and press the space bar, DEBUG will present you with byte 17 to edit. Enter the result and press Return.

Warning: It's very important that you enter the correct size for the FAT. If it's too small, DOS won't know what to do with the part of the disk that has no address in the FAT. If you run CHKDSK, even on an empty disk, it will report the unaddressed clusters as lost. No matter what you do at that point, your system will hang.

If the FAT is too large, some very strange things happen. Among them, the last sector of each FAT will be much larger than it should be, and the amount of storage allocated for the first file, and possibly the second, will be incorrect.

Hint: If you also want to change the size of the root directory, do it now. Proceed to the section called "Changing the Size of the Root Directory." Then, before you write your changes to the disk, return to this point in the chapter.

Changing the Size of the FAT Entries   If your hard disk volume is 10MB or less, you should also make a change to the first FAT sector to make sure it uses 16-bit entries. To do this, load the second sector from the disk into the area of memory that follows the space occupied by the first sector. As Figure 6.5 shows, this area starts at address 200 in DEBUG. The command will be

L 200 *N* 1 1

Now display the first line:

D 200 20F

Your screen should look like Figure 6.7. The values in the first four or five bytes are the FAT's own formatting information. The rest of the FAT should be filled with zeros, because there won't be any files on the disk since you formatted it.

```
-L200 2 1 1
-D200 20F
5F3E:0200  F8 FF FF FF 00 00 00 00-00 00 00 00 00 00 00 00   ................
```

Figure 6.7 ▲ *The Beginning of the File Allocation Table.*

Warning: If you dump more than the first line and see some bytes that have values other than zero, they may represent bad sectors. You will know whether the disk has any bad sectors from the report generated by the FORMAT command with which you started all this. If it said you

don't have any, and there are some nonzero values after the first four bytes, turn off your computer and start over.

If the fifth byte reads FF, you need do nothing. If it reads 00, you must change it so that it reads FF. To do this enter the command

E 204 FF

Writing the Results to Disk   Now that you've made all your changes, it's time to store those changes on the disk. It's best not to write more to the disk than necessary. Thus, if you didn't change anything in the FAT, just write the boot record back to the disk by entering the command

W 0 *N* 0 1

If you also changed the FAT, you will write two sectors to disk:

W 0 *N* 0 2

Now quit DEBUG by entering the Q command.

Completing the Task   Finally, you must turn off your computer, and then boot it from a DOS diskette. When you have your A > prompt, format the hard disk again. At this time you can transfer the system to it and add a volume label if you like. When the formatting is complete, if you did not transfer the system, note how many bytes are shown as free in the format report. If you did transfer the system, enter a DIR command and see how many bytes are free. Use the procedure outlined earlier in this chapter to find out your cluster size. If you did not transfer the system, and the size of the first cluster is not a multiple of 512, you got the size of the FAT wrong. If you repeat the process several times, and you find that other files use the expected amount of storage, you will have to correct the values in bytes 16 and 17. If the files still don't occupy the expected amount of disk space, you also got the value in byte 0D wrong. Repeat the procedure, and be careful with your arithmetic.

If everything is correct, restore your files from the backup medium. If you made an image backup using a tape, you will have to restore the files on a file-by-file basis. Because the structure of the disk has been changed, you will not be able to restore its previous image.

Changing the Size of the Root Directory

The root directory of a hard disk always allows space for 512 entries. Perhaps they figure you may not be smart enough to use subdirectories. However, hardly anybody who uses subdirectories needs anywhere near 512 root directory entries. You couldn't find anything in it if it were that big, anyway. If you have a multivolume hard disk, most of your volumes have only a few subdirectories as root directory entries. You can thus save a bit of space by cutting the root directory down to a reasonable size—say, 128 entries. It won't be anywhere near as much as you save by having an appropriate cluster size, but if you're changing the cluster size, you might as well shorten the root directory at the same time.

You change the size of the root directory with the same technique that you used to change the cluster size. However, it's much simpler. As you saw in Table 6.1, the size of the root directory is contained in bytes 11 and 12 (hex) of the boot record. As you can see in Figure 6.7, these bytes normally contain the values 00 02. Using the low-byte high-byte format, you can deduce that the value is

$$0 + (256 \times 2) = 512$$

or in hex,

$$0 + (100 \times 2) = 200$$

You can change the size of the root directory to any multiple of 16, because each sector contains 16 entries. However, to be on the safe side, make it a multiple of 32, and don't make it less than 64. Fortunately, it's easy to figure this out in hex because decimal 16 is 10 hex. Table 6.3 shows values to enter in bytes 11 and 12 for some reasonable directory sizes.

To enter your new directory size, enter the command

    E11

You will see something like

    -E11
    5F3E:000D 00._

Enter the value for byte 11 and press the space bar. Then enter the value for byte 12 and press Return. If you were creating a 128-entry directory,

NUMBER OF DIRECTORY ENTRIES	BYTE 11	BYTE 12
512	00	02
448	C0	01
384	80	01
320	40	01
256	00	01
128	80	00
112	70	00
96	60	00
80	50	00
64	40	00

Table 6.3 ▲ *BPB Values for Different Directory Sizes.*

your screen would resemble this:

```
-E11
5F3E:0011 00.80 02.00
-_
```

To finish the job, go back to the sections on "Writing the Results to Disk" and "Completing the Task," and follow the instructions given there.

Warning: If you change the size of the root directory, make sure that your FAT is large enough to include addresses for the extra sectors that will be freed for data storage. If you don't, DOS will use the default of 512 entries. DOS is smart enough to *try* to avoid trouble.

Using a Byte Editor

If you use The Norton Utilities or PC Tools, you can edit the boot record and FAT much more easily. Once the program is loaded you must choose the appropriate item. In Norton, use the Choose Item command, and select clusters 0 and 1 on the appropriate disk. In PC Tools, go to the special functions menu and select view/Edit. Either will place you in the boot record. With PC Tools, you must then press F3 to enter the edit mode. You can then move the cursor to the appropriate byte and enter the new value. With Norton, press Return twice to record your changes. With PC Tools, press F5. You will still have to follow all the other steps.

If you use Norton's Advanced Edition, you have a simple means of checking that everything has gone correctly. *After* you have completed the second format, as described above, invoke the NU program, and choose the newly formatted disk. Choose the Disk Information menu. Then choose Technical Information. The resulting screen will tell you the number and size of the clusters on your disk (you can get the same result with CLUSTERS.COM), and the number of root directory entries. Then go back to the Explore Disk menu, and select the FAT. Press End to get to the end of the second FAT. You should see a screen that's full of zeros and if you're lucky, the cursor will be resting on the last item on the screen and a message at the upper-right corner of the screen will inform you that it is cluster *NNNNN*, where *NNNN* is one more than the number of clusters shown on the Disk Technical Information screen. (Remember, the first cluster is number 2.) If the cursor is not on the last item on the screen, the FAT is larger than it needs to be. If you press PgDn and get another screenful of zeros, you have made your FAT too large. If the number you see when you reach the end of the FAT is *lower* than the number of clusters on the disk, your FAT is too small, and you will soon be in serious trouble. Check your arithmetic and repeat the procedures.

Changing the Interleave Factor

You change the interleave factor of your hard disk by doing a low-level format. The SpeedStor utility package will let you change the interleave factor for all or part of a hard disk without erasing your data. A public-domain utility called IAU.EXE (Interleave Adjustment Utility) will also let you change the interleave without erasing the disk, but it does not let you select a range of tracks. It will also tell you what it thinks is the ideal interleave factor. These programs pull off this neat trick by first reading a track at a time, then reformatting the track, and finally writing the data back to the track.

Another utility, Speed Utility from Ariel Corporation, will determine the optimum interleave and reformat your disk with it, optionally checking the surface for bad sectors at the same time. If you don't have any of these utilities, you can do a low-level format using DEBUG.

The catch is that you have to know what interleave factor you want to establish. (This is true with SpeedStor as well.) There's no easy way to do this. Unless you use one of the utilities that tells you what's best, you're reduced to trial and error.

Before you even think of doing a low-level format, *back up your hard disk completely!*

To find out if a different interleave factor is better than your present one without utility software, first do some timing tests. Use some commands or programs that require extensive reading from or writing to the disk. After the format, compare the time it takes to do the same things with the original times. If they take less time, your new interleave factor is more appropriate. If they take more, repeat the procedure with a different interleave factor.

To do a low-level format using DEBUG, first invoke the program, and then enter the command

RAX

You should see

AX 0000
:

The colon is a prompt for entering information. You enter a four-digit number. The first two digits are the logical number of the hard disk. At this point, however, disk C is 00, disk D is 01, and so forth. The second two digits specify the interleave factor. For example, to format drive C with an interleave factor of 2, enter

0002

At the next hyphen prompt enter

G = C800:5

This is the address of the diagnostic routine on a Western Digital hard disk controller. If you have another brand of hard disk controller, the address may be different.

Check the manual that came with your computer or your controller card. If the manual doesn't say, find out the correct address from your disk controller manufacturer's technical support department. The G command tells DEBUG to execute the routine.

When you press Return, you should see a series of prompts. To proceed, enter a Y for all of them. If you get cold feet, you can abort the process by pressing Ctrl-Break any time before it actually starts writing to your disk.

The low-level formatting will take anywhere from half an hour to several hours, depending on the size of your disk. Once it is done, you must create a DOS partition with FDISK, and then format your disk in the usual way.

Now you can restore some or all of your files and repeat your benchmark tests. (If you made an image backup on tape, you must restore the files on a file-by-file basis.) If you have to repeat the process, you need not back up the hard disk again, as you have already done so.

PROTECTING YOUR DATA

I T'S EASY TO IGNORE the importance of keeping your data secure. But you need to protect the data in your computer from deterioration of the media, unauthorized use, malicious damage, and your own mistakes. In this chapter we'll review some of the ways that data can become damaged or disappear, and we'll discuss some of the available remedies.

SOURCES OF PHYSICAL DAMAGE

The media on which your data is stored—hard disks, diskettes, and tapes—are subject to both deterioration and physical damage. If you use diskettes or tapes repeatedly, they simply wear out eventually.

On the back of many floppy disk envelopes you will find an illustrated list of things not to do with your disks: Putting your fingers through the oval-shaped hole in the case greases the magnetic surface. Placing magnets near floppy disks or storing disks at temperatures that are too high or too low scrambles the data. Using pencils or paper clips on them, spilling coffee on them, or bending them will physically damage the disks, making them unreadable.

You can inflict such damage unwittingly. You may store disks too close to your monitor, not realizing that it generates a magnetic field, or you may leave a disk underneath your printer, not realizing that it gets hot.

Tapes are subject to all the same sources of damage. Usually, they are a little more resilient because they have hard cases. However, they can be affected by vibration and shocks during storage, which may cause the tape to loosen from its spindle. You can correct this by retensioning the tape. It is a good idea to remove your tapes from the tape units when you're not using them.

You may wish it weren't so, but hard disks fail as well. Unfortunately, the operating system does not generally inform you of any problems. Then one day you get an unfriendly message such as

```
error reading drive C:
Abort, Retry, Ignore?
```

Retry very rarely succeeds but is always worth trying once. Ignore is usually dangerous if you're loading a program into memory, because DOS is telling you it's read something that's unlikely to be accurate. This inevitably leads to other system errors or even locks up the system.

The rate at which your hard disk degrades will vary depending on its construction and the demands made on it by the hard disk controller. Electroplated disks tend to be very reliable and work well with most types of hard disk controllers. Oxide coated, unplated disks work well with standard Western Digital hard disk controllers, but many exhibit problems with RLL (run length limited) controllers. An RLL controller optimizes the usable space on a hard disk by using special low-level formatting techniques. However, it makes extreme demands on the media. Simple coated disks will not stand up to these demands for long. You may suspect the disk is deteriorating when the available disk space disappears faster than your files are growing.

Treat hard disks carefully. Don't move your computer when it is plugged in, especially not when the hard disk is being read or written to. If you disk doesn't have a self-parking head, use the head-parking utility that came with your disk before you turn your computer off. (You'll know the head is self-parking if you hear a substantial clunk when you turn the computer off.) Although hard disks are fragile, a repair technician once dropped one of our computers on the floor from table height. The Seagate hard disk, with a self-parking head, survived unscathed, although we had to get a new case for the computer.

Another possible source of damage is a power outage. If the power goes out at the wrong time, the file allocation table of the disk currently in use can be wiped out.

The Best Defense

The solution is actually quite simple: make regular backups of your diskettes. Never run programs from the distribution diskette unless it's a copy-protected program requiring a key disk. Have at least two copies of every program and every important data diskette.

The best way to ensure integrity of backup tapes is to rotate them. Even if you make daily incremental backups from hard disk to tape, you should rotate several tapes for the purpose. This way, if you drop a tape in your cup of coffee, you won't lose the last eight days' work.

Always make backups of your hard disk. If you use the DOS BACKUP program, it's tempting to forget about it, because the procedure is so tedious. However, there are many fast and reliable backup software systems on the market that will download your hard disk to diskettes. If you have a hard disk of over 30MB, consider investing in a tape backup unit. As with tapes, you should have at least two sets of backup diskettes so you don't constantly overwrite your most recent data. For an extensive discussion of backup software and strategies, see *Power User's Guide to Hard Disk Management* by Jonathan Kamin (SYBEX, 1987).

To protect against power outages, there are continuous-power systems that will supply power to your computer for a given period of time. However, having a complete, recent backup may be quite sufficient.

PROTECTING YOUR DATA IN A SHARED ENVIRONMENT

The most obvious way to protect your system from everyone else is to use the lock that's built into the front of newer XTs and virtually all AT compatibles and 386 PCs. You can also lock your office, although it's always possible that someone else has a key.

The next most obvious step is to remove and lock up your data. This is easy to do with diskettes and tapes. If you have a hard disk and security is a vital issue, consider replacing your internal hard disk with a hard-disk cartridge system such as the Bernoulli Box. If all your data is on cartridges, you can lock up the cartridges as easily as diskettes.

You might want to lock up your disks somewhere away from your computer. For example, you might take your disks home from work. But then you risk forgetting to take them back or not having the ones you need with you. You also risk destroying your disks while you're carrying them around. (More on this later.)

Foiling Prying Eyes

You can make files unreadable by passing them through an encryption utility. Most encryption utilities ask you for a password or keyword and then rewrite the file you specify in an unreadable form. You cannot unencrypt the file unless you give the correct password. This does not protect files from being deleted, but it protects data in an environment where many individuals share a computer, or on a local area network. Other users are able to copy or look at the encrypted files, but without the password, the file appears to be gibberish.

A US government standard method of encryption called DES (for Data Encryption Standard) is incorporated in many utility programs. SuperKey offers a choice of DES encryption or a second proprietary system. Both are available from the main menu. If you use them, be careful that you don't switch between the two encryption systems, because they are incompatible. Moreover, you must not encrypt a file that's already been encrypted, or you may never be able to recover it.

SmartKey includes a separate encryption program called CRYPTOR. This program incorporates the DES standard and goes beyond it. When CRYPTOR encrypts a file it makes an encrypted copy, optionally deleting the original. If you ask it to delete the original, you can't recover it by any means—it's completely wiped from the disk.

The Disk Optimizer program from SoftLogic Solutions includes a pair of utilities called LOCK and UNLOCK. They work like the others, but they are smart enough to recognize a file that has been encrypted and will not attempt to encrypt it again. Nor will they decrypt an unencrypted file. They also let you process groups of files using wild-card characters.

A public-domain utility called CRYPTF lets you encrypt files with a password of up to 32 characters. The longer the key, the more difficult the encryption is to break. As an example, the sentence

The quick red fox jumped over the lazy dog.

was stored as a file and then encrypted. After encryption, the file read:

```
Wfb'uvgdl$qkc'blv'mqn ˜ bc$lxbu$wfb'hbt ˜ "li)
#
```

To use CRYPTF, enter a command of the form

CRYPTF *FILENAME.EXT*

CRYPTF will ask you for a keyword up to 32 bytes long. Having entered it, you'll be asked to enter it again to make sure you can remember it at least once. CRYPTF will encrypt a file in place; that is, it will not make a separate copy. Therefore, *don't abort the process halfway through,* because you'll end up with a corrupted file. CRYPTF operates like a toggle. You encrypt a file using a keyword, and decrypt the same file using the same keyword. You will get no warning if you have unsuccessfully decrypted the file. If it's still gibberish, then you have failed. If you can read it, then you have succeeded.

Restricting Access

A popular means of restricting access to data is to install a menuing system that requires you to enter a password before you can use a given file or directory. Several such systems are discussed in Jonathan's *Power User's Guide to Hard Disk Management.* We'll take a peek at two of the most powerful such systems here.

Each of these systems is a comprehensive security program. They not only restrict access via passwords, provide a file-encryption facility, and create audit trails, but they also lock users out of any files or directories that you specify. Both programs are also a bit of a bear to get running.

Protec Protec, from Sophco, is a combination master menu and security program. It installs itself automatically on your hard disk and rewrites your CONFIG.SYS and AUTOEXEC.BAT files, making them read-only files at the same time. It also automatically locks out the hard disk if you try to boot the system from a diskette. As a result, you can have a terrible time getting back into the system to reinstall your device drivers.

Like most security programs, Protec comes with two manuals—a difficult, 200-page manual for the security manager and a 50-page user's handbook. It is up to the security manager to figure out the large manual, and then keep it hidden in a safe place. Once the system is set up, it takes over the computer as soon as it is booted and presents a menu screen with the names of all the authorized users. To use the disk, you must cursor to your name and enter a user identification code and password.

The basis of the system is that Protec allows you to lock any user out of any file or directory. You can also lock users out of DOS. (A separate program included in the package can provide access to the ERASE, COPY, and TYPE commands, as well as to an encryption facility.) You can have Protec encrypt files automatically, or make encryption an option available to users.

Only the security manager has access to the entire system. As far as other users are concerned, the files and directories that they are locked out of do not exist.

The usage log includes records of all attempts to access files or directories that are supposed to be unavailable to a user, and all attempts to use unauthorized passwords. It also includes conventional records of time spent using each individual program. These records can be sorted for analysis.

You can set a minimum length for passwords, and you can make passwords expire after a given period of time. Users can select their own passwords, so you need not keep a record of them. If someone forgets a password, you can log on and allow them to enter a new one.

One additional facility worth noting is a device driver called NOCOPY. When it is installed in the CONFIG.SYS file, no one can copy files from specified directories. This is a good way to prevent software piracy.

Watchdog   If this is still not enough protection, you can pay $100 more and go for a program called Watchdog from Fischer International Systems. This one is copy protected, and it requires that you install your software through it, so you'll probably have to clean out your hard disk and start over before installing the program. Instead of locking people out of areas, Watchdog allows access (via passwords) only to files and directories that you specify. You can even specify which users can read or write files in specific directories, or only read old files, or only create new files. You can assign different passwords for different DOS commands. Moreover, the security manager must assign all passwords, so it is important to keep a master list in a safe place.

Watchdog provides even more comprehensive usage reports than Protec. It provides optional automatic file encryption and it can also prevent illegal copying. In addition, it locks out the keyboard during a boot, so that nobody can interrupt the process before the menu appears. While extremely difficult to install, Watchdog probably provides enough security for everything except state secrets. Either Protec or Watchdog can undoubtedly provide sufficient protection for sensitive business files.

Hiding Directories

One way to get some privacy on a shared machine is to not only hide files but also hide subdirectories themselves. Normally, DOS will not let you hide a subdirectory file by changing its attribute byte. To overcome this, you can use the script file MDH.DEB in Listing 7.1 to create MDH.COM, a utility you can use as an alternative to MD. The program will make hidden directories in the same way as MD makes non-hidden directories. The listing is somewhat long because it includes the same type of messages presented by the MD command. A full assembler listing can be found in Appendix A.

Even though the subdirectory is hidden, you can still access it with regular DOS commands. For example, RD will remove the subdirectory if it is empty. CD will make it current, and the path name will show up if you have set your DOS prompt to display it. So there is nothing magical about hidden sudirectories except that you can't see them without utilities such as The Norton Utilities.

Putting Passwords on Programs

PUTPASS is a utility that will patch any .COM file to require the user to enter a password before using it. Even though PUTPASS is not in the public domain, the authors have stated that it may be freely used, copied, and distributed. One useful application for this program is on FORMAT.COM, FDISK.COM, and SYS.COM in a shared environment. To add a password, enter a command of the form

PUTPASS *FILENAME*.COM

You must choose a .COM file no longer than 64,884 bytes. PUTPASS

```
A100
MOV     AX,CS
MOV     DS,AX
MOV     ES,AX
MOV     SI,0081
MOV     CL,[SI-01]
XOR     CH,CH
JCXZ    0167
MOV     AL,[SI]
CMP     AL,20
JNZ     0119
INC     SI
LOOP    0110
MOV     DI,025A
CLD
LODSB
CMP     AL,61
JB      0128
CMP     AL,7A
JA      0128
AND     AL,5F
STOSB
LOOP    011D
XOR     AX,AX
MOV     [DI+01],AX
MOV     DX,025A
MOV     AH,39
INT     21
JB      0177
MOV     CX,0002
MOV     AX,4301
MOV     DX,025A
INT     21
JB      0177
MOV     DX,0240
MOV     AH,09
INT     21
MOV     BX,025A
MOV     DL,[BX]
OR      DL,DL
JZ      015D
MOV     AH,02
INT     21
INC     BX
JMP     0150
MOV     DX,024E
MOV     AH,09
INT     21
JMP     016E
NOP
MOV     DX,0196
MOV     AH,09
INT     21
MOV     DX,0257
MOV     AH,09
INT     21
INT     20
XOR     AH,AH
MOV     BX,AX
ADD     BX,BX
MOV     DI,[BX+01B0]
ADD     AX,0030
MOV     [023D],AL
MOV     AH,09
MOV     DX,0220
INT     21
MOV     DX,DI
MOV     AH,09
INT     21
JMP     016E
OR      AX,200A
INC     SI
DB      6F
JB      020A
DB      61
JZ      01C0
```

```
DB      69
JNB     01C3
DEC     BP
INC     SP
DEC     AX
AND     [SI+69],AH
JB      0219
DB      61
DB      6D
DB      65
AND     [SI],AH
DAS
ADD     CH,[BX]
ADD     DL,DH
ADD     BP,SP
ADD     [BX],BP
ADD     DH,AH
ADD     [BX],BP
ADD     CH,[BX]
ADD     CH,[BX]
ADD     CH,[BX]
ADD     CH,[BX]
ADD     CH,[BX]
ADD     CH,[BX]
ADD     CH,[BX]
ADD     CH,[BX]
ADD     CH,[BX]
ADD     AL,[BP+SI]
ADD     CH,[BX]
ADD     CH,[BX]
ADD     AL,[BP+69]
DB      6C
DB      65
AND     [BP+6F],CH
JZ      01FF
DB      66
DB      6F
JNZ     0251
DB      64
AND     AL,50
DB      61
JZ      0251
AND     [BP+6F],CH
JZ      020E
DB      66
DB      6F
JNZ     0260
DB      64
AND     AL,41
DB      63
DB      63
DB      65
JNB     026D
AND     [SI+65],AH
DB      6E
DB      69
DB      65
DB      64
AND     AL,43
DB      61
DB      6E
JZ      0227
JB      026E
DB      6D
DB      6F
JBE     0272
AND     [BP+DI+75],AH
JB      0284
DB      65
DB      6E
JZ      0236
DB      64
DB      69
JB      027F
DB      63
JZ      028C
```

Listing 7.1 ▲ *MDH.DEB.*

```
JB      0298                          JB      02AC
AND     AL,0D                         DB      63
OR      AH,[BX+SI]                    JZ      02B9
INC     SP                            JB      02C5
DEC     DI                            AND     [SI],AH
PUSH    BX                            AND     [BP+DI+72],AH
AND     [DI+72],AH                    DB      65
JB      029A                          DB      61
JB      0267                          JZ      02BA
AND     [SI],AH                       DB      64
JB      0296                          AND     AL,0D
JZ      02A8                          OR      AH,[SI]
JB      02A3
AND     [BP+DI+6F],AH                 F25A L 40 00
DB      64                            F29A L 2 03 00
DB      65                            N MDH.COM
AND     [BP+DI],AH                    RCX
AND     [BX+SI],AH                    19A
CS:                                   W
AND     AL,0D                         Q
OR      AH,[BX+SI]
INC     SP
DB      69
```

Listing 7.1 ▲ *MDH.DEB (continued).*

will add the password and password checking routine and save the results to a file of the same name with the extension .CPM. To activate the protected program, rename the .CPM file so that it has a .COM extension. Before you do that, though, copy the original .COM file to a safe place such as a diskette that you lock up so you don't overwrite it.

It's a good idea to keep an unprotected copy of all your protected files, in case you forget the password. Note that there is no check to ensure that PUTPASS is working on anything other than a .COM file. As .COM files are the only ones that can be successfully modified, any other file will produce gibberish.

MALICE AFORETHOUGHT

Recently, two new threats to the integrity of computer data have reared their ugly heads; they go by the colorful names of Trojans and viruses. Trojans are modeled after the ancient horse of Troy in that they are not what they appear to be. When you install one on your hard disk, it does something unexpected and usually malicious, rather like setting off an electronic time bomb. Some Trojans simply print messages to the screen; others may destroy your disk directories and even trash your FAT.

Unlike Trojans, virus programs don't show up until some time after the infection. They spread their damage much less visibly. Virus programs can appear in many ways. For example, a virus program may be attached to any .COM file. The .COM file will behave as usual except that the virus program is also executed. The results of virus programs are often difficult to spot, but rapidly diminishing disk space or sudden strange system behavior may be symptoms of a viral infection.

Another sinister aspect of viruses is that that they can proliferate by cloning themselves, sometimes embedding themselves in other programs. Any copy of an executable file from a disk infected with a virus could contain the virus.

Unfortunately, viruses may not manifest themselves right away. Some are even time and data dependent. It is possible to write a program that looks like data until a specific time or event occurs. Then a small loader program relocates the embedded data into memory and executes it. This is extremely difficult to trace.

The shareware programs referred to throughout this book are obtained from remote bulletin board systems, or RBBSs. Files from many RBBSs can be uploaded by anyone with access. Although we have had success with the utilities we have reviewed, there is no guarantee of the integrity of a version you download. You don't know who uploaded the programs and you should treat all files obtained in this way as potential hazards to your system. Executing these programs from RAM disks and diskettes can reduce, but not remove, the impact of a malicious program. For more on downloading files, see Chapter 13.

Calling the Bomb Squad

The most reliable cure for viruses and Trojans alike is to call in the bomb squad. A pair of (naturally) public-domain utilities will scan the code for potential hazards and warn you of risks at run time.

CHK4BOMB   CHK4BOMB is a public-domain program you can use to scan a program to see if it performs any unusual operations that CHK4BOMB considers dangerous. Dangerous activity includes writing to absolute disk sectors, formatting a disk, or calling ROM code that could end up formatting a disk.

CHK4BOMB reads the program file from disk and attempts to spot dangerous code and suspicious messages. Unfortunately, it tends to miss concealed calls and other items that are not apparent until runtime.

Figure 7.1 shows a report generated by CHK4BOMB after examining the DOS external program SYS.COM. SYS.COM is a good example because it accesses absolute sectors. First it displays a message explaining what it is doing. Next, it displays everything that can be construed as ASCII characters. It takes this step because some malicious programmers want you to know how clever they are as they destroy your system, and will tell you what they are doing when it's too late to abort the process. You can see here that, as the introductory message points out, some machine code appears as gibberish ASCII characters. Following these characters are the messages normally generated by SYS.COM, and the text that SYS.COM writes to the boot record.

Finally, the warning messages draw your attention to the potential hazards of the program. Of course we would expect SYS.COM to write to absolute sectors—how else could it update the boot record? However, you would not expect a game program that you downloaded from a bulletin board to do this.

BOMBSQAD   BOMBSQAD, despite its name, is not a game. It is a RAM-resident program scanner that monitors the execution of any program. You can use it whenever you are suspicious of a program or unsure of its origins. You can also use it after CHK4BOMB to see if a suspicious program actually performs any unusual operations when running.

BOMBSQAD.COM intercepts BIOS calls and tells you what will happen next if you proceed. You can abort the program at any time, for instance, when there is an activity likely to be detrimental to your PC's health.

BOMBSQAD accepts several runtime commands, as shown in the following table. The more options that you select, the more frequently BOMBSQAD will interrupt you, except for the option that uninstalls BOMBSQAD itself. To use the program simply type

> **BOMBSQAD**

and one or more of the following letters:

R   Pause at a request to READ a sector

W   Pause at a request to WRITE to a sector

V   Pause at a request to VERIFY a sector

```
CHECKING FOR BOMBS AND ASCII CHARACTERS IN FILE SYS.COM.

Note that some machine code will print as ASCII characters and
appear as gibberish....other ASCII strings in the program will
be readable. Most programs have the code first, followed by data.

CHECKING 6193 BYTES


Converted
 0123456789ABCDEFabcdef
URQSPWV
<%t0
^_X[YZ].
<-t?<+tG<Lt><lt:<0r=<9w9<0u
<Xt&<ar
<Ct)<St
SYS 3.30P
%XXr
%XXs
&Xs
SQWV
^_Y[
PSQRVW
_^ZY[X
Cannot SYS to a Network drive
Cannot SYS to a SUBSTed or ASSIGNed drive
Incorrect DOS version
$Invalid drive specification
Invalid parameter
No room for system on destination disk
Incompatible system size
System transferred
No system on default drive
Insert system disk in drive %c
and strike any key when ready
Insert destination disk in drive %c
and strike any key when ready
IBMBIO.COM
IBMDOS.COM
IBMBIO.COM
IBMDOS.COM
A:\IBMBIO.COM
A:\IBMDOS.COM
A:\IBMBIO.COM
A:\IBMDOS.COM
A:\*.*
IBMDOS   COMIBMBIO  COM
IBM   3.3
IBMBIO  COMIBMDOS   COM
Non-System disk or disk error$
Replace and strike any key when ready
Disk boot failure$Copr. COMPAQ 1983-87
A:CON
A:\
*** (C) Copyright Compaq Computer Corporation 1987 ***§
****WARNING****
This program uses the ROM BIOS routines for direct disk access.
This program COULD format a disk or write to certain sectors without
updating the directory or File Allocation Table.
DO NOT RUN this program until checked by an expert, unless you
are familiar with the author or company.

****WARNING****
This program writes to absolute sectors.
The possibility exists to overwrite important data!


<END OF FILE>  6193 Bytes in file were read.
```

Figure 7.1 ▲ *Checking for Bombs and ASCII Characters in SYS.COM.*

F pause at a request to FORMAT a track

U Deactivate BOMBSQAD; you must either reboot or use a RAM management utility to unload it from memory

You can run BOMBSQAD many times. If you run it more than once, it will not load a second copy of itself into memory. However, you must enter the switches again, because it won't remember them.

IF BOMBSQAD detects a call to a suspect BIOS routine, it will pause only if it performs one of the operations you requested. After your intervention, you can terminate the routine or pass control back for it to continue. Figure 7.2 shows the results of setting just the R option.

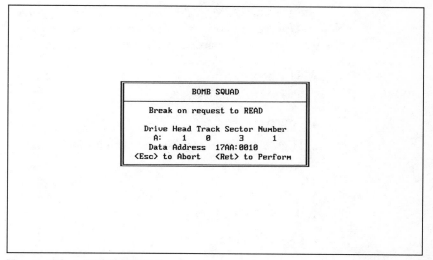

Figure 7.2 ▲ *BOMBSQAD Report.*

These are some of the elements in the report generated by BOMBSQAD:

- ▲ DRIVE is the requested drive
- ▲ HEAD is the diskette side or hard disk cylinder
- ▲ TRACK is the cylinder or track in decimal
- ▲ SECTOR is the starting sector number

▲ NUMBER is the number of sectors involved in the operation

▲ DATA ADDRESS is the address in hex where the data is read from or stored

You can press the Escape key whenever you think the BIOS call about to be executed is likely to perform an undesirable operation. This causes BOMBSQAD to exit the program, and the BIOS call will not be executed. Pressing the Return key causes the program to carry out the BIOS call and continue until the next one. Be aware that if you are intercepting read operations, you may have to press the Return key many times just to handle some of the preliminary DOS functions that call the BIOS.

When you use BOMBSQAD it's helpful to have something like The Norton Utilites on hand, so you can check and see to what file an absolute disk write belongs. In particular, a program should never write to:

▲ The boot record

▲ The FAT

▲ Any directory

▲ High clusters, especially the last cluster

▲ Any DOS file

▲ Any existing executable file

▲ AUTOEXEC.BAT

▲ CONFIG.SYS

It should never format a disk. There's no danger from a read or a verify. However, if a program reads any of the following, it may be about to do something destructive:

▲ IO.SYS

▲ MSDOS.SYS

▲ IBMDOS.COM

▲ IBMBIO.COM

▲ COMMAND.COM

> ▲ Unrelated subdirectories
>
> ▲ Unrelated files
>
> ▲ DOS external programs

BOMBSQAD can be configured to tell you when a program is about to read or write to an unrelated file or part of a disk. This is particularly helpful for locating viruses.

PROTECTING YOUR DATA FROM YOURSELF

There are an awful lot of ways to lose your data through carelessness. For example, you might enter a CD command, planning to delete all the files so you can remove the directory. But if you mistype the directory name and don't notice, you can delete all the files on a different directory before you reach the

Invalid path, not directory
or directory not empty

message, telling you about a mistake.

Similarly, its awfully easy to type

DEL *.BAS

when you meant to type

DEL *.BAK

especially at 3 a.m. when you're too worn out and frazzled to do anything about it.

The Big Three

To protect yourself from yourself, you should arm yourself with one of the big three utility packages: Mace Utilities, The Norton Utilities, or PC Tools. All three have facilities that will recover an erased file. Indeed, it was this facility alone that made The Norton Utilities so popular. In addition, the latest versions of these programs include a utility to stow a copy of the boot record, root directory, and file allocation table at a known location on your disk.

This latter utility can be very useful. If you accidentally format your hard disk, you can use it to restore the DOS reserved area. Most versions of DOS only erase the root directory and file allocation table when they format a hard disk. If you religiously update the files with the backup copies of these areas, you can run a companion program to rewrite the information to its proper location. This will allow you to recover any data that has not been changed since you last updated the backup file.

Additionally, Mace Utilities uses the information in this file to help you locate the clusters of an erased file when you want to get it back. Similarly, PC Tools Deluxe includes a new feature called Delete Tracking. If you install a small resident program, it will make a record on disk of the previous location of any file you delete, to help you recover it if necessary.

All three packages also include facilities to help you recover data when it's impossible to recover the DOS reserved area of your disk. In addition, all three include a facility to help recover data from bad sectors and write it to a safe location.

For a full discussion of these utilities, see Volume I of this series, Chapter 15, or *Power User's Guide to Hard Disk Management*, Chapter 4.

DBACK

DBACK is a public domain utility that will take a copy of your hard disk FAT and stow it safely on a diskette. Running DBACK from a diskette will restore the FAT back to the hard disk. This is useful if you format the hard disk under most versions of DOS; you can recover the allocation area and the actual data on the disk will be intact. Of course, this will not work with those versions of DOS that actually erase the entire disk. To use DBACK enter the command

DBACK [*drive*]

where *drive* is the drive to protect or restore. If you do not enter a drive name, it will operate on the current drive.

DBACK will back up both the FAT and root directory of a hard disk on another (floppy) disk and restore if disaster strikes. DBACK makes a read-only file called DBACK.DRx (where *x* is the backed up drive) in the drive's root directory.

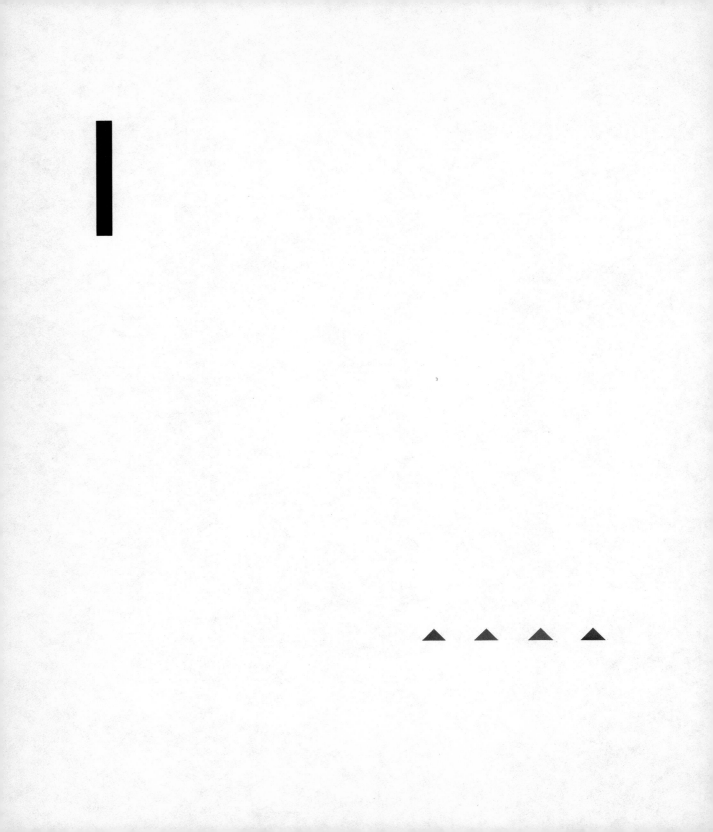

PART II

MULTITASKING

INTRODUCTION TO WINDOWED OPERATING ENVIRONMENTS

CHAPTER 8

HAVE YOU EVER WISHED you could stuff a Macintosh inside your PC? Many of us have envied Mac users for the ease with which they get around among their applications simply by dragging a mouse to an icon and clicking. The Mac world also deserves credit for standardizing a user interface that is both consistent across applications and easy to learn.

In addition, have you ever wished you could take a peek at some data in your spreadsheet without exiting your word processor? Mac users can employ part of the operating system—the Multifinder, which allows several programs to be open on the screen at once in different windows—to do just that. With another part of the operating system, the Clipboard, they can even cut data from one application and paste it into another. On the other hand, nothing on the Mac allows you to perform several jobs in succession, altering your environment in the process, the way a batch file can. Wouldn't it be nice if you could have the best of both worlds?

The good news is that there are several ways you can do both of these things—and more—on your PC. The "more" is something even more powerful: running several programs at once. The bad news is that it's going to cost you something—possibly a cherished aspect of your usual style of working. Each alternative provides some additional power and extracts a different price. What you have to give up depends on the solution you choose.

In this chapter, we'll introduce you to four rather different operating environments, all of which run in conjunction with MS-DOS: Microsoft Windows, DESQview, GEM, and Software Carousel. Three of these packages give you windowed operating environments, which emulate the Macintosh to one degree or another. In Chapter 9, we'll show you how three of these environments (not the same three) allow you to load several applications and switch freely among them. We'll also give some attention to how each of the four programs interacts with DOS. Two of them also give you a degree of multitasking if you have the hardware to support it. We'll give you a side-by-side comparison of these packages in Chapter 9, after we've presented them in some detail here.

WINDOWS

Microsoft Windows bids fair to become a major component of OS/2, having been endorsed by both IBM and Microsoft. For this reason alone it deserves special consideration. It will probably be the standard interface for programs designed for OS/2, and programs designed to run with it benefit greatly from it.

Windows uses your screen in graphics mode exclusively. This makes it easy to share text and graphics in a single application. One important feature of Windows is that you can cut text or graphics from one window and paste it into another, using a clipboard as an intermediary. On the other hand, because the graphics screen needs a great deal more memory to represent it than the text screen, Windows is relatively slow. Every change in the screen requires updating all of the video graphics memory.

You can have several windows open at one time, each with a different application. Or, if one program requires more of your memory resources, you can reduce the others to icons, which remain on the screen ready for you to pull them into the foreground with a double-click. Figure 8.1 shows the Windows 2.03 desktop with several applications loaded and a menu on display. Some applications are shown as windows while others are shown as icons.

You can access commands either by hitting an Alt-key combination to pull down a menu and then pressing a highlighted key, or by clicking on the menu with a mouse and selecting the menu item the same way.

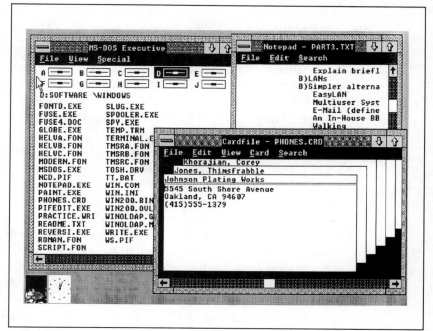

Figure 8.1 ▲ *The Windows Desktop.*

Every menu has a default item selected, which you can select just by double-clicking.

Menus stay in place until you select something from them or click elsewhere (or press Escape). You have access to the menus with any application that can run in a window.

When you have several programs in memory, those not currently active are swapped out, either to a hard disk or to expanded memory.

You can have Windows automatically load some programs when you invoke it. These programs can appear either as open windows or as icons. If you do not automatically load programs, Windows comes up in the MS-DOS Executive window, which contains the current directory with icons for all the drives in your system. You can move or change the size of the window at will, although its initial size is fixed.

Hint: It's much easier to move and size windows with a mouse than from the keyboard. It's a bad idea, however, to move the window so far

up the screen that the menu bar disappears. You can still invoke the
menu commands using the keyboard, but you'll be flying blind.

One design element that was *not* carried over from the Macintosh
environment is the way inactive applications and files are represented.
The only time files are represented as icons is when they are loaded but
in the background. These icons can be dragged around the desktop, and
zoomed open to become windows. However, in the MS-DOS Executive
window—the one where you have access to the operating system—files
are displayed by name only. While you can select several file names for
an operation such as copying or deleting, you can't drag them around or
rearrange them. Thus, you lack one of the principal advantages of a
windows-and-icons environment.

Where Windows really shines is with applications written especially
for it. When such applications are in memory, they run all the time, giving you timesliced multitasking. The multitasking within Windows is
especially well implemented because Windows knows what's happen-
ing in each application and assigns processor time to it as needed. In
contrast, most multitasking systems allot time to each application on
some arbitrary basis, whether they need it or not. (More on this in
Chapter 10.)

When an application is designed to use Windows, you have the
advantage of a user interface that is the same as that of all the other
Windows applications. This makes it easy to learn new applications,
and helps to keep you from getting confused when you switch from one
application to another.

One feature of virtually all Windows applications is that you can
select a portion of a window by clicking the mouse, holding down the
mouse button, and dragging to the end of the text you want to select.
Depending on the application, you can move the selected material to
another part of a window, delete it, or cut or copy it to the clipboard for
pasting into another application.

This can get a bit confusing if you also run applications that don't use
the mouse. For example, you can configure WordStar 4.0 to run in a
window by setting it up to use BIOS video calls instead of writing to the
screen. Similarly you can run dBASE III PLUS in a window effectively
if you select colors that show up as black and white. However, if you

switch to one of these applications from a Windows application, you may find yourself trying to select with the mouse. You can select a rectangular area to cut or copy to the clipboard, of course, but you can't select a block of text the way you would in a Windows application.

If an application cannot run in a window (as will be true if it writes to the screen directly) it will run in full-screen mode. Nothing on the screen will tell you that you are still in Windows. However, you can still return to the desktop by pressing Alt-Esc, or call the Control Menu (the one that determines whether a program is in the foreground or background and includes the cut and paste features). This menu is represented on the normal Windows screen by a small handle in the upper-left corner. In full-screen applications it appears as an inverse-video minus sign. In either case, you call it by pressing Alt-space bar.

If the program uses the keyboard buffer, however, you cannot use the cut-and-paste menu, and you cannot switch back to the desktop. You must exit the application to return to the desktop. However, you can capture an entire screen to the clipboard by pressing Alt-PrtSc. The text (or graphics) on the clipboard can then be pasted into any other window.

If the program uses the communications ports, it must run in real time. Hence, it cannot be swapped out of memory under any circumstances. Generally, you should load such programs first.

You can switch an icon to a window by double-clicking it, or by hitting Alt-Esc (which selects each icon in turn) until its name is highlighted and then pressing Return. The mouse driver doesn't appear to be very fast, at least with my PC-Mouse, so it ends up being easier to use keyboard commands most of the time.

Installing Windows

Installing Windows on your hard disk is easy. You place the Setup disk (one of its eight disks) in drive A and enter the command

```
SETUP
```

The program will take care of everything else, prompting you for details about your hardware, and modifying the code to take best advantage of your system as it installs the program.

Setting Up Your System for Windows

Windows can run on a standard 8088-based PC but you need some kind of graphics adapter. It requires a minimum of 512K to run, but it does better with 640K. It will run from diskettes, and it will run with a color graphics adapter.

However, Windows behaves much better the more powerful its hardware environment. Because it treats everything that appears on the screen as graphics, it tends to be slow. It takes some time to convert text into graphics. Therefore, you need an 80286 or 80386 processor before it stops seeming sluggish. And its color emulation on a CGA is, at best, messy. The better the graphics hardware environment you can give it, the better it looks. As a practical minimum, you should have a standard EGA and monitor, with 256K of EGA memory. A hard disk is highly recommended—preferably a large, fast one. (The program itself requires 1.6MB.) In addition, Windows will make use of as much expanded memory as you can give it. You can enter all its commands from the keyboard, but it usually works better and faster with a mouse.

To make Windows run at its best, you may have to make changes to your system configuration. Most important is Windows' relationship to the memory in your computer. You will probably want to create a new CONFIG.SYS file for Windows to load some special device drivers, which you will copy to your hard disk.

Windows deals quite differently with conventional memory, expanded memory, and extended memory. To begin with, you should give the program as much conventional memory as you can—Windows itself is large. The more memory you can give it, the larger the programs it can run, and the more programs you can keep in memory at once.

If you have the EMS 4.0 device driver for your expanded memory card, you can increase the number and size of programs that Windows can handle. DOS manages conventional memory, but EMS memory is "smart" memory and Windows controls it through the EMS device driver. (EMS 4.0 is packaged with Windows, but it may not work with your EMS board if your board is not 100 percent compatible with the Intel Above Board.) Therefore, you can maximize the control that Windows has by reducing the amount of conventional memory on your motherboard to as little as your computer will permit (probably 256K) and configuring your EMS board to assign enough of its memory to conventional memory to give you a total of 640K.

Windows can also use as much expanded memory as you can give it. If you can configure your EMS board as either extended or expanded memory, assign any that isn't filling out conventional memory to expanded memory.

Part of what Windows uses all that memory for is swapping programs out of memory when they are not active. The best place to swap programs to is expanded memory. However, you can also swap to a hard disk or a RAM disk.

Windows doesn't like RAM disks, even though it includes its own version of RAMDRIVE.SYS. (However, we've successfully used other RAM disks with it.) If you have extended memory, but no expanded memory, you can place a RAM disk in it (using Windows' own RAM-DRIVE.SYS driver) and use that disk as a swap area. It's more efficient, however, to use extended memory for Windows' own special disk-caching program, SMARTDRV.SYS, which is described below. If you have the facilities, then, this is the most efficient organization:

- ▲ Reduce your conventional memory on the motherboard to the least amount your computer can accept

- ▲ Fill conventional memory to 640K from an expanded memory board using the EMS 4.0 driver

- ▲ Configure the rest of your memory board for expanded memory

- ▲ If you have extended memory that *can't* be converted to expanded memory, use the SMARTDRV.SYS device driver to place a cache buffer in extended memory

- ▲ If you don't have any extended memory, use the SMARTDRV-.SYS device driver to place a smaller cache buffer in expanded memory

SMARTDrive   SMARTDRV.SYS, located on the Utilities 2 disk, is the device driver for Windows' own disk-caching program, SMART-Drive. It caches only programs that are currently in memory and is used primarily for programs that have been swapped out to a hard disk. You'll see shortly how to use a hard disk as a swap disk. If you have extended memory that can't be converted to anything else, you can assign all of it to SMARTDrive (unless you plan to run a normal DOS application that uses extended memory under Windows). If you don't have extended memory, you can allot some expanded memory to this program. Again, do not assign all of your expanded memory to SMARTDrive if you need some for programs that you plan to run.

To give SMARTDrive all of your extended memory, include the following command in your CONFIG.SYS file:

DEVICE = SMARTDRV.SYS

If you haven't placed the driver program on the root directory of your hard disk, precede the file name with a drive specifier and/or path name to its location.

To install SMARTDrive in expanded memory, use the /A switch. Its buffer will default to 256K unless you give it more memory. The command

DEVICE = SMARTDRV.SYS 1024 /A

will create a 1MB cache buffer in expanded memory.

Improving the Performance of EGAs   If you use an EGA and compatible monitor, you can use an additional device driver to improve the quality of the display when you run DOS applications under Windows. The driver is EGA.SYS, which is on the Utilities 2 disk. Copy it to the root directory of your hard disk. Then add a command to load it to your CONFIG.SYS file. If you use a mouse, and it is not a Microsoft mouse, add this line *before* the line that loads the mouse driver:

DEVICE = EGA.SYS

Because of Windows' own buffering, you need only a minimum of DOS buffers. The documentation recommends ten buffers. When you have made all of the changes described above, your CONFIG.SYS file will look something like Listing 8.1. This CONFIG.SYS file is for a system with an EGA and 3MB of expanded memory but no extended memory.

```
1: DEVICE=EMM.SYS 258,00;268,00
2: DEVICE=SMARTDRV.SYS 1024 /A
3: DEVICE=EGA.SYS
4: DEVICE=MSMOUSE.SYS /1
5: FILES=20
6: BUFFERS=10
```

Listing 8.1 ▲ *CONFIG.SYS File for Windows.*

The AUTOEXEC.BAT File Once you have your system configured, you'll want to optimize it for Windows at the DOS level. As you'll see later, Windows doesn't pay much attention to PATH and APPEND commands, so you need only a minimal path. The most important addition to your AUTOEXEC.BAT file is a command to establish a *swap disk*. This is where Windows will place programs that are loaded but inactive, if there is no room for them in memory. You do this with the environment variable TEMP. If you have one hard disk, the swap disk will be C. If you have more than one, use the one that has the most room to spare. You can also specify a subdirectory of a disk, or a RAM disk. Listing 8.2 shows an AUTOEXEC.BAT file that makes the root directory of drive C the swap disk. Notice that this AUTOEXEC.BAT file is about as minimal as you can get.

```
1: @ECHO OFF
2: PATH=C:\;C:\DOS;C:\WINDOWS;C:\WINDOWS\PIF
3: PROMPT $p$g
4: SET TEMP=C:\
5: CD\WINDOWS
6: WIN
```

Listing 8.2 ▲ *AUTOEXEC.BAT File for Windows.*

Configuring Windows for Your System

Windows has lots of configuration options. You can set many of them by running the CONTROL.EXE program from within Windows. Figure 8.2 shows the resulting "control panel." In this program, you can set:

- ▲ The date and time format
- ▲ The time between mouse clicks that Windows will recognize as a double-click
- ▲ The speed at which the cursor blinks
- ▲ The speed at which the mouse cursor moves
- ▲ National defaults for date, time, currency, and decimal delimiter
- ▲ Colors for all elements of the screen
- ▲ The default printer, the port it uses, the type of paper it uses, and whether to print in landscape (sideways) or portrait (normal) mode

You can also add or delete fonts. Any changes you make using the control panel are written to a file called WIN.INI. This file also lets you configure other aspects of Windows. It is heavily commented, so you can probably learn all you need to make the necessary changes just by reading it.

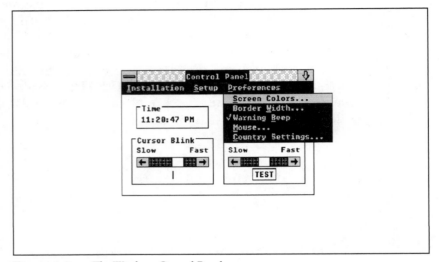

Figure 8.2 ▲ *The Windows Control Panel.*

Several points should be stressed here. First, if there are any changes you can make via the control panel, use the control panel. It's much easier. Second, pay special attention to the load= and run= commands. Third, you *must* configure your swap disk in WIN.INI as well as with the TEMP environment variable.

The latter points could use some further explanation. The load= command tells Windows to load whatever applications you list in it when you start Windows. These programs will be loaded as icons. From the point of view of memory management, you should load the *largest* program you intend to use first, even if you won't use it right away. Otherwise, you may not be able to reserve enough memory for it later, and you won't be able to run it at all unless you close some other programs.

The run= command loads applications as windows rather than as icons. You should place programs in this command line only if you intend to use them immediately.

There are two settings in WIN.INI that control the swap disk. One is swapsize=. This should be set to a size large enough to hold the largest application, its data, and memory to save its screen. The best approach is to set

SWAPSIZE = 0

or

SWAPSIZE = ?

With either of these settings, Windows will assign an appropriate partition size to the first standard application that uses a partition. Note that once the first application has been given a partition, the partition size applies to any subsequent standard applications that are loaded or swapped. (This is another reason to load your largest application first.)

In addition to the TEMP= environment variable, you should set up your swap disk in WIN.INI, using the swapdisk= command. If you have expanded memory, you can tell Windows to use expanded memory for the swap area by using the /E switch. You can also specify the same drive and directory you specified in the TEMP variable. Thus, if you edit the command to read

SWAPDISK = C:\ /E

Windows will swap programs to expanded memory if any is available, and then swap to a file in the root directory of drive C.

 Warning: If Windows terminates abnormally, you will be left with a huge file in this directory, which you will probably want to delete. You can recognize it because its name begins with the ~ character.

Configuring Your Programs for Windows

The key to using applications in Windows is the .PIF, or Program Information File. You must have one for every application you intend to use with Windows. (There is a set of standard defaults, but they don't work with very many programs, and they give you a bunch of extra dialog boxes to wade through.) You create these files using a special application called the PIF Editor. In it, you tell Windows:

▲ The file name, extension, and complete path name for the application.

▲ The name you want Windows to display at the top of the application's window.

▲ The parameters to be passed to the program (enter a question mark to have Windows prompt you for parameters).

▲ The directory where the application should come up—usually the directory where its data files are located.

▲ The minimum amount of memory the application needs, and the maximum amount it can use, if it can use more than the minimum.

▲ Information about the program's behavior. This includes whether it writes directly to screen memory (many popular programs do), whether it uses the keyboard buffer directly, and whether it uses any of the communications ports.

▲ Whether you might want to capture text, graphics, or both from the program to paste into other applications.

▲ Whether you want the window to close automatically when you exit the program.

Figure 8.3 shows the PIF Editor screen, so you can see what you have to deal with.

If you don't get the information right, the chances are your program won't run. You may have to modify the .PIF file as many as a dozen times before everything works the way you want it to.

If a program modifies the screen, you can't run it in a window. You can experiment with this one to see what happens. Be careful not use a vital file, because if the program writes to video memory and you say it doesn't, you may not see anything in the window. On the other hand, you may be able to modify your programs to run in a window. We were able to get WordStar 4.0 to do it using the WSCHANGE program to make WordStar use BIOS video calls instead of writing to video memory. (However, even though it takes up only about two-thirds of the screen, telling WordStar to use more than 25 lines was disastrous. Moreover, because it used BIOS calls, it was incredibly slow.) dBASE III

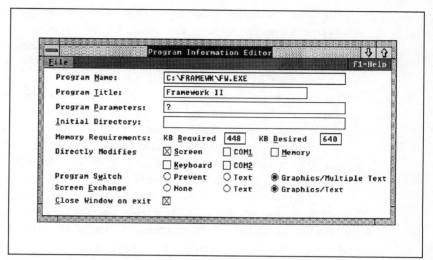

Figure 8.3 ▲ *The Windows PIF Editor.*

PLUS ran in a window when we modified the colors so that the menu highlight was black on white, and the text black on white (Windows reversed these colors).

DESQVIEW

DESQview gives you a windowed operating environment that can run effectively in a limited hardware environment. Because it is text-based, rather than graphics-based, it can run on any type of adapter and monitor. You can use it with either the keyboard or a mouse, and both are effective.

Among the most important of DESQview's features is the fact that it will let you not only load, but run, more than one program at a time. Unlike Windows, which permits the same thing, but only with programs written for it, DESQview will let you run *any* program in the background. And you don't have to upgrade from a PC or XT to use this feature.

There is a catch, however. You must have an enhanced expanded memory board that conforms to the AST/Ashton-Tate/Quadram EEMS standard. Although features of this standard have been built into the EEM 4.0 driver for Lotus/Intel/Microsoft memory, they won't give you multitasking without the special EEMS hardware.

Unlike many other systems that give you a simulation of multitasking (explained in detail in Chapter 10), DESQview even lets you run a telecommunications program while running other programs. The only restrictions are that you must load the telecommunications program first, and that you must have enough conventional memory to run other programs at the same time.

Among its many features, DESQview 2.01 can display either text or graphics or both on a monitor that is capable of displaying graphics, as Figure 8.4 shows. It provides a sophisticated cut-and-paste facility that lets you transfer text as a block or as a series of lines. In addition, it has a special mode for cutting to and from a spreadsheet or database. It can transfer formatted numbers as numeric data, rather than as ASCII characters. An additional built-in tool is a phone dialer that lets you dial any number on the screen by selecting it (if you have a modem).

DESQview includes a built-in macro recorder that is quite clever. You can have it execute a macro on startup to set up your applications the way you want them, or just to configure your screen. It has a learn mode, so you can record your keystrokes as you enter them. In addition,

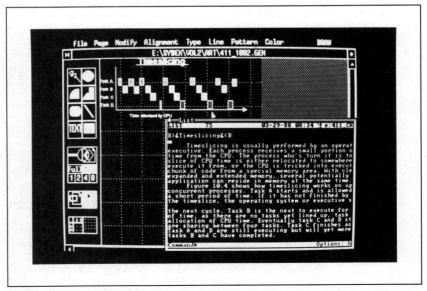

Figure 8.4 ▲ *Displaying Text and Graphics in Separate DESQview Windows.*

it's smart enough to remember which application was open when you recorded a macro. If you save your macros, DESQview will automatically load the appropriate set for any application you activate.

DESQview's mouse driver is quite lively. Unlike Windows, DESQview will use at least two of your mouse buttons (if your mouse has more than one). The left button always selects the main menu if no menu is on display, or the highlighted item on a displayed menu. The right (or center) button backs up to the previous menu, at least up to the main menu. To return from the main menu to your application, you press Escape, or else drag the mouse into the application's window and click once. Indeed, this is one way that DESQview takes excellent advantage of a mouse. If you configure your applications so that their windows don't cover one another completely, you can easily switch back and forth among them with only the mouse.

Figure 8.5 shows WordStar, a DOS window, SideKick, and the shareware program LIST all sharing the screen in an arrangement where they can be selected with only the mouse. The DESQview main menu appears in the upper-right corner. As you can see, you can choose any of its options with a keystroke, as well as with the mouse. If the option is not currently available, no key name appears next to the menu option.

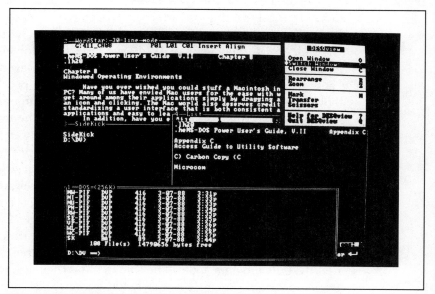

Figure 8.5 ▲ *DESQview with Four Selectable Windows.*

You open windows by choosing programs from the Open Program menu, which is one level down from the main menu. You can choose a program either by a two-character code that you assign, or by dragging the mouse cursor to the program's name and clicking. This means (of course) that you'll have to spend some time installing your programs on the Open Program menu. However, if you install DESQview in the normal manner, it will check your disk for familiar programs and install whichever ones it finds. It includes the information files for quite a few popular programs.

You don't have to install programs to use them however. You can install a DOS window large enough to run a variety of applications, and run the programs from a DOS prompt in that window.

Installing DESQview

Most of the time, you can install DESQview completely automatically. You insert the distribution diskette (that's right—there's only one) in drive A, and type

INSTALL

The program will ask you a few questions about your disk drives, and the name of the subdirectory to install the program to if you are using a hard disk, and then do everything else automatically. It includes .DVP files (the functional equivalent of Windows' .PIF files) for many popular applications. It also contains special loader files for some applications. These files make it possible for some of the popular "poorly behaved" applications to run in a small window or in the background.

In spite of all this, for reasons nobody—not even the technical support department at Quarterdeck—understands, we were completely unable to install DESQview on one computer using this method. The installation program doggedly refused to believe our answers regarding the drives in the system, and finally gave up. Fortunately, the technical support people helped us get around this hump. If you copy the right groups of files in the right order, you can actually get DESQview to work, although you will have to do some things manually that DESQview normally does for you. (If you just copy the files to a hard disk, the only program you will be able to run is the DESQview demonstration program.) Listing 8.3 shows all the commands you must issue to install DESQview if the normal procedure fails.

```
 1:  C:
 2:  MD \DV
 3:  CD \DV
 4:  A:
 5:  COPY SETUP.BAT C:
 6:  COPY *.COM C:
 7:  COPY DESQVIEW.DIR C:
 8:  COPY DVSETUP.DV C:
 9:  COPY DESQVIEW.DVH C:
10:     COPY DESQVIEW.DVO C:
11:  COPY DV.DVO C:
12:  COPY *.DVP C:
13:  COPY *.DVR C:
14:  COPY DESQVIEW.DVS C:
15:  COPY DV.EXE C:
16:  COPY READ.ME C:
17:  COPY NOFF.SHR C:
18:  COPY C:\COMMAND.COM C:
19:  COPY QEXT.SYS C:\
```

Listing 8.3 ▲ *Commands for Manual Installation of DESQview.*

If you use this manual procedure, you will then have to run the Setup program and use some of the advanced options to tailor DESQview to your system. You can do this either by selecting the program from DESQview's Open Program menu (described later), or by typing

SETUP

at a DOS prompt.

Setting Up Your System for DESQview

As with Windows, the most important consideration in how DESQview works for you is the amount and type of memory you have. If you have the EMS 4.0 device driver for your expanded memory card, you can increase the number of programs that DESQview can handle. Also, DESQview swaps programs in expanded memory four times faster than in extended memory. DOS manages conventional memory, but DESQview controls EMS memory through the EMS device driver. As we said before, it's a good idea to reduce the amount of conventional memory on your motherboard to as little as your computer will permit (probably 256K), and to configure your EMS board to assign enough of its memory to conventional memory, to give you a total of 640K.

However, it's with enhanced expanded memory that DESQview really shines. If you have an EEMS board, DESQview can run several of your standard DOS programs at once. Be aware that even though EMS 4.0 emulates the standards of the drivers originally developed for

EEMS boards, it is the special hardware on the board that makes this possible. If you like DESQview, you should consider investing in an EEMS board. Moreover, if you replace base memory with EEMS memory, you can actually run several very large programs at once. As an additional advantage, DESQview can switch between windows much more quickly, because EEMS memory moves much larger chunks of memory at a time than EMS memory.

If you have an AT, it's worthwhile to configure at least a little bit of your memory as extended memory. If you can set aside about 128K as extended memory, a special device driver will establish an invisible RAM disk, on which about 60K of its program code will be stored. This leaves you that much more conventional memory for your programs.

Except for this device driver, QEXT.SYS, the only way you can use extended memory with DESQview is to place a RAM disk in it, and use the disk for a swap area. This is not as efficient as using expanded memory for the swap area, but if you don't have disk space or expanded memory, it works perfectly well.

You may find yourself in a bit of a squeeze between the amount of memory taken up by the necessary device drivers and DOS 3.X, and the amount required to run your programs. In theory, you can get up to 605K for each application. However, on one of the systems we used, the absolute maximum we could get was 462K, after eliminating all the device drivers we could do without.

Like Windows, DESQview will make room in expanded memory for applications that use it, so you don't have to worry that you'll run out. Unlike Windows, DESQview has no problems with RAM disks. In one of our systems several applications were configured to use RAM disks. The only disadvantage was that the device drivers for the RAM disks occupied memory we would have liked to give to DESQview.

The one problem we've encountered (as you might expect) is that with the device drivers for expanded memory and QEXT and so on, it's difficult to run large programs. We could run Framework II after stripping everything essential out of the CONFIG.SYS file and making some changes in DESQview's Setup program (described below). However, to run something like Ventura Publisher, you have to strip out as many fonts as you can spare, and remove everything else that's absolutely nonessential.

Listing 8.4 shows a sample CONFIG.SYS program to set up a computer for DESQview. The system is an AT with a large expanded memory board, 128K of which is configured as extended memory, just to make room for QEXT.SYS. The RAM disk is included because some of the applications are configured to use it. (If this were not so, we could improve DESQview's performance by using a disk cache instead.) The number of buffers has been reduced to 14 just to conserve memory. The system is actually much more efficient with 32 buffers.

```
1: DEVICE=QEXT.SYS
2: DEVICE=EMM.SYS
3: DEVICE=VDISK.SYS 512 512 64 /A
4: DEVICE=MSMOUSE.SYS /1
5: FILES=20
6: BUFFERS=14
7: BREAK=ON
```

Listing 8.4 ▲ *A CONFIG.SYS File for DESQview.*

Listing 8.5 shows the AUTOEXEC.BAT file to run this system with DESQview using DOS 3.3. It has only a few peculiarities. First, the @ symbol in the first line suppresses the display of commands in the batch file, as we explained in Chapter 2. Second, the APPEND /E statement loads the code that manages appended directories in the environment so that lists of appended directories will appear there as well. (See Volume I, Chapter 8, for a full discussion of the APPEND command.) There's no point in appending any directories at this point, because DESQview ignores them. However, if you use the APPEND command with the /E switch you can append directories as needed when you load your applications. If you don't use the APPEND command, you will get a

TopView compatibility error

message. (You don't have this problem with the DOS 3.2 APPEND command. You can simply load your list of appended directories and DESQview will respond appropriately.)

```
1: @ECHO OFF
2: PATH C:\DOS;C:\BATCH;C:\UTIL;C:\;C:\KEY;C:\NORTON;C:\DICT;C:\EGA
3: APPEND /E
4: PROMPT $p$g
5: EMSSPOOL
6: DV
```

Listing 8.5 ▲ *An AUTOEXEC.BAT File for DESQview.*

The only other unusual feature in the batch file is the loading of a spooler in expanded memory. This lets you send text to the printer from any application. Without the spooler, printing is suspended when you switch from one application to another. This probably would not be true with EEMS memory installed, however.

Configuring DESQview for Your System

Once you have DESQview properly installed on your disk, you have quite a bit of control over how it behaves. The Setup DESQview program appears automatically on the Open Window menu. Do not ignore it. It can do a great deal for you.

When you select it and choose the Advanced Setup Options, you see the menu shown in Figure 8.6. Here's what its submenus can do for you:

▲ *The Auto Dialer submenu* tells DESQview which serial port your telephone is attached to, so you can automatically dial a phone number displayed on the screen.

▲ *The Colors submenu* lets you select the default foreground and background colors for each of the nine windows. (You can have any program override these defaults by selecting the Uses its Own Colors submenu when you install it, and you can change colors on the fly from the main menu as well.)

▲ *The Keyboard submenu* lets you install or uninstall the macro recorder, set the size of it's memory buffer, and change the hot keys. (The original hot keys are Alt for the main menu and Ctrl-Alt for the learn mode.)

▲ *The Logical Drives submenu* has two functions. First, it lets you assign subdirectory names to logical drives A through P. If you don't have DOS 3.1 or later (with its SUBST command), and you have programs that don't recognize path syntax, you can overcome this limitation by assigning the directories the programs need to use to drive letters. Second, if you don't have enough memory to use DESQview effectively, you can designate a drive and directory as a swap area. (If you do have enough memory, go into this menu and delete the swap drive.)

▲ *The Mouse submenu* lets you tell DESQview what kind of mouse you have and what port it's attached to.

▲ *The Performance submenu* is very important because it controls multitasking. If you have either a 386 PC or an EEMS board, you use this menu to tell DESQview how much time to assign to foreground and background operations. You can also use it to give yourself a bit more memory. DESQview defaults to 17K of "common memory" needed to run all programs under it. However, we have increased available memory by reducing this to 10K. There is also 2K assigned to an EMS buffer, which you can reduce to zero if you don't have EEMS memory.

▲ *The Video Monitor submenu* lets you tell DESQview what kind of video adapter and monitor you have. It also determines how simultaneous displays of text and graphics will be handled. If you want to display both at the same time, DESQview will convert the text in text applications to graphics so they can appear on the same screen. If you do not, DESQview will blank out the graphics portion of the screen when you make a text window active, which speeds up the display. This is a little faster. However, the former arrangement lets you look in a notepad, say, for a list of dimensions you need to correctly represent something in your drawing program.

▲ *The Window Positions submenu* lets you specify the default size and position of each of the nine windows. You can override these defaults when you install programs by setting their starting positions and window sizes in the Add/Change a Program menu. You can also change the size and position of an open window from the main menu.

Configuring Your Programs for DESQview

The procedure for installing programs on the Open Program menu is similar to creating .PIF files for windows. However, you have a great deal more control over the results. Although DESQview will probably have installed quite a few of your programs already, you may want to change the defaults.

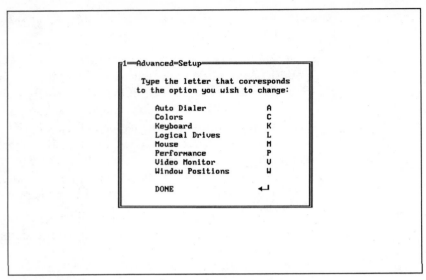

```
┌1═Advanced═Setup════════════════════════════┐
│                                            │
│     Type the letter that corresponds       │
│     to the option you wish to change:      │
│                                            │
│        Auto Dialer              A          │
│        Colors                   C          │
│        Keyboard                 K          │
│        Logical Drives           L          │
│        Mouse                    M          │
│        Performance              P          │
│        Video Monitor            V          │
│        Window Positions         W          │
│                                            │
│        DONE                     ↵          │
│                                            │
└────────────────────────────────────────────┘
```

Figure 8.6 ▲ *The DESQview Setup Menu.*

When you select Add a Program, a list of programs appears. To add these programs, just select the program name and press Return. To add a program that is not listed, select Other and press Return. You will be asked for its default directory. However, you should press F1 to get to the Program Information screen, which is shown in Figure 8.7. This is a lot like Windows' PIF Editor screen. You give the name of the program to display on the menu, the two keys to invoke it, the amount of memory it requires, the directory it should open in, and the parameters or a question mark. You also specify whether it writes directly to the screen, requires a diskette, displays graphics, or can be swapped out of memory.

If the program writes directly to the screen, it will run in full-screen mode. However, you can still get back to DESQview by pressing the hot key or clicking the left mouse button. The only kind of program you don't want to be swapped out of memory is a telecommunications program.

Pressing F1 a second time gets you to an Advanced Options screen, which appears in Figure 8.8. Here you can tell DESQview how many graphics pages your program uses, whether it should start in text or graphics mode, whether it uses its own colors, and whether the window should close automatically when you exit to DOS.

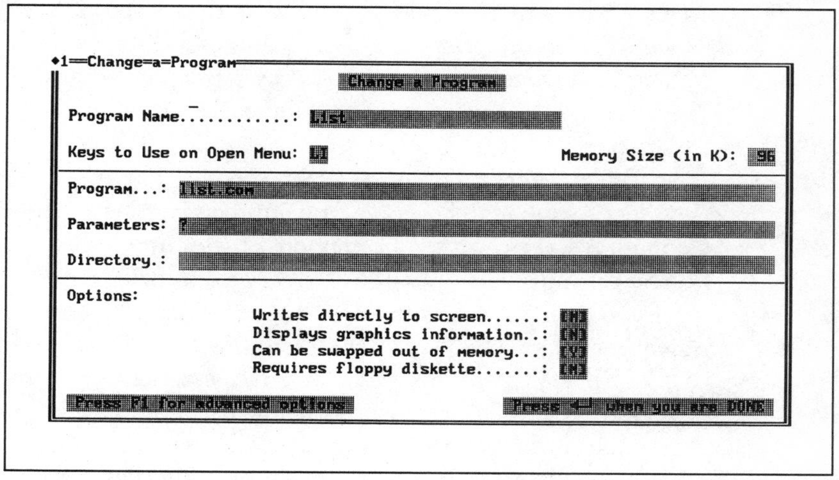

Figure 8.7 ▲ *The DESQview Program Information Main Screen.*

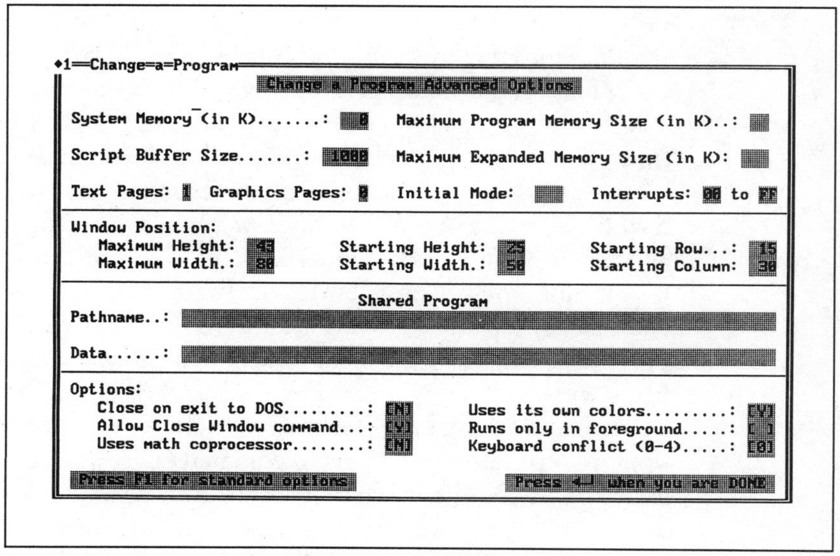

Figure 8.8 ▲ *The DESQview Program Information Advanced Options Screen.*

You may have to reinstall a program several times before it behaves just as you want it to. As you become familiar with the program, you'll see ways in which the performance of one program or another can be improved. You'll discover which programs should close the window on exit, and which shouldn't; and which ones should not be allowed to close when the program is active. You may discover some strange interactions between the colors used by a program in a window and those assigned to the window itself. (You can fix that by configuring the program to use its own colors.)

Once a program is on the Open Program menu, you can change it by selecting Change Program. You will be returned to the Program Information screen, with your previous entries intact. If you make changes, the previous version will be saved with a .BAK extension. Therefore, if you change something and make it worse, it's easy to return to the earlier arrangement. (For the record, the format of these file names is CC-PIF.DVP, where CC are the two characters you installed on the Open Program menu.) If you change the letters used to invoke the program from the menu, the program will appear on the menu twice. This lets you test the advantages of different installations.

The matter of closing windows has some interesting implications. If you expect you'll want to view text from a window in which an application has terminated (as you might in a DOS window, for example), you should set up the program so that its window does not close automatically. Then you will have a DOS prompt when the program terminates. You can close a window at this point either by selecting Close Window from the main menu, or by entering the EXIT command.

You can also elect to set up a program so that you can't close its window (thus, unloading it from memory) while the program is running. This might seem like a bad idea. After all, if you unload a program while it's running, you will probably lose the data file that it's using. However, there can be advantages to allowing a window to close at any time. Suppose, for example, you have a poorly behaved program that interacts badly with another program in memory, or with DESQview itself. The result can be a locked keyboard, which often leaves you only one option—a certain three-fingered command that will dump out the programs in all your open windows. However, it's quite possible that the mouse isn't also locked up. Thus, you can close the offending program's window from the DESQview main menu, and preserve the data in your other windows. Neat trick, huh!?

In addition, DESQview modifies the warm boot command. Ctrl-Alt-Del aborts only the process in the current window. To actually reboot the computer, you must press Ctrl-Shift-Del.

As you'll see in the next chapter, you don't have to give up either your batch files or your RAM-resident utilities to use DESQview. However, you may have to change the way you use them somewhat, and you may have to write new batch files.

GEM

GEM (an acronym for Graphics Environment Manager) presents quite a different set of opportunities and restrictions. It is by far the best emulation of the Macintosh desktop available on the PC. Applications are represented by icons, and you can choose an appropriate graphics symbol for each application. Subdirectories are represented by folders.

If your application uses a consistent set of extensions for its data files, you can tell GEM what extensions the program uses, and the data files too will be given appropriate icons.

Although your main desktop can have only two windows open, these windows can represent anything from your entire system (with each disk drive represented as an icon) to a single directory. Figure 8.9 shows the GEM desktop with one window open at the system level and the other in the GEM Applications directory.

GEM is, of course, at its best with applications designed for it. There are dozens available, and some are quite good. These applications run in the desktop environment, with the consistent user interface resembling that of the Macintosh. Perhaps the best known GEM application is Ventura Publisher. However, Digital Research, the publisher of GEM, sells its own series of applications, which work in concert to form a desktop publishing/presentation environment. They also work quite well independently.

In addition, GEM gives you complete file compatibility with Atari ST computers, which use GEM as their exclusive operating system. Files created with GEM applications on the PC can be used on Atari computers with no modification.

One of the especially nice features of GEM is its hardware drivers. With proper installation, you can get extremely good graphics output from dot-matrix printers, but HP LaserJet printers and PostScript devices are also supported, and the results are spectacular. Moreover, you can send printer output to a file specific to any printer you have

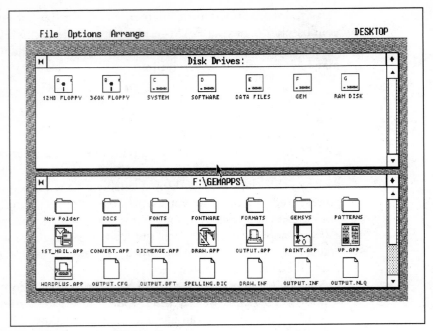

Figure 8.9 ▲ *The GEM Desktop.*

installed. These files can be sent to the appropriate printer with a command of the form

COPY *FILENAME.EXT* PRN

This lets you share files with someone who may have a different printer from you and who may not have GEM.

The mouse driver is well designed, and the screen drivers also take best advantage of your display adapter's features. Because GEM makes no attempt to represent text as graphics (except in its own text-oriented programs, such as First Word Plus), it is very fast. However, it lets you run non-GEM applications in full-screen text mode.

Installing GEM

It's easy to install GEM 3.0. You place the Gem Master Disk in drive A and enter

GEMSETUP

A menu asks you whether you are installing for the first time or changing an existing application. If you are installing for the first time, you will tell the program:

- ▲ What drive to install GEM on
- ▲ What kind of display adapter and monitor you have
- ▲ What kind of pointing device you have, and the port on which it's installed

If you wish, you can also install one or more printers, plotters, scanners, and cameras. (We're talking big-time graphics here.) When you finish answering questions, you choose Continue, and the program copies all the necessary files to the specified drive, creating directories as needed. You will have to swap disks several times so the setup program can find the appropriate drivers for your hardware. Once you are done, your screen may be a bit of a mess, because GEMSETUP redefines several characters for its own purposes, and leaves them redefined when you exit. This is easily remedied by rebooting.

The directory structure GEM creates can be confusing if you're used to keeping things simple. However, this needn't worry you, because you don't have to interact with it. The programs all know where to find what they need, and if you do by chance need to get into a directory, GEM makes it easy. Directories are represented by folders. You click on a folder to open it. Subdirectories are folders inside the preceding folder.

Figure 8.10 shows the directory structure of a hard disk containing the GEM desktop, GEM Draw Plus, GEM Paint, First Word Plus, and First Mail, along with some custom fonts.

If you need to load a file from a directory other than the default within a GEM application, a dialog box lets you enter the name of the directory or just the root directory of the disk. If you enter the root directory, subdirectories will show up in a selection box, marked with a diamond as shown in Figure 8.11. If you click on the name of a subdirectory, the files it contains will appear in the selection box.

Configuring Your Programs for GEM

You can run normal DOS applications from the GEM desktop. You don't gain any of the desktop's obvious advantages, but you do get a few

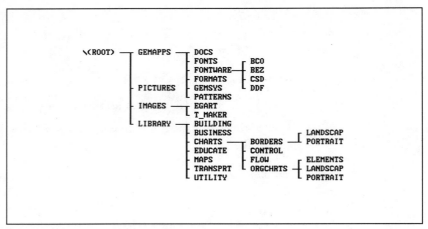

Figure 8.10 ▲ *GEM Directory Structure.*

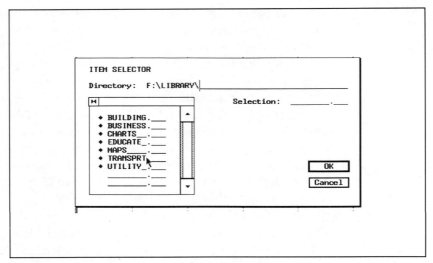

Figure 8.11 ▲ *Changing Directories in a GEM Application.*

benefits. You can run any program by clicking on its icon. However, if you install the programs first, you do get some significant advantages, especially if the program uses a consistent set of file name extensions that it doesn't share with any of your other programs.

To configure a DOS application, select it, and then choose Configure Application from the Options menu. From here you can enter the extensions used by the program's data files and the parameters you use to invoke the program. Or you can tell GEM to pause for parameters. You can also select an icon design appropriate to the type of application from a menu. If you enter one or more extensions, the files with that extension will also receive an appropriate icon design.

Once you have taken these steps, you can run a program by clicking either on its icon, or, if the program is on the search path, on the icon for one of its data files. You may have some trouble if several applications use the same extension for their data files.

Installing GEM Applications

Gem applications come with a special file called INSTALL.APP. (All Gem applications have the extension .APP.) It's marked with a "Programmer's Tool" icon—a hammer. You simply click on that icon, and GEM does the rest. It will inform you via dialog boxes, like the one shown in Figure 8.12, of exactly what it is going to do, and it will give you the chance to back out by choosing Cancel. If you choose OK, GEM will copy the program and supporting files to the \GEMAPPS directory and create whatever other directories it needs, copying the appropriate files to them. That's all there is to it. GEM applications come preconfigured with the appropriate icons and extensions, so you don't have to configure them.

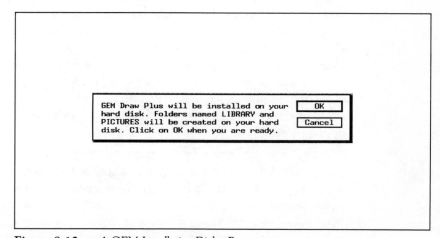

Figure 8.12 ▲ *A GEM Installation Dialog Box.*

SOFTWARE CAROUSEL

If you don't need to transfer information among programs, and you don't need to look at two programs at once, you might be interested in Software Carousel from SoftLogic Solutions. While it doesn't deliver as much as the programs already discussed, it costs less than half as much, and it works quite effectively.

This program allows you to set up a number of partitions in memory. Each can be as large as your available conventional memory less the overhead required by Carousel (32K), the operating system, and whatever is loaded by your CONFIG.SYS file. You can load a different program into each partition, and keep it up and running while you work in a different partition. It allows you to specify the amount of conventional memory, extended memory, expanded memory, and hard disk storage to be used for the entire configuration.

Warning: If you use a hard disk as part of your swap area, and Software Carousel terminates abnormally, you will be left with a huge file called ~CAROSEL.TMP in the root directory, which you will want to delete.

Once you load Carousel, the program in the first partition is executed automatically. The other partitions are not activated until you switch to them with a hot key. Therefore, you should give some thought to the order in which you activate your partitions. For example, the print spooler we use normally installs itself in expanded memory. However, we unthinkingly installed it in two partitions. By the time we loaded the second of these partitions, there was no extended memory available, so the spooler installed itself in conventional memory. This was no problem when we loaded the segment with the larger transient program first. However, when we reversed the order, the spooler in conventional memory took up just enough room that we were unable to run the application.

Warning: One partition locks out another completely. Thus, if you are printing a file via a spooler in one partition and you switch partitions, printing will stop until you return to the partition where printing began. You can thus safely have more than one spooler in memory, but you don't want to switch between them while a file is being printed.

If you have an application that uses extended or expanded memory, be sure that you do *not* assign all of that memory to Carousel, or your application will be unable to use it. Indeed, we found that, with normal overhead and Carousel, expanded-memory applications did not work, because there was not enough room in conventional memory to store the pointers to expanded memory locations. We had to set up an alternative configuration file for the application, which we used only with Carousel.

There is also a known bug in Carousel 2.0 regarding AT extended memory, which should be fixed soon. You can specify in the CAROUSEL.OPT file that the program activate itself automatically. If you do, however, and you tell it to use extended memory, the extended memory will not be initialized properly, and will not be available. You can overcome this by leaving out the AUTOMATIC command from the CAROUSEL.OPT file, adding the extended memory at the opening screen, and *not* saving the changes.

If you don't specify enough memory for a program, you may encounter an error message. However, you can still use your system by switching to another partition. You can also increase the memory in a partition by switching to the main menu, as long as there is no transient program active in the partition and you have allowed enough total memory to Carousel to absorb the increase.

If you get hung up badly enough to want to reboot, Carousel will display a list of the partitions, showing which ones still have applications running, and it will ask you if you really want to reboot now. This gives you the opportunity to close any open files, provided the partition they are in isn't locked up, before you reboot.

Once we had spent a day and a half getting all this stuff working, we found Carousel to be quite useful. Although not in the same class as DESQview or Windows, it still simplified quite a few tasks. One of the main advantages of this entire class of programs is that you can view several files in different applications without exiting from any of them.

Consider, for example, what's involved in writing a book like this. Without something that lets you switch among applications, you have to save your file and exit the word processor every time you want to check the exact wording of a message generated by a DOS command. It's not quite as easy to run the DOS command and read the message in Carousel as it is in a windowed environment—the message doesn't stay on the screen when you switch back to the word processor, for one thing. However, it's still a big advance over saving and exiting. It's also wonderful to have a DOS shell available for file management in one partition while running a program that allows no access to DOS in another.

Installing Software Carousel

Software Carousel 2.0 is not copy protected, although earlier releases were. You simply have to personalize your copy before you can use it. To do so, place the distribution diskette in drive A and enter

INSTALL A *drive*

where *drive* is the name of the drive you want to install it to. You will be asked some questions about your system—mainly concerning the amount and kinds of memory, and whether you want to use a disk as a swap area as well. This information is saved in a file called CAROUSEL.OPT, which is placed in the root directory and used when you invoke the program.

Configuring Software Carousel for Your System

CAROUSEL.OPT is the key to the way Software Carousel works. In addition to the memory information recorded on installation, you use it to specify

- ▲ The number of partitions
- ▲ The size of each
- ▲ A name for each, if you wish
- ▲ The name of a file to be loaded automatically the first time a partition is used
- ▲ The hot keys

You can specify the memory from Carousel's opening screen, and you can specify most of the rest of the information from its main menu, one setup for which is shown in Figure 8.13. The CAROUSEL.OPT file accompanying this configuration is shown in Figure 8.14. You might notice that the programs called by the file are all batch files. The way they work is described in Chapter 9 under "Using Batch Files."

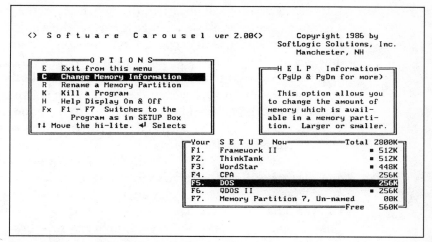

```
<> S o f t w a r e   C a r o u s e l  ver 2.00<>        Copyright 1986 by
                                                      SoftLogic Solutions, Inc.
                                                          Manchester, NH
        ╔══════════O P T I O N S══════════╗
        ║ E   Exit from this menu         ║   ╔══H E L P   Information══╗
        ║▐C   Change Memory Information▐   ║   ║(PgUp & PgDn for more)   ║
        ║ R   Rename a Memory Partition   ║   ║                         ║
        ║ K   Kill a Program              ║   ║ This option allows you  ║
        ║ H   Help Display On & Off       ║   ║ to change the amount of ║
        ║ Fx  F1 - F7  Switches to the    ║   ║ memory which is avail-  ║
        ║     Program as in SETUP Box     ║   ║ able in a memory parti- ║
        ║↑↓ Move the hi-lite.  ◄┘ Selects ║   ║ tion.  Larger or smaller.║
        ╚═════════════════════════════════╝   ╚═════════════════════════╝
                          ╔══Your   S E T U P  Now═══════════Total 2800K═╗
                          ║ F1.   Framework II              ▪ 512K       ║
                          ║ F2.   ThinkTank                 ▪ 512K       ║
                          ║ F3.   WordStar                  ▪ 448K       ║
                          ║ F4.   CPA                         256K       ║
                          ║▐F5.   DOS                         256K▐      ║
                          ║ F6.   QDOS II                   ▪ 256K       ║
                          ║ F7.   Memory Partition 7, Un-named  00K      ║
                          ╚═════════════════════════════Free  560K══════╝
```

Figure 8.13 ▲ *Software Carousel's Main Menu.*

```
DRIVE = C
FILE = 1600
EXPANDED = 304

PROGRAM1=E:FWCAR
PROGRAM2=E:TTSETUP
PROGRAM3=E:WSSETUP
PROGRAM4=E:CPACAR
PROGRAM5=E:SPARE
PROGRAM6=E:QDCAR
HOT KEY  = RSHIFT
TOGGLE KEY=41

SIZE 1   = 512
SIZE 2   = 512
SIZE 3   = 448
SIZE 4   = 256
SIZE 5   = 256
SIZE 6   = 256
NAME 1   = Framework II
NAME 2   = ThinkTank
NAME 3   = WordStar
NAME 4   = CPA
NAME 5   = Spare
NAME 6   = QDOS II
```

Figure 8.14 ▲ *A CAROUSEL.OPT File.*

HOW MUCH MACINTOSH DO YOU GET?

All the windowed programs invite comparison with the Macintosh. In this regard, Windows comes off pretty badly. The look of Windows suggests the Mac, but it doesn't have the feel. Menus stay open (which is nice). Instead of a menu bar for the entire screen, each window has one.

If it's not a Windows application, the only menu is the control menu. This menu basically lets you change the size of the window (if you don't have a mouse), reduce the application to an icon or restore it to a window, scroll the application within the window, or use the cut-and-paste facility. The windows have scroll bars and a size box like the Mac, so you can move the file around within the window, change its size with the mouse, or change its location by dragging. With Windows applications, you can click on a file to open the application (if you've installed the file's extension in WIN.INI).

There's an awful lot you can't do with Windows. You can't display applications as icons, except when they are loaded and in the background. You can't drag an icon from one window to another to copy a file; you often can't open a program by clicking on a data file (although this is supposed to work); and you can't change directories by opening a folder or closing a window. You can only see one directory at a time unless you open multiple copies of MS-DOS Executive. In addition, the mouse interface seems to require an awful lot of moving around, and the keystroke alternatives require too many keystrokes. Thus, you trade the advantages of multiple programs for the loss of batch file control, and you don't get simplified file management in return. This is the major tradeoff. It is in these areas that GEM shines, although GEM will not run several programs at once.

GEM gives you all the file-management advantages of a graphics desktop. In addition, with GEM applications, you can open several files at once in separate windows and control the size and position of each. You can transfer data from one window to another within an application just by selecting it and dragging it to the other window. (In Windows, you have to go through the clipboard.)

DESQview doesn't pretend to give you anything like the Macintosh desktop. What it does give you is the advantage of windowing in an otherwise familiar DOS environment. Moreover, the fact that you can use multiple programs on the same screen in multiple windows goes the Macintosh one better. Because DESQview can swap inactive applications to disk or expanded memory, your standard memory doesn't limit the number of programs you can have open at once. You can switch freely among up to nine applications, and there's nothing except your own tolerance for confusion to keep you from having several versions of a single program open at the same time, each with a different data file. Although you can't exactly drag text from one window to another, the sophistication of the cut-and-paste feature in handling numbers is unequaled.

And you get two extra advantages: first, DESQview will run in almost any PC hardware environment; second, in the right hardware environment, you get timesliced multitasking with any microprocessor.

Software Carousel, of course, makes no pretense to emulate the Macintosh. What you get is a limited version of the Multifinder without either windows or the clipboard. However, if you don't need to transfer data quickly between applications, Carousel can give you a significant increase in productivity at a modest cost.

USING WINDOWED
OPERATING
ENVIRONMENTS

T HE REASON FOR ADDING a windowed operating environment to your system is to simplify or enhance the way your applications work. Therefore, it's important to know how these environments interact with DOS and with your applications. There are several areas in particular where they differ dramatically. Differences from what you expect can have an enormous impact on the way you work. In this chapter, we'll review the way these environments handle batch files and path syntax, run programs, let you execute DOS commands, and manage your files. After that, we'll look at the ways they deal with multiple programs in memory at once, and sharing data among them.

RUNNING PROGRAMS

The first issue to consider is how these environments let you run programs. It is the most obvious part of the user interface, and it can profoundly affect the way you work.

Windows

There are three ways to execute a program in Windows. You can select its .PIF file (double-click with the mouse, or move the cursor to it and press Return); move to the file's directory and select the file name; or use the RUN command from the Files menu and enter the name of the program.

None of these methods works all the time. In any case, you should always install the complete path to an executable file in the .PIF file, even if the program is on the search path.

When you install Windows, it produces one subsidiary directory, called PIF. This directory contains the default versions of all the .PIF files. The first item in a directory is always selected by default. (Windows indicates this by placing the file name in inverse video.) Since directory names appear in the listing before file names, the PIF directory is always selected in the MS-DOS Executive window when it opens. To make the PIF directory current, just press Return or double-click the mouse. Unless you want to load some desktop utilities first, this is a good idea because you can execute programs in Windows by clicking on their .PIF files.

This is perhaps the easiest method to use. However, some programs don't execute properly—or at all—unless you first make their directory current. We had a bit of difficulty with Lotus 1-2-3, for example, unless its directory was current. (With such programs, you may want to place the .PIF file in the software directory.)

On the other hand, we had some problems attempting to run ThinkTank it any way other than by selecting its .PIF file in the PIF directory.

When you use the RUN command, you can in principle run programs for which you have not created a .PIF file. However, you will then have to go through the System Warning dialog box shown in Figure 9.1. Since the "standard defaults" referred to in this box include running the program in 55K of memory, you probably want to cancel the operation and create a .PIF file before you proceed.

DESQview

You run programs in DESQview by selecting them from the Open Program menu. You get to this menu by pressing O at the DESQview main menu, or by selecting Open Program with the mouse and clicking the left button. You can then select the program name with the mouse and click again, select it with the cursor and press Return, or enter a two-letter abbreviation that you assigned to it when you installed the program. As noted, you must install your programs on this menu using the Add Program command.

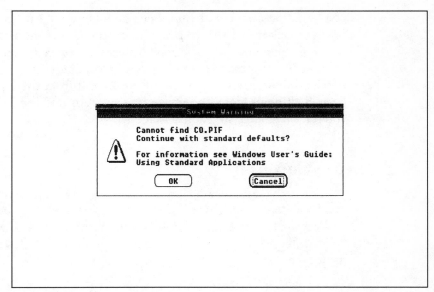

Figure 9.1 ▲ *Running an Application under Windows without a .PIF File.*

If your programs are small, you can run them in the DOS window. We've also tried adding a 448K window called Big Window to the Open Program menu. This program executes nothing more than a Prompt command. It's also big enough to run almost any program we may have forgotten to include on the Open Program menu.

GEM

When you use GEM, you are not restricted to GEM applications. You can still run DOS applications. You select an application by double-clicking its icon. If you have installed your programs properly, you can also run them by clicking on the icon for one of their data files. (One advantage of this method is that when you click on a data file, its directory becomes the default, even with GEM applications.) GEM itself remains in memory, however, taking up 176K, so you can't run extremely large DOS programs. When you exit the application, you will return to the GEM desktop.

You can also run nonGEM programs by selecting Enter DOS Commands from the Options menu of the desktop. This loads a secondary command processor, which takes up an additional 3 to 4K, depending on the version of DOS you use. This option is more useful for DOS internal commands, and for small utilities. If, for example, you want to use a utility that displays some system information on your screen and then terminates, you are better off running it from the Options menu than clicking its icon. Otherwise, you will return to the desktop before you have a chance to read the screen.

Software Carousel

When you have Software Carousel running, your computer is like several DOS computers sharing space in the same box. Running a program in Software Carousel is no different from running one at a DOS prompt. You just have a bit less memory to do it in, because Software Carousel itself takes up some RAM.

EXECUTING DOS COMMANDS

No matter how much of a front these environments put on DOS, you still have to interact with DOS itself at some point. There will always be some operation that's simply easier to complete when you can enter exactly the commands you need, rather than selecting something from a menu. Let's look at the pathways these environments create between themselves and DOS.

Windows

In Windows, the DOS external programs are supposedly accounted for in the WIN.INI file. However, Windows doesn't recognize XCOPY and REPLACE.

Windows' preferred method of giving you a handle on DOS is to have you choose the Run command from the Files menu in the MS-DOS Executive, and then enter the DOS command you want to execute. If you need to perform several DOS commands, you are supposed to enter COMMAND as the command to run. However, we've then been faced with the order:

Insert disk with COMMAND.EXE in Drive A

To get it to work properly, you either have to make the root directory current or enter

C:\COMMAND

as the command to execute. In any case, this requires quite a few keystrokes to accomplish.

Because of some of the peculiarities of Windows' memory management, you may be told that there is not enough memory to run some DOS commands, even when you know there is. The manual recommends that you exit Windows before you execute these commands if you see this message.

DESQview

DESQview gives you two avenues of access to DOS. Both are on the Open Program menu. One is a 128K DOS window, and the other is a DOS shell/file manager type of program called DOS Services. We've found that changing the 128K DOS window to a 256K window provides a lot more flexibility. You can use this window to enter any command that can execute in 220K or less, including programs that are not part of DOS. You can change directories freely, or execute anything on the path without changing directories. We've found it very handy to keep such a window open for quickly peeking at a directory, searching for a misplaced file, copying a file in from a diskette, and those innumerable other chores that always seem to crop up at inconvenient moments. Like all DESQview windows, this one is only three keystrokes away once it's been opened.

GEM

The GEM desktop has, as we have noted, an Enter DOS Commands option on its Options menu. If you select this option, GEM loads a secondary command processor, and you are to all intents and purposes in DOS. To return to the desktop, type the command

EXIT

Software Carousel

With Software Carousel, you never really depart from DOS. Each partition is controlled by a secondary command processor that is loaded permanently. You can have each partition start up at a DOS prompt, or, as explained below, have Software Carousel automatically invoke a batch file that loads an application, optionally installing one or more resident programs first. When you exit the application, you are, of course, returned to a DOS prompt. If you wish, however, you can reserve a small partition exclusively for entering DOS commands. The only problem you are likely to encounter is the confusion that will occur when you create or delete a file in a directory that's in use by another program. The program won't know about the change until it explicitly reads the directory again.

MANAGING FILES

All of the programs discussed here become truly convenient only if you also use a hard disk. At some point in every hard disk user's life—usually at least once a week—there comes a time when the disk requires housekeeping. Misplaced files have to be found and moved to the right location, irrelevant files have to be deleted, and the entire disk needs to be backed up on occasion. Only one of these environments gives you much help with these chores.

Windows

In Windows, you do your file management in the MS-DOS Executive window. This shows what is essentially a standard directory in wide format. You can open several MS-DOS Executive windows and display different directories in each, but you can't copy a file by dragging its name into another window. Instead, you have to highlight it (either by clicking with the mouse or by moving the cursor to it with the cursor keys and pressing the space bar), and then invoke the Copy command from the Files menu. A dialog box appears asking you where you want to copy the file to. You can select multiple files by holding the shift key down while you select. This is so cumbersome that you are better off doing your housekeeping either before or after you use Windows.

DESQview and Software Carousel

With either DESQview or Software Carousel you can devote one window to a file-management utility. This can be a notable convenience if you're careful not to do anything to files that are open in other windows.

DESQview's DOS Services program is such a utility. It lets you execute DOS commands from a menu, but it's nowhere near as powerful or easy to use as many of the file managers that are sold separately. However, it's no problem to delete it (and its .DVP file), and install another of your choice.

GEM

The GEM desktop is a marvelous environment for file management. You can copy a file from one directory to another by dragging its icon to the second directory's window, or to its folder in any window. You can delete an entire directory with all its subdirectories simply by selecting its folder and choosing Delete from the File menu. (This does have its dangers, of course.) If you have a diskette with subdirectories, and you want to erase it without reformatting it, you can do so by selecting the diskette's icon and choosing Delete from the File menu. This is the easiest way we've seen to do this, although it's not particularly fast.

You can also copy groups of unrelated files by holding the shift key as you select them with the mouse and then dragging them to their destination with the mouse.

PATHS AND DIRECTORIES

When you're working in unmodified DOS, you use PATH and APPEND statements to tell DOS where to look for programs to execute. However, the environments we are examining all do rather peculiar things to these statements. It's another factor to consider in setting up the environments.

Windows

The entryway to your directories and files in Windows is the MS-DOS Executive window. Unless you configure the WIN.INI file to open other applications when you load Windows, this is the window that first opens on the screen. It includes the name of the current directory, icons for all your disk drives, and the names of the files in your current directory. By default, the current directory is \WINDOWS, and the file names are in short form sorted by name. However, you can display the long form if you prefer, or sort by extension, date, or size and have Windows produce your preferred display as its default.

Changing directories in Windows is a bit of a chore unless the directory you want is above or below the current one. If it's below, you can just select the directory name. If it's above, you can click on its name in the display of the current path next to the disk drive icons. If it's neither, you must select the name of the current directory and click once. You will then have to type in the name of your target directory in a dialog box. Indeed, so many procedures present you with dialog boxes that you may quickly come to ignore the mouse.

Windows appears to pay very little attention to any PATH and APPEND statements. Even if a program is on the path, Windows won't find it unless you include its full path specification in its .PIF file.

DESQview

With DESQview, as with Windows, you have to install the full path to the executable program as part of the program name in the .DVP file. You should also install the default directory for the program to use in the Directory field if there is one. The screen where you enter this information is shown in Chapter 8, Figure 8.7. DESQview has no trouble locating programs on a search path. The program LIST.COM shown in Figure 8.7 is on the path and therefore does not need its complete path in the .DVP file.

If the program is not on the search path, DESQview appends the name of its directory to the current path. This makes it possible for DESQview to invoke the application while making the directory you specified as the default current. When you close the window, DESQview deletes the new directory from the search path, restoring it to the form it had before you invoked the application. Moreover, if you invoke your program from a batch file, you can include a search path in the batch file, and it will be active as long as the window is open.

As we said in Chapter 8, you have to be a bit wary of the APPEND command with DESQview. The APPEND command works with no difficulties in DOS 3.2. But the DOS 3.3 APPEND command must be loaded with the /E switch to work at all.

GEM

GEM operates within a normal DOS environment and does not alter it significantly. It's easy to change from one path or drive to another just by clicking on the appropriate icon. You can move up a level by clicking on the upper-left corner of a window, and down a level by clicking on a folder.

GEM follows whatever instructions you give it in PATH and APPEND statements. This is what makes it possible to run a DOS program by selecting one of its files.

As you have seen, GEM creates a rather complex path structure of its own. However, because its programs understand that structure, you needn't pay any attention to it. Its one annoying aspect is that the number of directories GEM adds to your root directory may seem unreasonably large. You can change this if you wish, by creating a directory called \GEM, and then using XCOPY with the /S switch to copy all the other GEM directories to it. For example, to copy the main directory, and all its files, to the \GEM directory, enter

> **XCOPY \GEMAPPS \GEM\ /S**

Alternatively, you can accomplish the entire process from within GEM by following these steps:

1. Invoke GEM.

2. Use the desktop to execute a DOS command to create the \GEM directory.

3. Open the GEM folder in one of the two desktop windows.

4. Open the root directory in the other desktop window by selecting your hard disk (if the disk icon is not visible when you start, keep closing the window until it is).

5. Drag all the folders for GEM directories from the root directory window to the GEM window.

6. Select the GEM directory folders (except the one you have created called GEM) in the root directory window and delete them.

GEM itself runs from a batch file. When you install GEM, it creates the file GEM.BAT on the root directory of your hard disk. This file contains the commands

```
CD \GEMAPPS\GEMSYS
GEMVDI %1 %2 %3
```

If you have changed the directory structure as described, you will then have to modify GEM.BAT. Add a SUBST command, so that GEM thinks the \GEM directory is a separate disk:

```
SUBST G: C:\GEM
CD \GEMAPPS\GEMSYS
GEMVDI %1 %2 %3
SUBST G: C:\GEM /D
```

Software Carousel

Software Carousel has one quirk when it comes to PATH commands. Because it immediately loads a permanent secondary command processor, it will not recognize a path that you installed via your AUTO-EXEC.BAT file. However, if you enter a PATH command in the first partition that you open, it will be recognized in all the other partitions as well. APPEND statements follow the same rules. Any change you make to your path or your list of appended directories in one partition carries over to all the other partitions.

 Warning: Software Carousel handles Display Master, the EGA control program described in Chapter 3, in the same way. If you put one partition in 35-line mode, you may find yourself in a mess of trouble when you switch to a partition containing a program that works only in 25-line mode. Color changes you make in one partition also carry over to other partitions, which can result in some terminally illegible screens.

USING BATCH FILES

In *MS-DOS Power User's Guide, Volume I,* Jonathan suggested that you create a series of batch files to establish defaults for your programs, make the appropriate directories current, load ancillary files, simplify access to directories, and otherwise take care of all your routine housekeeping. The extent to which you have done so will deeply affect your reactions to the operating environments discussed here.

Windows

If you've already set up your system to run from batch files, you'll be very unhappy with Windows. You can forget about using them for routine housekeeping before and after every application, especially if you use some of the small utilities that come in the big utility packages or from the bulletin boards. You have to have a .PIF file for every single utility you invoke, and some of your utilities will confuse Windows. You may find yourself running a familiar batch file twenty or so times until you've figured out which one of your utilities doesn't have a .PIF file or appears to stay in memory until the next program is loaded. At least Windows will tell you if the error is "directly modifies memory."

Windows generally doesn't like RAM disks (although it will accept its own). Therefore, setting up a program like RAMWS.BAT in Volume I can be a nightmarish project. You'll have to install Windows' RAM disk to start with. Then you'll have to make sure there are .PIF files for the XCOPY and REPLACE commands. And you can forget loading SuperKey and SideKick under WordStar. For more on the latter point, see "Using RAM-Resident Utilities," below.

If you have more than one data directory for a program, you can create a separate .PIF file for each one (and remember what all their names mean) or you can tell the .PIF file to pause and ask you for parameters, one of which is the path name, assuming your application can find its way to the directory. Otherwise, you can create simple batch files of the form

```
%1:
CD\%2
APP %3
```

in which you substitute the command that invokes the application for *APP*. Of course, you will have to create a .PIF file for this batch file and give it 55K in addition to whatever your application needs. When Windows prompts you to enter parameters, you enter the drive letter, the directory where the data file is located, and the file name. For example, for a batch file to call WordPerfect, where you wanted to open a file called OCTOBER.NTS in the directory D:\SALES\WEST, you would enter

D SALES\WEST OCTOBER.NTS

in the dialog box when prompted for parameters. Because a batch file such as this one includes only internal DOS commands, it should give you very little trouble. Be sure to put a question mark on the Parameters line in the .PIF file.

DESQview

If you are accustomed to using batch files to take care of some housekeeping before and after you run an application, you can still do so in DESQview. DESQview has no problems with batch files. You run most of your programs from its Open Program menu. The only change you need to make is to install the name of the batch file—not the application—in the .DVP file when you add the program to the Open Program menu.

If you want to copy some files to a RAM disk, invoke your application and have it open those files, and then copy the modified files back to a hard disk or diskette, you can use a batch file to do it. Be sure to use replaceable parameters in the batch file, so you can specify the relevant files and directories. Also, be careful to place a question mark on the Parameters line in the Add/Change Program menu. You may find that it simplifies matters a bit if you place the batch file itself in DESQview's home directory.

There are two other points to keep in mind when installing batch files in DESQview. First, in the Add/Change Program screen, set Close Window on Exit to No. Then end your batch file with the EXIT command. If you don't take these steps, any batch file commands executed after you exit the application will be bypassed, because the window will close at that point. The EXIT command closes the window automatically when the batch file has finished executing.

When you invoke a batch file that requires parameters, DESQview opens the window, enters the name of the batch file on a DOS command line, and pauses. The cursor waits for you to enter your parameters, and execution does not continue until you press Return. The only real change is that you'll be running in a window instead of using all of DOS.

GEM

GEM treats batch files the same as any other executable files. It doesn't need to know about their details, and it doesn't override their defaults. You can run them either by clicking their icons or by entering their names at a DOS prompt after selecting the Execute DOS Commands option.

As mentioned, GEM is executed from a batch file called GEM.BAT. Although there's a file called GEM.EXE, you don't run GEM by invoking this file. You need the batch file to load the GEM device drivers for your display adapter, printer, and other peripherals.

Because of the replaceable parameters, you can execute a GEM application, and have it open a file, by entering their names on the command line. For example, to start GEM Paint from a DOS prompt, and have it open a picture file called PICTURE, you would enter

GEM PAINT PICTURE.IMG

Software Carousel

With Software Carousel, running a batch file is no different from running a batch file in DOS. However, there's an extra benefit. You can include the name of a batch file to be executed as soon as a partition is selected in CAROUSEL.OPT, Software Carousel's configuration file. This is as good as having a separate AUTOEXEC.BAT file for each partition. Thus, you can configure several different working environments automatically.

USING RAM-RESIDENT UTILITIES

Your use of RAM-resident utilities will also have a profound effect on your preferences among these windowed environments. Some can coexist with them as well as any application can, while others cannot.

Windows

There's a hate-hate relationship between Windows and RAM-resident programs. Part of the problem has to do with Windows' memory requirements. You can load RAM-resident programs before you load Windows, but you can't access them in Windows. However, you can access them in full-screen applications. If you're addicted to your macro processor, you had best configure all the applications for which you use it as full-screen applications. (Check *Directly Modifies Screen* when you set up the program in the PIF Editor.) Naturally, this restricts the amount of memory left for program-switching and multitasking. It also puts a cap on the size of the largest program you can use.

You can actually load resident programs from within Windows. You must make sure that you have selected *Directly Modifies Memory* in the PIF Editor. Otherwise, Windows will tell you that the program directly modifies memory and refuse to run it. Once you have loaded such a program, you won't be able to switch back to Windows except by unloading the program.

At least, this is what the documentation says. We got the warning message when we tried to load the nonWindows version of PC Paintbrush Plus. This program wants to load a resident screen-capture facility before it starts up. Having forgotten about that, we dutifully went back to the PIF Editor and selected *Directly Modifies Memory*. PC Paintbrush Plus loaded and ran without a hitch (as a full-screen application). However, thereafter, nearly every other program returned a

Not enough memory to run

message. When we exited Windows, we found that the screen-capture program had remained in memory above Windows. This is at best a risky situation. (For the record, ZSoft makes a version of PC Paintbrush especially for Windows.)

Generally speaking, then, when you decide to run Windows, you also decide to give up your RAM-resident utilities. You may find yourself giving up your preferred application programs in favor of others designed strictly for Windows.

Windows takes a little of the curse off this restriction on residency by including its own analog clock, notepad, card file, and calendar. The latter two are among the best of their type that we've seen. Now if they'd just include a macro processor.

DESQview

DESQview, in contrast to Windows, is extremely hospitable to whatever you want to throw at it. Quarterdeck recommends loading utilities such as disk caches and print spoolers before you load DESQview. This makes them available to all your applications. (You may not want to give up the memory these conveniences require, however.) You don't need a cut-and-paste tool, because DESQview has an excellent mark-and-transfer facility.

There is also no problem loading resident utilities in a window. Indeed, if you make your windows large enough, you can load several utilities before you load your transient application, by calling them all from a batch file. We have loaded SuperKey, a thesaurus, and WordStar 4.0 in a single window with no problems whatsoever.

This flexibility gives you the option of loading your macro processor separately in each application's window, complete with its own macro file. You can even load different macro processors in different windows. (However, you may not need to once you get used to DESQview's Learn mode.) Indeed, you can choose a different set of utilities for each application, provided you can spare the memory.

If you like a desktop organizer such as SideKick, you can load that in a separate window. It's always only three or four keystrokes away. On the other hand, DESQview has a built-in phone dialer as well as its macro recorder, both of which are quite adequate. In addition, Quarterdeck sells a set of DESQview Companions comprising a notepad, an appointment-calendar/to-do list, an alarm clock, a calculator, and a terminal program. These are all designed to take special advantage of DESQview.

The one type of utility you *cannot* use with DESQview is a custom mouse menu. Some mice, such as the PC Mouse, come with software that lets you design mouse menus for programs not designed to use the mouse. Since DESQview itself uses the mouse (its mouse driver is especially zippy), it cannot share the space with another mouse driver. However, if an application normally uses a mouse, you can still use a mouse with it. You just have to use the hot key to get back to the DESQview menus.

GEM

GEM lets you load resident utilities before you invoke it. If you use them with standard DOS applications, you should encounter no problems. Be careful, however, not to call them up while the desktop is on the screen. We tried that with both SuperKey and SideKick. They appeared with no difficulty. However, when we sent them into the background, the desktop changed colors from black and lavender on white to light blue on black, and the mouse cursor disappeared. A single touch of the mouse caused the screen to go blank and the system to lock up, and even corrupted some supposedly nonvolatile RAM disks.

Software Carousel

Software Carousel is almost as good an environment as DESQview if you need only one program at a time but like to use different sets of utilities with each. You can set up a batch file to configure each partition as soon as you invoke it. The batch file can load whatever utilities you need. This is another instance where you can load your macro processor with the appropriate file in each program's environment.

The documentation suggests that you don't want to have a program like SideKick running with your applications, but rather in a separate window. However, this approach makes it impossible to transfer data between SideKick and your application. You may find it handier to include various configurations of SideKick in several of the partitions. The current revision of the program includes a separate program called POPOVER to make it possible to switch out of a partition while Side-Kick (or another resident utility) is open.

You can run into some peculiarities, however. For example, if you have SideKick in two different partitions, you may be surprised when you switch from one partition to another and find a different file in the notepad.

You can also load resident programs before you invoke Software Carousel. Indeed, this may be the only way to transfer information from one partition to another. However, resident programs will not pop up over Software Carousel's own menu. And of course, you lose some memory for your applications by using this approach.

Giving DOS More Memory

Hint: All of these programs except GEM have an annoying tendency to run out of memory. One possible solution is a peculiar little device called the All Card (for XTs and compatibles) or the All ChargeCard (for ATs and compatibles, and PS/2s). This card, manufactured by All Computers in Toronto, actually gives you 960K for DOS, and it turns all your extra memory into enhanced expanded memory.

Be forewarned that it is difficult to install. You have to take out your microprocessor, install it on the card, and then connect the card to the microprocessor's socket by means of a series of cables and connectors. Moreover, you have to be careful to get the right version of the card. There are several different physical configurations of the 80286 chip, for example, and they require different connectors. The one supplied with the card we examined was incompatible with the socket on the computer we tried to install it on, all because a little clip was designed differently from the one supplied.

The card, about the size of a credit card, works by moving video memory—which normally takes up the addresses from 640K to 960K—into expanded memory, and then using a device driver to redirect video BIOS calls to the proper address.

The documentation explains that you must patch programs that write to video memory directly. The procedure involves using something like DEBUG to search through each program's code for instructions that write directly to any of the video memory addresses, and then changing them all by hand. Since many popular programs do write directly to video memory, you could end up having quite a job installing all your software to run with the card. This is perhaps most feasible when you are part of a group in which one person can reconfigure all the software that everybody uses just once, and distribute the modified copies. (Be careful, however, that doing so doesn't violate your license agreement.)

It seems like an awful lot of trouble. However, many of us have been raging at the 640K barrier for some time. If you're not about to invest in a 386 PC, the ChargeCard is undoubtedly the shortest, least expensive route to true memory expansion. Moreover, with all your extra memory turned into EEMS, you can add DESQview and have multitasking now, with even your largest programs.

SWITCHING AMONG PROGRAMS

One of the principal reasons for using a windowed operating environment is to be able to switch among foreground and background tasks without unloading the applications from memory. GEM makes no provision for switching among programs, as it loads only one program at a time. However, let's look at how the other environments handle this situation.

Windows

With Windows, it's easiest to switch among applications if they are both open as windows on the desktop. However, most applications don't work well in windows that are less than 25 rows by 80 columns. The graphics-based text in the windows is scaled down somewhat, so 25 rows of text don't take the whole screen. Thus, you can have two overlapping windows, one at the top of the screen and the other at the bottom. For an example of overlapping windows, see Figure 8.1 in Chapter 8.

Normally, however, to conserve memory you'll want to reduce inactive programs to icons. If your currently active program is not a full-screen application, you can switch to another application by double-clicking its icon, if it's visible. If you don't have a mouse, or if the icon isn't visible, you can switch from one icon (or open window) to another by pressing Alt-Tab. As you hold down the Alt key, each time you press Tab, another application is highlighted. If it's in a window, its border changes color to show it's active. If it's in an icon, its name appears with a dotted line around it, even if it has to show through another window. When you release the Alt key, the chosen window appears in its default size in the foreground.

DESQview

DESQview gives you two methods of switching among programs. If the window for the program you want to switch to is visible on the screen, you just drag your mouse to it and click. (If you haven't used the program in a while, it may be buried somewhere deep in memory. Don't be alarmed if it takes some time to become active.) A box in the menu corner will say

Switching...

to let you know DESQview hasn't forgotten about your request. Since

DESQview can use an EGA's 43-line mode, you can fit quite a few programs on the screen at once if you have an EGA, as you saw in Figure 8.5.

If the window you want to use is not visible, you click the mouse button or press the hot key to display the main menu, and choose Switch Windows. A small box will show you which programs are in memory, and the numbers of the windows they occupy. You can select the program with the cursor, the mouse, or the number key for the window number. With the keyboard, this is just Hot-key, S, cursor, Return, or Hot-Key, S, Number. Either way, it's very fast.

Software Carousel

With Software Carousel, each partition is assigned an Alt-function key combination. Keys are assigned in the order in which the partitions are named in CAROUSEL.OPT, not in the order in which you invoked them. If you forget which partition is which, or if your application uses that particular Alt-key combination, there are two other ways to get around. A toggle key (Alt-Shift by default, but you can change it) switches from one partition to the next in sequence. A hot key (Alt-space bar by default, also changeable) brings you to the main menu shown in Figure 8.13 in Chapter 8.

SHARING DATA AMONG PROGRAMS

Another pricipal reason for using a windowed operating environment is the ability to see data files from different application programs together on the screen. When you can also transfer data from one application to another, this facility becomes even more useful.

Windows

In Windows, you transfer data by way of a clipboard. If you want to see what's on the clipboard, you can load CLIPBRD.EXE from the \WINDOWS directory in the MS-DOS Executive, but it works even if you don't load it. You can cut or copy text or graphics to the clipboard by selecting it with the mouse. In any application—DOS or Windows—

you can copy the entire contents of a window (the full screen in a full-screen application) to the clipboard by pressing Alt-PrtSc. In a nonWindows application running in a window, selecting the Control menu (the only one the window will have) automatically puts you in Copy mode, so that the mouse selects text to copy to the clipboard. You simply press the mouse button at one corner of the data to be selected, and hold it down until the highlighted rectangle includes everything you want to select. Select Copy from the Control menu and it will be transferred to the clipboard, replacing whatever was there.

In Windows applications, the Cut, Copy, and Paste commands are on the Edit menu. They work the same way as in full-screen applications. In full-screen applications, you must first press Alt-space bar to display the Control menu. You can then select text with the mouse, and it will be transferred to the clipboard when you select Copy. You can paste it back to your application from the clipboard using this menu, as well as paste it into another application.

Text cut to the clipboard remains text. However if you cut it into a graphics application, and then cut from there to the clipboard, it will be in bit-mapped graphics form.

DESQview

In DESQview, as we have noted, cutting and pasting are called marking and transferring. Both are options on the main menu. You can transfer text among any text windows, and, as noted, you can transfer numbers as numbers that you can use in mathematical operations, even if they were formatted with dollar signs and commas in the source application. You invoke the main menu, and press M to get the Mark menu. You then move the cursor (or the mouse—it's easier with the cursor keys) to the beginning of the area you want to transfer, and press B for Begin. You create a rectangle by moving the cursor or dragging with the mouse, and then press E for End. (If you're using the mouse, you can choose the commands from the menu with it.) If you are done, press Return.

However, there's more you can do. If you want to copy another part of the same—or even another—window to the same destination, press Escape to hide the menu. Then display the next section of text you want to copy. When you invoke the Mark menu, Press M for mark

More, instead of B. You can follow the same procedures as many times as you like, until the buffer is full. To transfer the text, choose Transfer from the main menu. You can transfer all the text at once, or transfer it line by line, or transfer one line at a time into each of several windows. The original text is not affected. This is an awfully nice way of, say, copying all the figure captions from a document into a separate file.

GEM

In GEM, you cannot transfer data among DOS programs. However, GEM applications use a consistent file structure. Therefore, you can, say, create a company logo in GEM Draw Plus or GEM Paint, and then open it in the word processor First Word Plus to use on a letterhead. Figure 9.2 shows how this is done. You simply open a second window, select the graphic, and drag it into the document window.

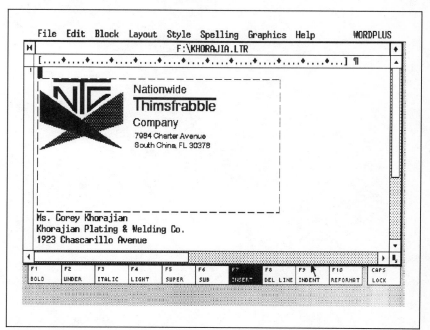

Figure 9.2 ▲ *Transferring a Graphic into a Text Program in GEM.*

Software Carousel

In Software Carousel, as we have noted, you cannot transfer data among partitions. This is its biggest drawback. Your alternatives are (as usual) saving the data as an ASCII file and loading it in another application, or giving up some of your program memory for a RAM-resident utility that has a cut-and-paste feature. Load the utility before you load Carousel.

Multitasking Operating Systems

D OS, AS YOU KNOW, runs only one program at a time. If you want to run more than one program at a time, you either need to add special types of hardware with appropriate software or use a different operating system. In this chapter we'll present three alternative operating systems: UNIX and its derivatives, OS/2, and Concurrent DOS. These systems allow you to use at least some of your DOS programs, and the way you set up your system will determine whether the new system will have exclusive use of your computer, or will share it with DOS.

We'll begin with a brief overview of multitasking and what it can do for you. At the end of the chapter, we'll look at multitasking on 386 PCs, and some of the programs that allow it.

WHAT IS MULTITASKING?

Multitasking, simply put, is performing several tasks at once. This isn't as difficult as it sounds. Have you ever read the newspaper while eating breakfast, or carried on a conversation while driving a car with the radio playing? Multitasking is actually the human way of dealing with the world, as every parent knows. But successful multitasking on a computer requires some planning and analysis.

Multitasking is possible on a computer because different programs perform different types of activities. Thus, the computer's resources can be allocated to various *tasks* (also called *processes*) as needed. You can assign some processor time to programs that are running *in the background* while you are working on another program *in the foreground*.

Multitasking can be implemented on a microcomputer in one of two ways. Either it can be built into the design of the microprocessor, or it can be emulated using a special operating system or control program.

A multitasking operating system, like any operating system, takes complete control of the computer. It creates an environment in which several programs can coexist sharing memory and peripherals efficiently. Figure 10.1 shows a single-tasking computer with three programs to execute, each of which contains several tasks. When a task requires reading from or writing to a disk, you can't do anything else until the task is completed. In a multitasking environment, in contrast, you might be entering text in your word processor while FORMAT.COM formats a diskette and your spreadsheet recalculates a complicated formula. Figure 10.2 shows how a multitasking operating system might manage your computer's resources.

True Multitasking

True multitasking occurs with a processor designed to activate *concurrent* processes. In other words, a second process can execute while the first process is still executing. In the PC world, the only way this has been implemented is through *virtual CPUs*. When a processor implements virtual CPUs (as does the 80386), it acts as though it were a series of separate, real CPUs—as though the computer contained several real PCs with memory and peripherals. Obviously, the processes share a single set of peripherals, but this is transparent to most programs. The 80386 implements these features in what is called its *virtual 8086 mode*.

Figure 10.3 shows an example of true multitasking, in which each process continues to receive full attention from the real processor. The impact on other concurrently running processes is minimal.

Timeslicing

Timeslicing is usually performed by an operating system or control program. Each process receives a small portion of execution time from the

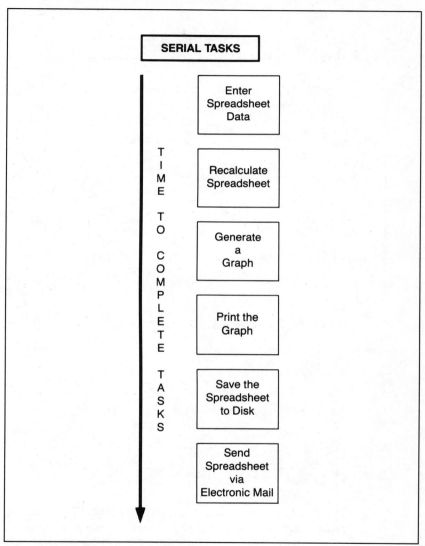

Figure 10.1 ▲ *A Single-Tasking Environment.*

CPU. The process whose turn it is to receive a slice of CPU time is either relocated to somewhere the CPU can execute it from, or the CPU is tricked into executing the next chunk of code from a special memory area. With clever use of expanded and extended memory, several potentially large applications can reside in memory at the same time.

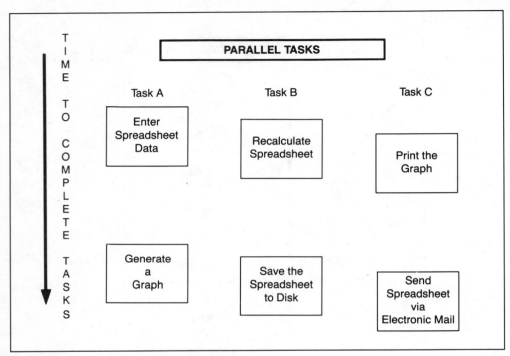

Figure 10.2 ▲ *A Multitasking Environment.*

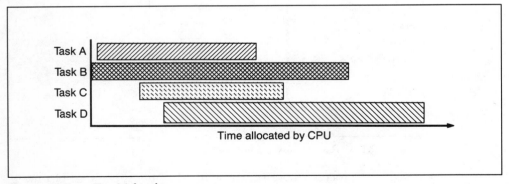

Figure 10.3 ▲ *True Multitasking.*

Figure 10.4 shows how timeslicing works on up to four concurrent processes. Task A starts and is allowed to execute for a short period of time. If it has not finished by the end of the timeslice, the operating system or control program stores any memory or screen locations so that the task can be picked up on the next cycle. Task B is the next to execute for the same amount of time. As there are no tasks yet lined up, task A gets another allocation of CPU time. Eventually tasks C and D start and now four tasks share the processor. Task C finishes as does task B. Tasks A and D continue; but they will get more CPU time because tasks B and C have completed.

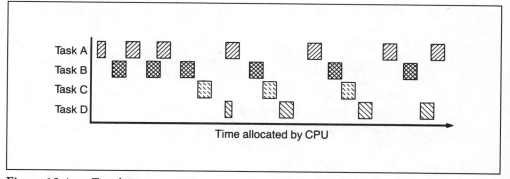

Figure 10.4 ▲ *Timeslicing.*

SHOULD I USE MULTITASKING?

Whether you should use multitasking on your computer depends on several factors. One is the way you work and the type of work you do. Another is the type of system you have. A third is the software you prefer to use.

Here are some of the ways a multitasking operating system can be a real benefit. A programmer might use separate multitasking sessions to compile one program, link another, and run a third to see if it produces bugs, all while editing a fourth program in the foreground. When the test run is finished, the programmer could then put the foreground program aside, link the compiled program, test run the linked program, and re-edit the tested program to eliminate the bugs.

Another circumstance in which multitasking is especially useful is telecommunications. You'll find lots of information about telecommunications in Chapters 12 and 13. However, we'll mention two examples here. Many of the programs discussed in this book are available on electronic bulletin boards. It may take over thirty minutes to transfer some of the longer programs from the bulletin board to your computer. If you can set up a telecommunications program to run in the background, you can be doing other work while waiting for the transfer to complete. Similarly, you may want to leave your telecommunications program running in the background in auto-answer mode, so others can transfer files to your computer without interrupting your work.

Here are two more situations in which multitasking can be helpful. The first is relatively easy to implement, the second quite complex.

You need to recalculate several Lotus 1-2-3 spreadsheets. You also need to produce a cover letter describing the effect of the recalculations in each spreadsheet. Let's assume that the spreadsheets take several minutes to recalculate. With a multitasking operating environment, you could have one spreadsheet recalculate in the background, while you bring a completed spreadsheet into a second window, and describe the changes in a third window.

Now let's assume that you are involved in trading stocks. A communications program is receiving stock data continuously in the background. Meanwhile, you need to manipulate a spreadsheet that contains snapshots of the data at specific times, and you need to produce a graph of price trends. Another specialized program is also monitoring several specific stocks and will sound an alarm if any of the stocks approach critical values. Along with the communications program, the graphing system and alarm program are running as background tasks while you work on the spreadsheet in the foreground. This level of sophistication requires a trustworthy package and significant horsepower on the PC itself. While the parts of this scenario are well integrated, it entails some risks. With so many programs active at once, there may be contention for your computer's resources. If this results in a crash, you could lose a great deal of critical data.

The most fundamental question to ask yourself on the benefits of multitasking is whether you will increase your productivity by making the necessary changes. First, you need to look at how you work. We'll discuss that next. Then we'll tackle some fundamental hardware constraints. Since the issues of software compatibility and some issues of hardware constraints depend on the particular operating system, we'll deal with them as they arise.

Do I Really Need Multitasking?

The way you use your computer will be the most important factor in determining whether you should use a multitasking operating system. First consider the following questions:

1. Do you use your computer for more than one hour a day?

2. Do you run more than one program a day?

3. Do your programs require the output of other programs as input?

4. Does any program tie up your PC for more than a minute at a time?

5. Do several people need access to the same data at once?

Now let's consider the implications of the answers to these questions. If you use your computer for more than an hour a day and you use more than one program, you may be able to increase your productivity by multitasking. However, if you spend four hours a day entering data in a single program, multitasking won't do much for you.

If you typically use the output of one program as input for another, you might as well stay with a single-tasking system, because there isn't much the second program can do until you finish with the first. However, you may benefit from one of the windowed operating environments described in Chapters 8 and 9.

If you use several programs, and one of them ties up your computer for long periods of time, you can definitely benefit from multitasking. For example, suppose your spreadsheet takes several minutes to complete a recalculation. Or suppose the printer driver in your word processor conflicts with your print spooler, forcing you to print without one. In these circumstances, you can definitely benefit from multitasking.

Finally, if several people need access to the same data, you may benefit from a multitasking operating system. One way to allow such access is through a local area network. Unfortunately, as you'll see in Chapter 14, LANs are expensive, and need a great deal of maintenance. However, there are several alternatives to networks that can accomplish the same thing. Some of these alternatives are based on multitasking operating systems. We'll present a few such alternatives in Chapter 11.

Before you plunge into the world of multitasking, there are other considerations. Against the gain in productivity, you have to balance compatibility, cost, and ease of use. If you have a large library of DOS programs that you don't want to give up, you are best off staying with DOS. There is no guarantee that all your programs will run correctly with another operating system, even if that system includes a means of running DOS programs. If this is so, your safest route to multitasking is to install some memory boards that use the EEMS specification and use DESQview (unless you have a 386 PC, a point we'll come to shortly). Be careful, though, that the boards you choose include the EEMS hardware, and not just the EMM 4.0 standard. EMM 4.0 will not multitask without EEMS hardware.

If ease of use is a primary consideration, stay with DOS and add a windowed operating environment. The graphic interfaces—especially GEM—can put an especially friendly face on DOS. Windows and DESQview, while somewhat less friendly, can add a great deal to what you can do within DOS.

Finally, if increasing your productivity is a primary consideration, you might try a multitasking operating system. However, you may find that some of your programs won't run, and that your system is no longer easy to use. While controlling one process may be easy, controlling several can present unforeseen pitfalls.

Can I Perform Multitasking on My System?

Any PC, regardless of its microprocessor, can be made to emulate multitasking via timeslicing. However, only an 80386 can offer true multitasking by virtue of its architecture. The 80386 has a way of providing multiple memory areas to multiple virtual 8086 machines; each treats each memory area as its own 640K.

Beyond the microprocessor, memory is also an issue. To run several tasks at once, you need to have memory in which to run them. The

80286, in contrast to the 8088 family, can directly address up to 16MB of memory, even if DOS can address only 640K. It addresses this memory as a linear address space. The memory above the 1MB address is known as extended memory. (Remember that the system uses memory from 640K to 1MB for its own purposes.) However, if you use DOS, the only way you can use extended memory is to put such things as RAM disks, disk cache buffers, and print spoolers in it. (A few programs do have memory drivers that can use extended memory, but you can literally count them on the fingers of one hand.) This is why most AT users configure any extra memory as expanded memory if possible. With enhanced expanded memory (EEMS memory), you can use DESQview to perform timesliced multitasking under DOS, as described below.

However, other operating systems do not have the same limitations as DOS. UNIX, for example, can address extended memory as linear memory.

Can I Get Multitasking from DOS?

DOS does not provide true multitasking, but the use of the RAM disk device driver and the PRINT command are examples of timeslicing applications that can run on any architecture.

As mentioned briefly in the previous chapter, Windows and DESQview provide a form of multitasking. Both do so by a variety of timeslicing, except on 386 PCs.

Windows applications will run in the background in Windows, even if they are reduced to icons. However, they run more slowly than they do in the foreground. DOS applications simply stop when they are in the background.

Windows is especially intelligent about the way it handles multitasking for its own programs. It keeps track of what the programs are doing and assigns some time to them only if they need it. If one program is sorting data in the background while another is waiting for input, for example, the program waiting for input will receive no processor time, and the other program's share of processor time will be adjusted accordingly.

DESQview provides multitasking only if you have an EEMS (enhanced expanded memory standard) board installed (or an All Card or ChargeCard, which turns your memory into EEMS memory). However, it will multitask any programs you can load. Thus, you really can format a disk in one window, copy a group of files in another, sort a database in a third, print a spreadsheet in a fourth, and enter text in your word processor in a fifth. You determine the proportion of time allotted to foreground and background tasks in the Setup DESQview program. You enter the amount of time each gets in the Performance submenu. The default is 9 clock ticks for the foreground task and 3 for background tasks.

These control programs, and Concurrent DOS XM as well, offer special support for 386 PCs that makes use of their virtual 8086 mode. Functionally, the systems appear the same, but special drivers in the 80386 versions allow them to apportion extended memory as expanded memory.

With the advent of OS/2, it is unlikely that Microsoft will implement multitasking within DOS itself. OS/2 offers a timeslicing approach to multitasking and allows application programs to use more than 640K. A later version of OS/2 is expected to offer full support (i.e., virtual 8086) for 386 PCs.

AN INTRODUCTION TO XENIX AND UNIX

UNIX is the name given to a family of operating systems developed at Bell Laboratories for 16- and 32-bit minicomputers. However, as microcomputers with similar power became available, UNIX and a vast array of derivatives and look-alikes began to appear. Originally, UNIX was used mainly in academic and research organizations. However, by 1988, many commercial applications began to appear for this operating system.

UNIX exists in many forms. In addition to the original Bell Labs versions, many manufacturers have released adaptations and extensions.

Among the versions of UNIX that run on PCs are AT&T UNIX System V, XENIX (Microsoft), and QNIX (Quantum Software). One major criticism of UNIX is its lack of standards.

We will consider two versions of UNIX: XENIX, which can run even on the original IBM PC; and AT&T's UNIX System V, Release 3, which has recently been made available for 386 PCs.

Hardware Requirements

UNIX systems require quite a bit of hardware. The average version of UNIX has over two hundred commands and utilities and occupies

200K of RAM when in use. Some versions require almost 9MB of disk storage. Thus, you can forget about using them without a hard disk. For comparison, consider that MS-DOS 3.3, with some forty commands and utilities, uses 65K of RAM and requires about 400K of disk storage. As a clue to the size and complexity of UNIX, note that the standard documentation includes two reference manuals, five user guides, and two system administration manuals.

You must have at least 2MB of RAM to run UNIX System V, Release 3. However, optimum performance requires at least 3 or 4MB. If several users will be linked to your computer, you should have upwards of 10MB.

Theoretically, you can load the system software using a floppy disk, but you will need a hard disk to operate UNIX as it was intended to be used. The bigger the hard disk, the better. Typically 70 to 100MB is optimum, although a 20MB disk will work—5 to 6MB will be used for system files and work areas. Interestingly, UNIX uses software device drivers that replace routines usually included in the hard disk controllers. This may mean that you'll either need to get a software ROM upgrade or another controller.

Setting Up UNIX

You can assign one of several partitions on your hard disk to UNIX, or devote all of your disk to it, by running FDISK and selecting a nonDOS partition. Only UNIX partitions can be used to store UNIX files.

UNIX can address only one logical drive. Therefore, on PCs, UNIX uses another area of your hard disk for its file management system, which is needed to organize and address the data on two or more physical disks. (Incidentally, this is why the JOIN command was added to DOS—to emulate this feature of UNIX.)

If you don't have enough RAM for UNIX applications, you can configure UNIX to use some of your hard disk space as a temporary storage area for code that is part of a program in memory but is not currently being used. This frees more memory for other tasks. If you want to use your hard disk in this manner, the faster your hard disk the better.

UNIX comes on a set of disks called a System Software Set. You begin by booting your computer from Disk 1. This will install the UNIX system kernel on your hard disk. This takes the place of DOS's hidden system files. It also formats the partition for UNIX and installs itself in place of the DOS boot record, so that you can boot your computer from the hard disk. (This is functionally equivalent to the FORMAT /S command in DOS.) You then reboot from your hard disk to continue the installation. You will be prompted to load the necessary supporting files and enter user IDs and passwords.

Next, you install your applications using a utility called INSTALLPKG. All UNIX programs conform to standards recognized by this utility and are ready to be installed by it. Therefore, you don't have to go through a different set of installation procedures for each program.

Using UNIX

Once you have installed UNIX, you interact with the shell, which is the command line editor. As in MS-DOS, you simply enter the commands followed by the appropriate parameters. If you are a C programmer, you can extend the shell by modifying its source code.

Some UNIX commands will be familiar to you. For example, wildcard characters such as * and ?. Because DOS borrowed redirection from UNIX, the redirection symbols <, >, and >> operate the same way. UNIX uses the slash as a path separator instead of the backslash, and it uses the minus sign instead of the slash as the switch character. UNIX uses the familiar directory commands MKDIR, RMDIR, CD, and so forth.

Although there are some similar commands and the file structure is similar, there are very few commands that are actually the same, and the command structure is different.

A typical UNIX command line might be

command *– option /arguments/more_arguments*

For example, the DOS command

DIR \TEXT*.*

would be replaced in UNIX by

ls −l /text

In this command, ls is the directory command, −l means use the long form, and /text is the name of the subdirectory, although the names of these items are different under UNIX.

If you don't want to give up all your DOS programs, you can use a software package called SoftPC, published by Insignia Solutions. This program emulates a standard PC through software routines.

Contrary to popular belief, literally thousands of application programs run in the UNIX environment, including spreadsheets, word processors, and communications packages.

Multitasking under UNIX

UNIX is usually used as the core of a multiuser system. The main reason to have UNIX on your PC is to communicate with other computers running UNIX, or to use some particular UNIX program on your PC.

Each user of a multiuser system has access to multitasking. However, UNIX supports only one background process in addition to the foreground process. Either can be any UNIX program. You simply execute the task in the background and continue to work on other tasks. For example, you can generate a report as a background task while modifying text in the foreground.

Every multiuser UNIX implementation must have a system console. This displays a summary of the work currently in progress. (On a single system, your computer is the system console.) It can be anything from a teletype machine to the console of the UNIX host machine itself. The host machine is usually a minicomputer, although a microcomputer with an 80386 or Motorola 68030 can also serve the purpose. Attached to it via serial cables are remote workstations. These can be dumb terminals or PCs running terminal emulation software.

A WORD ABOUT OS/2

On April 2, 1987 Microsoft and IBM jointly announced Operating System/2. This system is designed specifically to utilize the protected mode of the Intel 80286 and 80386 processors. A version that utilizes all the capabilities of the 80386 will be available in the near future.

OS/2 is a multitasking operating system that allows application programs written specifically for it to use up to 16MB of memory on ATs and 386 PCs. Although not generally available yet, the OS/2 presentation manager is an integral part of the OS/2 product, providing a graphics-based windowed user interface to the system. The OS/2 presentation manager is derived from Microsoft Windows 2.0.

If you are currently using an AT-class computer, you might ask why you need a new operating system. Consider the fact that the 80286 can address 16MB of RAM. DOS is not a multitasking operating system and has no way to address more than 640K without such additions as EMM device drivers. Thus, if 640K is not enough memory for your applications, or if you want multitasking, you must add quite a bit of hardware and software to your DOS computer to overcome DOS's limitations, even with an 80286. And you still aren't using the power of the chip.

The advantage of the 80286 is that it has a *protected mode*, in which no program can address memory directly. Instead, programs request a portion of memory from the processor, which assigns the memory to the various programs and ensures that each program's memory is protected from access by the other programs. When the program is finished with its memory, control is returned to the processor.

You will discover immediately that OS/2 is not designed for XT-class computers, because it is supplied only on 1.2MB diskettes or 3½-inch diskettes. You can't load it into a computer that has only 360K drives. Moreover, you must have a hard disk. It takes about 2MB of disk storage and 2MB of memory. However, you will need more if you want to run OS/2 at top speed, or run DOS programs, or use the presentation manager. To do all this, you need 4 to 5MB of RAM.

Installing and Starting OS/2

You can install OS/2 automatically. It comes on three high-capacity diskettes, an Installation Disk, a Program Disk, and a Supplemental Disk. You can boot your system from either of the first two and it will come up in OS/2. You will then see either the Session Manager screen, which allows you to start new tasks and switch among running tasks, or the protected mode prompt:

[A:\]

You install OS/2 from the Installation Disk by means of a menu. You can select either a standard installation or a custom installation. If you choose the latter, you will be asked a series of questions about your hardware. When you have finished, the installation program proceeds to partition and format your hard disk (if you have not already done so), create the directories it needs, copy the OS/2 files from the diskettes to your hard disk, and create OS/2's equivalent of AUTOEXEC.BAT and CONFIG.SYS files.

Alternatively, you can install OS/2 manually. OS/2 places about 130 files on your hard disk, 60 of them in the root. If you wish, you can place many of these files in subdirectories with careful use of the PATH command. Installing OS/2 involves replacing the hidden system files. However, you can still boot DOS from a diskette if you wish. If your disk is formatted with DOS, you can remove OS/2 and restore DOS with a SYS command.

With Microsoft's OS/2 (but not at present with IBM's), when the system boots from the hard disk, you are first asked whether you want to run OS/2 or MS-DOS. Your choice determines which operating system will control your computer until the next time you reboot.

OS/2 and DOS

What makes OS/2 different from other multitasking environments—such as DESQview and Windows running under DOS—is that the multitasking support comes from within the operating system itself rather than as an add-on to a single-tasking operating system.

At present, using OS/2 is a lot like using DOS. OS/2 includes all of the DOS commands and some new ones besides. Both OS/2 and DOS use a CONFIG.SYS file, and both can automatically execute a batch file on startup. However, there are two new components, CMD.EXE and STARTUP.CMD. CMD.EXE is the OS/2 equivalent of COMMAND.COM (which is also included so you can run DOS programs). STARTUP.CMD is the equivalent of the DOS AUTOEXEC.BAT file. (Batch programs under OS/2 are called *command files*, and have the extension .CMD.) Of course, when the presentation manager is released, using OS/2 will be more like using Windows than like using DOS. (However, programs written for Windows will not run under OS/2's presentation manager.)

OS/2 has a *compatibility box* in which you can run DOS applications. What this means is that along with the dozens of OS/2 programs on your software shelf, you can run one DOS program.

When you use the compatibility box, your computer will use a CON-FIG.SYS file set up especially for DOS. Thus, you actually have two CONFIG.SYS files, one for DOS and the other for OS/2.

DOS programs will run more slowly in the DOS compatibility box than in DOS. Moreover, they cannot be multitasked. Any DOS program running in the compatibility box will stop when in the background. Generally speaking, if you want to run DOS programs, you are better off using DOS than using the compatibility box.

This is especially true if you want to use telecommunications programs. There are as yet none written for OS/2. However, if you run a telecommunications program in the compatibility box, you will not be able to put it in the background, because real (8086) mode "goes to sleep" when it's in the background.

OS/2 does not recognize .COM programs and will not run them. All programs for OS/2 must be .EXE files. However, if you run a DOS .EXE program in OS/2's protected mode, or vice versa, your system will probably crash.

To benefit from OS/2, you must have applications that can not only run under OS/2 but also take advantage of it. Applications that run within OS/2 will fall into one of three categories: those that can run only under OS/2, those that can run under either OS/2 or DOS, and those that can run only in the compatibility box.

Generally, OS/2 applications must behave better than their DOS counterparts. Part of the memory limitation of DOS is the way in which memory is allocated. If a program needs memory, it simply goes out and grabs some. There is no checking to see if the memory is used by another program. Usually DOS will police well-behaved programs adequately to avoid this. Some poorly behaved programs write to specific areas of memory such as the video memory. Under OS/2, the program must request an amount of memory, which is then assigned by the operating system.

Unlike DOS, OS/2 requires all of its client programs to behave themselves. OS/2 strictly enforces a memory protection scheme that prevents programs from gaining direct access to physical memory. The major requirement for this is that the 80286 processor in protected mode uses paged memory rather than a linear address space. Protected mode is an appropriate name for the way the 80286 handles memory: it places barriers around memory access by using tables pointing to memory areas rather than physical addresses. When a program needs memory, it cannot specify the memory location as it can under DOS; it can only request a set amount and must accept whatever memory OS/2 allocates to it.

OS/2 also protects it own integrity, as Figure 10.5 shows. As you can see, access to the system files is severely restricted by this ring structure. Application programs run at level 3, which means that they cannot directly access parts of the operating system. Instead, they must request services in an orderly fashion.

At level 0 is the OS/2 kernel, which will be identical throughout all implementations of OS/2. The kernel loads all the supporting device drivers. Above that is level 1, which is not used currently. At level 2 are special I/O procedures. These can include specially written user applications. Finally, at level 3, you run applications.

The ring structure of OS/2 will allow a process operating at one level to access resources at either the same or a higher level. If a process attempts to access resources belonging to a lower level, then OS/2 will report an error and abort the program.

What benefits does OS/2 give you? Until you have a collection of programs written for it, not much besides increased speed. You won't be able to multitask DOS programs, and you won't get more than 640K for them. Moreover, if you have a computer with a processor in the 8086 family, you will need to add an 80286 card with some memory that is certified to run OS/2.

OS/2 and the 80386

You may have noticed that we haven't said anything about running OS/2 on 386 PCs. This is because the current release of OS/2 is not designed to take advantage of the special features of the 80386 processor. A 386 PC will run the current version of OS/2, but only in its 80286-emulation mode. An 80386 version is expected in the future.

Where Is OS/2 Taking Us?

So why should you upgrade from DOS to OS/2? In some respects, veteran DOS users have already gone through this once before. Remember

Figure 10.5 ▲ *OS/2's Ring Protection Scheme.*

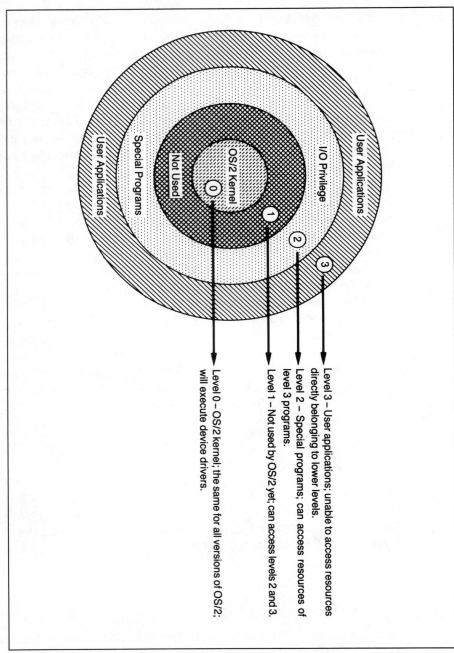

Level 0 – OS/2 kernel; the same for all versions of OS/2; will execute device drivers.

Level 1 – Not used by OS/2 yet; can access levels 2 and 3.

Level 2 – Special programs; can access resources of level 3 programs.

Level 3 – User applications; unable to access resources directly belonging to lower levels.

DOS 1.0? Of course, the problems were fixed in later versions, but it would be reasonable to argue that DOS 2.0 was a different operating system from DOS 1.0 rather than an upgrade.

OS/2 conforms to IBM's SAA (System Application Architecture). SAA is a very large set of rules and guidelines for application developers and operating system designers. The presentation manager conforms to what is known as UIA (User Interface Architecture), which is a subset of SAA. The intention is to provide a consistent set of interfaces. This means, for example, that a developer should always use the word Exit to terminate a program and not Quit, Kill, or Bye. This means that OS/2 will eventually give you access to a user interface that is standard across all programs.

If you use an AT clone, you may be concerned about your computer's ability to run OS/2. Actually, there are a few basic requirements. You have to be able to address memory above 1MB (thus some plug-in 286 cards such as the Orchid Tiny Turbo will never be able to run it), and you must have the mode switching hardware that is included in the AT to allow the operating system to switch from protected to real mode. Manufacturers of clones will have to approach Microsoft to get the adaptation materials and then produce an OS/2 version for their computers.

For older PCs, all is not lost if you wish to run OS/2. Many 80286- and 80386-based add-in boards will be able to run OS/2 if they have their own extended memory. One example is the Microsoft Mach 20 board.

CONCURRENT DOS XM

Digital research was one of the pioneers of multitasking operating systems for PCs. The company's current entries in the field are Concurrent DOS XM and Concurrent DOS 386. Concurrent DOS XM is a powerful operating system that supports large, multiple tasks and runs existing PC-DOS, MS-DOS, CP/M-86, Concurrent CP/M, and Concurrent DOS 86 application programs without modification. It runs on Intel 8088, 8086, 80186, and 80286 microprocessors.

All PCs have some ROM routines called the BIOS, or Basic Input/Output System. Concurrent DOS XM has an additional interface layer called the XIOS. This tailors the system to the processor in your computer, so that the standard version of Concurrent DOS XM will work without modification on any of the supported processors, and will allow two additional users to access the system from remote workstations.

The XM stands for expanded memory. However, Concurrent DOS XM handles Lotus-Intel-Microsoft expanded memory in the same way that DOS does. Thus, if your programs can use EMS memory, they will still be able to do so; however, there is no way Concurrent will make direct use of it. On the other hand, Concurrent uses enhanced expanded memory the same way DESQview does, as explained in Chapter 8. If you reduce your motherboard memory to 256K and use an EEMS board to fill out the remaining 384K, Concurrent will take over managing the memory. It can then swap program code as well as data to the extra memory, allowing you to run several reasonably large programs at once.

Concurrent DOS XM lets you configure many aspects of your system to your needs by using its SETUP command. This command displays a menu, shown in Figure 10.6, on which you can:

- ▲ Establish the size of the memory partitions to be used

- ▲ Allocate memory for a RAM disk in conventional memory

- ▲ Assign the various memory partitions to serial ports so that you can run a multiuser system

- ▲ Assign the number of timeslices each partition will have

Concurrent DOS XM works by assigning a *virtual console* to each of the tasks. That is, each program is fooled into believing it is running alone on a single computer, with its own keyboard and screen. However, only when you bring an application to the foreground will it access the real keyboard and screen.

There is some additional power built into this arrangement. If you run Concurrent DOS XM with programs especially designed for it, the output from one virtual console can be redirected to another virtual console, allowing data to be swapped between programs.

Concurrent DOS XM will use math coprocessor chips such as the 8087 if you have one. Both foreground and background tasks can use the coprocessor.

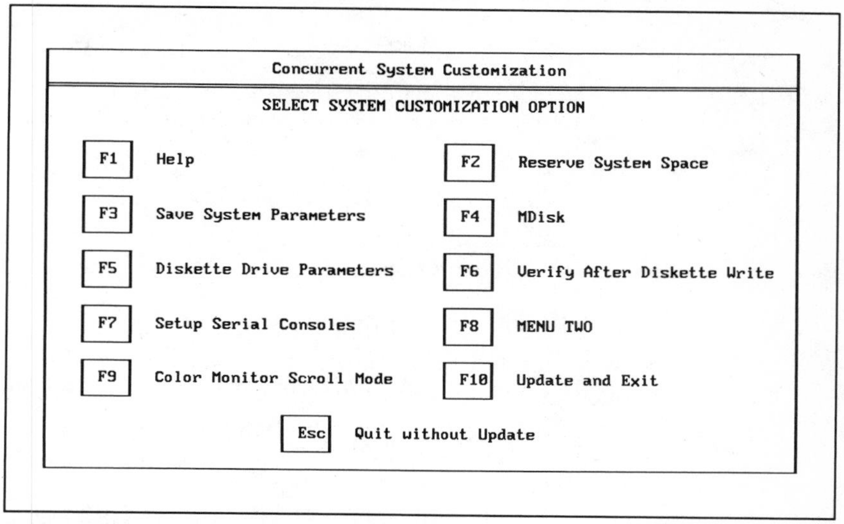

```
                    Concurrent System Customization
                 SELECT SYSTEM CUSTOMIZATION OPTION

   [F1]   Help                      [F2]   Reserve System Space

   [F3]   Save System Parameters    [F4]   MDisk

   [F5]   Diskette Drive Parameters [F6]   Verify After Diskette Write

   [F7]   Setup Serial Consoles     [F8]   MENU TWO

   [F9]   Color Monitor Scroll Mode [F10]  Update and Exit

                    [Esc]  Quit without Update
```

Figure 10.6 ▲ *The Concurrent DOS Setup Menu.*

Installing Concurrent DOS XM

There are basically two ways to install Concurrent DOS XM. You can either set it up as the primary operating system or so that it gives you a choice of using MS-DOS or Concurrent DOS. You must have formatted your hard disk using DOS, and you must have the system files and COMMAND.COM installed before you begin. Installation is a breeze—you simply put System Disk 1 in drive A (which you can boot from) and reboot the system.

The installation program then runs automatically. It first asks you which hard disk to install the program to, and whether you have any CP/M programs on your hard disk. (You have to take some additional steps if you do.) The installation program then installs some files in your root directory and creates a new directory called \CDOS to hold Concurrent's equivalent of the DOS external programs.

If you install the system so that you have a choice of DOS or Concurrent, the installation program adds the lines shown in Listing 10.1 at the beginning of your AUTOEXEC.BAT file. The LOADSYS command, which appears in line 3, is what actually loads Concurrent DOS XM, replacing DOS.

```
 1: echo off
 2: prompt $p$g
 3: if "%os%"=="" loadsys ask
 4: if "%os%"=="os%%" loadsys ask
 5: path %bootdrv%\cdos
 6: if "%os%"=="CDOS" echo Operating environment is Concurrent
DOS XM Release %ver%
 7: if "%os%"=="CDOS" echo current path is %path%
 8: if "%1"=="1" runmenu hdmenu.dat
 9: if "%os%"=="CDOS" exit
10: rem Existing autoexec.bat starts here.
```

Listing 10.1 ▲ *Lines Added to AUTOEXEC.BAT by Concurrent DOS.*

When you load Concurrent, it automatically removes from memory anything loaded under DOS, and takes over. This means that it removes any device drivers that CONFIG.SYS normally loads. If you want to use expanded memory, therefore, you must reinstall your expanded memory drivers, as well as any other device drivers you normally use.

You do so by means of a file called CCONFIG.SYS. You should include any drivers for external disks, or any hardware that doesn't initialize itself automatically. To do so, use the DEVICE command as usual. For expanded memory, however, you must use a different command. If you have standard EMS memory, you use a command such as

    EMM = EMM.SYS

If you have enhanced expanded memory, the command is EEMM, not EMM. To load an AST RAMpage driver, for example, you would include the command

    EEMM = REMM.SYS

You should then invoke a Concurrent program called SCEPTER to handle the memory-page-switching.

You can do a great deal more to make Concurrent fit well with your system. Begin with the SETUP program. If you have EEMS memory, you can use an internal EEMS driver installed from within this program instead of SCEPTER. If you do, you can also have it search system memory above 640K for any unused memory, which it can then utilize.

Concurrent inserts the following into the environment space:

    COMSPEC = C:\CDOS.COM
    OS = CDOS
    VER = 6.0

```
BOOTDRV = C:
TEMPDRV = C:
PROMPT = $p$g
PATH = C:\CDOS
```

As you can see, some of the ways Concurrent operates are the same as DOS, while others are not. However, you will probably want to use Concurrent's PATH and PROMPT commands and rewrite lines 2 and 5 of the revised AUTOEXEC.BAT file according to your system's requirements. You may also want to insert additional commands between lines 9 and 10.

To customize your system further, Concurrent includes a PIFED utility similar to the PIF Editor program in Windows, or the Add/Change Program menus in DESQview. However, instead of writing external files for loading the programs, it makes modifications directly to the program code. You invoke PIFED with a command of the form

PIFED *FILENAME.EXT*

and then you make the appropriate changes on a screen similar to the one shown in Figure 10.7. Fortunately, you can get online help for every item on this screen, so it's relatively easy to use. To remove the changes you have made to a program, enter a command of the form

PIFED *FILENAME.EXT* /R

```
                    The Digital Research Program Information Editor
         No Program Information currently installed in the file. Using defaults.

Program name:   123.exe

Memory usage:   Minimum memory required                    [  71]K bytes
                Maximum memory desired                     [1023]K bytes

Screen usage:   Directly writes to screen (ANSI, ROS, 25 line) [5]

Options:        Program requires a maths co-processor         [N]
                Program runs only in the foreground           [N]
                Program may run in banked memory              [Y]
                Program waits in idle loop                    [N]

Program makes direct access to COM1[N]  COM2[N]  LST1[N]  LST2[N]  LST3[N]

Program uses interrupt vectors [ 8]hex through [2F]hex inclusive.




    TAB or cursor keys to move between entries, ? or F1 for help, ENTER when done.
```

Figure 10.7 ▲ *The Concurrent PIFED Screen.*

Hint: If you have no expanded memory, use SETUP to adjust your maximum process size to less than 448K or you will only be able to operate in one process with any success. There is a trick to using this effectively. For example, we loaded WordPerfect and found that attempts to use any of the other processes resulted in the message

Insufficient memory

Then we loaded the smaller program processes first, and WordPerfect worked perfectly!

Using Concurrent DOS XM

If you install Concurrent DOS as a single-user system, each time you reboot the system, you will be asked

Load Concurrent DOS (Y or N)?

If you press N, you will be in DOS.

If you press Y, you will first see a report on your memory and hardware configuration, and then a title screen. At this point, you can press F10 to display the menu shown in Figure 10.8, or press Escape to display a DOS command prompt. You can also switch to another process at this point. The file manager referred to on the menu resembles many of the commercial DOS shell programs, such as XTree and QDOS II.

In addition to its other features, Concurrent DOS includes:

▲ A command stack, with which you can recall an immense number of commands that you have already entered

▲ A card file

▲ A printer manager

▲ A custom menu generator

▲ A Window Manager

If you load the Window Manager, you can change your window arrangement so that some or all of them are smaller than a full screen.

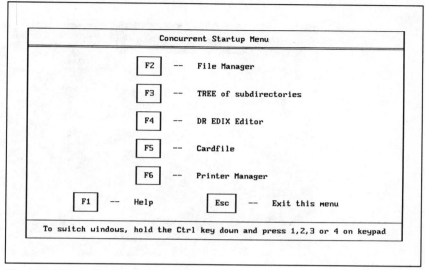

Figure 10.8 ▲ *The Concurrent DOS Main Menu.*

You can then display all your windows on the screen at once. Figure 10.9 illustrates a screen with the Window Manager in use. The active window is outlined with a double line.

If you have not loaded the Window Manager, each process runs in a full-screen window. To switch to another process, you hold down the Ctrl key and press the number of the process on the numeric keypad. A status line at the bottom of the screen tells you which window is current and what is active in the other windows (unless your current application uses the bottom line).

Concurrent DOS XM can run almost all standard DOS programs, such as Lotus 1-2-3, dBASE III PLUS, Paradox, Quattro, and WordPerfect. You cannot run more than one graphics program that writes directly to the screen at one time, because both will attempt to write to the same area of memory at once.

To run RAM-reesident programs, you must first load the command processor (CDOS). If you enter an EXIT command, you will automatically unload any resident programs in the partition.

Telecommunications programs are subject to the same limitations as they are in OS/2's compatibility box. However, Concurrent DOS XM

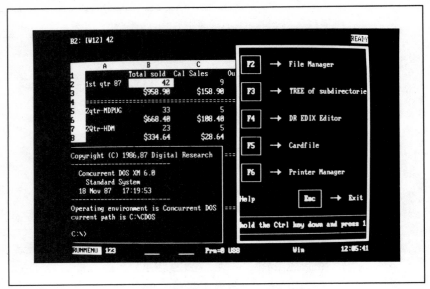

Figure 10.9 ▲ *The Concurrent DOS Window Manager.*

simply refuses to let you switch out of them until they become inactive, thereby protecting your telecommunications process.

386 OPERATING ENVIRONMENTS

The 80386 achieves multitasking through its virtual 8086 operating mode. You can have one or more virtual 8086 sessions active at once. Each virtual 8086 has up to 640K of virtual memory, a virtual console (i.e., keyboard and screen), virtual disk space, and so on. Obviously, you can use only one console (the main screen), one portion of memory, and one keyboard at a time. Only when you bring a process to the foreground will these devices become real. As far as a program running in one of these virtual 8086s is concerned, it is using real memory writing to a real screen and receiving input from a real keyboard. As far as the program can tell, it resides in its own computer.

Figure 10.10 shows how a 386 PC runs three virtual 8086 processes. The processes are labeled A, B, and C. Each 8086 process believes that it has a complete PC environment to itself. The 80386 maps the disk and memory storage of each virtual 8086 into its own real and virtual storage.

Even programs that write directly to the screen can run as virtual 8086 processes. The 80386 system can easily map the virtual console to its own display screen. While the other processes are still writing to their screens, they are not being displayed. Figure 10.10 shows the 80386 mapping the screen to process A.

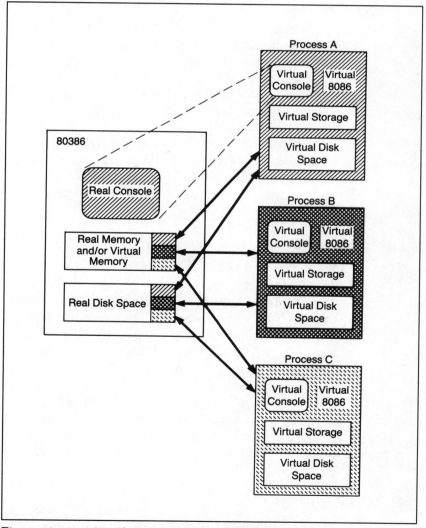

Figure 10.10 ▲ *How the 80386 Chip Allocates Multitasking.*

Several environments currently available can give you full use of the 80386. They include Concurrent DOS 386 from Digital Research, Microsoft Windows/386 and DESQview. Concurrent DOS 386 also has multiuser capabilities that we will touch on in Chapter 11.

Concurrent DOS 386

Concurrent DOS 386 is a specialized version of Concurrent DOS XM. It allows the use of some special features of the 80386 CPU. The most notable additional features of Concurrent DOS 386 are that it can support up to eight users—instead of the three supported by XM—and that it uses the 386's inherent multitasking capabilities. Thus, you don't have to go through as complex a setup procedure as you do with Concurrent DOS XM.

Concurrent DOS 386 has an especially efficient design. When you use it, your programs actually run faster than can be accounted for by the difference in processor speed alone. Moreover, you can run as many applications, of any size, as you like, if you have enough memory.

DESQview

When you use DESQview on a 386, you must install a special device driver (sold separately) called QEMM.SYS. This remarkable little driver converts your 386 extended memory into expanded memory. Since DESQview addresses expanded memory quite efficiently, you can then use DESQview as a control program for your 386. It takes advantage of the virtual 8086 mode to let you run as many DOS programs as you have memory for, up to nine.

Each program gets 530K with an EGA—more with a CGA or mono-graphics adapter. Thus, you can run all but the largest DOS programs at one time. Moreover, because QEMM.SYS converts the 386's extended memory to expanded memory, you can effectively run at full capacity those programs that make use of expanded memory.

! Windows/386

Windows/386 works much like DESQview to act as a control program for your 386 PC. You must use the expanded memory device driver that comes with the machine. Windows/386 can then multitask DOS programs as well as Windows programs. Each gets about 635K. However, Windows is somewhat slower than DESQview because it must write to the graphics screen. This requires addressing considerable memory each time the screen is updated.

PART III

CONNECTIVITY

WAYS OF CONNECTING COMPUTERS

CHAPTER

11

MOST OF US THINK of personal computers as just that—personal and for our use alone. However, there may come a time for many of us to move beyond the bounds of our own systems and link our computers in various ways with other computers. This procedure is called *connectivity*. This fancy name may conjure up images of spending lots of money but all it really means is sharing data, programs, and general information with other PC users.

There are many ways of providing connectivity, and the rest of this book is devoted to the subject. In this chapter we'll present a range of ways you can connect your computers to others. Chapter 12 will introduce you to the world of serial communications, which allows you to link computers directly, and to use the telephone system to access remote computers. Chapter 13 will demonstrate some practical uses for telecommunications. In Chapter 14, we'll present some hypothetical situations in which a network is appropriate and provide some details of installing and using networks. Finally, in Chapter 15, we'll explain some of the particulars of communicating directly with mainframes and minicomputers.

LINKS TO MAINFRAMES AND MINICOMPUTERS

There are basically three ways to link a microcomputer to a large-scale computer such as a mainframe or minicomputer. The simplest is to use a *modem* and dial in using *terminal-emulation* software on your own computer, as we'll explain in Chapter 12. Mainframe computers normally process jobs entered from *dumb terminals*. A dumb terminal essentially consists of a console (a keyboard and a screen). Terminal-emulation software is designed to fool the mainframe into thinking that your high-powered computer is nothing more than a keyboard and screen, and to present the mainframe with the communications protocols it needs to talk to your computer in this state. Many popular telecommunications software packages, including ProComm, which we use in the examples in Chapter 13, can emulate a wide variety of dumb terminals.

The second way of linking to a mainframe is by way of a local-area network (LAN). A LAN gains access to a mainframe system by way of a link known as a gateway, which is described later in this chapter.

Finally, you can use special adapter boards to hook directly into a mainframe's terminal network. These cards are often attached to a *cluster controller*, which is a distribution point for terminal cables from a mainframe. These cluster controllers usually have a single link to a high-speed mainframe connection and will split, or *multiplex*, the signal into the separate signals required by each terminal (or PC emulating one) attached to the cluster.

LOCAL-AREA NETWORKS

Local-area networks are basically a collection of PCs connected in such a way that they can share resources. On a network, each PC is considered a *workstation*. There are two types of workstations on a network: *servers* and *users*. Servers are PCs whose resources can be used by anyone on the network. These resources may include hardware, such as printers, disks, plotters, scanners, and modems. Equally important, network resources usually include files that can be shared by some or all of the PCs on the network. The network software ensures orderly access to these shared resources. Precisely what resources can be shared depends on the functions built into the network software.

It is possible for one computer to be both a server and a user. For example, one user's PC may be connected to a printer, which is shared via the network. When a single PC provides resources to the network and is also used by an individual, it is called a *nondedicated* server. Workstations that are exclusively servers or users are called *dedicated* workstations.

It is possible to link one LAN to another, or to a mainframe or minicomputer. To do so, you should have a dedicated server known as a *gateway*. The advantage of a gateway is that it can link two or more LANs of different types with different features.

A full-scale network requires rather extensive investment in both hardware and software. A *network card* must be installed in each PC and these cards must be connected to one another by means of special wiring. In addition, network software must be installed to run the network. Finally, if you want the network to give various users access to certain types of data files and programs, you may have to replace some of your software with versions of the same programs that are especially designed to be used on a network.

If you need to link a few computers and want to minimize the cost, you can probably use a network that handles all connections by means of serial ports. A serial port is standard equipment on ATs, 386 PCs, and most PC/XT clones. In addition, one is included on most of the popular memory-expansion boards. Thus, a network of this type requires nothing more than some serial cables and the network software. Of course, its functions are more limited than those of a hardware network. One such network is EasyLAN, which will be presented in a scenario in Chapter 14.

LANS will be further discussed later in this chapter, where we will offer some insights into what you can do with one so you can decide whether you really want one. In Chapter 14, we'll give you some guidelines for using the LAN safely and effectively.

SHARING PERIPHERALS

Although you can use a LAN for sharing peripherals, you often require little more than some extra wires and an A-B switch. Sharing peripherals can mean plugging a wire from a printer to a PC, then printing the job, unplugging the wire, and connecting it to a different PC. Of course, this is much easier with an A-B switch and some sort of agreement as to who gets to throw the switch.

There are many sophisticated devices in the marketplace that incorporate printer destination control, buffering, priority management, and print queue control. Even with all of this sophistication, they are still based on the A-B switch theory, and they are certainly not LANs. Peripheral sharing need not be limited to printers. Modems and plotters can also be shared, but they require more sophisticated equipment.

WAYS OF SHARING PROGRAMS AND DATA

Depending on what you need to accomplish, you can establish communications among PCs with systems that are much simpler than LANS. In this section, we'll look at these simple methods of connectivity: electronic mail, remote bulletin board systems, direct connections, and walking. But first we'll discuss multiuser systems.

Multiuser Systems

Multiuser systems generally allow several users to have all the features of a PC and some features of a LAN without even using a PC. Instead of a PC, each user has a dumb terminal, which is connected to a multiuser *host* by way of serial ports and serial cables. The host computer is ideally a high-performance AT or clone, or a 386 PC.

Multiuser systems are a safe means of allowing a small group of people to share data and peripherals. As an alternative to a single-processor host system, some manufacturers—such as Alloy Systems—offer a multiprocessor system where the host actually contains several identical processor boards. In effect, the host contains a series of PCs on boards, and the monitor and keyboard are attached using some very long wires. This means that the data can be shared and each user doesn't have to worry about disks or printers, because these are all attached to the host.

To run a multiuser system, you need a multiuser, multitasking operating system. Both UNIX and Concurrent DOS, which were discussed in Chapter 10, include multiuser capabilities. Perhaps the most inexpensive way to set up a multiuser system is to use a 386 PC running Concurrent DOS 386 as a host. This operating system is available in three-user and eight-user versions, and it can run virtually all software written for DOS. You need to link the host to a series of dumb terminals that include PC terminal emulation. We haven't seen it, but the Wyse 60 has been highly recommended to us for the purpose.

Electronic Mail

Electronic mail, often called *E-Mail,* is a general term for a system in which messages can be sent and received. It emulates the Postal Service in many particulars, except that the "mail" takes the form of electronic files, rather than paper. (As with regular mail, your missives can sometimes be misdirected, or disappear entirely.) E-Mail is frequently included in a LAN or multiuser system as an information service for users. It is an excellent way of passing around documents, ideas, reminders, and messages within a work group. E-Mail may also be part of a mainframe computer, a bulletin board, or any other means of electronic communication.

You can use E-Mail to send general bulletins to everyone on a LAN or to selected groups of users. If you send some documents to a server for storage or printing, the server can send an E-Mail note to let you know that the operation was successful or that the output has been printed. On a multiuser system, E-Mail is one of the few ways to communicate with another user through the system.

You can implement electronic mail without a network. If you have a multitasking setup, such as those described in Chapter 10, you can run a telecommunications program in *host mode* in the background. Then it will always be ready to receive electronic messages. Alternatively, some telecommunications programs, such as the telecommunications module in HomeBase or the one in Windows, can also run in the background.

Remote Bulletin Board Systems

You have already seen remote bulletin board systems, or RBBSs, mentioned in this book as a source of public-domain and shareware programs. However, RBBSs have many other uses. They are often used in companies or by special interest groups to collect and store messages, data, and programs. A PC makes an ideal RBBS host. All you really need is some form of RBBS software, a modem, and a connection to a telephone line. The software can be anything from the host mode of a telecommunications package such as ProComm, or a dedicated host program such as Mini-Host (a shareware product) to a complete, dedicated bulletin board system.

The latter normally includes a system for routing messages to various users, an area for file storage, a number of file-transfer systems, and a chat mode, or *terminal mode,* in which remote users can enter messages to one another at the keyboard.

If your company has a large outside sales force, you may find an RBBS especially useful. Each salesperson would have a portable computer with a modem. They could then call in daily to collect and leave messages, send in current orders, receive lists of clients to contact, submit spreadsheets of current sales figures, and so on. One great advantage of such a system is that it eliminates telephone tag. Anyone with access to the system can leave a message for anyone else. The message can be picked up, and a reply left, at everyone's convenience. We'll provide an extensive example of this in Chapter 13.

Direct Connections

Sometimes you need to share information with a variety of other computer users on an irregular basis. In these circumstances, the easiest solution is direct telecommunications. If you and those with whom you need to communicate have modems and telecommunications software, you can send files to one another by way of the telephone system. You can either make a voice call and arrange a time to make the transfer, or leave one computer running its telecommunications program in host mode, and let the other party transfer files at their convenience. Indeed, we could not have collaborated on this book, living over thirty miles apart, without transferring files to each other several times a week.

Walking

With all these ways of transferring data, it's easy to lose track of what you are really trying to achieve. If you want to transfer files to another user, it is often easiest to copy them to a diskette, walk down the hall, and hand over the diskette. This is often referred to as "CheapestNet," "WalkNet," or even "AdidasNet."

WHEN IS A LOCAL-AREA NETWORK APPROPRIATE?

As you have just seen, there are many ways of sharing data among users, at various levels of cost and complexity. You should consider carefully whether the time, effort, and expense involved in setting up a network is worthwhile for your purposes. There are many good reasons for *not* buying a network. Here are a few:

▲ You only have one PC with nobody to connect to.

▲ You have all the programs you need on your own computer, with all the peripherals you need attached to it, and you rarely need to share data with others.

▲ You need to share data so rarely that it's easier to use a modem or carry a diskette.

▲ You have a moderate amount of data to share but for security reasons you need to keep it physically locked up.

▲ You need to share data with other groups but you can't decide who will pay for a network.

▲ You can't spare anyone to manage the network.

▲ You want to do all of your company's data processing and storage handling on one machine. If so, you need a mini or a mainframe computer, not a network.

▲ Your work area is set up so that it is physically impossible to run any type of cabling between the workstations.

On the other hand, there are circumstances in which a LAN may be the ideal solution to a communications problem, or a way to boost productivity and lower costs. In the following circumstances you might find a LAN especially useful:

▲ You and several other PC users in your company or work group need frequent access to the same data.

▲ A large number of PC users in your unit need to use the same expensive software. It might save you a great deal of money to buy one network copy of the software, with appropriate licenses, rather than multiple copies of the individual version.

▲ Several users need access to expensive peripherals, such as laser printers, scanners, or optical storage devices.

▲ You need access to high-speed modems. In a large work group, it may be cheaper to install one or two such modems on a server than to install a modem and the requisite extra phone line for each PC.

▲ You need to maintain centralized control of data, to control access to certain files, and to ensure regular backups.

▲ Several LANs are already in use in your company, and you want your unit to be able to share resources with them.

▲ You want electronic mail facilities.

There are four distinct facilities that a network can provide:

▲ Shared data and disks

▲ Shared printers

▲ Access to other networks and larger computers via bridges and gateways

▲ Message services or E-Mail

Let's look at these facilities in detail.

Sharing Data and Disks

By sharing disks, we mean allowing several users simultaneous access to one physical disk storage device. Data can be shared on tapes, diskettes, and optical disks, as well as on hard disks. When hard disks were expensive, sharing them was one of the main reasons for installing a LAN. However, with the dramatic drop in prices for hard disks, this is no longer a good reason to buy a LAN.

When a disk is shared, several users can access the same data files. A typical example is when several people enter data into a large database file. Keeping the file on a shared disk ensures that the data is always current, and prevents the confusion that can ensue when several different updates of the database are floating around in different parts of the company. As a rule, a network includes some means of carefully controlling access to each file as well as to certain data elements. (See Chapter 7 for ways in which data can be protected.)

Networks are not always the most appropriate means for users to share data, however. If many users need access to the same file at once, or if the files are extremely large, it may be more efficient to place the files on a mini or mainframe system and provide access by way of a network cluster.

Sharing Printers

Networks are quite efficient for getting maximum use from expensive peripherals. However, if all you need to share is a single printer, there are devices for just this purpose. Usually, these are intelligent buffers with a series of ports to which you can attach several computers. They range from a simple A-B switch to intelligent multiway switches that allow spooling and multiple copies, and they can actually be controlled from the PC. Some of them allow access to more than one printer.

Bridges and Gateways

If several people in a work group need access to a mainframe, you can often arrange this by including a *gateway*, or *synchronous support server*. A gateway on the LAN can optimize access to the host and, in some cases, lower the cost. This works best when the need for access to the host is limited. A typical gateway is illustrated in Figure 11.1.

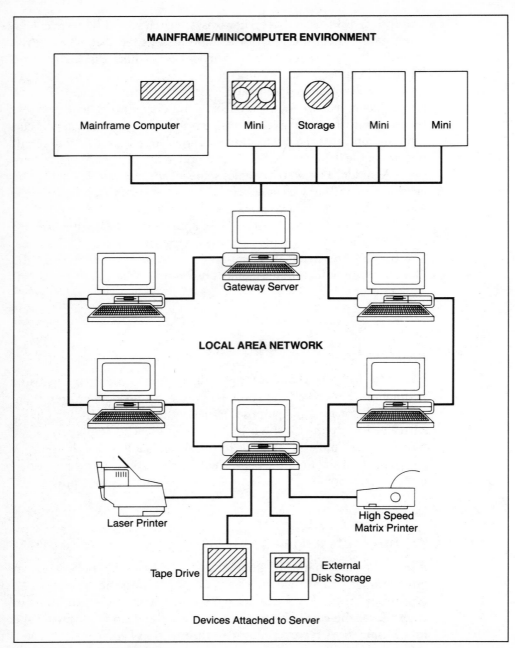

Figure 11.1 ▲ *A Network Gateway.*

If some workstations require very heavy access to the host, it can be far easier and less expensive to provide that access directly from the workstations using IBM 3274 controllers and SNA (synchronous network adaptor) cards.

If there are several LANs already in use in your organization, you might find it useful to link up with one or more of them. To do so, you use a *bridge*. This is a special type of server with two network cards, one for each of the networks it links.

A bridge maintains integrity of the data between the two LANs. In effect, with a bridge in place, two LANs become one. Figure 11.2 shows how two seperate networks use a bridge. Making this work properly requires specialized bridge software installed on each computer in both networks. With a bridge in place, workstations in either LAN can use devices attached to either server.

Network bridges have many uses. First, a bridge can effectively connect two distinct work groups. Second, it is one way to construct a *fault-tolerant system*, which maintains two copies of the files used by the network at all times. If one server fails, the files are still available on the other server, and the second server can take on the first one's work load until the first is repaired. Third, a bridge can link two networks with different topologies. For example, a bridge could be used to connect a token-ring LAN to a bus-based LAN. (These types of LANs are discussed later in this chapter.)

One unfortunate drawback to most bridges is that the workstation used to provide the bridge generally must be dedicated to that task and cannot be a user workstation also. You can use several bridges to connect as many LANs as are practical, as long as their network operating systems are compatible.

 Warning: Don't assume that you will be able to use E-Mail to send messages to users on a network that is linked to your own via a bridge. Unless both networks use the same operating system, their E-Mail systems will probably be incompatible.

The disadvantages of bridges in a multiple LAN environment usually revolve around coordination, control, and ownership of the bridge. We will discuss these organizational aspects later in this chapter.

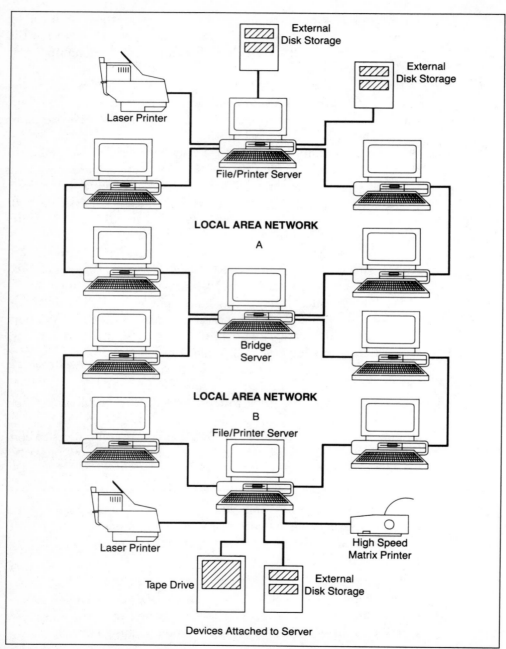

External
Disk Storage

External
Disk Storage

Laser Printer

File/Printer Server

LOCAL AREA NETWORK

A

Bridge
Server

LOCAL AREA NETWORK

B

File/Printer Server

Laser Printer

High Speed
Matrix Printer

Tape Drive

External
Disk Storage

Devices Attached to Server

Figure 11.2 ▲ *A Network Bridge.*

Messages and E-Mail

One of the features included in most networks is an E-Mail system. Every user on the network has a special network name. The network includes a place to store messages—usually on the main file server—where there is a "mailbox" for every name on the network roster. E-Mail systems vary in what they can deliver—from simple formatted messages to sophisticated file and documentation tracking systems. At the very least, one user can send a message to another on the same network.

E-Mail has many characteristics in common with regular mail. Registered E-Mail includes a request for acknowledgment that a message has been received. You can have mail returned to you if it didn't get to its destination. You can do bulk mailing by requesting that a copy of a message be sent to everyone on the network. You can also receive junk mail, of course.

Passing messages on a LAN is of limited value by itself. However, when the E-Mail system allows text formatting, time scheduling, attaching files to cover letters, storing documents, and tracking, it becomes a useful service for an office of almost any size.

Messaging is particularly useful on a larger LAN, where the LAN adminstrator can post warnings before performing system maintenance or reports on the status of shared files. E-Mail is also useful for getting information to the LAN administrator, or to others in your work group with whom you share data. You can, for example, post a message when you are about to open a file for your exclusive use, letting your group know when you will be finished with it. Then they won't try to access the file in circumstances that are sure to generate an error message.

NETWORK STRUCTURE

There are many types of networks, each using different combinations of hardware and software, and they can be structured in a variety of ways. The network's structure, or layout, is often called its topology, where each workstation is a *node* on the topographical map of the network.

Figure 11.3 shows a typical local-area network with six workstations. One of the workstations is the server. It allows workers at the other

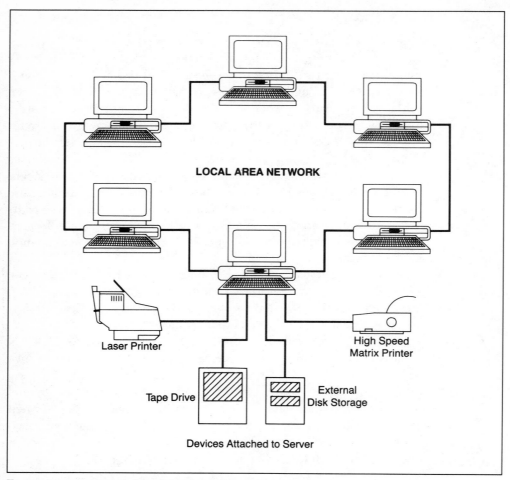

LOCAL AREA NETWORK

Laser Printer

High Speed
Matrix Printer

Tape Drive

External
Disk Storage

Devices Attached to Server

Figure 11.3 ▲ *A Typical Small Local-Area Network.*

workstations to use its attached devices; it might be dedicated or it might also be a user workstation.

There is no typical size for a LAN. They can range from two to a hundred or more workstations, with anywhere from one to ten servers. Most small LANs will use one machine as a server for files and peripherals. Larger setups may have several file servers, a print server, a modem server, and a host (usually mainframe) gateway server. Other servers may handle requests for use of specialized peripherals.

In this section we'll present various types of network topology, and we'll discuss their relative strengths and weaknesses. The major types are star, bus, and ring, and they are all popular. There are many versions of each available, and the differing versions don't generally talk to each other effectively. But first we'll look at the two types of cabling available.

Types of Network Cabling

All LANs are connected by some sort of wiring. There are two major categories of wiring: baseband and broadband. Twisted pair is a common type of baseband wiring; filter optic is a type of broadband wiring. In most cases, the wiring is used exclusively by the LAN. This type of wiring is called *baseband*. Its configuration is shown in Figure 11.4.

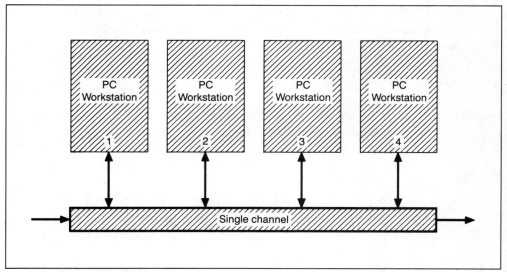

Figure 11.4 ▲ *Baseband Configuration.*

The other type of LAN wiring scheme can use existing wiring. This multiple-signal type is called *broadband*. Its configuration appears in Figure 11.5. In this configuration, many signals can be carried at different frequencies along the same piece of wire. Figure 11.5 shows two separate networks and cable television signals all carried on the same piece of wire. Broadband works because each signal is carried at a different frequency, which effectively keeps the signals apart.

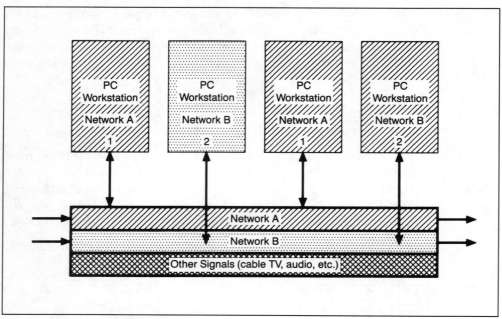

Figure 11.5 ▲ *Broadband Configuration.*

The advantages of using baseband wiring are that you can use long cables, and you often don't need to boost the signal. It's also faster than broadband, because the adapter card doesn't have to work as hard to decode the signal. The drawback is that you can't use the wiring for something else as well.

Broadband is a general-purpose network carrier. However, you can't use it as effectively when the computers to be linked are far apart, because other signals on the cable can introduce harmonics into the data signal and cause errors.

If you plan to install a LAN in an environment that does not already have cabling in place, you should consider whether you want to provide any auxiliary services, such as closed-circuit TV, or audio. If so, you may want a broadband system. If you need to install only a single network, you are better off with a baseband system because it is faster and more reliable.

LAN Topologies

LANs come in three basic topologies: ring, bus, and star. The ring style is based on what is called the Zurich Ring. It was invented in a communications laboratory in Zurich, Switzerland in the 1970s. In a ring configuration, all workstations are linked in a closed ring. One important aspect of the ring design is that the failure of one unit must not halt the operation of the rest of the ring. Figure 11.6 illustrates a ring network.

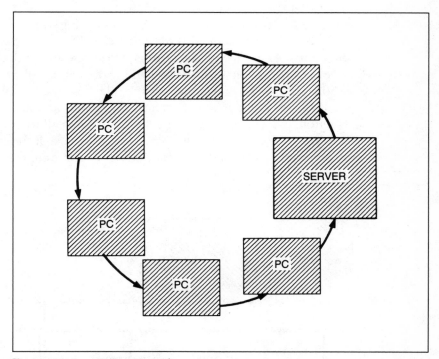

Figure 11.6 ▲ *A Ring Network.*

Here is how a ring network might operate. Let's say you want to use a file that is on the network file server. You log onto that drive, and enter the command that opens the file. DOS first processes your request to see if the drive is one of those in your own computer. If not, it passes the request to the network. That request then passes on to each workstation in the ring. Eventually, the server receives the request and either sends the data (attached to routing information) or sends back a message that the file is unavailable.

The routing information contains the address of the requester. It is usually attached to the data, forming what is known as a *packet*. On the way back, every intervening node gets to peek at the address of the packet and pass it on until the workstation that requested the data receives the packet and reads in the data. Assuming all this works, the receiving workstation sends an acknowledgment to the server inform-ing it that the transfer was successful.

The bus network has a linear rather than a ring structure. It is simply a signal cable with many workstations "teed" off the main cable at vari-ous points. The cable is usually grounded at one end or the other. This type of network usually uses baseband wiring, and is illustrated in Fig-ure 11.7. 3COM is one of the more popular bus-based LANs. It is espe-cially easy to install in circumstances where you can trace a continuous line from one workstation to the next, including all the workstations.

A bus network is especially vulnerable to damage. If the cable breaks, all workstations beyond the break will be cut off from the network, or

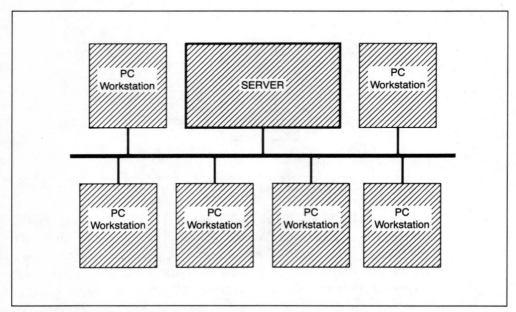

Figure 11.7 ▲ *A Bus Network.*

the whole network may shut down. Also, if someone disconnects the T connector from their computer, the network will shut down.

The star network is one in which many terminals are connected to the server either directly or through some form of multiplexing equipment. Each node on a star network radiates out from the server, as you can see in Figure 11.8. The advantage of a star network is that if someone damages the wiring running to one workstation—say, by running a chair over the cable—the rest of the network is not affected. The principal disadvantage of this type of network is that the cabling is messy at best. The Fox Research 10 net is a good example of a star LAN.

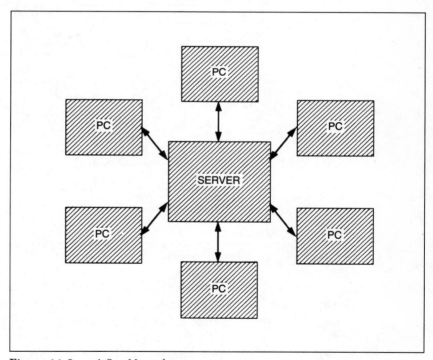

Figure 11.8 ▲ *A Star Network.*

IBM uses token-ring topology for one of its most popular networks. However, its appearance is more like a star because all nodes radiate from a hub called a multistation access unit (MAU) as illustrated in Figure 11.9. You might think of a token ring as a system in which the network has a single messenger (called a *token*), which can carry only one message at a time. This does not tend to be a problem because the token passes around the network several million times a second. If the token is free—i.e., not currently carrying any data—it will accept the next request for network access that it encounters. If it is carrying data, it will accept no requests until it first delivers the data it is carrying and then carries an acknowledgment back to the sender.

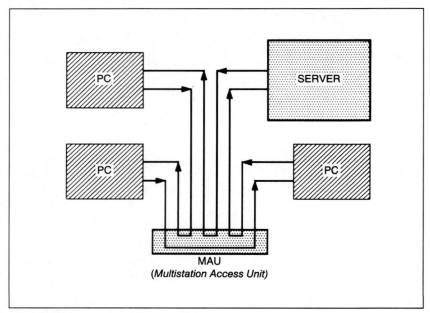

Figure 11.9 ▲ *A Token-Ring Network.*

The way IBM has implemented the token ring includes some clever ways of protecting the ring from internal damage. This is shown in Figure 11.10, where a break is detected in the ring itself. The token ring will loop back on itself if there is a break in the main cable. If one of the workstations is disabled, the relay will close in the multistation access unit causing the ring to bypass the broken circuit.

A LAN Checklist

Here are some criteria to use in selecting a LAN:

1. *Functionality:* One of the most important aspects of a LAN is resource sharing. Most LANs can share most, but not all,

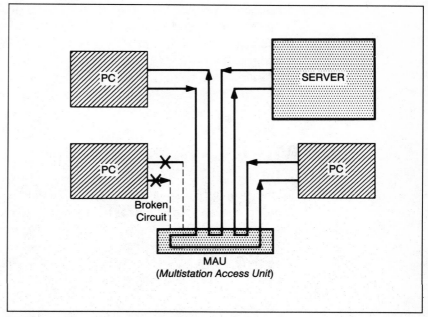

Figure 11.10 ▲ *IBM Token-Ring Network Fault Recovery.*

resources. For example, a typical LAN may be able to share data and peripheral devices such as printers, but may be unable to support input devices such as cameras, digitizers, and scanners.

2. *Security:* Security, or lack thereof, may be the downfall of many networks. Can users be locked out from files, directories, or entire systems? Are passwords effective?

3. *Operating system support:* Does the network you are considering require DOS 3.3 or will it work with earlier versions? Will the supplier support future releases of DOS?

4. *PC brands supported:* Does the network operate with only one brand of hardware? Does it work with a large number of application programs?

5. *Standards adhered to:* Standards often referred to include ISO (for network format), IEEE (for electrical specifications), and NET-BIOS (for IBM compatability).

6. *Simplicity:* If a network isn't simple to use, the trouble of getting it up and running may outweigh the benefits of having it in the first place. One major computer company's network advertising raised the question, "Is it worth the work to change the way you work when you think the way you work works just fine?" Of course, the advertiser thought so, but it may not be.

LAN SOFTWARE

We have already discussed the wide variety of LAN hardware alternatives and their strengths and weaknesses, but software has just as much effect on how the network performs as the hardware components. After all, the hardware simply provides the physical connection.

There are two types of network software to consider: network operating systems (NOS) and network-specific versions of application software. The NOS should tie in closely with the native operating system of the computers on the network.

The NETBIOS Standard

First of all, let us describe what NETBIOS is not; it is not a wiring scheme, nor a network card type, nor even some sort of chip. NETBIOS is a set of protocols that acts as a "glue" to allow a network operating system to use a particular type of network card and wiring scheme.

NETBIOS is a Microsoft product. It is an acronym for NETwork Basic Input/Output System. Having NETBIOS compatibility does not mean you can hook a token-ring card to a 3COM card. What it does mean is that you can run a program that uses NETBIOS on both the 3COM and token-ring networks.

Because NETBIOS is a published set of protocols, other manufacturers can implement their own NETBIOS support for different types of networks. IBM provides NETBIOS support for both their PC Network and Token-Ring products. How the NETBIOS support is provided is either by a ROM chip on the board itself or as a set of device drivers. The original PC Network offered NETBIOS in ROM on the adaptor card. For IBM's Token-Ring, NETBIOS is offered as either two device drivers, NETBEUI and TOKREUI (for DOS 3.2 and earlier), or as the LAN Support Program (for DOS 3.3 and higher).

Application programs such as dBASE III PLUS and Paradox 2.0 have been released in networking versions based on the NETBIOS protocol. This has helped to make NETBIOS a de facto standard. We expect more application programs will be written that can take full advantage of it.

NETBIOS is becoming accepted as a hardware standard as well. Most leading network suppliers, such as 3COM, Banyan, AT&T, and Novell use the NETBIOS standard. It would therefore be wise to adopt the NETBIOS interface, and to choose a LAN that supports it. This will ensure that the LAN will be compatible with the your current software and with products released in the near future.

Novell NetWare

One of the leading suppliers of network operating system software is Novell. Novell's NetWare can work with a wide variety of network adapter cards. With NetWare, you can use hardware cards from 3COM, IBM, Ungermann Bass, AT&T, and many others.

Different network operating systems interact differently with DOS, especially in how they handle disk space on the file server. Novell sets aside disk space on the server by creating what look like multimegabyte files to DOS. The users "attach" the server, and Netware then apportions pieces of these huge files to look like virtual disks to the user workstations. This approach has its drawbacks. For example, suppose only one small file within the network disk space is modified in a given day. Since the entire multimegabyte area looks to DOS like a single file, you must back up the entire area when you back up the server's hard disk, even though only a small portion of it has actually been modified.

In contrast, the IBM LAN program links directly to DOS so that actual DOS disk space is allocated. This approach is neater. However, it works only with specific versions of DOS, whereas Novell NetWare works with a broad range of DOS versions.

TOPS

TOPS is a network operating system that uses communications hardware built into the Apple Macintosh series of computers. The hardware is called Appletalk. Appletalk is designed to be very simple to use. For example, plug an Appletalk cable into some Macintoshes and an Apple Laserwriter printer, and you have an operational Appletalk network. Appletalk is really designed for sharing printers and other peripherals. TOPS, however, extends the capabilities of Appletalk to include sharing files. It can also be used to connect PCs to the Macintosh world, as Figure 11.11 shows. With a TOPS card for the PC and appropriate software, you can easily transfer files between systems.

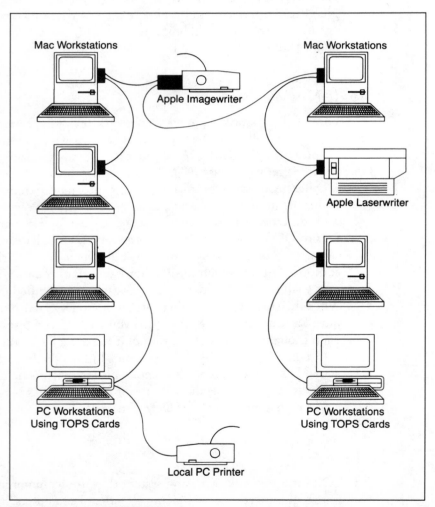

Figure 11.11 ▲ *A TOPS Network.*

If you are planning a network to include both MS-DOS and Macintosh computers but have not yet purchased the hardware, look into Radio Shack's Tandy PCs. Most of these have a built-in Appletalk connector, which greatly simplifies making connections.

INTRODUCTION TO SERIAL COMMUNICATIONS

W HEN YOU USE YOUR COMPUTER to communicate with other computers, the process is called *telecommunications*. Through telecommunications you can send information to computers anywhere in the world, and you can capture and store information you receive from them. You can also receive information from *services*, such as Dow Jones News/Retrieval, CompuServe, or The Source, and you can establish a direct connection with a computer on an adjacent desk.

In this chapter and the next, we'll introduce you to basic telecommunications processes and terms, and give you a perspective on its variety of uses. Telecommunications is a special application of serial communications, a term that will be explained shortly. You use serial communications when you send data to a plotter connected to your computer. If you have a serial printer or a serial mouse, you use serial communications when employing those devices as well. However, in this chapter, we will present serial communications as a prelude to telecommunications.

Before you begin, be forewarned that telecommunications is the least standardized function in the nonstandardized world of computers. To use telecommunications you need patience, dogged persistence, and a willingness to experiment. If you think Murphy watches over your computer enforcing his Law, you haven't seen anything until you've tried telecommunicating.

When you want two computers to talk to each other, there are a great many aspects of the process that you must attend to. The computers must be matched carefully in a number of respects before any communication can take place. In addition, there are many different types of telecommunications equipment and many different brands of each type. Every one of them has quirks that can disrupt the smooth flow of data communications if they have not been set up properly—or sometimes even if they have. The various computer programs that make telecommunications possible also have peculiarities, which complicates matters further.

Hint: If you know anyone who has already succeeded with the telecommunications feat you are attempting, you can save yourself hours of frustration by enlisting their help.

SERIAL COMMUNICATIONS BASICS

Telecommunications is a subset of the broader field of *serial communications*. It is this fact that accounts for its peculiar jargon, so different from Computerspeak. Serial communications developed with the telegraph machine in the 19th century, and the terminology developed with it. The problem with the jargon, therefore, is not that it is new, but that it is so old we have no reference points for it. (For an excellent treatment of the history of serial communications, including the development of the ASCII standard from the basics of telegraphy, see Joe Campbell's *C Programmer's Guide to Serial Communications* [Howard W. Sams & Co., 1987].)

Let's begin with a bit of theory. Normally, your computer represents data in the form of *bytes*—eight-place binary numbers. Each of the places in a byte is called a *bit*. Depending on your equipment, data flows among the parts of your computer one, two, or four bytes (8, 16, or 32 bits) at a time. This flow occurs along a type of channel called a *bus*. A bus is a set of parallel electrical paths, one for each bit. The type of bus your computer uses determines how many bytes can move at once.

In serial communications, however, there are only two electrical paths, one outgoing and the other incoming. This is an outgrowth of telegraph and telephone technology. Telephones, in fact, still use a two-wire technology.

Because communications between computers (with a very few exceptions) uses serial technology, the eight bits in a byte must be separated from one another and sent one at a time. Now, a bit can have only two possible values—0 or 1. Thus, in a series of bits, one bit looks rather like any other. When you send a stream of bits out of your computer, whatever receives them must have some way of organizing them back into bytes. Taking care of this translation is the job of the assorted paraphernalia and software associated with telecommunications. Let's examine the hardware and its functions first.

THE HARDWARE

Before any PC can communicate with another computer, both computers must have certain items of hardware. What hardware you need depends on several factors.

First, you can connect computers that are near each other by wiring them together directly. Second, if your office has a data-line facility built into its phone system, you can wire one computer to another by connecting to a serial port on the telephone. (Some systems made by Roelm and AT&T include this feature, which is called a data-switch.) Third, and most common, is to link with another computer by means of standard telephone lines.

The first two types of connection require a *serial communications port* and an *RS-232 cable*. The third requires a *modem*. Modems come in two varieties: internal cards that you install in your computer like any other expansion card, or external, self-contained units. If you have an external modem, you also need a serial port and an RS-232 cable. Let's examine these types of hardware and what they do.

The Serial Port

The serial port is the physical connection through which a computer communicates with the outside world. A serial port is *not* standard equipment on the IBM PC, although ATs, 386 PCs, and most compatibles do have one. To acquire one, you must purchase a *serial board*. IBM sells a serial board called the IBM Asynchronous Communications Adapter. However, if you have a memory-expansion board in your computer, it probably includes a serial port. The standard serial port for PC-class computers is a 25-pin, trapezoidal connector called a DB-25. ATs and 386 PCs use a 9-pin connector called a DB-9.

Unfortunately, there is very little that is standard about these thingies. IBM's DB-25 is male—that is, it has pins instead of holes. This distinguishes it from IBM's usual parallel printer port, which is female, but otherwise looks just like the serial port. Some clones have female serial ports. To add further to the confusion, the DB-9 looks just like a monitor port for anything but a VGA-class monitor.

So how do you know if you have a serial port? Most diagnostics programs (such as The Norton Utilities SI program) will tell you how many serial ports are installed in your computer. If you already have a parallel printer and monitor attached to your computer, and there is a vacant port of the type appropriate for your class of computer, it's probably a serial port.

The serial port is attached to the circuitry needed to convert parallel (8-bit) data into serial (single-bit) data. The circuitry performs this conversion before it sends the data out through the port.

The RS-232 Interface

The serial port is connected to the outside world by means of an *RS-232 cable*. RS-232 refers to a standard established by the Engineering Department of the Electronics Industries Association. It concerns the proper way of connecting *data terminal equipment* (such as your computer) to *data communications equipment* (such as your modem). These terms are conventionally abbreviated as DTE and DCE.

Now, you may have noticed that serial communication requires two wires, and serial ports have room for either 9 or 25. Perhaps you're beginning to get a clue as to why serial communication is such a potential quagmire. You need some of those other wires as well, for things like telling your modem to answer the phone, determining whether a connection is in progress, telling your modem that you are ready to send data, and other such chores. A full discussion of RS-232 interfacing is beyond the scope of this book. See *The RS-232 Solution*, by Joe Campbell (SYBEX, 1984) or *Mastering Serial Communications*, by Peter W. Gofton (SYBEX, 1986) for complete details.

In any case, to connect your serial port to anything else, you need a cable conforming to the RS-232 standard. It must have a connector on one end of the same type as your serial port (i.e., DB-25 or DB-9), but the opposite sex. The other end of the cable must have a connector appropriate to what you want to connect it to.

The details of internal wiring will differ depending on your purpose. To connect your computer to a modem, you generally need a "straight-through" cable—one on which the pins or sockets at one end are wired directly to the corresponding pins or sockets at the other. (The pins and sockets are numbered on the connector, but you may need a magnifying glass to read the numbers.) The only pins that carry data are pins 2 and 3. Pin 2 transmits data from the computer, and pin 3 receives data. Thus, if you are connecting the serial port of your computer directly to a serial port on another computer, you will need a cable in which pin 2 at one end is wired to pin 3 at the other, and vice versa. This is commonly referred to as having "pins 2 and 3 crossed."

It is possible to buy a crossed-pin serial cable with both a DB-9 and a DB-25 at each end. If you don't know what you'll be getting yourself into, you may find such a cable useful. You can also buy a cable with both male and female connectors at one end.

If you have a cable with a connector of the wrong sex at one end, you can use a sex-changer to complete the connection. A sex-changer is simply a small block or short cable connecting two DB-25s or DB-9s of the same sex, wired straight through.

If you have a straight-through cable, and you need to connect to another computer, you can add a *null modem* to the circuit. This is a device that looks superficially like a sex-changer. However, it has pins 2 and 3 crossed, and its connectors are of the same sex.

Warning: Sometimes you can end up with a mess of these little doo-hickeys strung together. You then run a serious risk of having the connection fall apart (physically) in the middle of a transmission. Feh! Maybe you need a new cable.

Hint: If all else fails, there's a mysterious device called a SmartCable, made by IQ Technologies. It has male and female DB-25s at one end, and a DB-25 attached to a box containing lights and switches at the other. The directions are printed right on the box. You just fiddle with the switches (following the directions) until certain lights come on, and you have a connection. It can be a godsend if you don't know what you're doing. Sometimes, even if you do.

The Modem

If you want to communicate with a computer that is more than a few feet away, you will also need a *modem*. A modem is a device that links a computer to a telephone line. The term is a contraction of *modulator-demodulator*, terms that describe the modem's principal functions: translating the digital information that arrives at the serial port into sound frequencies that can be transmitted by telephone, and converting arriving sound frequencies back into the digital information that the computer can understand.

Modems vary greatly. Some are boards that plug directly into slots in the computer. While they don't clutter up your desk, and don't require interfacing, they also usurp some of the computer's expansion room.

Free-standing modems come in two basic types: *acoustic couplers*, on which the telephone's handset is rested during transmission, and *direct-connect* modems, which are wired directly into the telephone lines. The latter generally transmit information more accurately than the former, because room noises cannot leak in and distort the signal. To connect a free-standing modem, you need a serial port and an RS-232 cable.

Free-standing modems have two notable advantages. First, they can be used with any computer that has a serial port conforming to the RS-232 standard. Second, they usually have a set of indicator lights on the front panel, which reflect the status of the various modem-control lines. These lights allow you to monitor the progress of a call, and help pinpoint the trouble if something goes wrong.

Either type of modem is connected to the phone lines with a standard telephone modular cable. You can either unplug your phone, or get an adapter that allows you to plug two modular plugs into the same line. Some modems have a jack into which you can plug the telephone directly. With this type of modem, you plug the modem into the wall jack and still have complete use of your telephone, except when the modem is using the line.

Another variation in modems is their top speed. At present the most common speeds are 300, 1200, and 2400 bits per second (bps), although some 9600 bps modems are now available.

Some modems are referred to as "smart." Smart modems can respond directly to commands sent to them from the computer. The smart modem was developed by Hayes Microcomputer Products, the company that owns the SmartModem trademark. Hayes established a set of commands for communicating with modems that have become an industry standard. These commands are known as the AT Command Set, because most of the commands begin with the characters AT. These characters signal the modem to pay *at*tention, because the following characters will be commands rather than data.

CONTROLLING THE FLOW OF COMMUNICATIONS

In order to engage in serial communications, your computer must know where to send the data. You must also, as noted, determine how the stream of bits is to be broken into bytes, and if you are using a modem, get the modem to behave correctly. You take care of the first point by installing your hardware correctly. The latter two are usually handled by telecommunications software. However, using DOS, you can treat your computer as a dumb terminal, format the data, and control the modem by entering commands from the AT Command Set at the keyboard.

Addressing the Port

DOS versions through 3.2 can address up to two serial ports. They are addressed by the names COM1 and COM2. (In DOS 2.X they have the names COM1: and COM2:. You can use these names with later versions of DOS, but the colon isn't necessary.) PC-DOS 3.3 can address up to four serial ports. OS/2 can address eight.

As a rule, you control the port address by the way you set up your hardware. A board with a serial port will probably have a jumper that allows you to configure it as COM1 or COM2. Some boards have software installation programs that will configure the board. Internal modems may have either switches or jumpers to select the port address. External modems take the port address of the serial port to which they are connected.

Every device attached to your computer uses a special memory channel called an *interrupt request* (IRQ) to tell the microprocessor when it needs attention. For example, IRQ0 is assigned to the internal timer, IRQ1 to the keyboard, IRQ6 to the diskettes, and IRQ7 to the printer.

By default, COM1 uses IRQ4 and COM2 uses IRQ3. On PC-class computers it is possible to use IRQ2 for a serial port. On ATs and 386 PCs that adhere to the AT architecture, you can configure one of the serial ports to use IRQ9 if the other two are in use. You can also use the third IRQ (IRQ2 or IRQ9) for COM3 if your DOS will let you address COM3. On PS/2 computers, you can have up to eight serial ports, and the hardware will automatically take care of assigning a port number and IRQ address to each.

Many boards and internal modems do not allow you to select the interrupt used by the serial port. If some other device is using the same IRQ, you must disable or disconnect one of the two devices before you can use the other. If you can change the IRQ used by a serial port, it is generally by setting a jumper on the board. If you find that you cannot access your serial port at all, you probably have more than one device using the same port address, or more than one device using the same IRQ. Consult your hardware documentation for details.

Formatting the Data

As you know, the data transmitted from the serial port is just a series of binary digits. These are transmitted as voltage levels. A modem converts the voltage levels into audible tones for transmission via phone lines, and vice versa. But to make sense of the flow of binary digits, they must be broken up into some kind of meaningful units. These units make up the *data format,* which consists of ten bits configured in any of several ways. The data format used to send the data must be the same as that used to receive it, or the result will be gibberish, also known as garbage.

The data format comprises four elements:

▲ The start bit

▲ Seven or eight data bits

▲ One or two stop bits

▲ The type of parity used

The line's "resting state" is represented by a binary 1. The *start bit* is a binary 0. It is a "wake-up" signal that tells the receiving modem to expect what follows to be data. There is always one start bit, so you don't have to set it.

The start bit is followed by either seven or eight *data bits*. Seven bits are adequate to represent numbers through decimal 127. Thus, as you will see if you examine the ASCII table in Appendix E, seven bits can represent all the normal text and control characters in the ASCII code. As a result, only seven data bits are needed to transmit text files.

In program files, in contrast, each byte is all or part of a machine-level instruction. These instructions may be represented by values from 0 to 255. It takes an additional bit to represent the numbers from 128 through 255. Therefore, program files are transmitted using eight data bits.

The data bits may be followed by a *parity bit*. Parity is a relatively simple form of error-checking. Parity may be EVEN, ODD, SPACE, or MARK. EVEN and ODD parity are based on the sum of the data bits. When EVEN parity is used, if the value of the data bits is an odd number, a 1 is placed in the parity bit to make the sum of the eight bits even. Otherwise, a 0 is placed in the parity bit. When ODD parity is used, a 1 is placed in the parity bit if the sum of the data bits is even, and a 0 is placed there if the sum of the parity bits is odd.

MARK parity always gives the parity bit a value of 1. SPACE parity always gives the parity bit a value of 0. These two forms of parity are not commonly used any more. The terms derive from early telegraph machines *marking* the dots and dashes on a strip of paper, and *spacing* between them.

With eight data bits, no parity bit is used. However, you must acknowledge this by setting parity to NONE. NO parity may also be used with seven data bits.

The end of the transmitted byte is demarcated by either one or two *stop bits*. With seven data bits and a parity other than NONE, or with eight data bits, one stop bit is used. With seven data bits and NO parity, two stop bits are used. The value of a stop bit is always a binary 1, or a return to the signal's resting state. Table 12.1 shows the valid data formats.

Establishing Communications Parameters

In addition to the data format, several other aspects of the communications process must be matched at both ends. You need to set the correct

DATA BITS	PARITY	STOP BITS
8	NONE	1
7	EVEN	1
7	ODD	1
7	NONE	2
7	MARK	1
7	SPACE	1

Table 12.1 ▲ *Acceptable Data Formats.*

transmission speed, the role of your computer as originator or answerer, and the direction of communication.

Transmission Speed   The transmission speed is measured in bits per second. Roughly, the transmission speed divided by ten will yield the number of *characters* transmitted per second. Modern modems allow transmission speeds of 110, 300, or 1200 bps. Many can also operate at 2400 bps, and some of the newer models can transmit at rates as high as 9600 bps. Matching transmission speeds is vital because it is the basis on which your machinery measures the length of a bit. Two 0 bits at 2400 bps look exactly like one 0 bit at 1200 bps. If the transmission speed at both ends does not match, garbage characters will pour onto your screen at an alarming rate.

As a rule, you should use the highest speed that both computers can handle. You may be paying long-distance rates, and some services charge for their time by the minute. The higher the rate at which you can transmit and receive data, the lower your ultimate cost of operation.

The transmission speed is often incorrectly called the *baud rate*. Baud rate, (named after J. M. E. Baudot, the inventor of the first fixed-length telecommunications code, the ancestor of ASCII) is actually the number of times a modem's signal is modulated per second. This number tends to be close to the bps rate at slow speeds. However, a high rate of bps actually represents a considerably lower baud rate.

Communication Roles   When two computers communicate, one must be designated as the source, or originator, of the communication, and the other as the answering computer. The originator is usually, quite logically, the computer that initiates the call. However, the important point is that the two computers take opposite roles. It doesn't much matter which is which, so long as they are different. When dialing up on-line services such as CompuServe, however, or logging onto electronic bulletin boards, you must set the role of your computer to Originate, because the remote service will always be set up to answer.

Direction of Communication   Data communications also involve "directionality." Data transmission can occur in one of three ways: in only one direction, in both directions at different times, or in both directions at the same time.

Transmission in only one direction is called the *simplex configuration*. It is rarely used with microcomputers. The other two configurations, *half duplex* (both directions at different times) and *full duplex* (both directions at the same time), are much more common, but most communication between microcomputers takes place in full-duplex mode.

When you type characters at your keyboard for transmission, they do not automatically appear on your screen. Rather, they go directly to the serial port. What you see on your screen is an *echo* of the characters that are received at the remote computer. This may seem a roundabout way of getting characters on your screen, but it ensures that what you send is being received. This echoing process is possible only in full-duplex mode. If you do not see characters when you type, you must change the duplex setting to full. Sometimes, you'll get a double echo—so that when you type

hello

you see

hheelllloo

on your screen. In this case, change your duplex setting to half. Some telecommunications programs allow you to turn on a *local echo*, which sends the characters you type directly to the screen, independently of the duplex setting.

Controlling the Serial Port through DOS

You can control a Hayes-compatible modem by redirecting output to the port at which it is addressed, and then entering commands from the

AT Command Set at the keyboard. If you prefer to use this cumbersome method, you must first set up the serial port using the DOS MODE command. A single MODE command sets the transmission speed and the data format. The form for the command is

MODE COM*N: BPS,parity,databits,stopbits*

where N is the logical address of the port you will be using. (In DOS 3.X, the colon is optional.) Valid transmission speeds include 110, 150, 300, 600, 1200, 2400, 4800, 9600, and 19,200. You can enter just the first two digits of the transmission speed. Parity is indicated by N for NONE, O for ODD, or E for EVEN. (The MODE command doesn't recognize MARK or SPACE parity.) Of course, you must specify either 7 or 8 data bits, and either 1 or 2 stop bits.

When configuring the serial port, you *must* enter a transmission speed. The other values have defaults of EVEN parity, 7 data bits, and 1 stop bit, except at a transmission speed of 110. At this speed the default is 2 stop bits. Thus, entering

MODE COM1 24

will configure your first serial port for 2400 bps, EVEN parity, 7 data bits, and 1 stop bit. The so-called universal data format is established by the command

MODE COM*N* 12,N,8,1

You can use default parameters by entering the commas without the parameters.

Having configured the port, there are then two ways to send data through it. If you are not using a modem, you can simply use the COPY command to send data to the port. A command of the form

COPY *FILENAME.EXT* COM*N*

will send the specified file, as a series of bytes, to the specified port.

Alternatively, you can redirect control to the serial port. The CTTY (for change *teletype*) command tells your computer to direct all input and output to the target of the command. Thus, if you enter

CTTY COM2

your computer will accept input only from the second serial port, instead of from the keyboard, and it will send all output only to the second serial port, instead of to the screen. This should make it possible to control your computer from another computer attached to the port by issuing DOS commands at that computer's keyboard. However, many programs will override DOS and refuse to accept input from a port. If you attempt to run such a program by this method, your system will lock up. Moreover, we have tried this many times, and have never had any success running a computer remotely by this method.

When you have redirected control to a port, the only way to restore control to your keyboard is to have the remote computer execute a batch file on your computer containing the command

CTTY CON

It won't work if the remote computer issues this command itself, because this will tell the remote computer to redirect output to the keyboard and screen, which presumably it's already doing.

USING TELECOMMUNICATIONS SOFTWARE

Although you can perform these operations from DOS, most people use various forms of telecommunications software for the purpose. Such programs generally allow you to set the communications parameters and data format from menus, save the settings for use with particular remote computers, and manage the session for you. A communications program can dial the phone, automatically execute the remote computer's log-on procedures, capture the text of a communications session to a file, take care of all the communications with your modem invisibly, and generally streamline procedures. Many also offer other facilities completely unavailable at the DOS level, such as providing error-checking protocols considerably more sophisticated than parity bits, and a script language that lets you automate a session.

There are many popular telecommunications programs on the market. However, one of the best is a shareware program called ProComm, from Datastorm Technologies. Since it is available from almost every bulletin board and user's group, and since many people who are serious about telecommunications prefer this program to the commercial products, we will base our examples on it.

 Warning: We are taking certain risks by using this program as our model. The documentation is written for people who already know a great deal

about telecommunications, and it includes terminology that reaches a level of obscurity considerably beyond that of this chapter. Moreover, the user interface is not entirely easy to navigate, as the main menu shown in Figure 12.1 indicates. However, the program's variety of options and degree of reliability and control make up for these deficiencies.

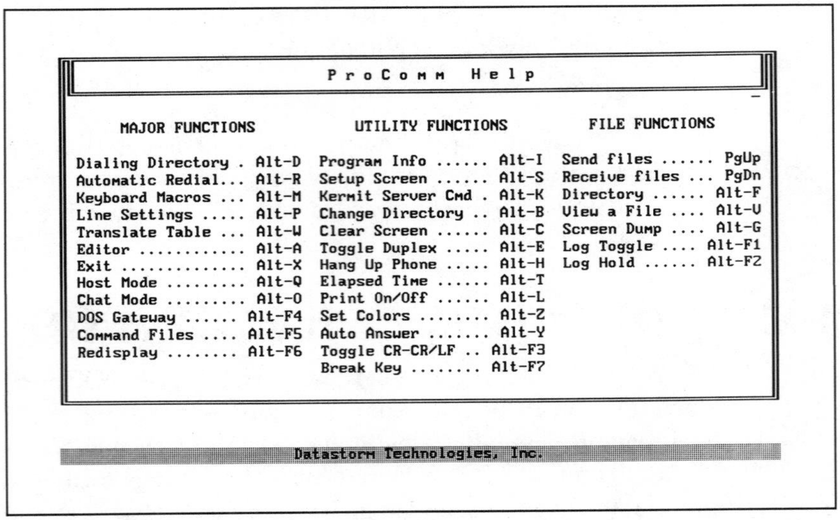

```
                          P r o C o m m   H e l p

          MAJOR FUNCTIONS        UTILITY FUNCTIONS        FILE FUNCTIONS

     Dialing Directory . Alt-D  Program Info ...... Alt-I  Send files ...... PgUp
     Automatic Redial... Alt-R  Setup Screen ...... Alt-S  Receive files ... PgDn
     Keyboard Macros ... Alt-M  Kermit Server Cmd . Alt-K  Directory ...... Alt-F
     Line Settings ..... Alt-P  Change Directory .. Alt-B  View a File .... Alt-V
     Translate Table ... Alt-W  Clear Screen ...... Alt-C  Screen Dump .... Alt-G
     Editor ............ Alt-A  Toggle Duplex ..... Alt-E  Log Toggle .... Alt-F1
     Exit .............. Alt-X  Hang Up Phone ..... Alt-H  Log Hold ...... Alt-F2
     Host Mode ......... Alt-Q  Elapsed Time ...... Alt-T
     Chat Mode ......... Alt-O  Print On/Off ...... Alt-L
     DOS Gateway ...... Alt-F4  Set Colors ........ Alt-Z
     Command Files .... Alt-F5  Auto Answer ....... Alt-Y
     Redisplay ........ Alt-F6  Toggle CR-CR/LF .. Alt-F3
                                Break Key ........ Alt-F7


                        Datastorm Technologies, Inc.
```

Figure 12.1 ▲ *The ProComm Main Menu.*

A new release of this program called ProComm Plus has recently come on the market. Like ProComm 2.4.2, you can try it before you buy it. However, the registration fee is somewhat higher. ProComm Plus includes all the features of ProComm 2.4.2. However, it has many additional features, including the following:

▲ Context-sensitive online help.

▲ Four transfer protocols in addition to ProComm's seven (which are described below), plus room to add three more as external programs.

▲ Six new terminal emulations, in addition to the original ten, including a special terminal emulation for making your computer into a dumb 3270 terminal attached to an IBM mainframe (for more on this point, see Chapter 15).

▲ A host mode that gives you direct control over who can access your computer by name. This feature makes ProComm Plus suitable for use as a BBS.

▲ A complete translation table for all 256 ASCII characters. This is useful for stripping control characters out of text files, or for translating ASCII into the code used on mainframes, as explained in Chapter 15.

▲ Room to install an editor or word processor and a file-viewing program for use without exiting ProComm Plus.

▲ Room to install two programs of your choice as pop-up utilities.

▲ Provision for up to eight serial port addresses instead of two, for compatibility with PS/2 computers. In addition, you can specify the memory address and IRQ line (up to 7) used by each port.

In addition, some of the command keys have been reassigned, and a few other changes also make the program easier to understand and use than ProComm. However, ProComm 2.4.2 will still be available on bulletin boards.

Before we go on, there are two areas that need explanation: the variety of ways you can transfer information via telecommunications, and the error-correcting protocols commonly in use.

Basic Telecommunications Modes

There are three fundamentally different ways to send and receive information through telecommunications. You can converse directly with another computer; transfer text files informally (character-by-character, without error-checking); and perform *protocol transfers*, which use error-checking routines that can be applied to all types of files. Let's see how these operations work.

Before you can engage in any of these activities, your telecommunications parameters must match those of the computer you want to link up with. When dealing with mainframes and online services, you must ensure that your computer conforms to the remote computer's standards. In connecting to another PC, you and the user of the other PC must agree on the standards you will use. You establish the match by setting the transmission speed, data format, role, and directionality, as discussed earlier.

Once you have configured your software properly for the remote computer, you can converse directly with other computer users or access the various online information services and electronic bulletin boards. In this mode, which is called *terminal* or *chat mode*, you type the information you want to send at the keyboard, and it appears almost simultaneously on the remote computer's screen. Similarly, information generated by the remote computer will appear on your screen. A great deal of recreational telecommunications consists of this type of conversation. Most telecommunications programs let you capture the text of such conversations.

But you can also capture data and upload and download text files. In ProComm, you can *capture* the contents of a single screen by pressing Alt-G. This appends the current screen to a previously designated file.

You can also open a file into which the text generated during the session will automatically be sent. In ProComm, you accomplish this by choosing ASCII from the Receive Files menu, which you activate by pressing PgDn. You may also want to configure the ASCII mode from the Setup menu, which you reach by pressing Alt-S. Capturing data in ASCII form is referred to as *downloading*.

In addition to downloading, you can also *upload* text files from your computer, and transmit them to a remote computer through terminal mode. This process is set up in ProComm by choosing ASCII from the Send Files menu, which you activate by pressing PgUp. (There is something a bit mnemonic in using PgUp for uploads and PgDn for downloads.)

In the *protocol transfer* mode, controlled by other options of the Send Files and Receive Files menus, you can send or receive any disk file, including programs. This mode of file transfer checks the transmission scrupulously for errors. It is especially appropriate for these three activities:

▲ *Transmitting and receiving word-processed text files.* The control codes used to format text in word-processing programs may also be used to control terminal communications, and they may have undesirable effects when transmitted through the terminal in ASCII mode. A protocol transfer prevents these undesirable effects from occurring.

▲ *Transmitting and receiving program code.* In a program, every character is significant, so you want to be sure that none are lost in the transfer process. Text files, in contrast, are relatively easy to reconstruct.

▲ *Transmitting and receiving heavily formatted data files such as spreadsheets or databases.* These types of files should be treated as though they were program code, because they contain a great deal of information other than text. This information can either be lost or disrupt communications if transmitted as ASCII.

Communications Protocols

Communications protocols are the routines that check the transmission for errors. They generally work by sending a block of characters at once, and then checking to see whether the block was received correctly. In contrast, when you send data as ASCII, you simply blow a series of bytes out through the serial port. The most important thing to know about communications protocols is that the sending and receiving computers must both be using the same protocol. However, they have different strengths and weaknesses, and they are used for different purposes.

ProComm offers you a choice of eight protocols, seven of which are variants on XMODEM. You choose them from the Send Files and Receive Files menus. These are the eight protocols:

▲ *XMODEM.* This is one of the most popular communications protocols. It is used on virtually all CP/M-based and DOS-based remote bulletin boards. It is part of most microcomputer telecommunications packages. Therefore, you may find it useful when communicating with other PCs, as well as with bulletin boards. XMODEM offers two types of error-checking: checksum and CRC (cyclical redundancy check). The latter is more accurate. ProComm will always check to see if the remote computer uses CRC. If so, it will use it.

▲ *MODEM7.* This is a variant of XMODEM that allows you to transfer several files at once using wild-card patterns.

▲ *YMODEM.* This is another XMODEM variant. It transfers data blocks of 1K, while data blocks in XMODEM and MODEM7 are only 128 bytes. Therefore, YMODEM is somewhat faster than XMODEM.

▲ YMODEM *batch.* This protocol allows you to transfer multiple files using the YMODEM protocol.

▲ *Telelink.* This is a protocol available mainly on FIDONET bulletin boards. It provides information about the size of the file and its date and time of creation before sending. It allows for wildcard transfers but is otherwise similar to XMODEM.

▲ *WXMODEM.* This is yet another XMODEM variant, found primarily on an online service called PeopleLink.

▲ *Kermit.* This protocol is used primarily when linking to mainframes. It has special routines for transferring files between systems using a 7-bit byte (as many mainframes do) and systems using an 8-bit byte.

▲ *CompuServe B.* This protocol is used on the CompuServe Information Service. It uses more control information than XMODEM, and therefore should be slower. However, it uses 512-byte blocks instead of 128-byte blocks. Because you must often access CompuServe via a time-sharing network, there are times when you will simply be waiting. Given these circumstances, the fact that CompuServe B uses larger blocks makes it more efficient.

There are many other protocols in use. CrossTalk and SmartCom, two popular commercial telecommunications programs, both include proprietary protocols that have an excellent reputation. However, as noted, the most important point is that both computers use the same protocol. If your telecommunications programs do not have any protocols in common, you must transfer the files as ASCII text.

You can transfer program files this way using an 8-bit data format. However, without error-checking, a few bytes can easily get mangled in transmission. If this happens, the person who receives the program file probably won't be able to use it.

A TELECOMMUNICATIONS CHECKLIST

As a summary, we present the following checklist of items that should be set before you link to another computer:

▲ Modem powered on and properly connected (if external)

- ▲ Modem switch settings
- ▲ Port address (and interrupt)
- ▲ Communications parameters (transmission speed, word length, number of stop bits, parity)
- ▲ Duplex
- ▲ Communications role
- ▲ Transfer protocol

If anything goes wrong with your telecommunications session, check these items first.

USING
TELECOMMUNICATIONS

13

I N THE PREVIOUS CHAPTER, we mentioned a variety of ways to make use of telecommunications. Now that you have learned the basics of telecommunications, we'll show you how to make it work for you.

TRANSFERRING FILES BETWEEN PCS

The most prosaic use of telecommunications is also one of the most vital: transferring files from one PC to another. There are many reasons you might want to do this. Most obviously, you might want to share a file with a friend or coworker. The simplest method of doing so is obviously WalkNet. But what if your file is too big to fit on a diskette?

You could transfer the file from your hard disk to diskettes using the BACKUP command. The BACKUP command splits files across diskettes when they are too large to fit on a single diskette. The RESTORE command then reconstructs the original file from all the diskettes. But there is a catch here. If you and your coworker don't use the same version of DOS, the structure of your backed up file may be incompatible with your coworker's RESTORE command. (This will be true if one of you uses DOS 3.3 and the other uses an earlier version.) You can't just send your RESTORE command over, either, because your coworker will get an

Incorrect DOS version

message when attempting to use it.

There are other situations too complex for WalkNet. What if your coworker's computer can't read the kind of diskettes that your computer writes? Or what if you need to transfer a dBASE II file created on a computer using CP/M to your PC, so you can convert it to a dBASE III file? Or better yet, what if your colleague uses WordStar under CP/M (some people still do) and you want to edit it on your PC in WordPerfect or Microsoft Word? You can convert the file to your word processor's format using a utility, but how do you get it onto your disk?

These are several good reasons for sending files directly from one computer to another. First, we'll talk about the least complex situation—one in which both computers are in the same room. To transfer a file in these circumstances, you need:

▲ A serial port on each computer

▲ An RS-232 cable with pins 2 and 3 crossed, or a straight-through RS-232 cable and a null modem

▲ Software that can receive data from the serial port on the receiving computer

▲ Software that can send data to the serial port on the sending computer

One great advantage of transferring data directly like this is that you can use the highest transmission speed of which your computer is normally capable—9600 or 19,200 bps. This is much faster than the highest speed most modems now on the market can handle.

Connect the serial ports using the RS-232 cables. Then configure the serial ports on the two computers to the same communications parameters. Finally, find a way to get the data to go out through the serial port of one computer and in through the serial port of the other.

At the very worst, the sending computer can redirect the file to the serial port. The receiving computer will then have to use a telecommunications program to download the incoming data as an ASCII file. If the file is a text file, or mostly a text file, and you have configured the serial ports so that their data formats match, the result should be reasonably successful.

At best, you will have telecommunications software on both computers with compatible transfer protocols. You can transfer files successfully using any telecommunications program that does not require you to have a modem online. This includes most of the popular commercial, public-domain, and shareware programs available today. The main difference between direct transfers and modem transfers (aside from the hardware involved) is that you don't have to dial a number. Once you have connected the serial ports and loaded the telecommunications programs with the appropriate parameters, the two computers will communicate directly.

To assure yourself that the computers are communicating, type a few characters on one computer's keyboard and see if they show up on the other's screen. If they don't, one of two things is probably wrong:

▲ Pin 2 on one computer's serial port is not connected to pin 3 on the other computer's serial port. Your cable may not be the correct type, or it may not be plugged in all the way. If you have a flat, ribbon cable, you can be sure that it's a straight-through cable; however, it may be damaged. Check the connectors to see that they are fully plugged in.

▲ Your communications parameters may not be the same on the two computers.

If the characters you type do not show up on your own screen, find the menu setting for Echo or Duplex and change it. Do the same if the characters show up twice. (In ProComm, Alt-E toggles between the two possible settings.)

The fact that you do not have to dial a number may mean a bit of extra work, depending on the telecommunications package you use. If your software stops sending modem commands when you tell it you have connected directly, you don't need to do anything. However, if it doesn't, you'll want to take some steps to ensure that the modem commands aren't transmitted, just to keep your screen relatively free of clutter.

If the characters you type show up once on both screens correctly, you are ready to begin.

Direct Transfers Using ProComm

Let's walk through a transfer using ProComm 2.4.2. You can follow this in ProComm Plus if you use the appropriate keystrokes to execute the steps described in the second column. We'll set you up on the sending computer first. With ProComm 2.4.2, follow these keystrokes:

Alt-P	Display the Line Settings Menu
12 Enter	Select option 12: 19,200 bps with 8 data bits
Esc	Return to the Terminal screen
PgUp	Display the Upload Menu
5 or 6	If you are sending one file, choose 5, YMODEM. If you are sending a group of files that can be specified using a wild-card pattern, choose 6, YMODEM batch.

We suggest YMODEM because it transfers large blocks of data at once. Thus, it's a bit faster than some of the alternatives. You will then be prompted with

Please enter filespec:

Type in the name of the file to send and press Return. A small status display box, such as the one shown in Figure 13.1, will report the progress of the transfer. If you have Alarm Sound set to ON in the General Setup Menu (which you reach from the Setup Menu), the computer will emit a double beep for the length of time you specify if the transfer fails, or when it it completed.

The procedure is quite similar on the receiving end. Instead of pressing PgUp for the Upload Menu, you press PgDn for the Download Menu, and select the same protocol you selected on the sending computer. You will then go directly to the transfer status window.

Transferring Files in Host Mode

You may find it more convenient to run the entire process from a single computer. To do so, use ProComm's *host mode*. You must be sure to configure the host mode appropriately for a direct-cable transfer first, however. On the receiving computer, press Alt-S to display the Setup Menu. Then follow these keystrokes:

5 Return	Select the Host Mode Setup Menu.

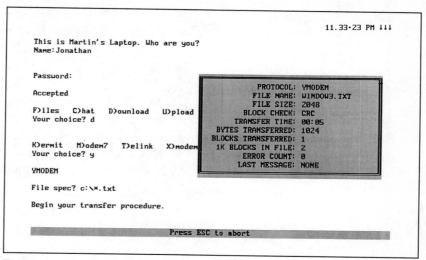

```
                                                              11.33·23 PM ↓↓↓

   This is Martin's Laptop. Who are you?
   Name: Jonathan


   Password:

   Accepted                            ┌─────────────────────────────────┐
                                       │        PROTOCOL: YMODEM          │
   F)iles   C)hat   D)ownload   U)pload│       FILE NAME: WINDOW3.TXT     │
   Your choice? d                      │       FILE SIZE: 2048            │
                                       │      BLOCK CHECK: CRC            │
                                       │    TRANSFER TIME: 00:05          │
   K)ermit   M)odem?   T)elink   X)modem│ BYTES TRANSFERRED: 1024         │
   Your choice? y                      │ BLOCKS TRANSFERRED: 1            │
                                       │ 1K BLOCKS IN FILE: 2             │
   YMODEM                              │      ERROR COUNT: 0              │
                                       │     LAST MESSAGE: NONE           │
   File spec? c:\*.txt                 └─────────────────────────────────┘

   Begin your transfer procedure.


  ▒▒▒▒▒▒▒▒▒▒▒▒▒▒▒▒▒▒▒▒▒▒▒▒  Press ESC to abort  ▒▒▒▒▒▒▒▒▒▒▒▒▒▒▒▒▒▒▒▒▒▒▒
```

Figure 13.1 ▲ *ProComm's Upload Status Window.*

2 Return Return — Select Auto Answer String, and delete it. (You do not want the host to answer the phone, because it will be receiving data directly.)

3 Return Return — Select Host Mode Password, and delete it. You don't want to have to enter a password just to access the other computer in the same room.

4 Return Return — Select DOS Shell Password and delete it. This password is normally used to prevent others from having access to DOS functions on the host computer. You may need to have access to DOS on the other computer, and it's just an extra annoying step. (*Never* leave this blank when you use host mode with a modem. Someone could easily wipe out all your files.)

5 Return — Select Auto Baud Detect. This normally adjusts the host's transmission speed to match that of the calling computer.

Space	Press the space bar to step through the alternative settings until the screen displays
	KEY HIT
	This instructs ProComm to make the adjustment on the basis of the first keystroke it receives. This is the most reliable setting to use in host mode whether you are doing director modem transfers.
6 Return Space Return	Select Connection Type, and change it from MODEM to DIRECT.
Esc	Return to the Setup Menu.
1 Return	Select the Modem Setup Menu.
1 Return Return	Delete the modem initialization string.
2 Return Return	Delete the dialing command.
9	Delete the hangup string.
Esc	Return to the Setup Menu. *Do not select Save Setup to Disk* unless you never expect to use host mode for modem connections.
Esc	Return to the terminal screen.
Alt-Q	Activate host mode.

Do not set both computers to host mode!
You must now configure the sending computer. Follow these steps:

Alt-S	Display the Setup Menu.
5 Return	Select the Host Mode Setup Menu.
6 Return Space Return	Select Connection Type, and change it from MODEM to DIRECT.
Esc	Return to the Setup Menu.
1 Return	Select the Modem Setup Menu.
1 Return Return	Delete the modem initialization string.

2 Return Return	Delete the dialing command
9	Delete the hangup string.
Esc	Return to the Setup Menu. *Do not select Save Setup to Disk.*
Esc	Return to the terminal screen.

You will use the receiving computer's host mode menus to control the receiving computer from the sending computer. As you can see in Figure 13.2, the host lets you view a directory, upload or download files, talk to the operator (which is irrelevant here), or execute DOS commands. You select Download, and then choose a transfer protocol. In the example, we've used YMODEM Batch. You then enter the file name, which may include wild-card patterns. When the host instructs you to begin your transfer procedure, you press PgDn to display the Download menu, and enter the protocol. Since the protocol is a batch protocol, you will not be asked for a file name. When you select the protocol, the progress of the transfer is reported in the transfer status window, as you saw in Figure 13.1. Figure 13.2 shows the screen after the transfer is completed.

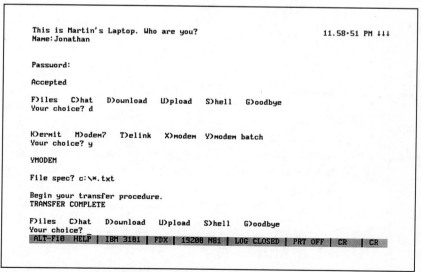

Figure 13.2 ▲ *A Completed Transfer in ProComm's Host Mode.*

Hint: If you expect to use this procedure often, you can simplify things a bit. On each computer, as soon as you complete the setup procedures, enter the following keystrokes and commands:

Alt-F4	Activate the DOS shell.
REN PROCOMM.PRM PROCOMM.REG	Rename the file that holds ProComm's default setup.
EXIT	Return to ProComm.
Alt-S	Display the Setup Menu.
S Return	Save the setup to disk.
Esc	Return to the terminal.

When you are done, rename the file PROCOMM.PRM, which will have been recreated by these steps, to HOSTXFER.PRM, and rename PROCOMM.REG back to PROCOMM.PRM. Then create the file HOSTXFER.BAT, shown in Listing 13.1.

```
1: ECHO OFF
2: CD\PROCOMM
3: REN PROCOMM.PRM TEMP.PRM
4: REN HOSTXFER.PRM PROCOMM.PRM
5: PROCOMM
6: REN PROCOMM.PRM HOSTXFER.PRM
7: REN TEMP.PRM PROCOMM.PRM
```

Listing 13.1 ▲ *HOSTXFER.BAT.*

What you have done is to create an alternative version of the file from which ProComm reads its settings. The batch file simply renames the regular setup file and the host-transfer setup file so that when you want to use this procedure, ProComm will automatically load the correct settings for it.

Using LapLink

If you find yourself having to do this sort of thing often, you might want to invest in LapLink, a hardware/software package from Traveling

Software. It's especially designed for downloading your work from a laptop computer to your main desktop computer when you return from the road, and vice versa. However, the package includes a cable with both a DB-9 and a DB-25 at each end, and has pins 2 and 3 crossed. Thus, you can use it to connect almost any two computers in the PC family.

The software comes on both 3½ and 5¼ inch diskettes. To transfer files, you simply connect the serial ports of the two computers and load the program on both. You will see a split screen, with your computer's current directory on the left, and the other computer's current directory on the right. Within one window is an inverse-video bar cursor. To select the computer you want to control, move the cursor to the appropriate window with the cursor-left or cursor-right key. Below these windows is a menu. You select items from the menu by their first letter. A sample screen appears in Figure 13.3.

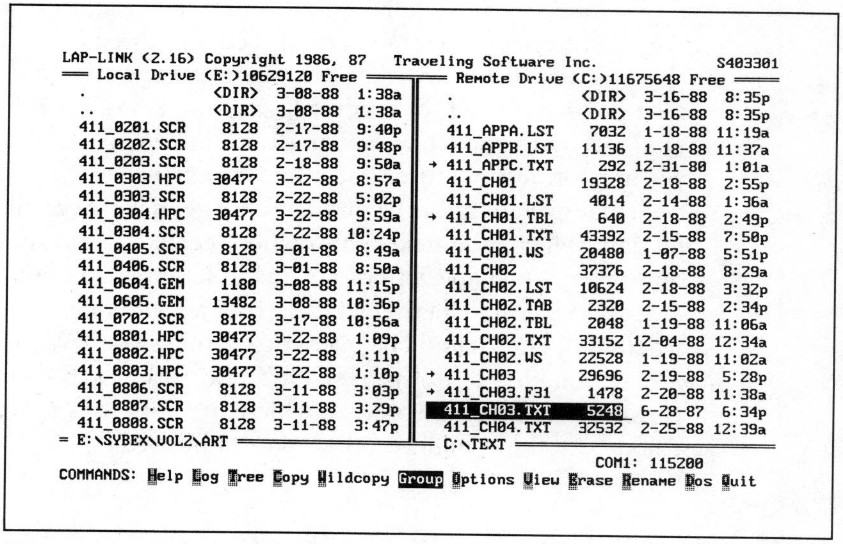

```
LAP-LINK (2.16) Copyright 1986, 87   Traveling Software Inc.              S403301
═══ Local Drive (E:)10629120 Free ═══╬═══ Remote Drive (C:)11675648 Free ═══
  .                <DIR>  3-08-88  1:38a    .                <DIR>  3-16-88  8:35p
  ..               <DIR>  3-08-88  1:38a    ..               <DIR>  3-16-88  8:35p
  411_0201.SCR      8128  2-17-88  9:40p    411_APPA.LST      7032  1-18-88 11:19a
  411_0202.SCR      8128  2-17-88  9:48p    411_APPB.LST     11136  1-18-88 11:37a
  411_0203.SCR      8128  2-18-88  9:50a  → 411_APPC.TXT       292 12-31-80  1:01a
  411_0303.HPC     30477  3-22-88  8:57a    411_CH01         19328  2-18-88  2:55p
  411_0303.SCR      8128  2-22-88  5:02p    411_CH01.LST      4014  2-14-88  1:36a
  411_0304.HPC     30477  3-22-88  9:59a  → 411_CH01.TBL       640  2-18-88  2:49p
  411_0304.SCR      8128  2-22-88 10:24p    411_CH01.TXT     43392  2-15-88  7:50p
  411_0405.SCR      8128  3-01-88  8:49a    411_CH01.WS      20480  1-07-88  5:51p
  411_0406.SCR      8128  3-01-88  8:50a    411_CH02         37376  2-18-88  8:29a
  411_0604.GEM      1180  3-08-88 11:15p    411_CH02.LST     10624  2-18-88  3:32p
  411_0605.GEM     13482  3-08-88 10:36p    411_CH02.TAB      2320  2-15-88  2:34p
  411_0702.SCR      8128  3-17-88 10:56a    411_CH02.TBL      2048  1-19-88 11:06a
  411_0801.HPC     30477  3-22-88  1:09p    411_CH02.TXT     33152 12-04-88 12:34a
  411_0802.HPC     30477  3-22-88  1:11p    411_CH02.WS      22528  1-19-88 11:02a
  411_0803.HPC     30477  3-22-88  1:10p  → 411_CH03         29696  2-19-88  5:28p
  411_0806.SCR      8128  3-11-88  3:03p  → 411_CH03.F31      1478  2-20-88 11:38a
  411_0807.SCR      8128  3-11-88  3:29p    411_CH03.TXT      5248  6-28-87  6:34p
  411_0808.SCR      8128  3-11-88  3:47p    411_CH04.TXT     32532  2-25-88 12:39a
═ E:\SYBEX\VOL2\ART ═════════════════╬═ C:\TEXT ══════════════════════════════
                                                          COM1: 115200
COMMANDS: Help Log Tree Copy Wildcopy Group Options View Erase Rename Dos Quit
```

Figure 13.3 ▲ *LapLink's Main Screen.*

You can transfer files in three different ways. From the main screen, you can simply move the cursor to a file name, in either directory, and press C to activate the Copy command. Using LapLink's turbo mode, the file will be transferred at 115,200 bps, as a status line just above the menu points out.

A second way to transfer files is with the Wildcopy option. You select this from the menu by pressing W, which displays the command line

Wildcopy: *.*

You can then edit the wild-card pattern. When you press Return, all files in the current directory, or the directory you specify, with names matching the pattern will be transferred.

The third method is to do a Group copy. You choose Group from the main menu, and then you can tag unrelated file names by pressing the T key. You can also tag groups of files matching a wild-card specification, and then untag selected files or vice versa. (Figure 13.3 shows several ragged files.) When you have selected your group, select Copy from this menu, not the main menu. LapLink will do the rest.

In addition, LapLink includes a fairly complete file management program. The Tree command displays a visual directory tree of the current disk on the selected computer, so you can make a directory current by moving the cursor to it. You can also change directories (or disks) with the Log command. In addition, you can view the contents of files, rename or erase files, or execute DOS commands, on either computer. (You may need the View, Rename, and Erase commands to make sure you are transferring the correct files, or to prevent older versions of files from being overwritten.) Thus, LapLink gives you everything you need for doing all your housekeeping on both computers. In addition, there's online help, and an Options command lets you configure the copying process to control whether wild-card copies will include subdirectories, whether old files should be overwritten, and so on. (Wildcopy can be a sort of combination of the XCOPY and REPLACE commands.) You can also determine the order in which directories are sorted, the screen colors, and the communications port to be used.

A Special Note for PS/2 Users

PC-DOS 3.3

PS/2 computers have a special built-in way of receiving files from another computer. The *parallel* (printer) port on PS/2s, unlike most other parallel ports, can receive as well as transmit data. However, in order to use it for the purpose, you must have a special kit called the IBM Data Migration Facility. You link the cable contained in this kit from the parallel port on another PC to the parallel port on a PS/2. You can then use the commands COPY35 and RCV35, which are included in PC-DOS 3.3, to transfer data to the PS/2.

Enter the command

RCV35

on the PS/2, and a command of the form

COPY35 [*drive*][*path*\]*FILENAME.EXT*

on the sending computer. You can include wild-card patterns in the file name. This command will send files to the default directory on the PS/2. However, you can send the files to other drives or directories by specifying the destination. The directories you specify must exist, however. Unlike XCOPY, COPY35 does not create directories as needed. The same parameters and restrictions that apply to the COPY command also constrain the COPY35 command.

LINKING TO ANOTHER PC VIA MODEM

Now that you've learned to work with two computers in the same room, let's see what happens when you link to a computer that's further away. For this, you'll need a modem, either internal or external, and access to a telephone line. Normally, when establishing a remote link to another PC user you will have to prearrange a time when you will both be ready to telecommunicate, and agree as to who should call whom. The procedures are quite similar to those you've just tried in ProComm. However, you also need to dial a phone number. In order to do that, you may have to set certain configuration options. Most important, you must tell your software how to interact with your modem. In ProComm, you do this from one of the submenus of the Setup Menu—the Modem Setup Menu, which is shown in Figure 13.4. If you don't configure these settings correctly, you may experience no end of frustration. As we said in Chapter 12, telecommunications is fraught with pitfalls and traps for the unwary. Here is one of them.

The details of this menu may be different from those on your telecommunications program, and some of the items may be on different menus, but you have to establish defaults for many of these settings with

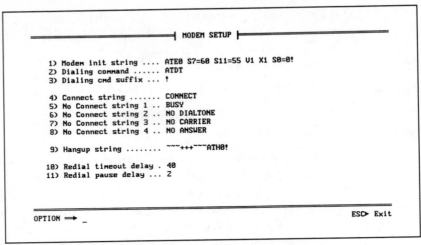

Figure 13.4 ▲ *ProComm's Modem Setup Menu.*

any telecommunications program. With all ProComm Setup menus, you select an item by entering its number and pressing Return. Let's look at the items on the menu. Item 1, the modem initialization string, prepares your modem for use. This default modem string uses the commands from the Hayes, or AT Command Set. If your modem is Hayes-compatible, you probably don't need to do anything to this entry. If it is not, consult your modem manual's command reference section to find out whether these codes are correct, or if you need to change them.

Item 2, the dialing command, is the Hayes command to begin dialing on a touch-tone phone. If you have a pulse phone, change this command to

ATDP

The exclamation point in item 3 is ProComm's representation of a carriage-return/line-feed combination—the characters sent when you press the Return key. This is normally needed to transmit the command to the modem.

Items 5 through 8 depend on your modem. These are responses sent by the modem to your computer to tell you whether it has successfully connected to another computer, or, if not, what has happened. You will find the exact phrases to enter in your modem manual.

Item 9, the hangup string, is the command that tells your modem to drop the line and break the connection. The tildes are ProComm's delay characters: they create a pause in the transmission to the modem.

The three plus signs are the Hayes command to tell the modem that the next characters it receives are to be treated as commands rather than data. From the time a connection is made until the modem receives these characters, it treats everything coming from your computer as data, and passes it along directly to the telephone line. Following the second delay is the Hayes command to hang up the phone, terminated again by a carriage-return/line-feed pair.

If you fail to make a connection on the first try, ProComm (and most other popular telecommunications programs) can keep trying the number until it gets a connection. Item 10 tells ProComm how long to wait after dialing to decide whether to give up and try again. If it takes a long time for the telephone to actually begin ringing, you may want to increase this number. Item 11 tells ProComm how long to wait after hanging up before trying again.

Dialing and Logging On

Now that you've told your software how to talk to your modem, you're ready to dial a number. Most telecommunications programs will dial a number for you, and they will also maintain a directory of phone numbers. If the remote computer requires you to log on by giving certain identifying information, or by entering a password, you can usually set up a procedure to handle that automatically as well. In ProComm, you press Alt-D to display the Dialing Directory, which is shown in Figure 13.5. From here, you maintain the directory and place your calls. You enter a new number, or change an old one, by pressing R for revise. You then enter or change the name of the party, the number to call, the communications parameters, and whether you need to turn the screen echo off or on. To dial a number in the directory, you select it by number. If you want to dial a number that's not in the directory, you press M for Manual dialing, and enter the number at the keyboard.

Once you have dialed, you may need to log on. If so, the remote computer will prompt you with a series of questions, which you answer from the keyboard. If you expect to call a particular computer more than once, open a download file before you begin. This will allow you to *capture the dialog* required for logging on. ProComm gives you two ways to capture the dialog. You can either choose ASCII from the Download menu and enter a file name, or press Alt-G to capture the current screen to a file. This file will have the name entered in the General Setup

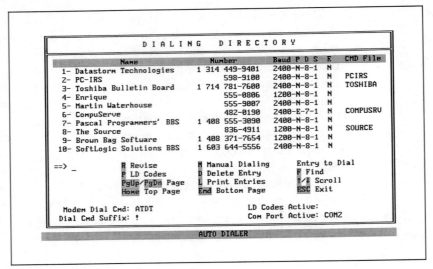

```
                      D I A L I N G   D I R E C T O R Y

                      Name               Number      Baud P D S E   CMD File
         1- Datastorm Technologies   1 314 449-9401  2400-N-8-1  N
         2- PC-IRS                         598-9100  2400-N-8-1  N  PCIRS
         3- Toshiba Bulletin Board   1 714 781-7600  2400-N-8-1  N  TOSHIBA
         4- Enrique                       555-0806   1200-N-8-1  N
         5- Martin Waterhouse             555-9007   2400-N-8-1  N
         6- CompuServe                    482-0190   2400-E-7-1  N  COMPUSRV
         7- Pascal Programmers' BBS  1 408 555-3090  2400-N-8-1  N
         8- The Source                    836-4911   1200-N-8-1  N  SOURCE
         9- Brown Bag Software       1 408 371-7654  1200-N-8-1  N
         10- SoftLogic Solutions BBS 1 603 644-5556  2400-N-8-1  N

         ==>  _          R Revise       M Manual Dialing     Entry to Dial
                         P LD Codes      D Delete Entry       F Find
                         PgUp/PgDn Page  L Print Entries      ↑/↓ Scroll
                         Home Top Page   End Bottom Page      ESC Exit

             Modem Dial Cmd: ATDT            LD Codes Active:
             Dial Cmd Suffix: !              Com Port Active: COM2

                                AUTO DIALER
```

Figure 13.5 ▲ *ProComm's Dialing Directory.*

Menu. If the file already exists, ProComm will append new screens, rather than overwriting the file.

When you have captured the log-on dialog, you can then enter this information in a *command file*. If you include the name of a command file in the Dialing Directory entry, ProComm will wait for the prompts you have specified, and it will automatically transmit the correct answers. The ProComm command language is well beyond the scope of this book. However, it contains all the commands and procedures to completely automate many types of telecommunications sessions. We'll show you a sample command file toward the end of the chapter.

Note that there are two ways to use command files with most telecommunications programs, and three with ProComm. If you invoke the program with the name of a command file as a parameter, ProComm will automatically execute the commands in the file. To set up a command file for this purpose, you should include the phone number to dial. Alternatively, you can include the name of the command file in the Dialing Directory. Once a connection is established, ProComm will execute the commands in the file automatically. Finally, you can execute a command file at any time by pressing Alt-F5. This displays a list of the command files in the directory, and prompts you for the name of the file to execute.

Answering a Call

If you are being called, rather than calling, you must instruct your modem to answer the call. Some modems can be set to auto-answer. If yours can, you can have ProComm tell it to do so by pressing Alt-Y. If you want to control answering, you can enter

+ + +
ATA

at the keyboard, or create a macro that sends the string

~ ~ ~ **+ + +** ~ ~ ~ **ATA!**

If you don't do one of these things, your modem will not answer the phone.

Remote Chatting

OK. So now you're hooked up to another computer, and communication is established. In ProComm, you will then find yourself in terminal, or chat, mode. In this mode, you and the other party can both enter characters at the keyboard, and they will show up on both screens. (If the characters you type don't show up on your own screen, change the Echo or Duplex setting.) ProComm has a special Chat mode, activated by Alt-O, that gives you a split screen. In this mode, what you type appears in a small window at the bottom, while your partner's messages appear in a large window at the top. This can help prevent confusion if you don't observe telecommunications etiquette. It's customary to type

-o-

(for over) when you have finished typing in something to send, and

-oo-

(for over and out) when you are ready to hang up, or move on to transferring files. However, many people don't observe these niceties, in which case the characters typed at each end will be all mixed up together on the screen (remember, communication flows both ways at once.) It's essentially the same as what happens when two people talk on the telephone at once.

If you want to record the conversation, some programs let you open a special download file, which stores everything that passes across your

Software. It's especially designed for downloading your work from a laptop computer to your main desktop computer when you return from the road, and vice versa. However, the package includes a cable with both a DB-9 and a DB-25 at each end, and has pins 2 and 3 crossed. Thus, you can use it to connect almost any two computers in the PC family.

Transferring Files

Now that you are properly connected, transferring files is a relatively simple matter. It's exactly the same as transferring files from one computer to another directly. You simply display the upload or download menu (depending on whether you are sending or receiving), select a protocol (having made sure that your partner will use the same one), and enter a file name (unless you're receiving in batch mode).

If you are receiving, the files will be written to a directory you have specified in an item in the General Setup Menu (Setup Menu 4). If you haven't set this item, and it points to a directory that doesn't exist, you may have trouble. Otherwise, the procedure should be familiar.

Using a Remote Host

If you and your partner cannot find a mutually convenient time to connect, one of you can leave the computer turned on with ProComm loaded in host mode. If you do, be sure to review the Host Mode Setup Menu. You must have your auto-answer string installed, and a password installed both for host mode and for the DOS shell. *Never* leave these blank when your host is connected to a modem. *Be very careful about who knows your DOS shell password.* It's all too easy for someone with a random-dialing device to make hash out of your hard disk if they know how to activate the DOS shell. Be sure also that your Connection type is MODEM, not DIRECT.

There are a few additional steps you can take. You can create a message for anyone who successfully logs on, by creating a file called PRO-COMM.MSG. You can have ProComm keep a record of who has logged on and what commands they have used in a file called PRO-COMM.HST. Finally, you must make sure that your partner knows the password. Once your partner has logged on, the menu you saw in Figure 13.2 will appear, giving your partner access to ProComm on your computer. Your partner can then upload and download files, leave messages, and so on. The Chat command will sound an alarm, so you can go online yourself if you are in the vicinity. Otherwise, it's just like using host mode on a computer that's connected directly.

Things to Watch Out For

We've made it sound as though everything will flow smoothly once you set a few parameters. 'Tain't necessarily so, though. If you get the transmission speed wrong, gibberish characters will probably flow across your screen with great alacrity, resisting all your attempts to stop them. Most telecommunications programs let you change the transmission speed on the fly. (In ProComm you press Alt-P to display the Line Settings Menu, and change them there.) This may help somewhat. However, once you have connected at the wrong speed, you may never get a clear signal unless you hang up and try again.

If the data format does not match that of the remote computer, you will also see nothing but garbage. However, it probably won't move as fast. The most likely solution is to switch to 7-1-EVEN. If this doesn't work, hang up and try again.

A third problem you can encounter is telephone line noise. When the telephone line is noisy, it interferes with the clear reception of the two pitches representing 0s and 1s. The result is that some extra characters will appear on your screen. Often, they are } characters. If you see lots of } characters that don't seem to belong, and your messages are not received correctly, hang up and try again.

BULLETIN BOARDS

Now that you've successfully connected with a friend, you may be ready to try something more adventurous. Once you are experienced with telecommunications, a vast world of information opens up to you.

We've mentioned remote bulletin board services (RBBSs) frequently in this book. There are literally thousands of them, and many are open to all at no charge. Many computer stores, user's groups, and hardware and software manufacturers run bulletin boards. Special interest groups of all types run bulletin boards as well. In addition to bulletin boards for specific types of computers, there are bulletin boards for astronomy buffs, programmers, single people, Bible students, political activists, and just about any other type of group you can name. Once you have reached one bulletin board, you can probably download a list of others. Most are free, but some ask for a one-time registration fee. Some offer access to more files once you have paid a fee, or have registered as a member.

What do these bulletin boards offer you? At the very least, they are a source of information. However, they may offer a great deal more. Most offer you the opportunity to leave a message for the system operator, or SYSOP. If you are having trouble finding a program or using the board, or if you have any questions at all, you can leave messages for the person with this job. The next time you log onto the board, you might see

You have two messages waiting

Some bulletin boards are download-only bulletin boards. This means that you can download public-domain and shareware programs from them, but you cannot send your own programs to them, which ensures that you will not receive any viruses or Trojans. Others serve as a program exchange, where users offer their programming efforts for public consumption.

In addition to public-domain and shareware programs, most bulletin boards offer a message service. Individuals call to post messages or queries, and others offer responses. Some upload all messages to a national bulletin board, so you have access to answers from all over the country. Others allow you to play games with other users; search databases on line (for example, real-estate foreclosures, or the PC Magazine index); or enter a dating service.

Many hardware and software manufacturers offer technical support through their bulletin boards. You leave a message concerning your problem, and call back the next day to find an answer addressed to you. You may find this considerably less expensive than calling a long-distance number and waiting on hold for twenty minutes or more. In addition, you may find special printer drivers, software patches, programs to convert file formats, and any number of useful utilities to help you get more out of the programs you use.

Using Archived Files

You should be aware that many, if not most, of the programs you can download from bulletin boards (and from online services as well), will be in *archived* form. You can recognize such files because they have the extension .ARC. These files contain versions of the operating files that have been reformatted so that they take less storage space. Shorter files take less time to transmit. Archiving also makes it possible to store all the files you need to use for a given program in a single file, which simplifies downloading.

Before you use any archived files, you must extract them from the archive. Two popular public-domain programs, PKXARC.EXE and ARC-E.EXE, can extract most archived files. If you do not have a copy of one of these files, you can generally download one from the same bulletin board from which you downloaded the archived files.

E-MAIL

One of the big problems with communicating by telephone is time-dependency. That is, if you want to talk to someone, they have to be there when you call. The fact that they often aren't leads to the frustrating game known as telephone tag. We've already looked at two ways computer telecommunications can help you avoid telephone tag: using host mode, and getting technical support from a bulletin board. E-Mail goes one better than these.

We've also looked at the way E-Mail is used as part of a local-area network. However, there are E-Mail services open to anyone willing to pay the price, which offer a great deal more. The big advantage of E-Mail is that it is not at all time-dependent. You call and upload messages at your convenience, and your correspondents call and check their mailboxes at theirs. This works fine as long as your correspondents actually check their mailboxes.

! **Hint:** When you're working with people who are scattered geographically, E-Mail may be the only reliable way to keep in touch, and it may also be the quickest way to transfer files for immediate comment or revision. If your correspondents check their mail regularly, you can reduce turnaround time to a few hours, or even less. If necessary, you can even call them by phone to remind them to check their mailboxes.

When your files are short enough that it takes less than half an hour to upload or download them, E-Mail can also save money. If your files are larger and time is not as critical, it may be cheaper to use an express service and send a disk.

How do you get E-Mail service? If you subscribe to an online service, you probably have access to an E-Mail service. CompuServe subscribers have a service called EasyPlex, through which subscribers can leave messages for one another by addressing their subscriber numbers. The Source has SourceMail. Dow Jones News/Retrieval includes access to MCI Mail for an extra fee. AT&T and Western Union also offer E-Mail services.

The most appropriate service for you will depend on your needs. CompuServe's EasyPlex, for example, lets you upload any type of file, using any of the transfer protocols available in CompuServe, but the files can be only up to 10K in length. This precludes sending long documents or complex spreadsheets. It generally precludes sending graphics as well. MCI Mail, in contrast, has no error-checking protocols, and can't handle binary files. However, it can accept files of any length.

E-Mail services often have other facilities in addition to the mailbox. You can generally scan or read your mail, leave it in a "hold" box until you are ready to reply, and save messages you have sent in an "out" box. Some services also have online editors, and most will send printed copies of your documents for an extra fee. Some will, for yet another fee, print the letters on a facsimile of your company letterhead, with a facsimile of your signature at the end, or guarantee next-day delivery.

When you use E-Mail, you can save a great deal of money in connect charges if you:

▲ Compose your messages before going online and upload them from disk, rather than use the service's editor while you are connected

▲ Download your mail to disk, print it out, and read it after you have logged off

ONLINE SERVICES

If you want still more telecommunications options than are afforded by bulletin boards and E-Mail, you can subscribe to one of the online services. These are a combination of many bulletin boards, plus E-Mail, and countless other services. The three largest are CompuServe, The Source, and Dow Jones News/Retrieval.

Features of Online Services

CompuServe and The Source are general-purpose services, while Dow Jones, as you might expect, is more specialized toward financial news and information. All offer E-Mail, shopping from online catalogs with online ordering, travel arrangements, banking and brokerage services, and access to the Official Airlines Guide. They all can search for information on selected topics and current events.

In addition, CompuServe and The Source have a chat mode, games that you can play with others who are online when you are, and numerous services for special interest groups. Besides computer-related interest groups, which we'll get to in a moment, CompuServe, for example, includes special interest information in the following forums, among others:

> Aircraft Owners and Pilots Association
> American Association of Medical Systems and Informatics
> Aquarium and Tropical Fish
> Auto Racing Forum
> Broadcast Profession Forum
> The Business Wire
> Comic Book Forum
> Consumer Electronics Form
> Disabilities Forum
> Executive News Service
> Journalism Forum
> Legal Forum
> Naked Eye Astronomy
> Religion Forum
> Science Fiction Forum

     Sports Forum
     SuperSite Demographic Information
     West Coast Travel

There are many other more specialized services. To name two examples, The Knowledge Index maintains a database of abstracts of articles from every source on technical subjects, and Lexis performs a similar service for the legal field.

There is, however, a catch to the online services—in your pocket. They all charge for connect time by the minute, and some services require an additional fee to register, or a monthly minimum-usage fee. Most also offer a premium service with extra benefits for another fee.

To take out some of the sting, you can usually call these services from a local number, so you don't also have to pay long-distance charges. Moreover, the rates at night and on weekends are considerably lower than those during the regular business day.

CompuServe Features for Computer Users

For serious computer users (that's you), three features of CompuServe make it probably the most useful service. First, it offers many public-domain and shareware programs, classified by computer and purpose. Second, several major hardware manufacturers and software publishers maintain online forums. You can read releases on the latest software upgrades; leave questions for the technical support department or other users; download printer drivers, screen drivers, and other utilities for specific programs; and gain access to the latest bug reports, along with patches or work-around procedures.

Third, many of the forums maintain a weekly conference schedule. A conference time is posted in the bulletin-board area of a particular forum. Logging onto the forum at the specified time allows you to communicate on line with others who share an interest, and to get the latest information from experts.

In the computer area CompuServe includes forums sponsored by, or pertaining to:

     Amiga
     Apple
     Ashton-Tate

Atari
Autodesk
Borland International
Commodore
Digital Research
Epson
Heath
Hewlett-Packard
IBM
Living Videotext
Lotus
MicroPro
Microsoft
Software Publishing
Tandy

In addition, there are special forums for programmers in Forth, Pascal, and LOGO. To give you an idea of the information you can glean from these forums, we found out how to produce the illustrations for our discussion of Concurrent DOS from the Digital Research Forum, and we found out about the reason for the conflict between disk caches and some programs that use expanded memory (mentioned in Chapter 5) in the IBM Software Forum.

Getting Started

To get started with CompuServe, you must subscribe. An introductory kit generally costs about $25. However, many telecommunications software packages include a coupon that is good for free membership and an hour of free time. You will be given an account number and password to use when you log on, and a local-access phone number.

Hint: The type of local-access phone number you use affects the service you get. There are two considerations. First, some local-access numbers work only at 300 or 1200 bps, while others work at 2400 bps as well. Second, some of these numbers are actually *network* numbers, while others are direct links to CompuServe. The networks are GTE, Telenet, and Tymnet. Calling one of these networks gives you local access to any number of services when you are a subscriber and provide the proper identifying information. However, because they are networks, you share them with many other users. This can result in interminable delays when the network becomes bogged down. Sometimes, CompuServe can appear to go dead on you. You might be tempted to hang up. If you do, you will be charged for an extra 15 minutes unless you call in again and log off properly. In addition, the networks add a surcharge to your CompuServe bill. You will do best with a CompuServe direct-access number that accepts your highest transmission speed.

Because CompuServe offers so much, you are likely to be overwhelmed at first. It pays to study the user information they provide before going online. However, that too can be overwhelming. For further assistance, you can buy a User's Guide. When you subscribe to CompuServe, you automatically receive a subscription to *Online Today*, a monthly magazine with tutorials and hints as to what's new. Even with all this help, however, you can expect to spend about $100 in connect charges before you've found the short routes to what's actually useful to you.

Hint: The very best way to get acquainted with CompuServe is to have an experienced user show you around. If it's on your time, change your password afterward.

When you log on for the first time, you may want to update your user profile. This includes a description of your terminal, your password, your preferred method of billing, and your billing address. If your screen shows too many line feeds or not enough, or otherwise doesn't match what your program can best display, you should change your profile. This is one of many items in the area called User Assistance. Any time you spend in this area is free.

You can get to any part of CompuServe via menus, or you can use GO commands as shortcuts. For example, you could enter

    GO PROFILE

at the CompuServe prompt (the exclamation point), to change your profile, or

    GO TERMINAL

to change just your terminal type and settings. To change your password, enter

GO PASSWORD

Alternatively, typing

HELP

at any exclamation-point prompt will produce the first menu that appears in Figure 13.6. As you can see from this figure, each menu displays submenus. The Terminal/Options Menu is two steps down from the main Help Menu. Once you are at this level, you will be guided by a series of prompts. You can go back and make further changes if the results are not what you desire.

You might also want to find out whether there is a better local-access number than the one you used. To do so, enter the command

GO PHONES

You will then be asked for the city and state from which you are calling. If you find a number that allows you to use a higher transmission speed, or a direct-access number you can use instead of a network number, by all means log off and call in again with the new number. The command to log off is

BYE

CompuServe includes some features that can save you a great deal of time if you pay attention to them. For example, whenever you log onto a forum, the screen will tell you the date you last logged on, and the number of the last message you read. You can then choose to exclude all items with a lower number or an earlier date when you browse through an area. You can also enter commands using three-letter abbreviations, whenever you have a prompt. For example, to browse through an area, use the command BRO. To download a file whose description you have just read while browsing, use DOW.

Automating Your Procedures

To give you some idea of how to log onto CompuServe, we have included a sample log-on dialog in Figure 13.7. This shows the screen messages both from ProComm and CompuServe when you call on a

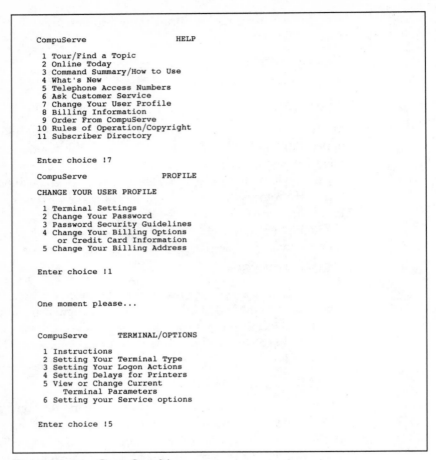

```
CompuServe                    HELP

  1 Tour/Find a Topic
  2 Online Today
  3 Command Summary/How to Use
  4 What's New
  5 Telephone Access Numbers
  6 Ask Customer Service
  7 Change Your User Profile
  8 Billing Information
  9 Order From CompuServe
 10 Rules of Operation/Copyright
 11 Subscriber Directory


Enter choice !7

CompuServe                    PROFILE

CHANGE YOUR USER PROFILE

  1 Terminal Settings
  2 Change Your Password
  3 Password Security Guidelines
  4 Change Your Billing Options
      or Credit Card Information
  5 Change Your Billing Address


Enter choice !1



One moment please...



CompuServe      TERMINAL/OPTIONS

  1 Instructions
  2 Setting Your Terminal Type
  3 Setting Your Logon Actions
  4 Setting Delays for Printers
  5 View or Change Current
      Terminal Parameters
  6 Setting your Service options


Enter choice !5
```

Figure 13.6 ▲ *CompuServe Menus.*

CompuServe direct-access line. (The steps are somewhat different when you use a network number.) We have taken the dialog all the way to the Opening Menu, which you can reach from any point in Compu-Serve by entering the command

GO TOP

This is precisely the sort of chore for which a command file is intended. In ProComm, you can recall the session by pressing Alt-F6. If you then dump the opening dialog to a printer, you can easily create a command file. The command file shown in Listing 13.2 is designed to

```
ProComm online to CompuServe
2400


  22OKC

Host Name:  CIS02

User ID: 70000,0007
Password:

CompuServe Information Service
 23:41 PST Monday 28-Mar-88

 Last access: 18:32 22-Mar-88

     Copyright (C) 1988
   CompuServe Incorporated
     All Rights Reserved

CompuServe                   TOP

  1 Subscriber Assistance
  2 Find a Topic
  3 Communications/Bulletin Bds.
  4 News/Weather/Sports
  5 Travel
  6 The Electronic MALL/Shopping
  7 Money Matters/Markets
  8 Entertainment/Games
  9 Home/Health/Family
 10 Reference/Education
 11 Computers/Technology
 12 Business/Other Interests


Enter choice number !GO MAIL

One moment please...
```

Figure 13.7 ▲ *Log-On Dialog on CompuServe.*

```
1: TRANSMIT "!"
2: TRANSMIT "!"
3: WAITFOR "Host name:"
4: TRANSMIT "CIS02!"
5: WAITFOR "User ID:"
6: TRANSMIT "70000,0007!"
7: WAITFOR "Password:"
8: TRANSMIT "MYOWN-PASSWORD!"
9: ALARM
```

Listing 13.2 ▲ *A ProComm Command File for Logging onto CompuServe.*

be used from the Dialing Directory. As you can see, it waits for Compu-Serve's prompts and automatically supplies the correct responses.

This is a relatively simple command file. The TRANSMIT command in the first two lines tells ProComm to transmit two carriage returns. You must transmit these characters to let CompuServe know that you are online. Following these characters, the command file uses the WAITFOR command to tell ProComm what prompts it should respond to, and more TRANSMIT commands to tell it how to respond. Of course, you replace the User ID and password with your own. Finally, when a connection is made, ProComm is told to issue the repeating double beep that is its alarm signal. This is useful because if the line is busy, ProComm will keep on redialing until it makes a connection. Without the alarm, you might walk away, unaware that you were connected.

This is only the merest hint of what you can do with command files. As you become familiar with CompuServe's offerings, you may want to create other command files for special purposes—one to check your mail and download it if you have any, another to go directly to your favorite forum and download a list of the newest software, or download the current prices of stocks you own, and so on. ProComm's command language includes conditional tests and branching, so you can, for example, have your command file check to see if you have mail, and perform the download procedures only if you do.

The one thing to be careful about is to watch the clock. Not only is it easy to get lost in the maze of menus, but you can also readily become fascinated and forget you're paying by the minute.

OPERATING A COMPUTER REMOTELY

There's one more purpose for which you might find telecommunications useful. Suppose you have a computer on your office desk, and you take some work home on a laptop. But your computer at work is connected to a network, with a laser printer, a huge hard disk, and many other facilities that your laptop doesn't have. Wouldn't it be nice if you could have access to all the power of your office desktop? Well, you can gain limited access by way of ProComm.

You leave your remote computer (your office desktop, in this case) in host mode, and you call in and use the Shell command. This gives you a DOS prompt on your remote computer, from which you can execute some, but not all, commands. You can execute any DOS internal commands, and most external commands. You can execute batch files so long as they don't call other programs that write directly to the screen. Once a program writes directly to the screen, you are lost. You won't see the remote screen on your local computer, and you won't know what's going on. You may not even know how to exit the program on the other end. When this happens, you have to reboot both computers. That's going to be awfully difficult from several miles away.

However, there is a solution. Several telecommunications utilities, when properly loaded on both computers, will allow you to operate the remote computer as if it were your local computer. One of the better ones we know about is Carbon Copy, from Meridian Technology. (You must purchase two copies of this program, one for each computer.) Its main purpose is for technical support. Say you're a consultant, and one of your clients is running into problems he can't explain properly. You each load one of Carbon Copy's modules, and then you watch as your client goes through the steps that create the problem. At the crucial moment, you step in and demonstrate the correct procedure. This can sometimes be a lot simpler than trying to understand a verbal explanation over the phone.

Carbon Copy is also useful for simply running one computer from another. To do so, you should first configure both computers using the CCINSTAL program. Its menu screen appears in Figure 13.8. With this program you set the communications parameters, determine which computer's printer will be used for data printed from the program, and configure the program for the computer it's running on. You can also change the hot keys (the default is Alt-Right Shift) to any combination

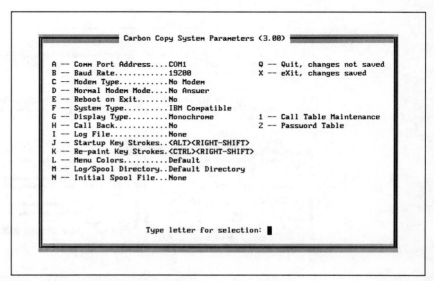

```
                  Carbon Copy System Parameters (3.00)

    A -- Comm Port Address....COM1         Q -- Quit, changes not saved
    B -- Baud Rate...........19200         X -- eXit, changes saved
    C -- Modem Type..........No Modem
    D -- Normal Modem Mode....No Answer
    E -- Reboot on Exit.......No
    F -- System Type.........IBM Compatible
    G -- Display Type........Monochrome     1 -- Call Table Maintenance
    H -- Call Back...........No             2 -- Password Table
    I -- Log File............None
    J -- Startup Key Strokes..<ALT><RIGHT-SHIFT>
    K -- Re-paint Key Strokes.<CTRL><RIGHT-SHIFT>
    L -- Menu Colors.........Default
    M -- Log/Spool Directory..Default Directory
    N -- Initial Spool File...None




                  Type letter for selection: █
```

Figure 13.8 ▲ *Carbon Copy's Installation Program.*

of the Alt, Ctrl, Left Shift, and Right Shift keys. You then load CC.EXE on the remote computer and load CCHELP.EXE on the local computer. You can, if you wish, set up a phone directory (called a Call Table in this program), and assign passwords to each phone number.

Once the programs are loaded, you can use the local computer to call the remote computer via your modem, and enter the password if necessary. Your screen will show the current screen of the remote computer. You can then run any program on the remote computer as if it were on your own. The only exception occurs if the two computers have different types of display adapters. If, for example, you have an EGA on your local computer and a CGA on the remote, or vice versa, the system will hang if you invoke a program that uses one of the modes unique to the remote computer's adapter.

If you need to communicate with an operator on the remote computer, you just press the hot keys, and the screen shown in Figure 13.9 appears. It is from this screen that you control the flow of communication, as well as communicate with the operator, capture screens, or print the output.

To remove the program from memory on the local computer, press Ctrl-Alt-Del. Unless you set the computer to reboot on exit when you ran CCINSTAL, these keys simply return you to DOS on your own computer and remove CCHELP from memory.

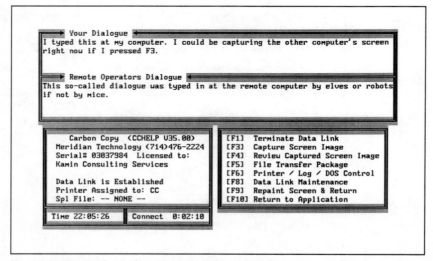

Figure 13.9 ▲ *The Carbon Copy Control Screen.*

By now you have some idea of the many ways telecommunications can expand your computer horizons and provide new ways to improve your productivity. We're sure you will think of many more.

INSTALLING AND
USING NETWORKS

A S YOU LEARNED IN CHAPTER 11, there are many different types of network hardware and many varieties of network software. Each software package has a different command structure. Thus, we cannot show you precisely how to install and use networks in a way that will apply to any network you might choose. Therefore, in this chapter we present a detailed overview of installing a token-ring network, and a summary of installing and using an EasyLAN network. We emphasize the issues to consider when choosing a network so you can be sure it suits your needs.

Then we present some of the details involved in using a token-ring network. Obviously, since these details are based on the network software, they do not necessarily apply to other types of networks. However, they should give you an impression of how using a network differs from using a PC that is not on a network.

Any time you share an environment with others, you need rules to maintain order. Therefore, we present some pointers on network etiquette. Finally, we present two scenarios in which a network can significantly increase office productivity.

INSTALLING A TOKEN-RING NETWORK

To give you an idea of what is involved with setting up a typical network, we will use an IBM token-ring LAN as an example. Installation can be broken down into three major stages:

1. Installing the hardware, including token-ring adapter cards, multistation access units, wiring, and the server or servers.

2. Installing the token-ring software on the workstations and servers, including both the LAN program and the LAN support program.

3. Installing shared applications and data on the servers and arranging for the workstations to access them.

Each stage requires careful planning. You must complete each stage before moving on to the next stage.

Installing the Hardware

It's fairly simple to install the adapter cards in the PCs. Once you have inserted the card, use the supplied diagnostics disk to ensure that the card is correctly installed and functioning.

Next, you need to install at least one multistation access unit (MAU). This is nothing more than a box into which every computer on the network is plugged—servers as well as workstations. All data passing through the network is directed by the MAU. As you saw in Chapter 11, Figure 11.9, the MAU is the hub of a star-shaped arrangement. Because of all the wiring, the MAUs should be placed in an area where there is little foot traffic. Nobody should have to get to the MAUs except to maintain and repair them, and they are better off left alone. The ideal installation is in a 19-inch equipment rack in a telephone cupboard. But you can use a storeroom, or an office that doesn't get used very often. Once you have installed the MAUs, you must test them to ensure that the relays are operating correctly, using the probe supplied. The MAU comes with pictorial instructions to guide you through the process.

To wire a token-ring network, you must have specialized knowledge of wiring standards. We strongly recommend that you hire a network wiring specialist. (You can probably find one in the yellow pages under Computer Repair and Installation.) A specialist can advise you on which type of cabling will best suit your needs. There are two main categories of cabling: coaxial and twisted-pair. There are many different wiring types within these categories. For example, for placement under office carpets, you would need shielded twisted-pair or flat coaxial cables. Some office telephone systems may carry extra pairs of wires that could be adapted to carry token-ring signals. As you can imagine, with all these different types of wiring, you can't simply plug in to the existing wiring. Many types of wiring will require a media jumper at one end to match the signal to your adapter card, and a media filter at the other to connect to the MAU.

Selecting servers, and deciding on the right number of servers, requires careful planning. The first question to ask yourself is which applications and data will be shared. If you plan to run two or more major applications on the system, you may want to include a file/ application server for each application.

If you plan to create many reports from the shared data, you may need a printer server in addition to the file server. You may not know if you need one until you see how much traffic the printers get. It's easy to add servers to most LANs if you install some extra wires near your servers when you set up the network.

As to what kind of server you need, the manufacturer's specifications are the best place to start. For example, if you need to share 500MB of data, you'll need servers and support programs capable of handling that much data.

Cost will play an important role in your decision and so will the types of media the network can use. If you already have certain types of wiring installed in your office, the wiring may limit your choice of LAN hardware, and consequently the types of servers you can use.

You should consider what functions each server will have, because this will determine the most appropriate types of hardware. It's possible, for example, that a file server need be nothing more than the shell of a 386 PC with a couple of very large hard disks and a tape backup unit. Once the hard disks have been formatted, all you have to do to start the network is turn on the server, and let the AUTOEXEC.BAT file take care of everything else. In any case, there probably won't be enough memory in a file server to do any local tasks once the network software is loaded. However, you may want to attach a screen for the network to display status messages, and a keyboard from which the network administrator can perform maintenance. (You can perform the maintenance remotely from a workstation, but you can't display status messages anywhere else.)

If you need bridges to other networks, or gateways to minis or mainframes, you will need a server for these functions as well. These, too, may simply be hardware boxes.

If your network will be running 24 hours a day, as in a banking application, you might want some form of redundancy in the system so that it can continue to operate even if one unit fails. If so, you might include two servers, one to back up the other in the case of failure.

Installing the Network Software

In this section we discuss installing the IBM LAN program, release 1.2. Earlier releases of the LAN program are considerably slower; release 1.2 runs only with DOS 3.3.

As we discussed, you should install token-ring software on the server before any applications. Unlike some other network systems, all workstations on a token-ring network use the same network operating program. However, it's configured differently for users and servers.

The LAN program comes with configuration and installation aids. The configuration aid will decide what device drivers you need to interface with DOS. The installation aid will set up a network subdirectory; install the token-ring files; and ask you what directories you want to share on the server, with what type of access, and whether you want to use passwords.

 Warning: The installation aid should install the LAN program on a disk with DOS already installed. But when we tried to run it, the program refused to install itself without first installing DOS. Apparently, it wants to be sure you have the right DOS version.

The configuration aid will determine the requirements for the LAN support program by asking you questions and selecting device drivers based on your answers. An example of the configuration aid is shown in Figure 14.1.

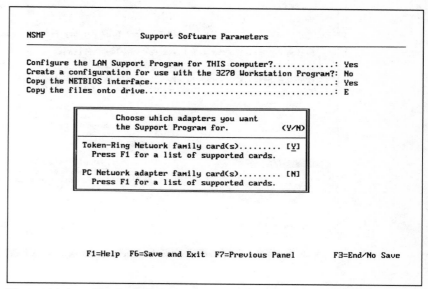

```
NSMP                    Support Software Parameters

Configure the LAN Support Program for THIS computer?.............: Yes
Create a configuration for use with the 3270 Workstation Program?: No
Copy the NETBIOS interface......................................: Yes
Copy the files onto drive.......................................: E

              ┌─────────────────────────────────────────────┐
              │        Choose which adapters you want        │
              │        the Support Program for.      (Y/N)   │
              │                                              │
              │  Token-Ring Network family card(s)........ [Y]│
              │     Press F1 for a list of supported cards.  │
              │                                              │
              │  PC Network adapter family card(s)........ [N]│
              │     Press F1 for a list of supported cards.  │
              └─────────────────────────────────────────────┘



         F1=Help  F6=Save and Exit  F7=Previous Panel      F3=End/No Save
```

Figure 14.1 ▲ *The Configuration Aid.*

Before running the installation aid program, you should have a useful network name for each server on the network, and a name for each user on each workstation (you can use initials as a substitute).

For later reference, you will want to be able to see what the installation aid sets up for you. Attach a printer to the server, and use Shift-PrtSc to make a copy of each significant screen. An example of the installation aid is shown in Figure 14.2.

Installing Applications Software

If you wish, you can have the installation aid install applications for you. This is actually more trouble than it is worth, because the installation aid can only install programs it knows about. You probably won't find too many applications that you can install with this facility.

Installing applications on a network is complex because your PCs can have varying configurations. For example, Figure 14.3 shows two workstations. One has two diskette drives (A and B) and a hard disk designated C. The other has two hard disks (C and D), a RAM disk (E), and a diskette drive (F). As the workstations access drives on the server, network drives would normally receive the next available drive

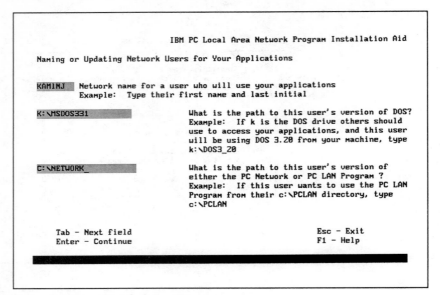

```
                    IBM PC Local Area Network Program Installation Aid

        Naming or Updating Network Users for Your Applications

        KAMINJ    Network name for a user who will use your applications
                  Example:  Type their first name and last initial

        K:\MSDOS331          What is the path to this user's version of DOS?
                             Example:  If k is the DOS drive others should
                             use to access your applications, and this user
                             will be using DOS 3.20 from your machine, type
                             k:\DOS3_20

        C:\NETWORK           What is the path to this user's version of
                             either the PC Network or PC LAN Program ?
                             Example:  If this user wants to use the PC LAN
                             Program from their c:\PCLAN directory, type
                             c:\PCLAN


        Tab - Next field                        Esc - Exit
        Enter - Continue                        F1 - Help
```

Figure 14.2 ▲ *The Installation Aid.*

designation on each workstation. Thus, the network virtual disks start at D on workstation A and at G on workstation B, as Figure 14.3 shows.

This can cause problems if, for example, you run a batch file on the server from your own workstation to attach a server directory to your system. If the batch file includes a drive designation that is lower than the highest logical drive designation on any of the workstations (lower than G, in Figure 14.3), the batch file won't work. Therefore, in this case, the server directory will be on drive G on both workstations. As an alternative, you can use the DOS ASSIGN command on each workstation to make sure that common applications have the same drive letter.

In summary, the IBM token-ring system is one of the easiest network systems to install. However, it needs a lot of fine tuning. In other words, it's easy to get it up and running but not so easy to get it up and running effectively. Paul Berry's book *Operating the IBM PC Networks* (SYBEX, 1986) offers guidance in these areas.

INSTALLING AN EASYLAN NETWORK

EasyLAN release 3 is a simple software solution for connecting two or more personal computers. It is one of a class of LANs called "zero-slot

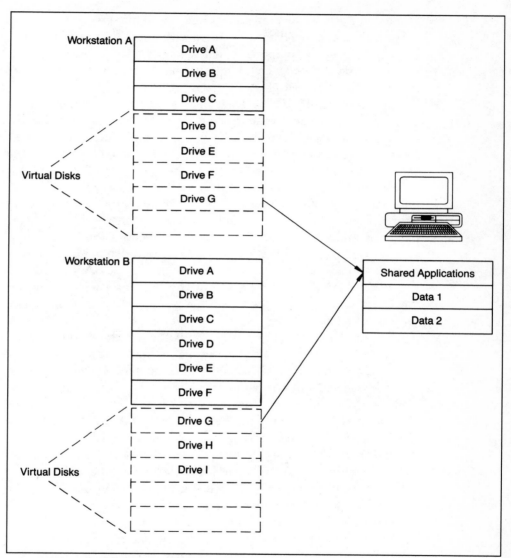

Figure 14.3 ▲ *Virtual Disk Mapping.*

LANs" because it requires no additional hardware. Instead, it uses the existing serial ports. Of course, it can't do as much as a hardware-based LAN, and it is considerably slower. However, it's also considerably cheaper and very easy to use.

You don't get the advantages of a high-speed file server, but you also don't get the high overhead associated with one. If you need a method to share files among computers and don't mind relatively low-speed file transfers, EasyLAN may be for you. It's also an uncomplicated way to share one-of-a-kind peripherals such as printers.

EasyLAN is configured as a star network with one computer designated as the hub. The workstations are connected to the hub by RS-232 connections, which can be modems, null-modem cables, or PBX switched-circuit connections. With this type of connection, no unit can be more than a thousand feet from the hub.

Since there are no network control cards to bother with, EasyLAN's hardware requirements are simple: an available serial port and some RS-232 cable. The package includes 30 feet of cable with a 25-pin connector on each end, a 9-pin connector for connecting to a PC/AT serial port, a copy of the EasyLAN software for each computer to be connected, and a supplemental diskette containing EasyLAN utility programs. EasyLAN is controlled entirely through its software. Moreover, you can disconnect from the network if you need to use the serial port for something else.

All communications are routed through the hub computer. Since that computer handles all traffic between all other computers on the network, you must limit the number of computers on the network so that the hub can still be used for other tasks. The limit is 19 workstations plus the hub. To use this many computers on the network, you must have two serial ports (the usual COM1 and COM2) plus three multiport adapters, each of which has six serial ports. Of course, in this configuration, the hub is zero-slot in name only since you need a card for each multiport adapter, and at least one for the serial ports.

EasyLAN, as its name implies, is quick and easy to install. Users who already have a serial port installed need only snap the cable to the 25-pin connectors. You prepare the multiport adapters the same way. It's just as easy to install the software. The installation program is menu-driven and requires no particular expertise. Even novice LAN users won't get too anxious, since the user's manual thoroughly explains the installation options.

All printers, no matter which computer they're physically connected to, can be shared via EasyLAN. Any network computer, even one without a printer port, can use a network printer. Unfortunately, all output is spooled, and there's no way to bypass the print queue without removing the printer from the network. Some EasyLAN users have complained of network crashes when using virtual printers, but the problem was not evident in the EasyLAN release we evaluated.

Operating an EasyLAN network quickly becomes automatic. Since there's no specialized file server, the software provides the paths for all network disk operations. To discriminate network commands from DOS commands, EasyLAN's commands have an EZ prefix. For instance, to display the directory of a remote computer, you use the command EZDIR, with appropriate parameters. There are similar commands for other disk operations.

The presence of these specialized disk commands points out one of EasyLAN's shortcomings. It doesn't allow you to share disks across the network. To use a remote computer's files, you must direct EasyLAN to copy those files across the network onto your computer's disk. You can lock a remote file, however, so that when you obtain a file from another computer, no one else can use it until you return the updated copy to the originating computer.

If you need to have several computers sharing a database, EasyLAN probably isn't the answer. However, before you write it off, try monitoring typical file use on the computers you want to connect. If your programs constantly access relatively small disk files, EasyLAN may best suit your needs. If you're not familiar with networks, you can easily become confused when evaluating network speeds. On RS-232 networks, you can't get high-speed operation. Therefore, zero-slot LANs that allow disk sharing add a burden to the system that slows it down greatly. If your system requires frequent access to shared disks, consider a hardware-oriented network.

LIVING ON A TOKEN-RING NETWORK

What you can do on a network depends on how your workstation was installed. After you have installed the IBM LAN network, there are four types of workstations, each a subset of the previous one:

> server
> messenger
> receiver
> redirector

Any or all of these can be user workstations.

The server can share disks and printers, send messages, receive messages, and use disks from another server on the network (if there is one). The messenger can send and receive messages and can use the disks shared by the server. The receiver can only receive messages and use shared files. Finally, the redirector can use only shared files.

Network Commands

All commands concerning network access begin with the keyword NET, followed by a command. Entering NET by itself will display a menu from which you can select the services you require. On the workstations that are started as servers or messengers, you can also pop up the NET menu by pressing Ctrl-Alt-Break.

To make your workstation available on the network, you must first have installed the network support program on your workstation, which places several device drivers in your CONFIG.SYS file. You then issue the NET START command at the DOS prompt or from a batch file. The parameters you use depend on the role your workstation will have on the network. The general form of the command is

NET START *role name*

where *role* is one of the four types of workstation: To make your workstations a server, use SRV. To make it a messenger, use MSG. To make it a receiver, use RCV. To make it a redirector, use RDR. *Name* is the name your workstation will be known by. You can use any name of up to 14 characters, but it helps if you use something meaningful.

In addition to your station's network name, there are many other parameters used for fine-tuning performance and allocating memory, but they are beyond the scope of this book. Tuning the network may take as little as changing the FILES and BUFFERS configuration commands on the server or the workstations. At the other extreme, you could set up RAM disks on workstations to load executable and run-time files that are accessed often. Then you'd have to read them from the server only once. This greatly reduces network traffic, which makes the network run faster.

To share a disk (or more often a subdirectory) on the network, you use a command of the form

NET SHARE *name* = C:*path* /*switch*

where *name* is what the disk is to be known as on the network and *path* is the real subdirectory name on your workstation. The switches you can use are /R for read, /W for write, and /C for create. You can combine them with a single slash; for example

/RWC

allows anyone who uses the named directory to read, write, create, and delete files on the disk. Thus, the command

NET SHARE DOS33 = C:\DOS /R

would allow anyone on the network to use the disk DOS33. However, they could only read the files, not update nor delete them, nor create new files on that disk. To use the DOS33 directory from your workstation, you would enter the command

NET USE *drive:* *servername*\DOS33

where *drive* is the designation the network drive will have on your workstation, and *servername* is the network name of the server on which the DOS33 directory actually resides. The drive designator must refer to a disk that is not already on your workstation. Unless you have a LASTDRIVE command in your CONFIG.SYS file that lets you access higher drive designations, the designation you use must not be greater than N. If access to the disk required a password, you would append either an asterisk or the password to the command. The asterisk tells the network software to prompt you for a password. If you don't add the asterisk or a password, you will fail if you try to access a password protected disk. Thus, for example, if the password were BEATIT, you could enter

BEATIT

Or, to have the network prompt you for a password, you could enter

NET USE H: \\\\RATIOCINATION\DOS33 *

It's better to use the asterisk, because otherwise anyone can see—and use—your password. When you use the asterisk, you enter the password blind. The network administrator sets the password for each shared disk and is responsible for deciding who knows about it.

A server can also share printers by using a command of the form

NET SHARE *printername* = LPT*N*

where *printername* is the network name by which the printer is known, and N is 1, 2, or 3. To use that printer from your workstation, you would enter a command such as

NET USE LPT3 \\HALLUCINATORY\OUTOFTHISWORLD GUNCH

where HALLUCINATORY is the name of the printer server, OUTOF-THISWORLD is the name of the printer, and GUNCH is a password. A password is optional and can be requested when the NET SHARE command is issued.

You have some flexibility in the logical name you use for a printer. Thus, for example, you might already have an LPT1 and LPT2 attached to your local workstation. If you wanted to use a network printer, you could refer to it as LPT3 and still retain access to your local printers. Alternatively, you could refer to it as LPT1, in which case any output directed to logical printer port 1 will actually be sent to the network printer you are attaching, instead of to the printer on LPT1 on your workstation.

Notice the double backslash that precedes the path names used for network drives and devices. It is a convention used by IBM's LAN program to designate the server name that controls the devices you want to attach. This distinguishes remote shared disks from you local drives. Thus, if you have SERVER1 and SERVER2 and they both share disks called TEXT, then you would want to know whether you are talking to \\SERVER1\TEXT or \\SERVER2\TEXT.

Among the many other NET commands, NET PRINT sends printer output to the specified server, NET SEND sends messages to other computers on the network, NET PAUSE temporarily removes you from the network, and NET NAME finds out whether a name is in use on the network.

Network Etiquette

When you have to share space and resources with others, you need some rules to keep things orderly. Below are some general guidelines, perhaps the "ten commandments" of networking. Depending on the sophisticated of your network, you may need considerably more rules, but these will do for a start.

1. Know who your network administrator is, and make full use of his or her expertise.

2. Keep personal data off the network. (You can keep it on floppies or on your own hard disk.)

3. If you take a printer off-line to remove your output, remember to put it back online.

4. Use RAM disks where possible to copy and execute shared programs. It puts a lot less strain on the network's resources if you can read overlays from a disk in your own computer rather than from a remote computer.

5. If you place data on the network, use E-Mail to tell other users and the network administrator about it.

6. Similarly, if you place programs on the network, inform the network administrator and users of what it does. Ideally, only the network administrator should place shared data and programs on the network, but this is not always practical.

7. Do not disconnect network cables without first consulting your administrator.

8. If you receive a broadcast message to log off the network, do so immediately. It may be your data that is at stake.

9. Always log off the network if you leave your machine unattended or when you won't need network access for a while. This will usually improve performance for other users.

10. *Never* turn off the file server.

Let's expand on these points. When you share common facilities, there are obvious productivity gains. However, they require that everyone using the network cooperates. It's relatively simple to share peripherals on most networks, but there must be some commonly accepted rules about who controls them and the ways in which they should be used. Abuse of the network facilities can make it impossible for other members of the LAN to do their work effectively.

For example, bus networks, as we mentioned in Chapter 11, have workstations attached by T connectors. These do not cause problems if the T is left in place. However, removing the T will break the network circuit because it forms part of the bus. This often requires a complete restart. Generally speaking, you should handle the T connectors with extreme caution, because they tend to wear out.

You should plug only LAN cables into the LAN adapter board connector. Do not connect the LAN cable to anything else. Another board, such as a mainframe link card, may have the same kind of physical connector. However, if you plug the T connector into other types of cards, you may cause the network to hang.

Some networks require you to log out of the system. Otherwise, you may hang up any devices that you have attached during your network session. This problem may not even be apparent until the end of the day when the system administrator attempts to perform maintenance functions. Logging out will effectively relinquish your hold over any resources that are still attached.

On a server workstation, not logging out could expose your files to tampering. Try not to reboot while using a server in nondedicated mode. If other network users are using files on your computer, doing so will lock up their screens. This is an instance in which electronic mail is useful for informing users of the situation. This is also why file servers should be dedicated machines.

You may be fascinated by the novelty of E-Mail, but you may also find that it's easy to abuse. For example, you can clutter up the system with junk E-Mail, such as sending thanks for the thank-you note you received.

Printers can be particularly frustrating in a shared environment. For example, no matter when you want to use a laser printer, you find it out of paper. If you have just run off a large print job, check the paper tray, and refill it if necessary.

It's also helpful to have a place to stack output. Often people will print a document and not pick it up for hours or even days! Some LAN printer sharing facilities can generate a separator page with the user's name on it at the beginning a print, which makes identifying its owner simple. Unfortunately, not all printer sharing software is this helpful.

Using a RAM disk to store program overlay files can speed up execution time for large-scale applications. You should copy all the overlays and any other ancillary files used by the application to your RAM disk. If you don't, every time the program needs overlays, it must transfer them over the network before it can use them. If everyone on the network did this, performance would decline dramatically.

The Network Administrator

A network administrator is responsible for many tasks related to smooth operation of a network. Without someone in charge, a network can quickly degrade into a state of chaos. The person responsible should have some technical knowledge but needn't be a guru. The most important requirements are a willingness to accept the responsibility, commitment to the task, and good organizational skills.

A network administrator's tasks may include:

- ▲ Organizing shared data.
- ▲ Authorizing use of the network.
- ▲ Restricting access rights for some users.
- ▲ Enforcing rules.
- ▲ Loading and maintaining shared applications.
- ▲ Making sure that software licenses are adhered to.
- ▲ Maintaining the network operating system on the server.
- ▲ Making sure that the network software on the workstations is of the same release as the server.
- ▲ Making sure that peripherals on the network are functioning correctly.
- ▲ Removing serious violators of network rules from the network.
- ▲ Testing applications for potential network conflicts *before* loading them on the network.
- ▲ Ensuring the security of any modems that allow remote access to the network.

These are just a few of the requirements of the network administrator. It's a tough job but somebody has to do it! We offer below ten commandments of network etiquette for the network administrator.

1. Put the ten commandments for the user into operation.

2. If network administration is not your primary job, be prepared to make adequate time available from your other duties.

3. Obtain authority to allow you to strictly enforce the rules.

4. Exercise care when giving special privileges to users.

5. Change master access passwords often.

6. Be sure that correct software licensing procedures are followed for any commercial software packages on the network.

7. Inform users when changes are made that may affect them.

8. Back up the server daily. Make an incremental backup daily and a full backup biweekly.

9. Thoroughly test any program on a non-networked computer before you install it on the network.

10. Periodically inspect all peripherals (especially printers).

TWO NETWORK SCENARIOS

In order to give you some idea of the circumstances in which a network can provide productivity benefits, we have constructed two scenarios. The first concerns a dental/orthodontic practice. You might wonder how such a relatively small-scale business might profit from a network. However, we have chosen this example precisely because networking can bring unique benefits. The second scenario involves automating a real estate office. In this scenario, the network is useful because it provides several workers with access to the information they need.

Scenario 1: A Dental/Orthodontic Practice

Our first case study is a dental/orthodontic practice. In addition to the dentist and his assistant, the office employs two clerks. As you might expect, one clerk updates the dental records, which are stored in a massive database on one computer. A billing clerk extracts information from this on procedures performed the previous day for billing purposes. Each procedure has a numeric code, and each code is assigned a fixed price. The billing clerk needs to extract from all records updated the previous day the name and address of the patient, and the codes for the procedures performed.

Without a network, each clerk would have to input a great deal of the same information separately from the same paper records. However, with a network, data can be entered once. The single database will contain all pertinent information, which helps to ensure the integrity of the data.

This might seem an ideal situation for a simple connection such as EasyLAN. The network initially includes two computers and one shared graphics printer. The record clerk's computer has the database and the database management program on its hard disk. Since the Easy-LAN software uses only serial ports (which most PCs already have), this is an inexpensive way of seeing if a network provides a solution.

To save time, the billing clerk's computer also has a copy of the database program. However, all records are extracted from the main patient database on the records clerk's computer. Records of payments, insurance claims, and other pertinent financial information are entered by the billing clerk into the remote database. Maintaining only one database ensures integrity of the records. Because the database is so large and complex, the records clerk's computer has a 40MB hard disk.

The billing clerk also carries out mass mailings, takes care of insurance forms, and sends out late-payment notices and appointment reminders. Therefore, the billing clerk uses a word processor and mailmerge program, as well as the database program. The billing clerk's computer is attached to a dot-matrix printer, in which billing forms are permanently loaded. Whenever the billing clerk needs to print anything other than the billing forms, he sends the printout to the graphics printer attached to the records clerk's computer.

However, let's assume that this dentist wants to make more creative use of technology. He adds a third workstation in his office. On this workstation, he can call up dental records for each patient as he works, and enter any special procedures he performs immediately, thus updating one aspect of the patient records.

In addition, to aid in his orthodontic work, the dentist uses a graphics program to record changes directly to the tooth diagrams. He enters the information by digitizing the dental X-rays. Once digitized, the X-ray images can be manipulated to illustrate the effects of orthodontic procedures. For general cases, the dentist can use digitized X-rays and add comments and indicators to the final image. These images are printed on a laser printer attached to the records clerk's computer and used by the dentist as he works on a patient.

With the addition of the graphics workstation, more LAN hardware is needed to provide the required performance. Without the additional hardware, the time it would take to pass the graphics data from one workstation to another would make the whole system function too slowly to be acceptable. The final version of the network is shown in Figure 14.4.

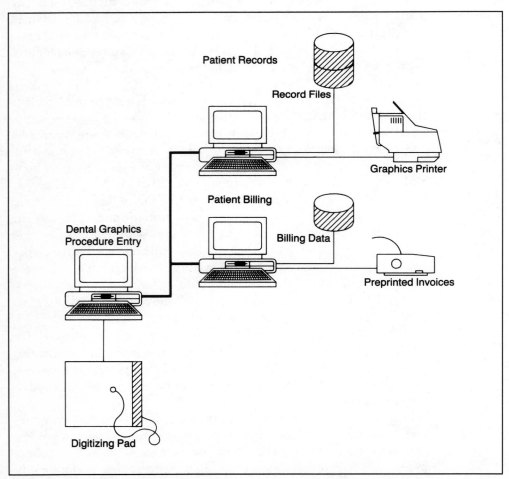

Figure 14.4 ▲ *A Dental Office Network.*

Scenario 2: A Real Estate Office

Another prime candidate for office automation is a medium-sized real estate office. Each agent must access the multiple listing service (MLS) several times a day to get housing information targeted to their clients' specific needs. The MLS functions as a bulletin board, from which agents request records meeting specific criteria and download them. However, downloading is expensive in time and money. Moreover, because all the output goes directly to paper, it is hard to update.

There are many other functions performed in the office, quite a few of which involve filling out forms. Some centralized control could greatly reduce the redundancy and improve efficiency.

With this in mind, we set about designing a networking system for a real estate office. These were the main requirements:

1. The daily updates to the MLS should be collected automatically.

2. The agent requests should be collected and used to determine what will be downloaded from the MLS.

3. If the data downloaded from the MLS does not meet the agents' requirements, the agents should be able to download the data they need. Any such data should be placed in the local download of the MLS file.

4. All access to the MLS will be via a shared modem.

5. The agents should have access to the network when they are in the field.

6. Other information not coming from the MLS, such as bank repossessions, for sale by owner, and foreclosures should be incorporated into the MLS file.

7. All the specialized forms required by the real estate industry, state and federal governments, insurance and financial institutions, should be produced locally and filled out automatically.

The solution is illustrated in Figure 14.5. There are six workstations. Four of them are used by the agents, one is a file server, and the last is a modem server. The file server is also attached to a modem. It is programmed to download the MLS during the night when the office is

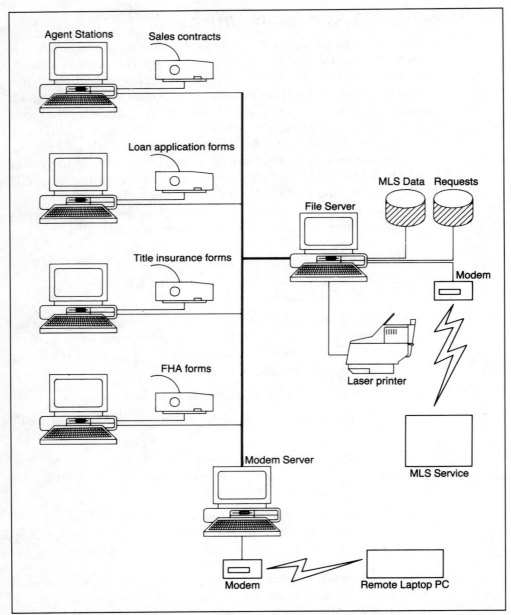

Figure 14.5 ▲ *A Real Estate Office Network.*

closed. When the network is brought up in the morning, the latest listings are available to all the agents. The modem server is attached to a separate phone line, which is used by agents in the field, who are supplied with laptop computers. Every one of the six workstations also acts as a printer server. Five printers are permanently loaded with the most commonly used forms. The sixth is a laser printer, which is attached to the server. All other forms are produced and filled out on this printer.

ACCESSING MAINFRAMES AND MINICOMPUTERS

CHANGES IN PC TECHNOLOGY over the past few years have altered the way in which corporations view information centers. The major areas of change are in LANs, database technology, electronic mail and host connectivity products.

In many companies, PCs are no longer stand-alone systems. They are rapidly becoming nodes (or integral parts) of LANs or host networks. This may mean that you no longer own your PC data files. Rather, they are considered a company resource to be centrally managed. In these circumstances, your actions as a PC user may threaten the integrity of the system.

We have already heard of one major company that controls the contents of its employees' PCs. In this company, you must leave your PC attached to the network at all times. If you don't, your supervisor gets a complaint—electronically, of course. Some time during the wee hours a mainframe computer will look at your PC's hard disk to see that all your software, including the operating system, is of the current release. If not, it will download new software to your PC and upgrade you on the spot. This handy little maintenance program will also erase any programs that it doesn't like the look of! So if you want to use noncorporate software on your PC, you had better keep it on a floppy disk. This may sound like Orwell's 1984; it's definitely here in many companies, and others are anxious to install such a system. All we can say is *caveat usor.*

The vaunted speed of mainframes may not always be an advantage, because they serve many users. In fact, many 386 PCs will run popular applications faster than they could run if they were attached to a mainframe as one of many workstations. If this is so, why would you want to link to a mainframe? The answer may lie in the thousands of megabytes of storage available, or possibly in the ability to run mainframe applications. In other cases, you could be sharing the programs and application data with hundreds of other users in a timesharing system.

It is possible that you have already been linking your PC to a mainframe without even realizing it. If you use CompuServe or The Source, you will have already had a taste of timesharing. If you use an automatic teller machine, you are using the equivalent of a PC connected via a modem or coaxial cable to the main banking computer, which is invariably a mainframe or minicomputer. If you do home banking from your PC, you are usually dialing in to a multiuser mainframe.

LINKING TO A MAINFRAME

There are basically two ways to link a PC to a mainframe or minicomputer. Either you dial in via modem following procedures similar to those outlined in Chapter 13, or you have a terminal-emulation card in your PC linked to the mainframe by a coaxial cable. Once you are linked, you communicate with the mainframe using a *terminal-emulation* program. This is a piece of software that makes the mainframe think your PC is a dumb terminal with no processing power of its own. (ProComm, the telecommunications program discussed in Chapter 13, can emulate ten types of terminals. Many telecommunications programs include a number of terminal-emulation protocols.)

If you need only occasional access to a mainframe, dialing in should be sufficient. However, if you must work extensively with a mainframe application, you will do better if you have some type of network access card in your PC.

One of the principal problems in linking to a mainframe is the fact that mainframes use *synchronous* communications, while telecommunications on a PC is based on *asynchronous* communications. Synchronous communications are faster but need more expensive hardware, usually including a special type of wire. To perform the conversion you need to connect your PC to a *protocol converter,* which is attached to the mainframe by a *coaxial cable.* You also need terminal-emulation software, and either a terminal-emulation board or a modem.

We can't go into detail on how to link to a mainframe, or how to use one once you are linked, because every installation is different. Most mainframes use customized software specific to the company's needs. Even the operating system itself may be customized.

Direct-Link IBM 3270 Emulation

By far the most common terminals for an IBM mainframe are the 3270 series teminals, which include the 3278, 3279, 3178, and 3179. As we discussed in Chapter 11, terminals are usually connected to a mainframe through an intermediary device called a network cluster controller. Each controller attaches to one or more terminals, usually via coaxial cables. The maximum data rate of these coaxial cables is 2.35 megabits per second.

The 3270 series terminals are generally unintelligent devices. The "smart" part of the network is the cluster controller. The mainframe communicates with the terminals in pages or screens of data rather than line by line. You can actually have thousands of 3270-class terminals on one network, which can also incorporate several mainframes. To provide this connectivity, IBM developed a wide-area networking (WAN) protocol called SNA (Systems Network Architecture).

To allow PCs the same type of access to mainframes that was available from dumb terminals, several manufacturers marketed a 3270 adapter card that could be installed in a PC. This took care of making the hardware look like a dumb terminal. To use it, you also need terminal-emulation software. Figure 15.1 shows a typical micro-mainframe link using a mixture of 3270 terminals and PCs pretending to be 3270 terminals. These are connected using SNA via cluster controllers. The cluster controllers are in turn connected either directly or via communications controllers and synchronous modems.

IBM is not the only manufacturer to offer this facility. Digital Communications Associates (DCA) has released a 3270 IRMA card with IRMALink software. More recently, Attachmate has released a 3270 adapter with emulator software called Extra. Attachmate's software will run on IBM, IRMA, and Attachmate adapter cards, whereas most other manufacturers' software will work only with their own adapters.

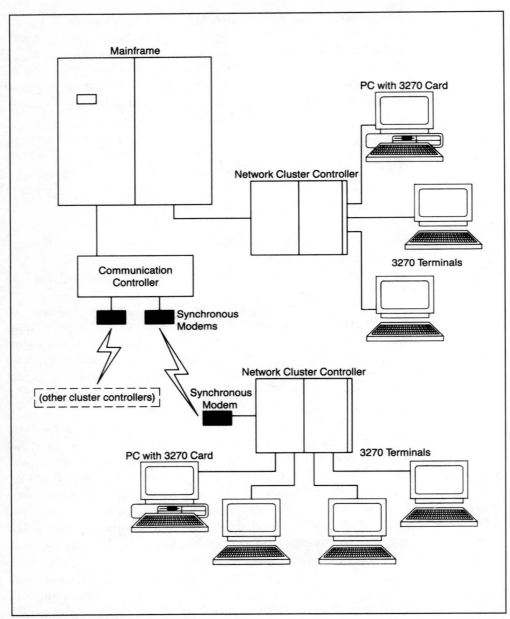

Figure 15.1 ▲ *Typical Micro-Mainframe Links.*

Because 3270-class terminals are dumb devices, they are not expected to transfer files. Therefore, each emulation package includes a set of file transfer utilities that allow you to move data between the PC and the mainframe. The speed of file transfers depends on whether you are attached to a network cluster controller hooked directly to the mainframe, or linked to it via a synchronous modem. As you would expect, a direct link is fastest, followed by a cluster controller. A modem is usually the slowest type of link. The exceptions to this are the more recent high-speed error-correcting modems that can achieve data speeds in excess of 9600 bits per second. Unfortunately, these modems tend to be expensive.

Dial-In Access

If you don't work in a company that has a 3274 cluster controller, you must use dial-in access. To do so, you go through a *rotor* of modems to a protocol converter attached to the mainframe, as shown in Figure 15.2. The protocol converter is usually a minicomputer. The rotor permits a variety of terminal types to link to an SNA network. The IBM mainframe expects your terminal to be an IBM 3270-class device attached to a 3274 cluster controller. With a protocol converter, the terminal could be any type of terminal or personal computer. On the mainframe side of the converter everything looks like a 3270 terminal.

Dialing in using a telecommunications program offers some, but usually not all, of the features of a terminal attached by coaxial cables. Specifically, you will probably lack an appropriate error-checking protocol for binary file transfers. Most telecommunications programs include some such protocols, but they are not generally the ones available on mainframes. About the only one that might be useful is Kermit, but this requires a similar version of Kermit on the mainframe.

If you use a dial-in terminal-emulation package, you need several layers of protocol conversion. For example, you could set your communications package to emulate a DEC VT-100 terminal and dial up to a modem attached to a protocol converter. You inform the converter that you are using a VT-100. The protocol converter will then send you sequences to control the screen of a VT-100. It tells the mainframe that

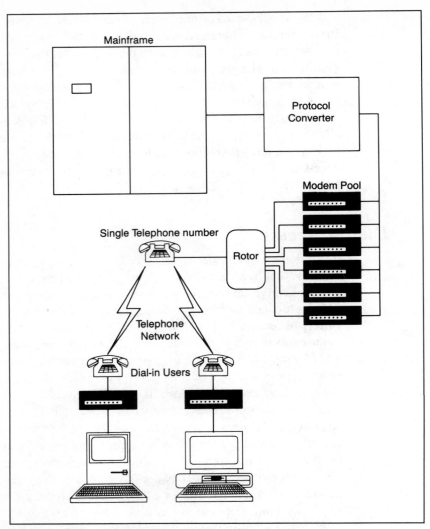

Figure 15.2 ▲ *Mainframe Dial-in Access.*

you are really a 3270 terminal with 12 or even 24 function keys. If you can't map the function keys to something you can use, you may encounter a world of problems. (Note that ProComm Plus includes a separate keyboard-remapping utility for this purpose.)

COOPERATIVE PROCESSING

One very good reason for attaching PCs to mainframes is to spread the workload sensibly among the PCs and the mainframe. This is known as *cooperative processing,* and it has many applications. In this chapter, we'll look at two: using a database that is too large to fit on a PC, and using company-wide E-Mail.

Cooperative processing is particularly useful in very large data entry applications. What cooperative processing is all about is selecting the right tool for the job. Mainframes are excellent at managing large databases, but very inefficient at spotting simple data entry errors.

A typical mainframe data entry system may involve accepting data from several hundred terminals. Each time you press the Return key on a terminal, a special editing program is executed on the mainframe. This program checks the data entries for such errors as being out of range, or being of the wrong type (e.g., is it between 1 and 99, is it numeric?).

Let's assume that the most common error is putting alphabetic characters in a numeric field. This problem may take the mainframe program only the tiniest amount of time to discover. Unfortunately, getting the screen to the mainframe and receiving it back with the errors flagged takes quite a bit of mainframe processing. The PC could easily check the entered data for errors, but unfortunately it doesn't have access to the database, nor does it know what errors to check for. If this task could be broken down so that the PC could check the data for errors before transmitting it to the mainframe, a great deal of time would be saved. In order to break down this job, first let's consider what the mainframe does best:

- ▲ Storing large amounts of data and retrieving it quickly
- ▲ Wide-area networking
- ▲ Printing reports at very high speeds
- ▲ Running applications that require sharing lots of data

Now consider the strengths of a PC:

- ▲ Controlling its own screen
- ▲ Validating the data entered on it

▲ Responding to the user quickly

▲ Local-area networking

Figure 15.3 illustrates a typical example of a cooperative processing application. The PC initiates a procedure that will attach to the mainframe and download the information it needs to edit the data—such items as lookup tables, screen layouts, data entry screens, and valid ranges and data types. Using the latest version of the application's data entry validation tables, the PC can edit the data entries locally. It won't have to interact with the mainframe until the data meets the validation requirements. Once the data has been validated, it can be safely transmitted to the mainframe. The mainframe can assume that the data is acceptable and continue with the processing.

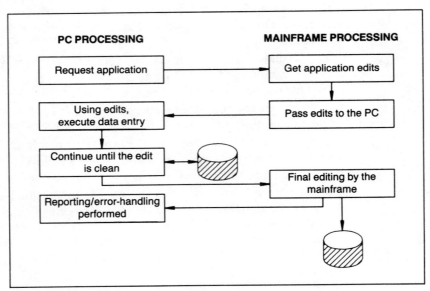

Figure 15.3 ▲ *Cooperative Processing.*

With this type of arrangement and some careful planning and education, cooperative processing can greatly increase the productivity of a department. In addition, you have centralized control over the form in which data is entered. If your procedures for validating data have been updated, you can expect that everyone else who enters similar data is using the same procedures and standards as you are.

Not very many such systems are currently in use. However, with new CPU architectures and industry trends toward the distributed database (discussed later this chapter), a growing number of cooperative processing applications are beginning to appear.

Large Databases

A large database is one of the traditional reasons for employing a mainframe. It used to be that the only way you could use one was via a terminal. However, by the early 1980s, PCs running terminal emulation began rapidly filling that role.

Examples of large database applications include airline reservation systems, online encyclopedias, and census and demographic information. With an airline reservation system, not only must the system be available to all the airline staff but also to myriad travel agents. With this many users involved, it's cheaper (by a few hundred dollars per workstation) to use a terminal rather than a PC and a terminal-emulation package.

Figure 15.4 shows a scaled-down example of a centralized database application. It uses a mixture of workstations that are all hooked into a common IBM mainframe SNA communications network. In this example, the PCs could use 3270 terminal emulation by way of an IRMA 3270 card and IRMA software. (Macintoshes can use similar products, such as DCA's Appleline.)

Only the mainframe can add, change, or delete data in the database. However, you can use a PC to produce reports. To do so, you have to use terminal-emulation software to extract the data. You then download the data to your PC and produce the report from it.

In this situation, you must enter your data on the mainframe using a host-based data-entry system. This ensures the security of the data and allows the data files to be processed centrally. However, it relegates your PC to a dumb terminal.

SQL Servers

Another reason to link to a mainframe is to make use of Structured Query Language (SQL). SQL can be used to create and delete databases; to supply security on a multiuser system; and to add, delete, or

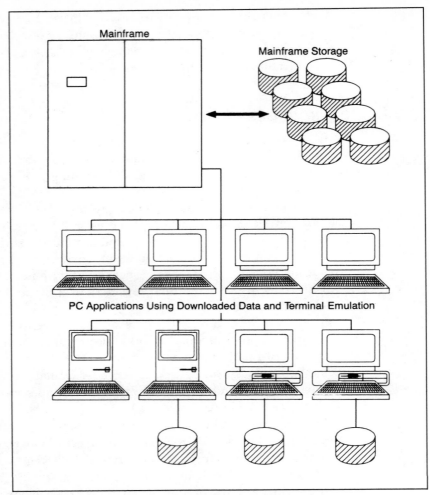

Figure 15.4 ▲ *A Traditional Large-Scale Mainframe Database Network.*

modify database records. Many publishers of database software for the PC market are beginning to include SQL compatibility in their products. Oracle, Ashton-Tate, Borland/Ansa and several other companies have announced or included SQL compatibility in their latest versions of database packages.

SQL is not a newcomer to the computer marketplace. It has been an established database management language in the mainframe and minicomputer world for some time. IBM offers SQL/DS and DB2 for its mainframe systems and plans for SQL to be part of its OS/2 Extended Edition.

So what has SQL got to do with connecting to a mainframe? SQL offers a global standard unparalleled by any other database language. This means that you could write an application based around SQL and port the entire system to another machine—such as a mainframe—and have it work with little or no conversion. Compared to dBASE or R:base, SQL is a very compact language. Functions that require over a hundred lines of dBASE code can be accomplished in three to four lines of SQL.

Distributed databases will be an important area for SQL standardization. In a distributed setup where data is scattered over LANs, mainframes, and micros, it would be almost impossible to operate the system successfully if a database standard language such as SQL were not in use. The main task of distributed database management is to make a hodge-podge of data look like one file. SQL should be able to find the necessary data on any computer in the system whenever the application is executed. Figure 15.5 illustrates a typical distributed database.

USING E-MAIL ON A MAINFRAME

One feature that a mainframe can provide is E-Mail. You have already seen something of how E-Mail is implemented on a network and read about the public E-Mail services such as MCI Mail and EasyPlex.

Mainframe E-Mail is considerably more sophisticated than LAN E-Mail. For example, you can use some E-Mail systems to check the schedule of everyone involved in a project, to find the first available time at which they could all meet. You could then send a message to all concerned, letting them know about the meeting and request an acknowledgment, so that you're sure everyone has received your notice. If a group of people is working on a project requiring centralized control of documents, you can use E-Mail to retrieve the documents you need and route them to all concerned parties. You can also keep track of who has received which documents.

If you have more than one mainframe in the system, you can have each one's E-Mail talk to the others. Figure 15.6 shows how PROFS (IBM's electronic mail system) allows E-Mail to pass between two or more mainframes. Most terminals and PCs with 3270 cards will be connected via SNA. Those that aren't can dial in using a standard modem.

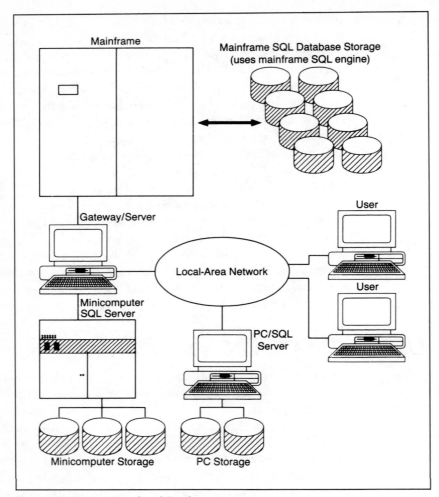

Figure 15.5 ▲ *A Distributed Database.*

PROFS exists over all systems and is aware of users on both. The systems need to be connected by communications controllers as shown in the figure. PROFS uses a master directory that associates a nickname with a real user ID and mainframe. For example, the ID on mainframe A could be XWALT and on B, XFRED. PROFS knows them as WALT and FRED. When FRED sends WALT a note, PROFS tells the mainframe operating system to send a note from XFRED at MAINA to XWALT on MAINB.

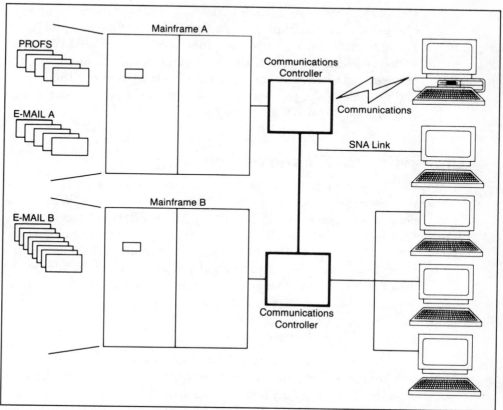

Figure 15.6 ▲ *E-Mail Access between Mainframes.*

You can even link a mainframe E-Mail system to outside E-Mail services. This makes it possible to send E-Mail between all types of computer systems. You use a public-access E-Mail network, such as MCI Mail or CompuServe, to link mainframes to a single company's minicomputers or mainframes at different locations. Without this link, the company would have to have its own satellite network.

USING MICRO-MAINFRAME COMMUNICATIONS: PROBLEMS AND PITFALLS

Whenever PCs and mainframes interact, problems are bound to occur. There are many variables that come into play including PC and mainframe operating system updates, communications equipment changes, and protocol upgrades. Any one of these can pose a problem to a manufacturer trying to remain compatible, but several can cause severe problems. In spite of this potentially hostile environment, the problems have been surprisingly few. In this section, we will attempt to outline some of the problems you may encounter, and where possible, suggest ways to circumvent them.

Converting the Character Sets

One significant difference between microcomputers and mainframes is that they use almost completely different character sets. While most personal computers use ASCII, or a variation of it, mainframes (at least, IBM mainframes) use EBCDIC, a 7-bit character code. Many of the ASCII characters do not have an equivalent in EBCDIC. You must use some kind of translation protocol if you want to use the file on the mainframe (e.g., if you want to print it on the mainframe's printer).

Converting New Lines

Another difference is that IBM mainframes and PCs control their newlines in completely different ways. PC text files have lines separated by carriage-return/line-feed pairs, while on the mainframe the definition of a "line" of text is established in a file header known as a data control block (DCB). If the record format is fixed, then each line is the same length, and PC lines of different lengths must be extended or truncated; if the record format is variable, then the mainframe file must have block or record descriptor words to tell it the length of the line. This is generally handled by the communications software that links you to the mainframe.

Finally, mainframes have special carriage control just for printers. For example, if you set your printer width to 133, and you can set up the printer to accept ASA control codes, then you can use characters in the first column to control page ejects, carriage suppression, double spacing, and so forth. The most common control character is the "new-page" code, which is 1. Double spacing is 0 and line-feed suppression is -.

Control Program Problems

Most software to manage systems attached by coaxial cable is memory resident and activated by using hot-key combinations. One of the popular ones is the Alt-Escape combination. This may conflict with RAM-resident pop-up utilities like SideKick or SuperKey. Most of the more recent control programs allow you to select the hot-key combination to avoid this conflict.

The size of many terminal-control programs can cause you problems as well. Quite a few of them use over 100K. If you also use some RAM-resident utilities, you may not have any room to run your local applications. The newer control programs can load themselves into expanded memory, leaving a small resident portion in conventional memory.

Hardware Conflicts

As with any card you install in a PC, you may find that your terminal-emulation board wants to use the same DMA channel, port address, or IRQ line as another card you have already installed. Unfortunately, 3270 connection cards have more than their share of these conflicts. Most cards use DMA channel 3 and several port addresses. To illustrate this type of conflict, early versions of the Quadram EGA card will stop a 3270 card from functioning properly. To resolve the conflict you must use a utility supplied with the EGA called QEGA.COM. Copy this program to your hard disk's root directory and add the line

QEGA CGA:ON

to your AUTOEXEC.BAT file, or to the batch file that loads your 3270-emulation program.

LOOKING TO THE FUTURE

The trend of the future is toward greater standardization. You can expect that applications will come to look the same whether they run on PCs, mainframes, or LANs. Protocols for networks will also become standardized. You can expect higher data speeds, and closer integration between voice and data communication.

System Applications Architecture

System Applications Architecture (SAA) is IBM's declared strategic direction over the next five years. SAA is a comprehensive attempt to standardize the way programmers develop applications. If it is successful, any application—word processors, spreadsheets, or communications programs—should offer you the same control tools.

Virtually all technical aspects of operating systems, communications, application design, graphics, windows, and databases, as well as the way systems are integrated, will be incorporated. IBM has often been criticized in the past for offering a diverse set of systems that had severe problems conversing with each other. With SAA, we may see applications running on a PC that look and feel the same as one running on a mainframe, or for that matter a minicomputer.

Communications protocols are a critical part of SAA because an application should be able to request a piece of data regardless of its location. Instead of having to select a file, perform an ASCII/EBCDIC translation, move the file, and store it, the user should simply be able to request a piece of data; it is up to the system to know where that piece of data is and in what format, and what translations to apply.

Advanced Program-to-Program Communication

IBM is also investing vast resources into its APPC (Advanced Program-to-Program Communication) standard. APPC is not something you can buy. It is a set of general rules that other packages will implement, both from IBM and other developers. APPC is part of IBM's SNA plan for linking all IBM devices.

Without going into too much detail, APPC can set up communications between anything connected via SNA—PCs, IBM mainframes, IBM minicomputers, and minicomputers from other companies such as Wang and DEC. These communications can initiate a process on a remote machine. Thus, a PC could call a minicomputer and activate a program to be run on that machine. The output could be routed back to the PC after the job had been run. Similarly, a mainframe could invoke a process on a PC. For example, you might wish to maintain standard data files on several local-area networks. The mainframe could attach to the LAN server, get the server to list its contents, and transfer the updated files to the server's hard disk. Conversely, a mainframe could poll several PCs and extract daily summary files. All this could be performed late at night when the PCs are not being used.

Cable TV

Cable TV companies are as yet an untapped resource for data communications. Cable television is available in millions of homes and is in effect a broadband network, as described in Chapter 12. The television signals occupy only a part of the available spectrum the cable can handle. This leaves lots of room for carrying signals for such uses as networks and other forms of high-speed data transfer.

With a special card (yet to be designed) you might be able to transmit and receive data via the TV cable at extremely high speeds. The high speed would allow you to transmit such complex data as a photograph of your granddaughter in Australia. In addition, you could examine illustrated catalogs online, or receive detailed blueprints for repairing your car. The possibilities are limited only by the imagination of system design engineers.

PART IV

APPENDICES

APPENDIX A

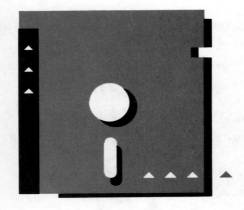

SOURCE CODE FOR ASSEMBLY-LANGUAGE PROGRAMS

T HE FOLLOWING LISTINGS provide the assembly-language source code for programs presented in Chapters 2, 3, 6, and 7.

```
page        55,132
title  STARTAT:        Use in BAT files to control start time.
;
;-----------------------------------------------------------------------
; Environment        PC DOS 2.00 or Higher - IBM PC/AT/Compatible.
; DOS Syntax -       STARTAT HH:MM:SS
; M P Waterhouse July 17, 1987
; Requirements: An accurate DOS time would be useful.
;-----------------------------------------------------------------------
; Setup so that EXE2BIN can convert the program to .COM format
CSEG        segment para public 'CODE'
            assume  cs:CSEG,ds:CSEG,es:CSEG,ss:CSEG
            org     100H                   ;all COM files start here
START:      jmp     GO                     ;leap over the data area
;-----------------------------------------------------------------------
BY10        db      10                     ;when we need a div by 10
PARM        db      128 dup(0)             ;Parm stow area init to 0
STHH        db      00
STMM        db      00
STSS        db      00
;-----------------------------------------------------------------------
MAIN        proc    far                    ;keep it clean
GO:         MOV     SI,80H                 ;Point string index at parm
            MOV     DI,OFFSET PARM         ;Point to our PARM area
            MOV     CX,128                 ;Set up counter
            CLD                            ;Forward
            REP     MOVSB

            CMP     PARM,9                 ;Check length 8 + 1 (space)
            JNZ     ERROR
            MOV     AL,PARM+2              ;Get first char
            CMP     AL,30H                 ;See if it's not numeric
            JL      ERROR                  ;Error if less
            CMP     AL,32H                 ;See if it's more than 2
            JG      ERROR                  ;Error if more
            SUB     AL,30H                 ;Convert to Binary.
            MUL     BY10                   ;Set decimal value to 10X
            MOV     STHH,AL                ;Stow in hour save

            MOV     AL,PARM+3              ;Get Next  char
            CMP     AL,30H                 ;See if it's not numeric
            JL      ERROR                  ;Error if less
            CMP     AL,39H                 ;See if it's more than 9
            JG      ERROR                  ;Error if more
            SUB     AL,30H                 ;Convert to Binary.
            ADD     STHH,AL                ;Add to hour save
            MOV     AL,STHH                ;Some more checking
            CMP     AL,23                  ;make sure valid hour
            JG      ERROR                  ;Hours GT 23 - invalid
            MOV     AL,PARM+4              ;Get Colon
            CMP     AL,3AH                 ;See if it's not a colon
            JNZ     ERROR                  ;Error if less


            MOV     AL,PARM+5              ;Get Next  char
            CMP     AL,30H                 ;See if it's not numeric
            JL      ERROR                  ;Error if less
            CMP     AL,35H                 ;See if it's more than 5
            JG      ERROR                  ;Error if more
            SUB     AL,30H                 ;Convert to Binary.
            MUL     BY10                   ;Set decimal value to 10X
            ADD     STMM,AL                ;Add to minute save

            MOV     AL,PARM+6              ;Get Next  char
            CMP     AL,30H                 ;See if it's not numeric
            JL      ERROR                  ;Error if less
            CMP     AL,39H                 ;See if it's more than 9
            JG      ERROR                  ;Error if more
```

Listing A.1 ▲ *STARTAT.ASM.*

```
            SUB     AL,30H                  ;Convert to Binary.
            ADD     STMM,AL                 ;Add to minute save
            JMP     BYPASS                  ;This just gets round the
                                            ;128 byte limit on Label
                                            ;jumps.
            MOV     DX,offset msg1          ;user anxiety
            MOV     AH,9                    ;Get dos display function
            INT     21H                     ;print msg -> by dx
            JMP     EXIT

            MOV     AL,PARM+7               ;Get Colon
            CMP     AL,3AH                  ;See if it's not a colon
            JNZ     ERROR                   ;Error if less

            MOV     AL,PARM+8               ;Get Next  char
            CMP     AL,30H                  ;See if it's not numeric
            JL      ERROR                   ;Error if less
            CMP     AL,35H                  ;See if it's more than 5
            JG      ERROR                   ;Error if more
            SUB     AL,30H                  ;Convert to Binary.
            MUL     BY10                    ;Set decimal value to 10X
            ADD     STSS,AL                 ;Add to second save

            MOV     AL,PARM+9               ;Get Next  char
            CMP     AL,30H                  ;See if it's not numeric
            JL      ERROR                   ;Error if less
            CMP     AL,39H                  ;See if it's more than 9
            JG      ERROR                   ;Error if more
            SUB     AL,30H                  ;Convert to Binary.
            ADD     STSS,AL                 ;Add to second save
            MOV     DX,offset msg2          ;Reassure User
            MOV     AH,9                    ;Get dos display function
            INT     21H                     ;print msg -> by dx


LOOPIT:
            SUB     AX,AX                   ;Clear reg
            MOV     AH,2CH                  ;Function 44
            INT     21H                     ;Xfer to DOS

            MOV     AL,STHH                 ;Retrieve start hour
            CMP     AL,CH                   ;Test for same
            JNZ     LOOPIT                  ;If not loop again

            MOV     AL,STMM                 ;Retrieve start minute
            CMP     AL,CL                   ;Test for same
            JNZ     LOOPIT                  ;If not loop again

            MOV     AL,STSS                 ;Retrieve start second
            CMP     AL,DH                   ;Test for same
            JNZ     LOOPIT                  ;If not loop again

EXIT:       XOR     AL,AL                   ;Return zero
            MOV     AH,4CH                  ;Terminate
            INT     21H                     ;Call DOS
MAIN        ENDP
;------------------------------------------------------------------------
; Data area declarations
;------------------------------------------------------------------------
msg1        db 'Format is : STARTAT HH:MM:SS',10,13,'$'
msg2        db 'Waiting...',10,13,'$'
;------------------------------------------------------------------------
CSEG        ends
            end     START
```

Listing A.1 ▲ *STARTAT.ASM (continued)*.

```
;
;--------------------------------------------------------------------
; Environment          PC DOS 2.00 or Higher - IBM PC/AT/Compatible.
; DOS Syntax -         EGASIZE
; Returns    -         Number of 64K banks in EGA
; M P Waterhouse Feb  13, 1988
;--------------------------------------------------------------------
; Setup so that EXE2BIN can convert the program to .COM format
CSEG           segment para public 'CODE'
               assume  cs:CSEG,ds:CSEG,es:CSEG,ss:CSEG
               ORG     100H                     ;all COM files start here
START:         JMP     GO                       ;leap over the data area
;
MAIN           PROC    far                      ;keep it clean
GO:            MOV     AH,12H                   ;Return EGA info
               MOV     AL,0
               MOV     BL,10H                   ;Alt function select
               MOV     BH,0
               MOV     CX,0                     ;keep it clean
               INT     10H                      ;Call video interrupt.
               MOV     AH,0                     ;Remove high AX
               MOV     AL,BL
               MOV     AH,4CH
               INT     21H
               RET
MAIN           ENDP

CSEG           ends
               end     START
```

Listing A.2 ▲ *EGASIZE.ASM.*

```
;
;--------------------------------------------------------------------
; Environment          PC DOS 2.00 or Higher - IBM PC/AT/Compatible.
; DOS Syntax -         CURSOR ssee where ss is start line; e.g., 01
;                      ee is end line; e.g., 09
; Example    -         CURSOR 0107 (Cursor box between lines 1 and 7)
; Returns    -         Error code of 1 if wrong format given
; Sets       -         Cursor Start/End
; M P Waterhouse Feb  23, 1988
;--------------------------------------------------------------------
; Setup so that EXE2BIN can convert the program to .COM format
CSEG           segment para public 'CODE'
               assume  cs:CSEG,ds:CSEG,es:CSEG,ss:CSEG
               ORG     100H                     ;all COM files start here
START:         JMP     GO                       ;leap over the data area
BY10           DB      10                       ;when we need a div by 10
PARM           DB      128 dup(0)               ;Parm stow area init to 0
SVAL           DB      00                       ;Store Start Value
EVAL           DB      00                       ;Store End Value
;
MAIN           PROC    FAR                      ;keep it clean
GO:            MOV     SI,80H                   ;Point string index at parm
               MOV     DI,OFFSET PARM           ;Point to our PARM area
               MOV     CX,128                   ;Set up counter
               CLD                              ;Forward
               REP     MOVSB

               MOV     AL,PARM+2                ;Get first char
               CMP     -AL,30H                  ;See if it's not numeric
               JL      ERROR                    ;Error if less
               CMP     AL,39H                   ;See if it's not numeric
               JG      ERROR                    ;Error if more
               SUB     AL,30H                   ;Convert to Binary.
               MUL     BY10                     ;Multiply by 10
               MOV     SVAL,AL                  ;Stow in start val
```

Listing A.3 ▲ *CURSOR.ASM.*

```
            MOV     AL,PARM+3              ;Get second char
            CMP     AL,30H                 ;See if it's not numeric
            JL      ERROR                  ;Error if less
            CMP     AL,39H                 ;See if it's not numeric
            JG      ERROR                  ;Error if more
            SUB     AL,30H                 ;Convert to Binary.
            ADD     SVAL,AL                ;Stow in Start value

            MOV     AL,PARM+4              ;Get third char
            CMP     AL,30H                 ;See if it's not numeric
            JL      ERROR                  ;Error if less
            CMP     AL,39H                 ;See if it's not numeric
            JG      ERROR                  ;Error if more
            SUB     AL,30H                 ;Convert to Binary.
            MUL     BY10                   ;Multiply by 10
            MOV     EVAL,AL                ;Stow in end val
            MOV     AL,PARM+5              ;Get fourth char
            CMP     AL,30H                 ;See if it's not numeric
            JL      ERROR                  ;Error if less
            CMP     AL,39H                 ;See if it's not numeric
            JG      ERROR                  ;Error if more
            SUB     AL,30H                 ;Convert to Binary.
            ADD     EVAL,AL                ;Stow in End value

            MOV     AH,01H                 ;Set cursor
            MOV     CH,SVAL
            MOV     CL,EVAL                ;keep it clean
            INT     10H                    ;Call video interrupt.
            JMP     ITSOK                  ;jumps.
ERROR:                                     ;Set return code
            MOV     AL,1                   ;Problem
ITSOK:      MOV     AH,4CH                 ;Value in AL - set func
            MOV     AL,0                   ;Clean finish
            INT     21H
            RET
MAIN        ENDP

CSEG        ends
            end     START
```

Listing A.3 ▲ *CURSOR.ASM (continued).*

```
;
;------------------------------------------------------------------------
; Environment     PC DOS 2.00 or Higher - IBM PC/AT/Compatible.
; DOS Syntax -    VMODE
; Returns    -    Number relating to video mode.
; M P Waterhouse Feb 23, 1988
;------------------------------------------------------------------------
; Setup so that EXE2BIN can convert the program to .COM format
CSEG        segment para public 'CODE'
            assume  cs:CSEG,ds:CSEG,es:CSEG,ss:CSEG
            ORG     100H                   ;all COM files start here
START:      JMP     GO                     ;leap over the data area
;
MAIN        PROC    far                    ;keep it clean
GO:         MOV     AH,0FH                 ;Request mode
            MOV     AL,0
            MOV     CX,0                   ;keep it clean
            INT     10H                    ;Call video interrupt.
            MOV     AH,4CH                 ;Value in AL - set func
            INT     21H
            RET
MAIN        ENDP

CSEG        ends
            end     START
```

Listing A.4 ▲ *VMODE.ASM.*

```
;
;--------------------------------------------------------------------
; Environment        PC DOS 2.00 or Higher - IBM PC/AT/Compatible.
; DOS Syntax -       SETVID
; Returns     -      DOS ERRORLEVEL of 1 if there is a format eror.
; Example     -      SETVID 19 would set up a VGA in 320X200 256 color mode
; Sets        -      Video mode
; M P Waterhouse Feb  23, 1988
;--------------------------------------------------------------------
; Setup so that EXE2BIN can convert the program to .COM format
CSEG          segment para public 'CODE'
              assume  cs:CSEG,ds:CSEG,es:CSEG,ss:CSEG
              ORG     100H                          ;all COM files start here
START:        JMP     GO                            ;leap over the data area
BY10          DB      10                            ;when we need a div by 10
PARM          DB      128 dup(0)                    ;Parm stow area init to 0
MVAL          DB      00                            ;Store Mode Value
;
MAIN          PROC    FAR                           ;keep it clean
GO:           MOV     SI,80H                        ;Point string index at parm
              MOV     DI,OFFSET PARM                ;Point to our PARM area
              MOV     CX,128                        ;Set up counter
              CLD                                   ;Forward
              REP     MOVSB

              MOV     BL,PARM+2                     ;Get first char
              CMP     BL,30H                        ;See if it's not numeric
              JL      ERROR                         ;Error if less
              CMP     BL,39H                        ;See if it's not numeric
              JG      ERROR                         ;Error if more
              SUB     BL,30H                        ;Convert to Binary.

              MOV     AL,PARM+3                     ;Get second char
              CMP     AL,30H                        ;See if it's not numeric
              JL      SINGDIG                       ;Only one DIGIT
              MOV     MVAL,AL                       ;Stow in Mode value
              MOV     AL,BL                         ;Get first digit
              MUL     BY10                          ;Multiply by 10
              ADD     MVAL,AL                       ;Add to mode save
              JMP     DOIT

SINGDIG:      MOV     MVAL,BL                       ;Stow in Mode value

DOIT:         MOV     AH,0H                         ;Set mode
              MOV     AL,MVAL
              MOV     CX,0                          ;keep it clean
              INT     10H                           ;Call video interrupt.
              JMP     ITSOK                         ;jumps.
ERROR:        *                                     ;Set return code
              MOV     AL,1                          ;Problem
ITSOK:        MOV     AH,4CH                        ;Value in AL - set func
              MOV     AL,0                          ;Clean finish
              INT     21H
              RET
MAIN          ENDP

CSEG          ends
              end     START
```

Listing A.5 ▲ *SETVID.ASM.*

```
page      55,132
title  CLUS:      Use to display cluster info foe default drive
;
;--------------------------------------------------------------------
; Environment        PC DOS 2.00 or Higher - IBM PC/AT/Compatible.
; DOS Syntax -       CLUS
; Returns     -      Cluster size, number, Sectors etc for dflt drive
; M P Waterhouse Mar 7, 1988
;--------------------------------------------------------------------
```

Listing A.6 ▲ *CLUS.ASM.*

```
; Setup so that EXE2BIN can convert the program to .COM format
CSEG        segment para public 'CODE'
            assume  cs:CSEG,ds:CSEG,es:CSEG,ss:CSEG
            ORG     100H                    ;all COM files start here
START:      JMP     GO                      ;leap over the data area
SPC         DW      0                       ;Sectors per cluster
AVC         DW      0                       ;Available Clusters per drive
BPS         DW      0                       ;Bytes per cluster
CPD         DW      0                       ;Clusters per drive
;
MAIN        PROC    FAR                     ;keep it clean
GO:         MOV     AH,36H                  ;Request free disk space
            MOV     DL,0                    ;Set for default drive
            INT     21H                     ;Call DOS
            MOV     SPC,AX                  ;Save Sec per clus
            MOV     AVC,BX                  ;Save Avail clusters per drive
            MOV     BPS,CX                  ;Save Bytes per sector
            MOV     CPD,DX                  ;Save Clusters per drive
            MOV     CL,4                    ;Set shift value
            SHR     AX,CL                   ;Get first nibble
            CALL    CONB                    ;Convert AH to disp fmt
            MOV     AX,SPC                  ;Now disp second nibble
            AND     AH,0FH                  ;Just the low part
            CALL    CONB
            MOV     AX,SPC                  ;Now disp second byte
            MOV     AH,AL
            MOV     CL,4                    ;Set shift value
            SHR     AX,CL                    ;Get first nibble
            CALL    CONB                    ;Convert AH to disp fmt
            MOV     AX,SPC                  ;Now disp second byte
            MOV     AH,AL
            AND     AH,0FH                  ;Just the low part
            CALL    CONB                    ;Convert AH to disp fmt
            MOV     DX,offset MSG1          ;Point to offset of MSG1
            CALL    OUTMSG                  ;Display msg

            MOV     AX,AVC                  ;Get avail clus
            MOV     CL,4                    ;Set shift value
            SHR     AX,CL
            CALL    CONB                    ;Convert AH to disp fmt
            MOV     AX,AVC                  ;Now disp second byte
            AND     AH,0FH                  ;Just the low part
            CALL    CONB                    ;Convert AH to disp fmt
            MOV     AX,AVC                  ;Get avail clus
            MOV     AH,AL
            MOV     CL,4                    ;Set shift value
            SHR     AX,CL
            CALL    CONB                    ;Convert AH to disp fmt
            MOV     AX,AVC                  ;Now disp second byte
            MOV     AH,AL
            AND     AH,0FH                  ;Just the low part
            CALL    CONB                    ;Convert AH to disp fmt
            MOV     DX,offset MSG2          ;Point to offset of MSG2
            CALL    OUTMSG

            MOV     AX,BPS                  ;Get bytes per sector
            MOV     CL,4                    ;Set shift value
            SHR     AX,CL
            CALL    CONB                    ;Convert AH to disp fmt
            MOV     AX,BPS                  ;Get bytes per sector
            AND     AH,0FH                  ;Just the low part
            CALL    CONB                    ;Convert AH to disp fmt
            MOV     AX,BPS                  ;Get bytes per sector
            AND     AX,00F0H
            MOV     CL,4                    ;Set shift value
            SHL     AX,CL
            CALL    CONB                    ;Convert AH to disp fmt
            MOV     AX,BPS                  ;Get bytes per sector
            MOV     AH,AL
            AND     AH,0FH                  ;Just the low part
            CALL    CONB                    ;Convert AH to disp fmt
            MOV     DX,offset MSG3          ;Point to offset of MSG3
            CALL    OUTMSG
```

Listing A.6 ▲ *CLUS.ASM (continued).*

```
                MOV     AX,CPD            ;Get clusters per drive
                MOV     CL,4              ;Set shift value
                SHR     AX,CL
                CALL    CONB              ;Convert AH to disp fmt
                MOV     AX,CPD            ;Get clusters per drive
                AND     AH,0FH            ;Just the low part
                CALL    CONB              ;Convert AH to disp fmt
                MOV     AX,CPD            ;Get clusters per drive
                AND     AX,00F0H
                MOV     CL,4
                SHL     AX,CL             ;Set shift value
                CALL    CONB              ;Convert AH to disp fmt
                MOV     AX,CPD            ;Get clusters per drive
                MOV     AH,AL
                AND     AH,0FH            ;Just the low part
                CALL    CONB              ;Convert AH to disp fmt
                MOV     DX,offset MSG4    ;Point to offset of MSG4
                CALL    OUTMSG
                MOV     AH,0              ;Terminate
                INT     21H

                RET
MAIN            ENDP
OUTMSG          PROC    NEAR
                MOV     AH,9              ;Set to display msg
                INT     21H               ;Call DOS
                RET
OUTMSG          ENDP


CONB            PROC    NEAR              ;Convert hex to display fmt
                CMP     AH,09H            ;See if 0-9
                JBE     LESSA             ;
                ADD     AH,'A'-'0'-10     ;If not assume 1-9
LESSA:          ADD     AH,'0'
                MOV     DL,AH
                MOV     AH,02             ;display Character
                INT     21H               ;Call DOS
                RET
CONB            ENDP
MSG1            DB      ' (HEX) Sectors per cluster',10,13,'$'
MSG2            DB      ' (HEX) Available clusters',10,13,'$'
MSG3            DB      ' (HEX) Bytes per cluster',10,13,'$'
MSG4            DB      ' (HEX) Clusters per drive',10,13,'$'
CSEG            ends
                end     START
```

Listing A.6 ▲ *CLUS.ASM (continued).*

```
        TITLE   MDHIDDEN [MDH.COM]

LF      EQU     10
CR      EQU     13

CODE    SEGMENT
        ASSUME DS:CODE, SS:CODE, CS:CODE, ES:CODE
        ORG     100H

START:          MOV     AX,CS
                MOV     DS,AX             ;Get extra seg/data seg
                MOV     ES,AX             ;pointing to CS.
                MOV     SI,81H            ;Point to command parm
                MOV     CL,-1[SI]         ;Get parm length
                XOR     CH,CH
                JCXZ    INVMSG
CHKPARM:        MOV     AL,[SI]
                CMP     AL,' '            ;See if it's blank
                JNE     MOVNAME
```

Listing A.7 ▲ *MDH.ASM.*

```
        INC     SI                      ;Advance to first non-blank byte
        LOOP    CHKPARM                 ;Get another byte
MOVNAME:    MOV     DI,OFFSET DNAME
        CLD
LDCHAR:     LODSB                       ;Move name to ASCIIZ string
        CMP     AL,'a'
        JB      STCHAR
        CMP     AL,'z'
        JA      STCHAR
        AND     AL,5FH                  ;Converting to upper case
STCHAR:     STOSB
        LOOP    LDCHAR
        XOR     AX,AX
        MOV     1[DI],AX                ;Add null terminator
        MOV     DX,OFFSET DNAME
ENDIT:  MOV     AH,39H                  ;Function 39 - Create Subdir
        INT     21H                     ;Create directory
        JC      ERROR                   ;If a problem on create
        MOV     CX,2                    ;Attribute byte (hidden)
        MOV     AX,4301H                ;Set file attributes
        MOV     DX,OFFSET DNAME         ;Using the DIR name
        INT     21H                     ;Set directory attribute
        JC      ERROR                   ;A problem ?
        MOV     DX,OFFSET DMSG          ;Tell user it worked
        MOV     AH,9                    ;Disply msg
        INT     21H
        MOV     BX,OFFSET DNAME         ;Add DIR name to string
SHONAME:    MOV     DL,[BX]
        OR      DL,DL
        JZ      ADDED
        MOV     AH,2                    ;Character output
        INT     21H
        INC     BX
        JMP     SHORT SHONAME
ADDED:      MOV     DX,OFFSET CRMSG
        MOV     AH,9                    ;String output
        INT     21H
        JMP     DONE
INVMSG: MOV DX,OFFSET NOPARM
        MOV     AH,9                    ;String output
        INT     21H
DONE:   MOV     DX,OFFSET CRLF
        MOV     AH,9
        INT     21H                     ;Print CR, LF
QUIT:   INT     20H                     ;Terminate
ERROR:      XOR     AH,AH
        MOV     BX,AX
        ADD     BX,BX
        MOV     DI,ERTBL[BX]    ;Point to error description
        ADD     AX,30H
        MOV     ERCODE,AL
        MOV     AH,9
        MOV     DX,OFFSET ERHDR
        INT     21H                     ;Dos error
        MOV     DX,DI
        MOV     AH,9
        INT     21H                     ;Print specific error message
        JMP     SHORT DONE

NOPARM      DB      CR,LF,' Format is MDH dirname $'
ERTBL       DW      ERMSG,ERMSG,ERR2,ERR3,ERMSG,ERR5,ERMSG,ERMSG
        DW      8 DUP(ERMSG)
        DW      ERR16,ERMSG,ERMSG
ERR2        DB      'File not found$'
ERR3        DB      'Path not found$'
ERR5        DB      'Access denied$'
ERR16       DB      'Cant remove current directory$'
ERHDR       DB      CR,LF,' DOS error: $'
ERMSG       DB      'return code # '
ERCODE      DB      ' .$'
DMSG        DB      CR,LF,' Directory $'
CRMSG       DB      ' created$'
CRLF        DB      CR,LF,'$'
DNAME       DB      64 DUP(0)
CODE    ENDS
    END     START
```

Listing A.7 ▲ *(continued).*

APPENDIX B

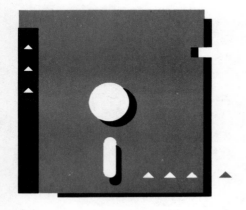

SOURCE CODE
FOR TURBO
PASCAL PROGRAMS

T HE FOLLOWING LISTINGS provide the Turbo Pascal source code for programs presented in Chapters 2, 3, and 6. These programs are written in Turbo Pascal 3.0. If you are using Turbo Pascal 4.0, you can modify these programs with the Upgrade utility to make them compatible with release 4.0.

```
program STARTAT;
{
  Turbo Pascal version
  Martin Waterhouse.
  Format STARTAT HH:MM:SS
  This is not one of the best examples of a Pascal program as it uses
  GOTO statements. It does however, illustrate how unorthodox
  Turbo Pascal really is.
}
const
  false = 0;
  true  = 1;
type
  registers = record
    ax, bx, cx, dx, bp, si, di, ds, es, flags: integer;
    end;
var
  timestr : string[8];
  REGS: registers;
  alarm,I : integer;
  HH,MM,SS :integer;

label
  errorlbl;

  begin
  alarm := false;
  if ParamCount <> 1 then goto errorlbl;          {Check no of parms}
  timestr := ParamSTR(1);
  if length(timestr) <> 8 then goto errorlbl;     {Check length}
  if copy(timestr,3,1) <> ':' then goto errorlbl;
  if copy(timestr,6,1) <> ':' then goto errorlbl;
  val(copy(timestr,1,2),HH,I);
  if HH > 23 then goto errorlbl;
  val(copy(timestr,4,2),MM,I);
  if MM > 59 then goto errorlbl;
  val(copy(timestr,7,2),SS,I);
  if SS > 59 then goto errorlbl;
  clrscr;
  writeln('Start Time: ',ParamSTR(1));
  writeln('Current Time: ',ParamSTR(1));
  with regs do
    begin
      while alarm = false do
        begin
        ax := $2c00;                {set AH for the DOS get time function}
        MSDos (regs);
        gotoxy(15,2);
        writeln (hi(cx),':',lo(cx),':',hi(dx));
        If hh = hi(cx) then
            if mm = lo(cx) then
                if ss = hi(dx) then
                    alarm := true
        end;
    end;
  exit;
  errorlbl:
  writeln('Format is STARTAT HH:MM:SS');
end.
```

Listing B.1 ▲ *STARTAT.PAS.*

```
{ Martin Waterhouse - July 1987 - WHATVID.PAS}
{ Turbo Pascal program to indicate the monitor type and video}
{ set up in your system.}

TYPE

   T_REGS = RECORD
      AX,BX,CX,DX,BP,SI,DI,DS,ES,FLAGS : INTEGER
   END;

VAR
   REGISTER   : T_REGS;
   MONTYPE    : INTEGER;
   PCTYP      : STRING [13];
   MON3270    : INTEGER;

BEGIN
   WITH REGISTER DO
   BEGIN

{ See whether the monitor is set to color or mono in the }
{ equipment list.}

      INTR ($11,REGISTER);
      MONTYPE := AX AND $0030;
      IF (AX AND $0030) = $30 THEN
         WRITELN ('Monitor type: Monochrome')
      ELSE
         WRITELN ('Monitor type: Color');

      {Test to see if this is a PS/2 or VGA present}



      AX := $1C00;     {service 1C only applies to PS/2s}
      CX := $FFFF;
      INTR ($10,REGISTER);
      IF LO(AX) = $1C then Writeln('VGA system available');

      AX := $0F00;
      INTR ($10,REGISTER);
      CASE (AX AND $00FF) OF
         0 :WRITELN('40X25 text B/W CGA  ');
         1 :WRITELN('40X25 text 16 Color CGA');
         2 :WRITELN('80X25 text B/W CGA  ');
         3 :WRITELN('80 column color text.');
         4 :WRITELN('320X200 4 Color CGA  ');
         5 :WRITELN('320X200 4 Grey  CGA  ');
         6 :WRITELN('640X200 1 Color CGA  ');
         7 :WRITELN('Monochrome           ');
         8 :WRITELN('160X200 16 COLOR PCjr');
         9 :WRITELN('320X200 16 COLOR PCjr');
        10 :WRITELN('640X200 4 COLOR PCjr');
        11 :WRITELN('** EGA Internal use');
        12 :WRITELN('** EGA Internal use');
        13 :WRITELN('320X200 16 COLOR EGA');
        14 :WRITELN('640X200 16 COLOR EGA');
        15 :WRITELN('640X350 Mono Graphics EGA');
        16 :WRITELN('640X350 64 COLOR EGA');

         ELSE WRITELN('Unknown graphics adaptor.');
      END;

{ Now we will check to see if we have an EGA installed.   }
{ We can't simply tell what is installed by assuming the  }
{ EGA is set to a mode only an EGA can use. Therefore, we }
{ must interrogate the graphics controller chip.          }

      AX := $1200;
      BX := $0010;
      INTR ($10,REGISTER);
      CASE (BX AND $00FF) OF
         0 :WRITELN('EGA with 64K installed');
         1 :WRITELN('EGA with 128K installed');
         2 :WRITELN('EGA with 192K installed');
```

Listing B.2 ▲ *WHATVID.PAS.*

```
        3 :WRITELN('EGA with 256K installed');
          ELSE WRITELN(' adaptor installed');
      END
        AX := $3000;                      {Check to see if this is a}
        CX := $0000;                      {3270 PC}
        DX := $0000;
        INTR ($10,REGISTER);

                                          {If CX or DX change then this}
                                          {is a 3270 PC}



     IF (CX > 0) OR (DX > 0)
        THEN BEGIN
           PCTYP := '3270 PC or AT'; {Here we go overlaying things}
           MON3270 := MEM[CX:DX+2]; {again, but it's in a good cause
           WRITELN ('                     ');{Remove EGA}
                                                    {Message}
        CASE (MON3270) OF
           0 : WRITELN('3270PC 5151/5272 Display    ');
           1 : WRITELN('3270PC 3295 Display         ');
           2 : WRITELN('3270AT 5272 XGA Display     ');
           3 : WRITELN('3270PC/G 5279 Display       ');
           4 : WRITELN('PC/GX 5379 C01 Display      ');
           5 : WRITELN('PC/GX 5379 M01 Display      ');
           ELSE WRITELN('Unknown 3270PC Display     ');
           END;
        END;
  END;
END.
```

Listing B.2 ▲ *WHATVID.PAS (continued).*

```
{SETVID.PAS - Martin Waterhouse}
{ Turbo Pascal program to set the video mode from a toggle window}

TYPE

   T_REGS = RECORD
     AX,BX,CX,DX,BP,SI,DI,DS,ES,FLAGS : INTEGER
   END;

VAR
   REGISTER    : T_REGS;
   COUNTER     : INTEGER;
   KEYCHAR     : CHAR;
   MODESET     : ARRAY [0..16] of STRING[25];

BEGIN
   WITH REGISTER DO
   BEGIN


   { See whether the monitor is set to color or mono in the }
   { equipment list.}

        CLRSCR;
        GOTOXY(15,7);
        WRITELN('Q to quit, all other keys select.');
        MODESET[00]:='40X25 text B/W CGA       ';
        MODESET[01]:='40X25 text 16 Color CGA  ';
        MODESET[02]:='80X25 text B/W CGA       ';
        MODESET[03]:='80 column color text.    ';
        MODESET[04]:='320X200 4 Color CGA      ';
        MODESET[05]:='320X200 4 Grey  CGA      ';
        MODESET[06]:='640X200 1 Color CGA      ';
        MODESET[07]:='Monochrome               ';
```

Listing B.3 ▲ *SETVID.PAS.*

```
               MODESET[08]:='160X200 16 COLOR PCjr     ';
               MODESET[09]:='320X200 16 COLOR PCjr     ';
               MODESET[10]:='640X200 4 COLOR PCjr      ';
               MODESET[11]:='** EGA Internal use       ';
               MODESET[12]:='** EGA Internal use       ';
               MODESET[13]:='320X200 16 COLOR EGA      ';
               MODESET[14]:='640X200 16 COLOR EGA      ';
               MODESET[15]:='640X350 Mono Graphics EGA ';
               MODESET[16]:='640X350 64 COLOR EGA      ';

               AX := $0F00;                          {Get display mode}
               INTR ($10,REGISTER);
               AX:=AX AND $00FF;                     {Get rid of AH}
               GOTOXY(15,5);                         {Move to central part of
               IF AX < 17 then
                 WRITELN(MODESET[AX])                 {Print it out}
               else
                 begin
                    WRITELN('Unknown graphics adaptor.   ');
                    EXIT;
                 end;
                 repeat until(keypressed);            {Any key will trigger}
                 READ(KBD,KEYCHAR);
                 IF (KEYCHAR = 'Q') or (KEYCHAR = 'q') then HALT;
                 GOTOXY(15,7);                         {Move to central part of scr}
                 WRITELN('S to Set, Q to quit, all other keys select.');

               FOR COUNTER := 0 to 16 do
                  BEGIN
                     GOTOXY(15,5);
                     WRITELN(MODESET[COUNTER]);        {Print selection}
                     repeat until(keypressed);         {Any key will trigger}
                     READ(KBD,KEYCHAR);
                     IF (KEYCHAR = 'Q') or (KEYCHAR = 'q') then HALT;
                     IF (KEYCHAR = 'S') or (KEYCHAR = 's') then BEGIN
                        AX := $0000;                   {Set display mode}
                        AX:=AX + COUNTER;              {Add count to AH}
                        INTR ($10,REGISTER);           {Set Video mode}
                        HALT;                          {Terminate program}
                     END;
                  END;
               END;
        END.
```

Listing B.3 ▲ *SETVID.PAS (continued).*

```
{SETCRSR.PAS - Martin Waterhouse}
{ Turbo Pascal program to set the cursor size and starting height}

CONST
     MAXSTART = 11 ;
     MAXEND   = 12 ;

TYPE

   T_REGS = RECORD
      AX,BX,CX,DX,BP,SI,DI,DS,ES,FLAGS : INTEGER
   END;

VAR
    STARTLN   : INTEGER;
    ENDLN     : INTEGER;
    Result_s  : INTEGER;               {Used for error reporting}
    Result_e  : INTEGER;               {Ditto}

PROCEDURE SETPROC(VAR Startln,Endln : Integer);
VAR
```

Listing B.4 ▲ *SETCURSR.PAS.*

```
      REGISTERS  : T_REGS;
      BEGIN
       WITH REGISTERS DO
         BEGIN
           AX := $0100;                      {Set cursor DOS function}
           CX := Startln * $00FF + Endln;    {Mult by $00FF to put in CH}
           gotoxy(20,16);
           writeln(CX);
           INTR ($10,REGISTERS);
         END;
      END;

      {Main Procedure}
      BEGIN
       {First check to see if parameters were passed}
       {Two are needed - Start and end line numbers}

         if ParamCount < 2 then               {Check no of parms}
            BEGIN                              {Other than two}
                                               {Clear the screen as we are}
              Clrscr;                          {going to prompt for values}
              Gotoxy (8,6);
              Writeln('Change cursor size/shape');
              REPEAT
                Gotoxy (8,8);
                Writeln('Enter cursor start line');
                Readln(Startln);
              UNTIL ((STARTLN > 0) AND (STARTLN < MAXSTART));
              REPEAT
              Gotoxy (8,10);
              Writeln('Enter cursor end line');
              Readln(Endln);
            UNTIL ((ENDLN > 0) AND (ENDLN < MAXEND) AND (ENDLN > STARTLN));
              Setproc(Startln,Endln);
              Clrscr;                          {Reset the screen}
                                               {show new cursor}
         END
         ELSE
         BEGIN
              VAL(ParamSTR(1),Startln,Result_s);   {Two parms supplied}
              VAL(ParamSTR(2),Endln,Result_e);     {Convert incoming st
              If (Startln > MAXSTART) AND (Result_s = 0) {to integers, rpt er
              THEN                                 {Check for validity}
              BEGIN
                  Writeln('Invalid Cursor starting line');
                  halt;
              END;
              If (Endln > MAXEND) AND (Result_e = 0)   {Check for validity}
              THEN
              BEGIN
                  Writeln('Invalid Cursor ending line');
                  halt;
              END;
              Setproc(Startln,Endln);
         END;
      END.
```

Listing B.4 ▲ *SETCURSR.PAS (continued).*

```
   {EGAMSIZE - is used to determine how much EGA memory you have installed}
   TYPE
      REGS = RECORD
         AX,BX,CX,DX,BP,SI,DI,DS,ES,FLAGS : INTEGER
      END;

   VAR
      REGISTER  : REGS;

   BEGIN
         REGISTER.AX := $1200;
         REGISTER.BX := $0010;
```

Listing B.5 ▲ *EGAMSIZE.PAS.*

```
        INTR ($10,REGISTER);
        CASE (REGISTER.BX AND $00FF) OF
           0 :WRITELN('EGA with 64K installed');
           1 :WRITELN('EGA with 128K installed');
           2 :WRITELN('EGA with 192K installed');
           3 :WRITELN('EGA with 256K installed');
           ELSE WRITELN ('EGA not installed');
        END;
END.
```

Listing B.5 ▲ *EGAMSIZE.PAS (continued).*

```
{ Turbo Pascal program to set the cursor size and shape}

CONST
    MAXSTART = 11 ;
    MAXEND   = 12 ;

TYPE

    T_REGS = RECORD
        AX,BX,CX,DX,BP,SI,DI,DS,ES,FLAGS : INTEGER
    END;

VAR
    STARTLN   : INTEGER;
    ENDLN     : INTEGER;
    Result_s  : INTEGER;                {Used for error reporting}
    Result_e  : INTEGER;                {Ditto}

PROCEDURE SETPROC(VAR Startln,Endln : Integer);
VAR
REGISTERS  : T_REGS;
BEGIN
 WITH REGISTERS DO
  BEGIN
    AX := $0100;                        {Set cursor DOS function}
    CX := Startln * $00FF + Endln;      {Mult by $00FF to put in CH}
    gotoxy(20,16);
    writeln(CX);
    INTR ($10,REGISTERS);
 END;
END;

{Main Procedure}
BEGIN
 {First check to see if parameters were passed}
 {Two are needed - Start and end line numbers}

  if ParamCount < 2 then               {Check no of parms}
     BEGIN                             {Other than two}
                                       {Clear the screen as we are}
        Clrscr;                        {going to prompt for values}
        Gotoxy (8,6);
        Writeln('Change cursor size/shape');
        REPEAT
           Gotoxy (8,8);
           Writeln('Enter cursor start line');
           Readln(Startln);
        UNTIL ((STARTLN > 0) AND (STARTLN < MAXSTART));
        REPEAT
           Gotoxy (8,10);
           Writeln('Enter cursor end line');
           Readln(Endln);
           UNTIL ((ENDLN > 0) AND (ENDLN < MAXEND) AND (ENDLN > STARTLN));
            Setproc(Startln,Endln);
            Clrscr;                     {Reset the screen}
                                        {show new cursor}

        END
        ELSE
```

Listing B.6 ▲ *CURSR.PAS.*

```
          BEGIN
              VAL(ParamSTR(1),Startln,Result_s);          {Two parms supplied}
              VAL(ParamSTR(2),Endln,Result_e);            {Convert incoming st
              If (Startln > MAXSTART) AND (Result_s = 0)  {to integers, rpt er
              THEN                                         {Check for validity}
              BEGIN
                  Writeln('Invalid Cursor starting line');
                  halt;
              END;
              If (Endln > MAXEND) AND (Result_e = 0)      {Check for validity}
              THEN
              BEGIN
                  Writeln('Invalid Cursor ending line');
                  halt;
              END;
              Setproc(Startln,Endln);
          END;
END.
```

Listing B.6 ▲ *CURSR.PAS (continued).*

```
{$p256}
Program CLUSTERS;
{ This program will illustrate the cluster size of your present hard-disk
{ setup. Set the default drive to the one you want to test and type the
{d:\path\CLUS the "d:" is for drive and "path" is for the entire path
{to the location of the CLUS program}

type
    registers= record                              { main registers}
        ax,bx,cx,dx,bp,si,di,ds,es,flags:integer;
    end;

var
    regs:       registers;    { Set/Return register area.          }

BEGIN
    with regs do Begin;
          ax := $3600;
          dx := 0;              {0 = default disk}
          MSDOS(Regs);
          if AX = $FFFF
              then writeln('*** Invalid drive ***')
              else
                  begin
                      writeln('Bytes per sector   : ',CX);
                      writeln('Clusters per drive : ',DX);
                      writeln('Available clusters : ',BX);
                      writeln('Bytes per cluster  : ',(CX * AX)); {AX contains
                                                                  {of sectors
                                                                  {cluster}
                  end;
      end;
end.
```

Listing B.7 ▲ *CLUSTERS.PAS.*

A P P E N D I X C

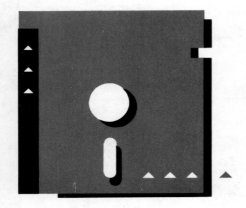

A C C E S S G U I D E
T O U T I L I T Y
S O F T W A R E

COMMERCIAL UTILITIES

Carbon Copy
Meridian Technology
1101 Dove Street
Suite 120
Newport Beach, CA 92660
(714) 261-1199
Suggested retail price: $195

Command Plus
ESP Software Systems
11965 Venice Boulevard
Suite 309
Los Angeles, CA 90066
(213) 390-7408
Suggested retail price: $79.95

Cruise Control
Revolution Software
715 Route 10 East
Randolph, NJ 07869
(201) 366-4445
Suggested retail price: $59.95

DESQview 2.01 and
Quarterdeck Expanded Memory Manager
Quarterdeck Office Systems
150 Pico Boulevard
Santa Monica, CA 90405
(213) 392-9701
Suggested retail prices:
  DESQview: $129.95
  QEMM.SYS: $39.95

Disk Manager
Ontrack Computer Systems
6222 Bury Drive
Eden Prairie, MN 55344
(612) 937-1107
Suggested retail price: $124.95

Disk Optimizer 2.0 (LOCK and UNLOCK)
SoftLogic Solutions
530 Chestnut Street
Manchester, NH 03101
(800) 272-9900
Suggested retail price: $49.95

Display Master 3.01
Intersecting Concepts, Inc.
4573 Heatherglen Court
Moorpark, CA 93021
(800) 422-8018
(805) 373-3900 in California
Suggested retail price: $69.95

Fontasy Release 2
Prosoft, a division of TTSC
P. O. Box 560
North Hollywood, CA 91603
(818) 765-4444
Suggested retail price: $69.95

GEM Desktop 3.0
Digital Research, Inc.
Box DRI
Monterey, CA 93942
(408) 649-3896
Suggested retail price: $49.95
(Packaged free with GEM applications)

LapLink
   Traveling Software, Inc.
   19310 North Creek Parkway
   Bothell, WA 98011
   (206) 483-8088
   Suggested retail price: $129.95

Mace Utilities 4.10
   Paul Mace Software
   400 Williamson Way
   Ashland, OR 97520
   (800) 523-0258
   (503) 488-0224
   Suggested retail price: $99

Microsoft Windows 2.03
   Microsoft Corporation
   P. O. Box 97017
   Redmond, WA 98073
   (206) 882-8080
   Suggested retail price: $99

The Norton Utilities Release 4.0 and Advanced Edition
   Peter Norton Computing
   2210 Wilshire Boulevard
   Santa Monica, CA 90403
   (213) 453-2361
   Suggested retail prices:
      Release 4.0: $99.95
      Advanced Edition: $150

PC Tools R3.23 and PC Tools Deluxe R4.11
   Central Point Software
   9700 S.W. Capitol Highway
   Suite 100
   Portland, OR 97219
   (503) 244-5782

Suggested retail prices:
PC Tools: $39.95
PC Tools Deluxe: $79.95

Personal REXX
Mansfield Software Group
P. O. Box 532
Storrs, CT 06268
(203) 429-8402
BBS Phone: (203) 429-3784
Suggested retail price: $125

PolyBoost Utilities
Polytron Corp.
P. O. Box 787
Hillsboro, OR 97123
(800) 547-4000
Suggested retail price: $79.95

Protec
Sophco, Inc.
P. O. Box 7430
Boulder, CO 80306
(303) 444-1542
Suggested retail price: $195

SmartKey V5.2 (CRYPTOR)
Software Research Technologies, Inc.
3757 Wilshire Boulevard, #211
Los Angeles, CA 90010
(213) 384-5430
(800) 824-5537
Suggested retail price: $49.95

Software Carousel

SoftLogic Solutions
530 Chestnut Street
Manchester, NH 03101
(800) 272-9900
Suggested retail price: $59.95

SpeedStor

Storage Dimensions
981 University Avenue
Los Gatos, CA 95030
(408) 395-2688
Suggested retail price: $99

Speed Utility

Ariel Corporation
P. O. Box 866
Flemington, NJ 08822
(201) 788-9002
(201) 788-2788
Suggested retail price: $39.95

Watchdog 4.0

Fischer International Systems Corp.
4175 Mercantile Avenue
Naples, FL 33942
(800) 237-4510
Suggested retail price: $295

PUBLIC-DOMAIN AND SHAREWARE UTILITIES

We have often spoken of two types of noncommercial software: *public-domain software* and *shareware*. Public-domain software consists of programs that have been released to the public at no cost by their creators. The programs may or may not be copyrighted, but you are free to use them, copy them, and give them away.

Shareware refers to programs that you may *obtain* for free, but which you are expected to pay for if you use. Such programs are copyrighted and are the property of their authors. They are released to the public on the assumption that you have the right to try them before you buy them. Generally, a license fee establishes you as a registered user and gets you a printed manual (in place of a disk file) and access to technical support and upgrades. Sometimes, you even get a commission if someone registers a copy they received from you.

You can obtain these types of programs at most user's groups. They are also available on many bulletin boards, from which you can download them by modem. In addition, several mail-order companies will sell you disks full of public-domain and shareware programs for a nominal fee. Listed below are sources of the shareware programs discussed in this book.

BOMBSQAD *and* CHK4BOMB
Andy Hopkins
526 Walnut Lane
Swarthmore, PA 19081
BBS Phone: (302) 764-7522
No fee

CRYPTF
Christopher Blum
509 West Main, Front
Ashland, OH 44805
CompuServe: 76625,1041
No fee

DBACK
Eric Gans
French Department
UCLA
Los Angeles, CA 90024
No fee

Extended Batch Language
Seaware Corp.
P. O. Box 1656
Delray Beach, FL 33444
(305) 392-2046
BBS Phone: (305) 395-2816
Registration fee: $49.95

Imageprint
Image Computer Systems
P. O. Box 647
Avon, CT 06001
(203) 678-8771
Registration fee: $20

Interleave Adjustment Utility
Dave Bushong
Fremont Street
Concord, NH 03301
CompuServe: 70441,2456
$10 donation requested for technical support

LaserJet Setup Utility
Guy Gallo
P. O. Box 344
Piermont, NY 10968
BBS Phone: (212) 924-6598
Registration fee: Voluntary

LJ2UP
Joe Barnhard
1470 Townview Avenue
Santa Rosa, CA 95405
Compuserve: 76174,1573
No fee

NANSI.SYS
Daniel Kegel
2648 169th Avenue, SE
Bellevue, WA 98008
No fee
Permission required for commercial use

ProComm and ProComm Plus
Datastorm Technologies
P. O. Box 1471
Columbia, MO 65205
(314) 474-8461
BBS Phone: (314) 449-9401
Registration fee (ProComm): $25
Complete package (ProComm): $50
Complete package (ProComm Plus): $75

Pro-Set Utility
Fred Willshaw
207 Oak Lane
Cranford, NJ 07016
BBS Phones: (201) 568-7293
          (201) 963-3115
No fee

PUTPASS
John R. Harrington
1147 Willowood Drive
Milford, OH 45150

Danny D. Cornett
2417 Monatana Avenue #B6
Cincinnati, OH 45211
BBS Phones: (513) 243-0188
          (301) 480-0350
No fee

TDPRT
Saxman Software
Jim Standley
2350 Winstead Circle
Wichita, KN 67226
(316) 688-0235
BBS Phone: (316) 684-8744
Registration fee: $15

APPENDIX D

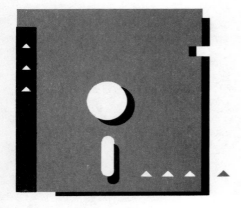

ANSI ESCAPE SEQUENCES

GRAPHICS DISPLAY

The codes in Table D.1 establish the foreground and background colors on a color display. On a monochrome monitor, they establish the attributes of the displayed text. The syntax is

   ^ [[*N;...;N*m

where *N* is any value from Table D.1.

   Any number of values may be included in a single escape sequence, as long as they are separated by semicolons. However, there must not be a semicolon between the final value and the terminating code *m*. Note

COLOR	FOREGROUND	BACKGROUND
Black	30	40
Blue	34	44
Green	32	42
Cyan	36	46
Red	31	41
Magenta	35	45
Yellow	33	43
White	37	47

VIDEO MODES	PARAMETERS
All attributes off	0
High-intensity text	1
Underlined text*	4
Blinking text	5
Inverse video	7
Concealed text	8

*Available in monochrome only.

Table D.1 ▲ *Graphics Display Codes.*

that the code for blue text will result in underlined text on a mono-chrome monitor (if the background is black), and the codes for black text on a white background will appear as inverse video on a mono-chrome monitor.

VIDEO MODE

The codes in Table D.2 are used to establish the video mode. They are equivalent to specific parameters to the MODE, SETUP, or CONFIG command. The syntax for establishing the video mode is

^ [[= Nh

or

^ [[= Nl

where N is any value from Table D.2.

VIDEO MODE	CODE	EQUIVALENT MODE COMMAND
40 × 25 black & white	0	MODE BW40
40 × 25 color	1	MODE CO40
80 × 25 black & white	2	MODE BW80
80 × 25 color	3	MODE CO80
320 × 200 color graphics	4	MODE COGR
320 × 200 black & white graphics	5	MODE BWGR
640 × 400 high-resolution graphics	6	MODE HIGR

Table D.2 ▲ Video Modes.

WORD WRAP

To establish word wrap on the screen (the default setting) use the sequence

^ [[?7h

To eliminate word wrap, so that lines longer than 80 characters are truncated, use the sequence

   [[?7l

CURSOR POSITIONING

The escape sequences in Table D.3 establish the position of the cursor on the screen.

ESCAPE SEQUENCE	EFFECT
^ [[*row;column*H	Moves the cursor to the specified row and column. When no parameters are given, places the cursor in the home position.
^ [[*row;column*f	Has the same effect as the H terminating code.
^ [[*row*A	Moves the cursor up the specified number of rows.
^ [[*row*B	Moves the cursor down the specified number of rows.
^ [[*column*C	Moves the cursor forward the specified number of columns.
^ [[*column*D	Moves the cursor backward the specified number of columns.
^ [[s	Records the position of the cursor at the time the escape sequence is issued.
^ [[u	Restores the cursor to the position recorded by ^ [[s.
^ [[2J	Clears the screen, and places the cursor in the home position.
^ [[K	Erases from the current cursor position to the end of the current line.
^ [[*row;column*R	Reports on the screen the position of the cursor at the time when the escape sequence was issued.

Table D.3 ▲ *Escape Sequences for Positioning the Cursor.*

REASSIGNING KEYBOARD FUNCTIONS

Keyboard functions can be reassigned by inserting the decimal ASCII code (or the extended ASCII code from Table E.2) for the key to be defined, followed by the new value for the key, expressed either as an ASCII code or a string in quotation marks. To have the string end in a carriage return, end the sequence with ASCII code 13. Extended ASCII codes are prefaced with a 0 and a semicolon. The new value is separated from the old value by a semicolon, and each ASCII value or string is separated from the others by semicolons. The sequence is terminated with a *p*. Table D.4 shows some examples.

ESCAPE SEQUENCE	EFFECT
^[[65;80p	Pressing shifted A displays an uppercase P.
^[[72;"Help";13p	Pressing shifted H displays the word Help, followed by a carriage return.
^[[0;68;"DIR B:";13p	Pressing F10 issues the command DIR B:.

Table D.4 ▲ *Sample Key Reassignment Codes.*

To clear key assignments, you must assign them to themselves. For example, to clear the assignments illustrated in Table D.4, issue the following escape sequences:

```
^[[65;65p
^[[72;72p
^[[0;68;0;68p
```

APPENDIX E

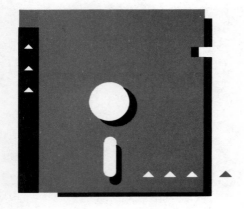

ASCII TABLES

ASCII	PRINTS	HEX		ASCII	PRINTS	HEX
0	*	0		32	**	20
1	☺	1		33	!	21
2	☻	2		34	"	22
3	♥	3		35	#	23
4	♦	4		36	$	24
5	♣	5		37	%	25
6	♠	6		38	&	26
7	•	7		39	'	27
8	◘	8		40	(	28
9	○	9		41	)	29
10	◙	A		42	*	2A
11	♂	B		43	+	2B
12	♀	C		44	,	2C
13	♪	D		45	-	2D
14	♫	E		46	.	2E
15	☼	F		47	/	2F
16	►	10		48	0	30
17	◄	11		49	1	31
18	↕	12		50	2	32
19	‼	13		51	3	33
20	¶	14		52	4	34
21	§	15		53	5	35
22	▬	16		54	6	36
23	↨	17		55	7	37
24	↑	18		56	8	38
25	↓	19		57	9	39
26	→	1A		58	:	3A
27	←	1B		59	;	3B
28	∟	1C		60	<	3C
29	↔	1D		61	=	3D
30	▲	1E		62	>	3E
31	▼	1F		63	?	3F

*Nonprintable character   **Space

Table E.1 ▲ *MS-DOS Printable ASCII Characters.*

ASCII	PRINTS	HEX	ASCII	PRINTS	HEX
64	@	40	96	`	60
65	A	41	97	a	61
66	B	42	98	b	62
67	C	43	99	c	63
68	D	44	100	d	64
69	E	45	101	e	65
70	F	46	102	f	66
71	G	47	103	g	67
72	H	48	104	h	68
73	I	49	105	i	69
74	J	4A	106	j	6A
75	K	4B	107	k	6B
76	L	4C	108	l	6C
77	M	4D	109	m	6D
78	N	4E	110	n	6E
79	O	4F	111	o	6F
80	P	50	112	p	70
81	Q	51	113	q	71
82	R	52	114	r	72
83	S	53	115	s	73
84	T	54	116	t	74
85	U	55	117	u	75
86	V	56	118	v	76
87	W	57	119	w	77
88	X	58	120	x	78
89	Y	59	121	y	79
90	Z	5A	122	z	7A
91	[	5B	123	{	7B
92	\	5C	124	:	7C
93	]	5D	125	}	7D
94	^	5E	126	~	7E
95	_	5F	127	△	7F

Table E.1 ▲ *MS-DOS Printable ASCII Characters (continued).*

ASCII	PRINTS	HEX
128	ç	80
129	ü	81
130	é	82
131	â	83
132	ä	84
133	à	85
134	å	86
135	ç	87
136	ê	88
137	ë	89
138	è	8A
139	ï	8B
140	î	8C
141	ì	8D
142	Ä	8E
143	Å	8F
144	É	90
145	æ	91
146	Æ	92
147	ô	93
148	ö	94
149	ò	95
150	û	96
151	ù	97
152	ÿ	98
153	Ö	99
154	Ü	9A
155	¢	9B
156	£	9C
157	¥	9D
158	₧	9E
159	ƒ	9F

ASCII	PRINTS	HEX
160	á	A0
161	í	A1
162	ó	A2
163	ú	A3
164	ñ	A4
165	Ñ	A5
166	ª	A6
167	º	A7
168	¿	A8
169	⌐	A9
170	¬	AA
171	½	AB
172	¼	AC
173	¡	AD
174	«	AE
175	»	AF
176	░	B0
177	▒	B1
178	▓	B2
179	│	B3
180	┤	B4
181	╡	B5
182	╢	B6
183	╖	B7
184	╕	B8
185	╣	B9
186	║	BA
187	╗	BB
188	╝	BC
189	╜	BD
190	╛	BE
191	┐	BF

Table E.1 ▲ *MS-DOS Printable ASCII Characters (continued).*

ASCII	PRINTS	HEX	ASCII	PRINTS	HEX
192	└	C0	224	α	E0
193	┴	C1	225	β	E1
194	┬	C2	226	Γ	E2
195	├	C3	227	π	E3
196	─	C4	228	Σ	E4
197	┼	C5	229	σ	E5
198	╞	C6	230	μ	E6
199	╟	C7	231	τ	E7
200	╚	C8	232	Φ	E8
201	╔	C9	233	Θ	E9
202	╩	CA	234	Ω	EA
203	╦	CB	235	δ	EB
204	╠	CC	236	∞	EC
205	═	CD	237	ø	ED
206	╬	CE	238	∈	EE
207	╧	CF	239	∩	EF
208	╨	D0	240	≡	F0
209	╤	D1	241	±	F1
210	╥	D2	242	≥	F2
211	╙	D3	243	≤	F3
212	╘	D4	244	⌠	F4
213	╒	D5	245	⌡	F5
214	╓	D6	246	÷	F6
215	╫	D7	247	≈	F7
216	╪	D8	248	°	F8
217	┘	D9	249	·	F9
218	┌	DA	250	·	FA
219	█	DB	251	√	FB
220	▄	DC	252	ⁿ	FC
221	▌	DD	253	²	FD
222	▐	DE	254	■	FE
223	▀	DF	255		FF

Table E.1 ▲ MS-DOS Printable ASCII Characters (continued).

ASCII Value	Control Character	Hex Value	Keyboard Equivalent	Device Control Effect
00	NUL	00	Ctrl-@	Null
01	SOH	01	Ctrl-A	
02	STX	02	Ctrl-B	
03	ETX	03	Ctrl-C	
04	EOT	04	Ctrl-D	
05	ENQ	05	Ctrl-E	
06	ACK	06	Ctrl-F	
07	BEL	07	Ctrl-G	Beep
08	BS	08	Ctrl-H	Backspace
09	HT	09	Ctrl-I	Tab
10	LF	0A	Ctrl-J	Linefeed
11	VT	0B	Ctrl-K	Cursor home
12	FF	0C	Ctrl-L	Form feed
13	CR	0D	Ctrl-M	Carriage return
14	SO	0E	Ctrl-N	
15	SI	0F	Ctrl-O	
16	DLE	10	Ctrl-P	
17	DC1	11	Ctrl-Q	
18	DC2	12	Ctrl-R	
19	DC3	13	Ctrl-S	
20	DC4	14	Ctrl-T	
21	NAK	15	Ctrl-U	
22	SYN	16	Ctrl-V	
23	ETB	17	Ctrl-W	
24	CAN	18	Ctrl-X	
25	EM	19	Ctrl-Y	
26	SUB	1A	Ctrl-Z	
27	ESC	1B	Ctrl-[or Esc	Escape
28	FS	1C	Ctrl-\	Cursor right
29	GS	1D	Ctrl-]	Cursor left
30	RS	1E	Ctrl-^	Cursor up
31	US	1F	Ctrl-_	Cursor down

Table E.2 ▲ *ASCII Control Codes and Their Effects.*

The codes in Table E.3 must be preceded by an ASCII 0 (null); for example, for F10 use 0;68. The numerical order of the codes for alphabetic characters follows the keyboard layout, rather than their order in the alphabet.

KEY OR CHARACTER	CODE
Null	3
Shift-Tab	15
Ctrl-PrtSc	114
Alt –	130
Alt-1	120
Alt-2	121
Alt-3	122
Alt-4	123
Alt-5	124
Alt-6	125
Alt-7	126
Alt-8	127
Alt-9	128
Alt-10	129
Alt-=	131
Alt-A	30
Alt-B	48
Alt-C	46
Alt-D	32
Alt-E	18
Alt-F	33
Alt-G	34
Alt-H	35

Table E.3 ▲ *Extended ASCII Codes.*

Alt-I	23
Alt-J	36
Alt-K	37
Alt-L	38
Alt-M	50
Alt-N	49
Alt-O	24
Alt-P	25
Alt-Q	16
Alt-R	19
Alt-S	31
Alt-T	20
Alt-U	22
Alt-V	47
Alt-X	45
Alt-Y	21
Alt-Z	44

FUNCTION KEYS

F1	59
F2	60
F3	61
F4	62
F5	63
F6	64
F7	65
F8	66
F9	67

Table E.3 ▲ *Extended ASCII Codes (continued).*

F10	68
Shift-F1	84
Shift-F2	85
Shift-F3	86
Shift-F4	87
Shift-F5	88
Shift-F6	89
Shift-F7	90
Shift-F8	91
Shift-F9	92
Shift-F10	93
Ctrl-F1	94
Ctrl-F2	95
Ctrl-F3	96
Ctrl-F4	97
Ctrl-F5	98
Ctrl-F6	99
Ctrl-F7	100
Ctrl-F8	101
Ctrl-F9	102
Ctrl-F10	103
Alt-F1	104
Alt-F2	105
Alt-F3	106
Alt-F4	107
Alt-F5	108
Alt-F6	109
Alt-F7	110

Table E.3 ▲ *Extended ASCII Codes (continued).*

Alt-F8	111
Alt-F9	112
Alt-F10	113
CURSOR KEYPAD KEYS	
Home	71
Cursor-Up	72
PgUp	73
Cursor-Left	75
Cursor-Right	77
End	79
Cursor-Down	80
PgDn	81
Ins	82
Del	83
Ctrl-Home	119
Ctrl-PgUp	132
Ctrl-Cursor-Left	115
Ctrl-Cursor-Right	116
Ctrl-End	117
Ctrl-PgDn	118

Table E.3 ▲ *Extended ASCII Codes (continued).*

213	209	184		214	210	183	
╒	╤	╕		╓	╥	╖	
198	216	181		199	215	182	
╞	╪	╡		╟	╫	╢	
212	207	190		211	208	189	
╘	╧	╛		╙	╨	╜	
201	203	187	205	218	194	191	196
╔	╦	╗	═	┌	┬	┐	─
204	206	185	186	195	197	180	179
╠	╬	╣	║	├	┼	┤	│
200	202	188		192	193	217	
╚	╩	╝		└	┴	┘	

Table E.4 ▲ *Box and Border Characters.*

PROGRAM INDEX

Note: The programs listed here are available on disk. Fill out the coupon to obtain a copy.

SUBJECT INDEX

Selections from The SYBEX Library

DOS

ABC's of MS-DOS
(Second Edition)
Alan R. Miller
233pp. Ref. 493-3

This handy guide to MS-DOS is all many PC users need to manage their computer files, organize floppy and hard disks, use EDLIN, and keep their computers organized. Additional information is given about utilities like Sidekick, and there is a DOS command and program summary. The second edition is fully updated for Version 3.3.

Mastering DOS
Judd Robbins
572pp. Ref. 400-3

"The most useful DOS book." This four-part, in-depth tutorial addresses the needs of users at all levels. Topics range from running applications, to managing files and directories, configuring the system, batch file programming, and techniques for system developers. A major book.

MS-DOS Handbook
(Third Edition)
Richard Allen King
362pp. Ref. 492-5

This classic has been fully expanded and revised to include the latest features of MS-DOS Version 3.3. Two reference books in one, this title has separate sections for programmer and user. Multi-DOS partitons, 3 1/2disk format, batch file call and return feature, and comprehensive coverage of MS-DOS commands are included.

MS-DOS Power User's Guide,
Volume I
(Second Edition)
Jonathan Kamin
482pp. Ref. 473-9

A fully revised, expanded edition of our best-selling guide to high-performance DOS techniques and utilities – with details on Version 3.3. Configuration, I/O, directory structures, hard disks, RAM disks, batch file programming, the ANSI.SYS device driver, more.

MS-DOS Power User's Guide,
Volume II
Martin Waterhouse/Jonathan Kamin
350pp, Ref. 411-9

A second volume of high-performance techniques and utilities, with expanded coverage of DOS 3.3, and new material on video modes, Token-Ring and PC Network support, micro-mainframe links, extended and expanded memory, multitasking systems, and more.

Performance Programming
Under MS-DOS
Michael J. Young
436pp. Ref. 420-8

Practical techniques for maximizing performance in MS-DOS software by making best use of system resources. Topics include functions, interrupts, devices, multitasking, memory residency and more, with examples in C and assembler.

The ABC's of PC-DOS
Alan R. Miller
231pp. Ref. 438-0

A beginner's guide to PC-DOS for users of the IBM PC and compatibles – everything from working with disks and files, to using built-in commands, customizing the system, recovering from errors, and adding some handy utilities.

Essential PC-DOS (Second Edition)
Myril Clement Shaw/ Susan Soltis Shaw
332pp. Ref. 413-5
An authoritative guide to PC-DOS, including version 3.2. Designed to make experts out of beginners, it explores everything from disk management to batch file programming. Includes an 85-page command summary.

The IBM PC-DOS Handbook (Third Edition)
Richard Allen King
350pp. Ref. 512-3
A guide to the inner workings of PC-DOS 3.2, for intermediate to advanced users and programmers of the IBM PC series. Topics include disk, screen and port control, batch files, networks, compatibility, and more.

DOS Instant Reference SYBEX Prompter Series
Greg Harvey/Kay Yarborough Nelson
220pp. Ref. 477-1; 4 3/4x8
A complete fingertip reference for fast, easy on-line help:command summaries, syntax, usage and error messages. Organized by function – system commands, file commands, disk management, directories, batch files, I/O, networking, programming, and more.

OTHER OPERATING SYSTEMS AND ENVIRONMENTS

Essential OS/2
Judd Robbins
367pp. Ref. 478-X
This introduction to OS/2 for new and prospective users offers clear explanations of multitasking, details key OS/2 commands and functions, and updates current DOS users to the new OS/2 world. Details are also given for users to run existing DOS programs under OS/2.

Programmer's Guide to OS/2
Michael J. Young
400pp. Ref. 464-X
This concise introduction gives a complete overview of program development under OS/2, with careful attention to new tools and features. Topics include MS-DOS compatibility, device drivers, services, graphics, windows, the LAN manager, and more.

Programmer's Guide to GEM
Phillip Balma/William Fitler
504pp. Ref. 297-3
GEM programming from the ground up, including the Resource Construction Set, ICON Editor, and Virtual Device Interface. Build a complete graphics application with objects, events, menus, windows, alerts and dialogs.

Programmer's Guide to TopView
Alan R. Miller
280pp. Ref. 273-6
A guided tour through every features of the TopView multitasking, windowed, operating environment for the IBM PC, with programming techniques and examples showing proper use of system resources. Includes assembly-language programming.

Power User's Guide to Hard Disk Management
Jonathan Kamin
315pp. Ref. 401-1
Put your work, your office or your entire business literally at your fingertips, in a customized, automated MS-DOS work environment. Topics include RAM disks, extended and expanded memory, and more.

Mastering CP/M
Alan R. Miller
398pp. Ref. 068-7
An advanced guide to using, altering and adding features to CP/M, with an introduction to macro programming and a useful macro library. Full details on BIOS and BDOS operations, and the 8080 and Z80 instruction sets.

How to Get the Programs in This Book

All the programs that appear in this book, along with most of the public-domain utility programs we discuss, are avaiable on disk.

To obtain a copy of the disk, complete the order form below, and return it with a check or money order for $19.95 in U.S. funds. (California residents please add appropriate sales tax for your county. Overseas orders please add $1.00.)

You will receive a disk by first-class mail.

Martin Waterhouse
P.O. Box 2011
Danville, CA 94526-2011

Please send me a copy of the companion disk for *MS-DOS Power User's Guide, Volume II.*

Name _____

Address _____

City/State/Zip _____

Enclosed is my check or money order.
(Make check payable to *Martin P. Waterhouse.*)
Price includes postage within the United States.
(California residents please add appropriate sales tax for your county. Overseas orders please add $1.00.)

This offer is made solely by the author, and SYBEX assumes no responsibility for any defect in the disk or programs.

SYBEX Computer Books are different.

Here is why . . .

At SYBEX, each book is designed with you in mind. Every manuscript is carefully selected and supervised by our editors, who are themselves computer experts. We publish the best authors, whose technical expertise is matched by an ability to write clearly and to communicate effectively. Programs are thoroughly tested for accuracy by our technical staff. Our computerized production department goes to great lengths to make sure that each book is well-designed.

In the pursuit of timeliness, SYBEX has achieved many publishing firsts. SYBEX was among the first to integrate personal computers used by authors and staff into the publishing process. SYBEX was the first to publish books on the CP/M operating system, microprocessor interfacing techniques, word processing, and many more topics.

Expertise in computers and dedication to the highest quality product have made SYBEX a world leader in computer book publishing. Translated into fourteen languages, SYBEX books have helped millions of people around the world to get the most from their computers. We hope we have helped you, too.

For a complete catalog of our publications:

SYBEX, Inc. 2021 Challenger Drive, #100, Alameda, CA 94501
Tel: (415) 523-8233/(800) 227-2346 Telex: 336311
Fax: (415) 523-2373

ASCII	PRINTS	HEX
128	ç	80
129	ü	81
130	é	82
131	â	83
132	ä	84
133	à	85
134	å	86
135	ç	87
136	ê	88
137	ë	89
138	è	8A
139	ï	8B
140	î	8C
141	ì	8D
142	Ä	8E
143	Å	8F
144	É	90
145	æ	91
146	Æ	92
147	ô	93
148	ö	94
149	ò	95
150	û	96
151	ù	97
152	ÿ	98
153	Ö	99
154	Ü	9A
155	¢	9B
156	£	9C
157	¥	9D
158	₧	9E
159	ƒ	9F

ASCII	PRINTS	HEX
160	á	A0
161	í	A1
162	ó	A2
163	ú	A3
164	ñ	A4
165	Ñ	A5
166	ª	A6
167	º	A7
168	¿	A8
169	⌐	A9
170	¬	AA
171	½	AB
172	¼	AC
173	¡	AD
174	«	AE
175	»	AF
176	░	B0
177	▒	B1
178	▓	B2
179	│	B3
180	┤	B4
181	╡	B5
182	╢	B6
183	╖	B7
184	╕	B8
185	╣	B9
186	║	BA
187	╗	BB
188	╝	BC
189	╜	BD
190	╛	BE
191	┐	BF